D1034218

FLORIDA STATE
UNIVERSITY LIBRARIES

JUN 22 1997

TALLAHASSEE, FLORIDA

Aesthetic Politics

*Political Philosophy
Beyond Fact and Value*

EDITORIAL BOARD

Jean-Marie Apostolides

K. Anthony Appiah

Louis Brenner

Ngwarsungu Chiwengo

Jocelyne Dakhlia

Hans Ulrich Gumbrecht

Sandra Harding

Françoise Lionnet

Hervé Moulin

Gayatri Chakravorty Spivak

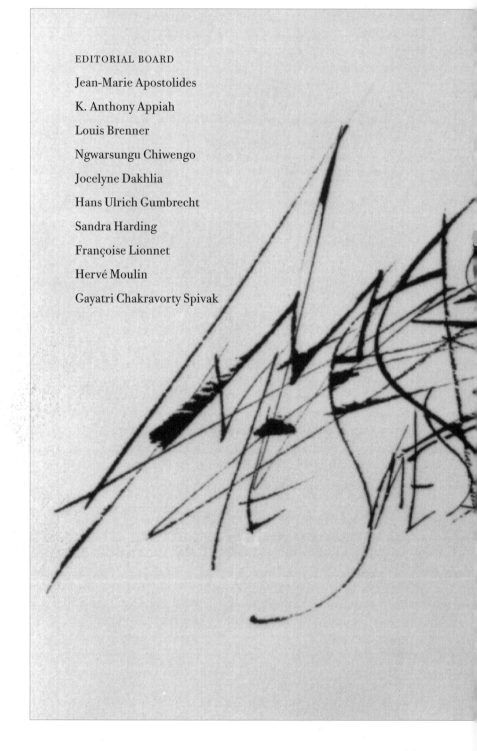

Mestizo Spaces
Espaces Métissés

V. Y. Mudimbe
EDITOR

Bogumil Jewsiewicki
ASSOCIATE EDITOR

Aesthetic Politics

Political Philosophy Beyond Fact and Value

F. R. Ankersmit

Stanford University Press
Stanford, California

JA
71
A585
1996

Stanford University Press
Stanford, California

© 1996 by the Board of Trustees of the
Leland Stanford Junior University

Printed in the United States of America

CIP data appear at the end of the book

Stanford University Press publications are
distributed exclusively by Stanford University
Press within the United States, Canada, Mexico,
and Central America; they are distributed exclusively by Cambridge University Press
throughout the rest of the world.

Cover illustration: Contemporary engraving of
Frederick V (1596–1632), Count Palatine, on the
Wheel of Fortune. A leader of the Protestant forces
in Germany, Frederick allowed himself to be elected
King of Bohemia in 1619, but shortly lost the crown
to Emperor Ferdinand of Austria at the battle of
White Mountain (1620) and fled to the Netherlands
(personified in the engraving as the fishermen).

"The problem is to know the highest truth that the people will bear and to preach and inculcate that."

—W. Bagehot, *The English Constitution*, p. 180

Acknowledgments

First of all I would like to express my gratitude to the readers of the manuscript of this book: John Pocock, Hans Gumbrecht, the anonymous reader from Wesleyan University, and especially Hayden White, whose continuous support is one of the best things in my life. I am most grateful to Anthony Runia for having corrected my English in his usual efficient and accurate way. A special debt I owe to Ann Klefstad, who copyedited the manuscript: she succeeded in projecting herself into the argument in a way that deeply impressed me and that proved to be an important condition of the clarity and cogency of the text in its final form. Without her this book would have been quite different from what it presently is. I would like to thank Harry Bracken for his many most useful comments on both the text itself and on deficiencies of the argument. But the greatest debt I owe to my former teacher Ernst Kossmann—both he and I know why.

The two last chapters in this volume were previously published in a slightly different form, as "Metaphor in Political Theory," in F. R. Ankersmit and J. J. A. Mooij, eds., *Knowledge and Language. Volume III: Metaphor and Knowledge* (Dordrecht, 1993), 155–203, © 1993 by Kluwer Academic Publishers; "Tocqueville and the Sublimity of Democracy," Parts 1 and 2, in *Tocqueville Review* 14, 15 (1993, 1994).

I am grateful to the publishers for their permission to reprint these essays here.

Contents

Preface

The origins of this book go back to the middle of the eighties, when I had finished my book on narrative logic. In that book I had hoped to give a version of historism that might satisfy the requirements of late-twentieth-century philosophy of language. Since historism was not only a theory of history but also had its political implications—implications that were so obvious and ineluctable that historism profoundly changed the face of political philosophy in the nineteenth century—I now naturally asked myself what consequences my modernized form of historism might have for political philosophy.[1]

The beginning of an answer was provided by the insight that the argument from historical to political theory was best conducted via the notion of representation. Historians represent the past and political representation may well be seen as the heart of parliamentary democracy. Both in my work on historical theory and in this book on political philosophy I have openly welcomed and embraced all the aestheticist connotations of the term "representation." Moreover, it is no coincidence that historism and parliamentary democracy both came into being at exactly the same time in Western history: for the historists' ideal of an "objective" representation of the past is the historian's counterpart of the democratic politician's search for the *juste milieu* in the conflict of interests and ideologies. Both historism and democracy are typical products of the Restoration, when Europe came to itself again after the fall of Napoleon.

The common factor in my conceptions of historical and political representation is that there are no algorithms that link the represented to its representation. Obviously, that is what we have art for: the interest of art lies in the fact that there are no fixed and generally accepted rules to link the represented and its artistic representation. When asking myself what this might mean for politics, I found the answer in Machiavelli's insight into the "brokenness" of political reality. There is no continuity between the ruler (or representative) and the ruled (or represented). Far from regretting this, as most people are apt to do, we may discern here not a *threat* to civil freedom and all legitimate political power but precisely their origins. It is here that this book opposes almost all of contemporary political philosophy, for which brokenness—if recognized at all—is an obstacle to be overcome rather than the beginning of all (political) wisdom.

But my greatest difficulty lay elsewhere. The polarity between the represented and the representative (suggested by this crucial term "representation") seems to be gradually disintegrating in our contemporary political world. The distinction between the state, the political party, and the representative, on the one hand, and society and the citizen (or represented), on the other, is nowadays losing much of the clarity that it used to have. So how to react to this?, I asked myself.

Should the notion of representation and of an aesthetic political philosophy be used for explaining this gradual erosion of the state and its loss of contours, and for presenting this evolution as a desirable inevitability that will introduce us into a new and happy "post-state" political world, as theorists like Jean-Marie Guéhenno have recently so convincingly argued? Just as, according to Arthur Danto, contemporary art aims at a leveling of the traditional barriers between the representation and what it represented? Or is this loss of the contours of the state precisely our major political problem and ought aesthetic political philosophy be seen as our best intellectual instrument for restoring to the state its contours and its self-confidence?

I believe that no theoretically convincing answer to this dilemma can be given. One may well argue with the postmodernist that in our world "all that is solid melts into the air," and that the state is just another victim of the process. On the other hand, one may argue that we need the state, since, for better or worse, it is the only collective institution we possess that can help us solve our political problems. So, in the end, if I am not mistaken, the dilemma can only be decided by means of practical arguments, that is, by a maximally open-minded assessment of our present political predicament. Practice, not theory, must be decisive.

Such practical arguments, then, made me opt for the second approach to the dilemma. For after the short euphoria of 1989 we have discovered the number and the size of our collective problems, and we shall have to solve them in one way or another in the next few decades. Problems such as the depletion of oil reserves, multiculturalism, unemployment and "jobless growth," climatological change, crime, overpopulation, ethnic conflicts, the social and physical disintegration of our large cities—these we cannot even think of addressing with the helpless and impotent state we presently have. A stronger state seems inevitable if we wish to deal with problems like these.

So, in the end, what decides the question is one's view of the future. If one believes that all our future collective problems can and will effectively be solved by experts, networks (financial or otherwise), lobbies, bureaucracies, and all these institutional microorganisms that have grown up between the citizen and the state—if one believes that politics has truly come to its end in our age in the way predicted by Fukuyama—one will feel little affinity with the argument in this book. If, on the other hand, one believes that the experts, the networks, and all the rest (may) generate their own kind of problem, often belittled or even wholly unnoticed by themselves, and that even in the future, at least *somewhere* in the body politic, *some* effort must be made to see how these problems hang together and how we could effectively deal with them, then one will concur with the plea for a stronger state that is presented in this book.

But this *stronger* state should not be identified with the *meddlesome* state that socialism and social democrats have always striven for. For the meddlesome state inevitably is a weak state, since its meddlesomeness results from its lack of strength to resist the invitations of civil society to get entangled in issues where there is no credit to be gained by the state. The large state is *sui generis* a weak state, unable to pronounce the word "no"; its largeness is the unmistakable sign of its flabby weakness and of its incapacity to avoid involvement in issues in which it can only compromise itself. The strong state is the lean and autonomous state that is aware that it can serve civil society only when it does not forget about its nature, its possibilities, and its inherent limitations—in short, the state knowing that it should only attempt to do what it can do *well*. Obviously, for the politician this means that he or she can do democracy no worse disservice than to suggest to the public that the democratic state might be able to solve a certain kind of political problem, while being quite well aware that it will be beyond the state's capacity to do so. There is no form of political misbehavior by the politician that will more readily sow the seeds of justified frustration, distrust, and contempt in the heart of the citizen and that will more strongly reinforce these two main innate vices of democracy, which are immoderateness and the tendency to ignore the facts. Nothing will compromise democracy more than unclarity about what (democratic) politics can and cannot do.

Violating the democratic state's nature by attempts to transcend its possibilities may, admittedly, create the illusion of the state's omnipotence (the seductive illusion that is the source of those two main vices just mentioned), but will ultimately result in its impotence. This insight will give us the right synthesis and the *juste milieu* between the traditional right-wing argument in favor of a small and weak state and the traditional left-wing argument in favor of a strong and large state. The good state is the small and strong state that I shall be arguing for; the bad state is the large and weak state that we presently possess in most Western democracies. The smallness of the good state will prevent it from overestimating its possibilities; this will guarantee, next, that it only does what it can do well; and here we have, finally, the source of its real, and not merely apparent strength.

Yet the experiences of this century with strong (and large) states have been such that we know that without democracy a strong state can unleash the worst of terrors. Even smallness would not necessarily and under all circumstances be a sufficient guarantee against such terrors. How, then, to reconcile our love of democracy with the necessity of a stronger state? It is my conviction that only within the parameters of an aesthetic political philosophy can an answer to that most urgent question be given.

F.R.A.

Anloo, September 1995

Aesthetic Politics

Political Philosophy
Beyond Fact and Value

Against Ethics

In 1971 John Rawls published his famous *A Theory of Justice*. It is often said that the publication of this book symbolized the rebirth of political philosophy in our time. Certainly many good arguments can be given in favor of this assessment of the book's significance. Academic political philosophy antedating Rawls's book was an anemic discipline primarily interested in a conceptual analysis of terms such as "ought," "obligation," "freedom," and so on. So-called ordinary philosophy of language as developed and practiced by Gilbert Ryle, the later Wittgenstein, and John Austin provided this variant of political philosophy with its disciplinary matrix. In spite of the intellectual precision and the ingenuity that were so amply displayed in this kind of political philosophy, its practical significance was next to nil; however, in conformity with the philosophical asceticism reigning in those days, one could not venture further. Certainly there were a number of political theorists like Karl Popper, Friedrich Hayek, Michael Oakeshott, or Reinhardt Koselleck, who did not hesitate to transgress these narrow disciplinary limitations and who tried, in their work, to offer a more substantial and ambitious analysis of existing political reality and to pronounce on the political issues of the day. But precisely because of their interest in more concrete aspects of political realities their work was generally regarded with an *air de dédain* by academic political philosophers. Irrelevance to contemporary political issues was considered a most praiseworthy virtue

in political philosophy, rather than a shortcoming. It was believed that the
discipline should present us with timeless insights into the nature of our
political conceptual apparatus and leave such mundane matters as the discussion of the advantages or disadvantages of Western capitalist democracy
or of Soviet-style communism to unsophisticated amateurs such as politicians, journalists, or party ideologues.

Rawls radically changed this. He developed in his book a number of
principles for distributive justice—that is to say, for how welfare and income ought to be distributed in a just society. The result of his inquiry
was, roughly, that inequalities could be justified if and only if these inequalities would also be in the interest of those who are least well-off in a
society. The two main methodological instruments that enabled Rawls to
come to this conclusion were his notions of the "original position" and the
"veil of ignorance"; Rawls introduced these two notions because he believed, first, that we can only meaningfully discuss issues of equality and
distributive justice if and to the extent that we succeed in eliminating all
the contingent and historical factors that make us into the concrete human
individuals that we are, and, second, that with the help of and in terms of
these two notions these factors could be successfully discarded. History is
thus in Rawls's methodology the main villain, the dimension that has to be
ruthlessly and relentlessly driven out. In short, by imagining ourselves into
an "original situation" thanks to this "veil of ignorance" behind which our
present situation in life is completely concealed, we will succeed in preventing our conception of the just society from being distorted by our present
interests. In this way Rawls paid a perhaps unintended compliment to the
Marxist notion of ideology, since his whole method is apparently inspired
by the wish to avoid the ideological seductions of what the Marxists always
referred to as "false consciousness." And, surely, political theorists less inclined to share the Marxist paranoia about false consciousness would feel
no need to have recourse to such a ruthless abstraction from history and
contingency as was required by Rawls's methodology; on the contrary, they
would urge that a reliance on historical insight can only contribute to the
practical value of what the political philosopher wants to tell us, and would
aid in avoiding sterile abstraction. Anyway, in this paradoxical way Rawls's
tacit Marxism prompted him to return to the kind of political philosophy
preceding Marx, a kind that one might associate with (Stoic) natural law
philosophy and, more specifically, with Kant's practical philosophy. Indeed,

this last was reverently praised by Rawls precisely because of its relentless antihistoricism.

Two aspects of Rawls's argument are of specific significance in this context. In the first place his political philosophy could be used to justify a political program belonging to the liberal left and coming quite close to how social-democratic parties in postwar continental Europe wanted to distribute welfare and income. Academic political philosophy thus gained a practical significance that it conspicuously lacked before Rawls. Second, Rawls's political philosophy was primarily intended to be an answer to the question of how welfare and income *ought* to be distributed in the just society. It was aimed, therefore, at a reduction of politics to ethics. Politics is, for him, applied ethics, and ethics is, within the matrix of his political philosophy, the foundation of all political philosophy. These two aspects surely justify the view that with Rawls a new form of (academic) political philosophy had come into being.

The influence of *A Theory of Justice* can hardly be overestimated: Robert Nozick's similarly discussed *Anarchy, State and Utopia* was a first reaction to it; since then political philosophy has been mainly a debate of the kind of questions that Rawls had put on the agenda of political philosophy. Sometimes colleagues were critical, as with Michael Sandel's *Liberalism and the Limits of Justice*; sometimes they were enthusiastic, as in the case of Richard Rorty's comments on Rawls's (later) writings, but in all cases they did not seriously venture to move outside or beyond the coordinates that Rawls had set. Contemporary political philosophy, the kind of political philosophy we will find in the writings of Ronald Dworkin, Bruce Ackerman (in the United States) or of Brian Barry (in Great Britain) should all be located within the disciplinary matrix that was created by Rawls and subsequently detailed by him in a quickly expanding oeuvre.

In a fiercely polemical essay the British political philosopher John Gray recently launched a frontal attack on Rawls and the kind of political philosophy that had so much been promoted by him.[1] Gray attacked Rawls on his elimination of all historical, sociological, and anthropological dimensions of political action:

> Because recent political philosophy in the Anglo-Saxon mode remains for the most part animated by the hopes of the Enlightenment, above all the hope that human beings will shed their traditional allegiances and local identities and unite in a universal civilisation grounded in generic humanity and a rational

morality, it cannot even begin to grapple with the political dilemmas of an age in which political life is dominated by renascent particularisms, militant religions and resurgent ethnicities. As a result, the main current in recent political philosophy condemned itself to political nullity and intellectual sterility.

By eliminating these aspects mentioned by Gray, Rawls was accused of having stripped the political domain of all those nasty and refractory problems that politics and the politician come across daily and must try to solve as well as they can. Rawls's political philosophy, says Gray, gives an ethical jurisdiction for a society consisting exclusively of reasonable and self-denying intellectuals, as exemplified by Rawls himself (as we may hope). And all that distinguishes the scholar's study from the brute and harsh realities of political practice is now lost from sight. Therefore we need not be surprised, says Gray, that Rawlsian political philosophy has had virtually no repercussions in politics itself. Neither the politician, nor the citizen, nor political parties (with the exception of some party ideologues) have ever demonstrated any interest in this kind of political philosophy, nor have they ever had any reason to react otherwise.

And here we may discern the fatal shortcoming of Rawlsian political philosophy if compared to that expounded in the writings of theorists from a remoter past, such as Bodin, Hobbes, Locke, Montesquieu, Tocqueville, or Constant. These theorists responded to the great political challenges of their time—whether it be the great European religious civil war of the sixteenth and seventeenth centuries, in the case of Bodin or Hobbes; or what the relationship between the prince and parliament would have to be like in order to avoid the kind of conflicts resulting in the events of 1649 and 1688, in the case of Locke; or the question of the best constitution for a parliamentary government, as in the cases of Montesquieu or Constant. It is certainly true that these theorists were by no means averse to abstract reasoning and often they liked, no less than Rawls, to speak the idiom of natural law philosophy. But the use of this idiom was merely a rhetorical ploy for convincing their audience. It was an appeal to the language used and respected by the intellectual community they wished to address, and emphatically not an attempt to get lost in the technicalities of the idiom, or to evade urgent political problems existing in their times. And whenever a political philosopher did indeed mistake the language of his argument for its essence—as was the case with a theorist such as Christian Wolff—the political message rarely survived its messenger.

Put differently, for theorists such as Hobbes, Locke, or Montesquieu a quasi-universalist argument couched in the idiom of natural law was always intended to offer a solution to some well-defined, concrete, and urgent political problem with which western European society saw itself confronted in some phase of its history. What is of interest in their arguments down to the present day is not whether they offered a more or a less believable form of natural law philosophy or whether their conclusions were always warranted by their premises, but in what way their writings have enabled them to conceptualize these most urgent problems, and could thus contribute to a new balance of political powers between western European states or within these states. What remains of permanent interest in their writings is their inventory of the most urgent political problems of their time: how these problems should be addressed and conceptualized and what language and concepts would be needed for solving them. They knew that a political theorist can only be of value for practical politics if he or she has the capacity and the "Fingerspitzengefühl" to identify those cogwheels in the political machinery that prevent it from functioning satisfactorily; they knew that the political theorist has to be a mechanic rather than a designer of political machines, and that the universalism of the designer of completely new political machines will inevitably doom the political theorist to academic irrelevance. The political philosopher must primarily possess Lynceus's sharp eye, to see through all the complexities of the fabric of society and through all the conceptual veils in which it is wrapped in order to discover, in the end, where the political cancer is hidden. Nothing is harder than that. It will require the political philosopher to objectify his or her own time, to step outside it to a certain extent. Only by looking at the existing political machinery as if one were seeing it for the first time can one become aware of its defects.

This is where the method of meaningful political philosophy differs so conspicuously from that of Rawls: he transcends history in order to be able to forget about it; here, however, one is required to step outside or to transcend history in order to get the best grasp of it. But only to the extent that the political philosopher is successful in this task can he or she expect to be heard by those who will be needed to cut out the political cancer. Only then will the political philosopher be of practical significance to his or her own time. And if political philosophy fails in this task—as is the case with Rawls and with all political philosophy taking ethics as its guide and foundation—it can be seen as merely adding to the confusion and to the number of problems that we already have. Indeed, universalist or ethically inspired political philosophy does not solve problems, but only creates new ones by suggesting desiderata that hitherto nobody felt tempted to put on the political agenda. The political philosopher who wishes to discover the ethical foundation for the just order is not a problem solver, but rather a problem maker—though it must be added that few people will attribute any urgency to the new kind of problems that the philosopher suggested, and they will tend to subsume these "new" problems under the kind of problems that exist already. This is, for example, how Rawls was used in social-democratic party programs.

More specifically, only if a kind of political church would come into existence where the revelations of, for example, *A Theory of Justice* are taught; and only if we would all have become the true believers of this new political gospel; only under such extremely unlikely circumstances could a book like this one have any real political impact, or help solve our social and political problems. But as long as human beings will remain the same old Adam that they have always been, with their unpredictable mixture of egoism and altruism, rationality and irrationality, as long as political problems are "lived" problems rather than newly invented ones, books like *A Theory of Justice* will remain merely an occasion for idle debate and the harmless topic for academic conferences. In sum, then, we have every reason to agree with Gray's devastating conclusion that "political philosophy may have been reborn in 1971 [the year in which *A Theory of Justice* was published], but it was a stillbirth."

Certainly we will now be much interested in what Gray has to offer in return. Gray praises Joseph Raz's *The Morality of Freedom* and Berlin's *The Crooked Timber of Humanity*, since it is recognized in these books that different individuals, and certainly individuals representing different cultures and backgrounds, will also have different opinions of what the good life is (Raz) or that the values that are dear to us unfortunately often tend to come into conflict with each other (what we like to forget because of Berlin's so-called Ionic fallacy).[2] Certainly these corrections of the dreams inspired by natural law philosophy are most welcome, but one may doubt whether they would be sufficient for producing a meaningful political philosophy that may actually help us to repair, wherever necessary, the political house in which we are presently living. For what books like these still have in common with the Rawlsian paradigm is a concentration on the world of the individual citizen and on what is, from that perspective, the most desirable political order, as well as what problems one might expect in the attempt to realize that order. The shared presupposition of these books and Rawls's approach is that the political order is constructed and understood from the point of view of the individual or individual citizen.

And, more generally, if it is customary nowadays to discern three traditions in mainstream contemporary political philosophy—the liberal tradition (as exemplified by Rawls or Dworkin), that of republicanism (as exemplified by John Pocock), and that of communitarianism (as exemplified by Alasdair MacIntyre, Charles Taylor, or Amitai Etzioni)—then this same criticism can be leveled at each of these three traditions. The first of the three discovers the foundation of the political order in what the rational individual will conceive as the just political and social order; the second looks for this foundation in the individual's willingness to identify him- or herself with the public interest; and the third sees this foundation in how the individual can realize the self and all its potentialities in the social or political order. But these three traditions have two aspects in common: the individual is always considered to be the basis or "foundation" of the social and political order; and no clear distinction is made between the social, or pre-political, and the political order. Put differently, the political order is always seen as an emanation or aspect of the individual (to which all the essential properties of that political order can ultimately be reduced). Strangely enough, individualism thus goes together in all these three traditions of contemporary political philosophy with the absence of an effective barrier against the complete politicization of all interhuman relationships. That is, paradoxically, the result of this extreme individualism. For if the individual is so consistently and so persistently seen as the foundation of all aspects of the social and political order, we will inevitably lack the means to distinguish between society and the domain of politics. In none of these traditions will we, ideally, transgress an invincible barrier guaranteeing the individual's sanctity in moving from the individual to the state or vice versa. Each of these three traditions is therefore, to greater or lesser extent, tainted by (or at least vulnerable to) the seductions of totalitarianism inherent in much pre–nineteenth century political thought. Hence, strangely enough, the most effective protection against the totalitarian seduction is not to be found in individualism (as we often like to think, in spite of the wise lessons of Jakob Talmon) but, on the contrary, in the recognition of the existence of a sphere that cannot have its foundation in the individual and that possesses its own autonomy with regard to the individual citizen. Our real freedom is a freedom rather "found" than "founded" (or "made").

Paradoxically, it is not individualism but a certain collectivism, a qualified recognition of the autonomy of the collectivity in its relationship to the individual, that will prove to be the best friend and ally of the sphere of individual freedom. For if the individual is considered to be the sole and ultimate foundation of all social relationships between citizens, there is, in principle, nothing that will be outside the reach of what is collectively willed and desired by individuals. And it has been this Jacobin conviction that nothing in political reality is outside the reach of the (collectivity of the) individual(s) which lies at the root of all variants of totalitarianism. The only solid "foundation" of the individual's freedom must, by contrast, be situated in the recognition that there is a sphere that will forever and inexorably remain beyond the reach of even our collective will. This is the absolutely essential paradox that each of the three paradigms in contemporary political philosophy mentioned just now has been unable to comprehend. For where collectivism successfully challenges each attempt to reduce the collectivity to the individual—hence, where the collectivity unambiguously demonstrates its autonomy with regard to the individual—we will find, at the same time, the *locus* where the individual, in its turn, possesses *its* autonomy with regard to the collectivity. For if there is, so to speak, an imaginary line beyond which a tree becomes a mere part of a wood, this line *eo ipso* also indicates where the individual tree has its unique and irreducible individuality. The best argument in favor of the sanctity and the integrity of the individual (citizen) therefore paradoxically presupposes a preliminary concession to collectivism, and whoever refuses to make this concession will, in the end, often come to the painful discovery of having become entangled against his will in the webs of totalitarian patterns of thought.

This may also explain why we may discern the strongest checks on the totalitarian seduction not in contemporary political philosophy (with some shining exceptions, such as the work of Popper, Talmon, Hayek, or Aron),[3] but in the simple fact that most politicians in Western democracies had the good sense to recognize, for practical reasons, that there are certain limits to their aspirations. They were aware that there are collective forces in the body politic that neither they nor their most brutal or most mellifluous colleague would ever be able to overcome. This insight, to which we owe our freedom, was movingly formulated by the Guizot of after 1848: "We know our limits, the limits of our political comprehension and of our will. We have been powerful, immensely powerful; and yet we have been unable to accomplish our will because it disagreed with the laws of an eternal sagacity; and against these laws our will was broken like a piece of glass [*contre ces lois notre volonté s'est brisée comme une verre*]."[4] Our freedom has had its truly effective safeguard not in some theorem of political philosophy that had been put forward by a Locke or a Kant or some other hero of contemporary political philosophers, but in the witting or unwitting recognition by politicians that there exists in political reality an element of sheer inertia, an immense and immovable weight that even the collective can never succeed in overcoming—in the same way that even the most persistent collective will of all stockholders to become richer is, in itself, insufficient to move the Dow Jones an inch in the direction so arduously desired by all.

Similarly, Soviet-style totalitarianism did not fall because of arguments that could in any way be related to the dogmas of contemporary democratic political thought but, once again, because of the simple fact that a certain *decency* (as amazingly embodied in the person of Mikhail Gorbachev) filtered into the ethos of the Soviet leaders. And by political decency I mean the following two things: first, the readiness to recognize and to respect that dimension of passive and invincible inertia present in the political domain to which I referred a moment ago and, second, the capacity to creatively adapt one's political goals to the given of this dimension of inertia, instead of trying to attack it with all means available. This decency can also be considered perhaps the most important part of all political wisdom, if we think of the old adage that in politics the difference between the wise man and the fool is that the former does at once what the latter does only in the end, and therefore too late. For it is characteristic of the political fool that he is incapable of accepting the social and political realities for what they are; whereas the wise man has the (profoundly un-Kantian) decency to recognize that he may sometimes have to sacrifice to reality even his most rational, most praiseworthy, and most cherished goals because under such circumstances the stubborn pursuit of these goals could only prove to be disastrous to all concerned.

What we may lose by surrendering the purism of the Kantian *fiat iustitia, pereat mundus* is more than compensated by the welcome insight that there exists this intrinsic relationship between the notions of political wisdom and that of political decency: so that, from a political point of view, it truly is unwise not to be decent. Or, to return to Gorbachev, not "glasnost" or "perestroika" meant the end of Soviet-style communism but the political decency of just this man — that is, Gorbachev's wisdom in recognizing that it would make no sense to try to weather the storms that he had unwittingly unleashed by attempting to remove, again, its causes. Gorbachev had the *decency* not to start eliminating his opponents in the traditional Soviet style because he had the *wisdom* to see that an outright confrontation with the new realities of Russian society would be disastrous both for himself and his people. And both in the case of the statesmen in Western democracies and in that of Gorbachev these twin virtues of decency and wisdom originated in an awareness of the *autonomy* or recalcitrance of the domain of politics with regard to the will of the individual or of individual statesmen. They all recognized that all that the politician can meaningfully do is to try to deal as successfully as possible with this domain lying beyond what is collectively willed and desired, without ever having the power to completely dominate that domain. They recognize that the realm of politics is like a second domain of nature: we can only bend or transform it in certain ways, but never form it completely according to our wishes. It is this practical recognition of the autonomy of the political domain that has proved to be the best safeguard of human freedom. All responsible politics and political theory therefore mainly consists in the task of trying to find the narrow optimum between freedom and the necessity that rules the political domain.

The irrelevance and the dangers (a strange company!) of contemporary political philosophy alluded to in the previous paragraph have their common origins in the latter's orientation to ethics. Ethics attempts to answer the question of how I ought to act under certain circumstances. Because of this way of putting the ethical question, ethics could never transcend the sphere of what the individual could and would do. As soon as we enter the domain where politics possesses the autonomy attributed to it just now, we will have left the domain of ethics and of the domination of the social by individual action. I hasten to add the two following qualifications. In the first place, it emphatically is not my purpose to deny the significance of ethics for certain aspects of our dealings with each other (or with animals). Ethics is all right as far as it goes; but it does not go very far, and the restriction to ethics will only too easily invite political stultification. What I am attacking is, in the end, the *reduction* of all politics to ethics that is advocated by contemporary political philosophy. Politics is not a department of ethics, but something else and something essentially more than that. Second, this plea for the recognition of the autonomy of politics with regard to ethics and the pretensions or scope of ethics does not in the least imply, as one might perhaps be tempted to infer, the acceptance of holistic, collectivist, or totalitarian assumptions.

This brings me to the essence of my argument in this introduction. When Bodin or Hobbes proposed the notion of sovereignty in order to check the religious civil war that was fought in their days, this was because they were acutely aware that, under the circumstances obtaining then, an ethical condemnation of that civil war (however justifiable and necessary) would be as useless as preaching to a tree—to paraphrase Frederick the Great. For the simple fact is that the majority of the Catholics and the Protestants of the sixteenth and seventeenth centuries sincerely believed that fighting this war was their supreme moral duty. But furthermore, supposing that the overwhelming majority would actually have believed that to kill one's neighbor for religious reasons was morally wrong, even *this* would not have meant that *eo ipso* one now had the means to realize the religious peace supposedly desired by all. For even if we all wish to achieve a certain goal, this does not mean that we now also have an answer to the subsidiary question of how to realize our collective will. To return to my earlier example, all the speculators at the stock exchange want to become richer—and under certain circumstances this actually happens, for the stock exchange is no zero-sum game—and yet they are unable to permanently realize these circumstances. Hence, even if an ethical commandment would actually coincide with our collective wish, this is, in itself, insufficient for solving the relevant political problem.

It is in this resistance to our collective will and desire that the autonomy of the political domain (and its transcendence of the domain of ethics) most clearly reveals itself. For just as Renaissance "virtù" enabled the Machiavellian prince to put certain restrictions on the unpredictable behavior of the Goddess of Fortune, so the autonomy of politics with regard to the will of the individual does not imply that we are entirely powerless in our transactions with it.[5] To return to the example mentioned above, the intention of the authors of *Les six livres de la République* and of the *Leviathan* was to develop, in terms of the notion of sovereignty, a conceptual instrument for lessening the autonomy and inertia of the political domain and for putting an end to the horrors of the religious civil war. In other words, like all great political theorists Bodin and Hobbes did in fact recognize in the political domain a dimension that we might properly associate with the notions of holism and collectivism. More specifically, this is what they identified as

the main political problem to be addressed in their writings; hence, as precisely *that* manifestation of political inertia that could not be allowed to
continue to exist if a collective European suicide were to be avoided. Certainly, they saw that there is a dimension of holism or collectivism in the
political domain that we encounter when political reality seems to possess
a will of its own stronger than that of all the individuals put together. And
they knew that this is the very essence of what we experience as a political
problem. To mention a contemporary example, we now all know that there
is something fundamentally wrong in the relationship between the citizen
and the late twentieth-century democratic state that we all want to mend —
but we simply do not know how to mobilize our collective will. Bodin's
and Hobbes's recognition of this dimension of politics was the point of departure of their argument and their proposals for how to regain sufficient
control of it. Their conception of sovereignty was the notion that permitted
them — and the political practice of their days — to regain the upper hand
over the inertia or holism of the political reality of their time. And, indeed, if it became possible to end the religious civil war, this was at least
partly thanks to the notion of sovereignty that they had defined and developed theoretically. In this way political philosophy actually saved the lives
of many of our ancestors. In sum, we shall first have to submit to the dictates of collectivism and holism in order to subsequently overcome them at
a later phase. Or, to put it in the idiom of sixteenth-century political theory,
if we do not begin with recognizing the powers of the Goddess Fortune we
will never be aware of how our virtù can restrain her.

Contemporary academic political philosophy does not aspire to this pur-
poseful appropriation of the political domain that we observed in the cases
of Bodin and Hobbes, simply because it has forgotten that we may discern
here the primary assignment to political philosophy.[6] Its ethical inspiration
forces it into the narrow circumscriptions of methodological individualism. Two factors may explain this self-paralysis of contemporary political
philosophy. In the first place, our century has had such disastrous experiences with political collectivism and holism that anything even remotely
seen as the slightest concession to them is immediately and automatically
strongly distrusted. But, as so often in politics, an understandable over-
reaction invited precisely what it intended to avoid. Political philosophers'
self-inflicted blindness to the holist and collectivist mechanisms in contemporary politics has contributed to the unchecked reign of unintended
consequences that is the major political problem of our age. We could only

recognize these holist and collectivist mechanisms for what they are and perhaps counteract them to the extent that the political philosopher has made us aware of them and able to take them in.[7] Next, democracy is, in contrast to what one might have expected, intrinsically opposed to all forms of collectivism. For what seems initially a more reasonable assumption than that if we all want the solution to a certain political problem it must, in principle, be within our reach, if we live in a democracy? Where and how could a mysterious collective force come into being that might counteract our collective democratic will? Hence, democracy engenders a feeling of omnipotence, ruling out an awareness of the presence in political reality of a dimension that is not reducible to the collective will of the individual citizens. From that perspective democracy has an innate resistance to holism and collectivism.

And even though our more recent experiences with Western democracies, especially since the dissolution of the Soviet threat, are those of an increasing collective impotence and of a state that is less and less capable of preventing all its actions from disintegrating into a cloud of unintended consequences, this has not stimulated till now an increased awareness of the inertia or autonomy of the political sphere discussed here. On the contrary, our ethically and democratically inspired anticollectivism and our ensuing blindness to the forces of political inertia have resulted in a free and unchecked proliferation of all kinds of unsuspected and unexpected mechanisms. These have succeeded in removing the results of our collective actions from their original intentions at a scale hitherto unparalleled in the whole history of mankind. More than ever before we changed the social and physical realities of the world in which we live, but we are less capable of determining the nature of that change than ever before. Surely, if future historians would decide to refer to our time as "the Age of Unintended Consequences," what more appropriate label could they find for characterizing (and condemning) the political world that we have shaped? Our exploitation of the environment, the discrepancy between the ethical ideals of the welfare state and the way the welfare state undermined its own economic basis and presuppositions, the relationship between individualism and crime—all these will provide the future historian with rich examples of how our age systematically restricted its horizon to what seemed good ideas from a technological and moral perspective without being sufficiently interested in the unintended consequences of attempts to realize these ideas. And I hasten to add, new examples would be provided if one were to see here a sufficient argument for abolishing individualism, the welfare state, and so on. For unintended consequences have the unpleasant habit of imperturbably creating new unintended consequences if one tries to counteract them merely by taking away their causes.

My argument has been predominantly negative so far, in the sense of being a critique of the main current in contemporary academic political philosophy. Obviously, I should not leave the matter there. I now want to devote some remarks to what conditions, in my opinion, political philosophy has to satisfy if it may plausibly expect to contribute to the solution of our most urgent political problems. I want to recall, in this context, the Renaissance notion of "virtù" that was mentioned a moment ago. Virtù is the statesman's capacity to take in a complex situation at a glance and to penetrate to its essence. It is the talent of the statesman to see what course of action is to follow from such an insight, to possess furthermore the personal power and charisma to make his or her will and presence felt, and, most of all, a fine instinct for the right moment for political action. It is closely related to "prudentia," which classical authors such as Cicero saw as the supreme political virtue. The latter's ingredients have recently been summed up by Andreas Kinneging:

> Cicero called it *ars vivendi* and "the knowledge of things to be sought for and to be avoided," i.e., virtues and vices. . . . Related notions are judgment, tact, *Urteilskraft*, good taste, and common sense. The fact that prudence and its virtual synonyms seem more and more to disappear from our vocabulary indicates that the modern mind is ill at ease with these notions.[8]

"Virtù" and "prudentia" go beyond what ethics requires us to do, not in the sense that they are completely opposed to morality, but rather in that they see that morality is merely one of several considerations lying at the basis of political action. They are amoral or supramoral rather than immoral.

Both are political or practical virtues in the sense that they require the politician to combine knowledge and action, instead of creating an insurmountable barrier between the two, as we have learned to do since Descartes and Kant. One might argue, though, that all these connotations are more pronounced in "virtù" than in "prudentia" since the classical notion still presupposed the presence of that Stoic ontology with which Roman political thought was permeated. In Renaissance Italy "virtù" fed precisely on the absence of such an order and on an intense awareness of the necessity to create one, more or less *ex nihilo*. "Prudentia" is suggestive, therefore, of what might contribute to the restoration of a (Stoic) order that is lost, or which threatens to become so; "virtù," on the other hand, expresses the insight that politics is essentially the creation of something new, in the sense that we can only properly appreciate the work of art by focusing on its "newness."

The contemporary discipline that comes closest to the intellectual world of "prudentia" and "virtù" is not, as one would have expected, political science, but history. In his *Die Idee der Staatsräson in der neueren Geschichte* from 1924, still one of the most brilliant studies in intellectual history written in this century, Friedrich Meinecke demonstrated that there is a direct line from the world of "virtù" and of "raison d'état" to that of historical writing. Both share a rejection of the clear and transparent world of moral argument, both recognize the ever-present dimension of the unintended consequences of all human action; the former insofar as it cut the ties between moral intentions and the welcome consequences to be expected from their implementation, and the second because the object of historical writing can be identified almost completely with the domain of unintended consequences.[9] We may infer from this that meaningful political philosophy will have more affinity with the aims and methods of history than with that of ethics, political science, or any other discipline attempting to cover political reality with some rationally constructed conceptual web. Truly meaningful political philosophy does not find its expression in perky moral certainties nor in statistics or theories about the behavior of politicians and the electorate, but in individual, unsuspected, and surprising insights into the functioning or the dys-functioning of the existing political machinery — in short, in the insights typically offered in the best that has been written by historians. Neither is meaningful political philosophy the result of a continuous refinement of previous insights (as is the case, for example, in the sciences), for, in a way, each real insight is here essentially a new beginning. The refinement of these insights is always quickly subject to the law of diminishing returns. Or even worse, such refinement can and will often result in the disintegration of political insight into a set of meaningless fragments.

When saying that this kind of insight is best exemplified by historical writing, I certainly do not wish to imply that we could not possibly find them outside historical writing. On the contrary, the insight having its origins in the way of thinking suggested by "virtù" does not respect any disciplinary circumscriptions. We will find it most often, it is true, in the writings of historians such as Marx, Burckhardt, Meinecke, or Talmon —

but it can also be found in political theorists like Hobbes or Rousseau; law-
yers like Bodin or Montesquieu; statesmen like Machiavelli, Burke, Guizot,
or Tocqueville; philosophers like Locke, Hegel, or Popper; sociologists like
Weber or Simmel; economists like Smith, Schumpeter, or Friedman; or
even novelists like Stendhal, Balzac, or Orwell. Examples of this kind of
understanding would be Tocqueville's insight into the inherent conservatism of democracy, Foucault's insight that in democracy power functions
bottom-up instead of top-down, Claude Lefort's insight that we presently
have an "empty place" where power formerly had its visible center, or, to
take a more recent example, Michel Albert's thesis about the differences
between Anglo-Saxon and continental forms of democracy.

But what all these theorists, of whatever disciplinary denomination, have
in common and what the insights proposed by them all share is best exemplified by *historical insight*. And that is, essentially, the recognition that
subtlety here has to do with new and original ways of looking at what is
most banal, trivial, and best known to everybody. Subtlety here is not a
moving away, by abstraction or theoretical refinement, from the (political
and social) world we all know. Indeed, the highest achievements of both historical insight and the kind of insight political philosophy should primarily
aim for is the proposal of a new way of looking at what we have been familiar with all along. Insight is here not an ever-deeper penetration into the
depths of the familiar (as we may find in the sciences). It rather requires the
talent, or the virtù, to find the most rewarding perspective from which to
see most of our political reality and the problems politics has to deal with.

It is here, moreover, that we may observe what political (and historical)
insight has in common with aesthetics. For the genius of painters like Ruis-
dael, Watteau, or Cézanne is not that they teach us new truths about trees,
landscapes, or human beings, but that their paintings so powerfully suggest
a way of looking at these familiar elements of our daily world so new that we
will never see them in the same way again. Subtlety is here a predicate of
the observer and his or her position vis à vis (political) reality, rather than
of an analysis of it. It has its locus in a *representation* of (political) reality,
rather than in the attempt to structure reality *itself* by means of either a
(socio-scientific) conceptual web or by moral laws. In sum, political insight
is not part of the realm of facts or of values, but of aesthetics—and this is
what it shares with historical insight. Both historical and political insight
are, essentially, *beyond fact and value*. It should not be forgotten that this
kind of insight is the most difficult to develop: nothing is harder than to

notice the obvious that was not noticed before. Abstraction requires mere intelligence; but seeing the obvious that hitherto remained unnoticed truly requires genius.

Like great art, the great ideas in the history of political thought are not very complicated and abstract insights; they do not require the highest effort of the mind in order to be properly understood. The ideas that inspired the French Revolution, most of the reactions to it, or contemporary democracy are not really very "deep" ideas, but are fairly easily accessible to all of us. In this way meaningful political philosophy is necessarily "democratic" as great art is "democratic" in the sense of being accessible even to the artistically unsophisticated. And, indeed, they could not possibly have the intellectual sophistication of the kind of ideas that are developed in the sciences, or even only in the social sciences, since they can only be effective on condition that most people can understand them, assess them, and pronounce on the way they have been put into practice. This does not rule out, however, that it may take centuries of political development and the gradual evolution of a complex and sophisticated "political mentality" before a population may become responsive to them.

This is not a plea for a banalization of politics; rather, it is an exhortation to both the politician and the political philosopher to remain aware at all times of the inverse relationship existing between the abstractness and the efficacy of political ideas. Both should never forget that it is their highest challenge to always find that narrow optimum between concreteness, abstraction, and efficacy that will show them the way to the citizen's mind and heart. Undoubtedly, this is what Bagehot had in mind when he wrote that "the problem is to know the highest truth that the people will bear and to teach and inculcate that." Political decision-making presupposes the political "Bildung" of the electorate and is powerless without it.

This book is not the first attempt to expound an aesthetic political philosophy transcending the limitations of fact and value. In his *The Aesthetic State: A Quest in Modern German Thought* (1989) Josef Chytry has given an impressive and erudite account of the effort of German theorists over the last two centuries to use aesthetics as the point of departure for a political philosophy. There is, however, one crucial difference between the German tradition of an aesthetic political philosophy, at least since Schiller (as expounded by Chytry), and the one that is advocated here. What primarily attracted these German theorists to an aesthetic political philosophy was the intuition that the work of art always effects a harmonious integration of its components. The atomization of society that Schiller already observed for his own time could, according to him, only be successfully counteracted by impulses toward synthesis that he considered to be the defining characteristic of the aesthetic state or society. It is only in the aesthetic state, Schiller believed, that justice can be done to all the faculties of the individual human being, and that these can most completely develop in the fullest interaction with others. And, as has recently been demonstrated by Pieter Duvenage, this is still true for Jürgen Habermas's attempts to aestheticize politics.[10] This German conception of aesthetic politics is of course not wholly alien to the disastrous derailments of twentieth-century German political history.

The kind of aesthetic political philosophy proposed here is, however, diametrically opposed to the German one, since aesthetics is invoked here not in order to argue for the *unity* but precisely for the *brokenness* of the political domain. The hero of this study is therefore not Schiller but Machiavelli, since the latter, as will be demonstrated in Chapter 3, gave us the first, and till this day the most forceful defense of the thesis of the brokenness of political reality. More specifically, whereas the German tradition tended to focus on the unity of the work of art, the basic insight in this book is the insurmountable aesthetic *barrier* between the represented and its representation. "Brokenness," "alienation," and conflict, which the German tradition of (aesthetic) political philosophy always attempted to undo, are regarded here as the unmistakable signs of the well-functioning political machine. Thus in the first chapter the guiding principle is the claim that it is no coincidence that the word "representation" may refer to both an aesthetic and political representation. This principle is used to uphold the relative autonomy of the representation (the state) with regard to the represented (the electorate) and the unbridgeable aesthetic gap that separates the two. Legitimate political power originates in this gap, hence the nature of political power is essentially aesthetic. In Chapter 2 it is explained why, in practice, we all accept an aesthetic conception of the tasks, purposes, and legitimate action of the state, whereas we tend to favor anti-aesthetic or Stoic intuitions as soon as we start to theorize about the relationship between the citizen and the state. It is argued that the all-pervasive Stoicism and anti-aestheticism of contemporary philosophy has generated and stimulated our incomprehension of the nature of politics.

Without wishing to exaggerate the importance of philosophical reflection, I believe it nevertheless probable that a continuous gap between theory and practice is not without its dangers even for political practice. More specifically, in Chapters 2 and 3 the relevance of aesthetic political philosophy for a proper grasp of the nature of democracy is expounded. And it is argued that if several Western democracies have begun to show signs of dys-function since the demise of the Soviet empire in 1989, the explanation can be found in an insufficient awareness of the aesthetic moments in a properly functioning democracy. This is no coincidence. In politics there is always an intimate relationship between foreign and home affairs, and it seems likely that the disappearance of a serious and universally recognized foreign threat has also effected a slackening of the forces and tensions that used to stretch the political order. Now that the pressure is gone, Western democracies resemble tents from which the tentpoles have suddenly been removed: there is a kind of universal collapse and the "moral maps" of politicians and citizens are now so much confused that political aims and priorities can no longer be defined and the vision of the future rarely goes beyond the next elections.[11] Mistaken or misleading intuitions about the relationship between the state and the citizen become a stronger determinant of the nature of political reality in such times than when the dimensions of political problems are such that even those parts of the political machinery unnoticed by ourselves (or by political philosophers) are kept in motion. With the disappearance of pressure the political machinery will tend to adapt itself to our intuitions about its nature. Then incomprehension can really become dangerous. It is, so to speak, in the anti-crisis of our time that its true crisis must be discerned. This is why the victory of the West in the Cold War had the paradoxical side effect of revealing not the strengths but the weaknesses of our contemporary democracies.

In representation we may discern three dimensions: that of represented reality, that of the process of representation, and the dimension of the representation itself. If the first three chapters focus on the first two dimensions, the latter becomes the subject of investigation in the last three. More specifically, the presupposition is that political philosophy will customarily have the character of a *representation* of political reality. This invites us to ask in what way the nature of this representation of political reality is a product of, or is at least co-determined by, its formal features. Or, to put the question as Hayden White has, what is the *content* of the *form* of the representation of reality in political philosophy? Following, once again, White's suggestions, this question can be answered mainly by an investigation of how several tropes structure the political philosopher's text. Chapter 4 focuses on irony, Chapter 5 on why metaphor is the preferred trope of political philosophy and why we may have our doubts with regard to it. Chapter 6 is a detailed investigation of Tocqueville's historical and political writings, and concludes that what is referred to as "the sublimity of democracy" can only be discerned if we opt for paradox as the trope best suited to a political philosophy of democracy.

The conclusion is a plea to reestablish the state at the center of interest of political philosophy. Without the state—and without a philosophically sophisticated understanding of the nature of the democratic state—we will fatally fail to solve the many and immense political problems that will face us in the next millennium—or even before then.

1. Political Representation

The Aesthetic State

Up until the present day, all thinking concerning politics, the state, and society has moved around between norm and fact. Seventeenth- and eighteenth-century natural law was normative, present-day political philosophy has been normative since its recent rebirth brought about by Rawls and Nozick. Nineteenth- and twentieth-century political theory drew its main inspiration from history and the social sciences: the historical, sociological, economic, and political facts about the evolution of state and society were considered to be the only reliable basis for all meaningful political thought. I do not wish to suggest that the transition from natural law philosophy to the fact-oriented political theory of the nineteenth and the twentieth centuries could properly be described as the abandonment of the realm of norms for that of historical, sociological, or political facts. The gap between norm and fact has never been very wide in history or in any of the other social sciences—certainly not as wide as some people following in the footsteps of Weber or of the logical positivists would have liked. On the one hand, natural law often hoped to derive its norms from the facts it was thought possible to establish concerning the nature of Man or of a hypothetical natural society. And, on the other hand, a great number of the conclusions reached by sociologists, political scientists, and others proved to be *values* rather than factual truths. Similarly, the return to a normative political philosophy in the work of theorists like Rawls, Dworkin, or Ackerman has a peculiar affinity with the kind of rational choice theories that have been developed mainly by economists and political scientists.

Hence, what is and what ought to be were always the two questions giving rise to the perspectives from which politics, the state, and society were seen. Traditionally, however, a third domain, besides the question as to what *is* and what *ought* to be, is ascribed to philosophy; I am referring here to aesthetics, to the question of beauty and of the aesthetic representation of reality. Yet aesthetics has seldom been seen as a suitable partner for political philosophy. Nevertheless, there is at least one eminent exception to this rule if we think of Friedrich Schiller.[1] Schiller considered it a shortcoming of the Kantian system that aesthetics, the theme of the third *Critique*, was not explicitly given the highest position in it. It deserved this place, in Schiller's opinion, on the basis of the interrelations of the three *Critiques*. He therefore wanted to place aesthetics above ethics in order to aestheticize political philosophy. Schiller remained too much within the Kantian system to be able to correct Kant in this respect in his *Über die ästhetische Erziehung des Menschen* (1795). Schiller distinguished here between the so-called dynamic state, in which we are still "in the terrifying empire of force"; next, the ethical state, in which Man is "in the sacred empire of law";[2] and last, the highest of the three, the aesthetic state. It turns out, however, that this aesthetic state only *motivates* our subjection to the ethical law, to what "Tugend" requires of us. The aesthetic state's definition is not then substantially different from that of the ethical state. Aesthetics may give us an argument for ethical behavior while leaving the nature of the latter out of consideration. Because of this we may say that even Schiller's "aesthetic" state does not really escape from the well-defined bounds that were indicated by Kantian ethics. For as far as the ethical law itself is concerned, Schiller remained faithful to Kant. In sum, Schiller could and would go no further than the following statement: aesthetics, good taste, "provides the mind with the right moral orientation, since it removes the inclinations that might obstruct the latter, while awakening those that are favorable to it [gibt also dem Gemut eine für die Tugend zweckmässige Stimmung, weil er die Neigungen entfernt die sie hindern, und diejenigen erweckt, die ihr günstig sind]."[3]

In the following I would like to move further than Schiller did in replacing ethics by aesthetics as a partner and source of inspiration for political philosophy. The subject of political representation immediately presents itself to this end. For we say that the artist "represents" reality in the work of art, and the nature of the aesthetic representation of reality has always been an important topic in debates between aestheticians. Even at first sight, we can ascertain a number of obvious parallels between political representation and artistic representation—certainly if we think of their attitudes toward fact and norm. Neither invites an empirical and fact-oriented or an ethically inspired approach. As various writers since Guizot have observed, whether a state represents its people is a question of taste, of a feeling on the part of those represented, just as is the question of whether a work of art represents reality properly.[4] To be more precise, in both cases correct representation will always be a matter of dispute and can never be objectively ascertained in the way we can ascertain the factual truth of a statement. In both cases the debate on the correctness of representation seems more important—seems a more indispensable condition for aesthetic and political success—than a consensus on "correct" representation, either artistic or political. There is an intrinsic relationship between aesthetics on the one hand and debates that are in principle undecidable on the other. And, from this perspective, a normative approach must be seen as even less satisfactory: norms will have here the practical effect of an attempt to suppress present and future debate about representation on the basis of alleged ethical certainties. And so it is in art: the question as to how the artist ought to represent reality—assuming we consider this question to be a meaningful one—will immediately be recognized by us as an aesthetic question and phrased as such. It may seem, therefore, that both in aesthetic and in political representation, the normative or ethical dimension is immediately reduced to irrelevance by the aesthetic dimension. And since representation can well be seen as the heart of politics— because all politics presupposes the self-awareness of the political collectivity that is paradigmatically exemplified by (political) representation— this may suggest the priority that we must ascribe to an aesthetic approach over an ethical approach to politics.

I will begin my argument by making a number of terminological agreements concerning what I take political representation to mean. I will then give a brief survey of the debate on political representation. Third, I will make an attempt to solve the problems that arose in this debate. To that end, political representation will (as may be clear from the foregoing) be interpreted aesthetically. Finally, I shall mention the most important consequences of an acceptance of what I shall refer to as aesthetic political representation.

1. *Terminological Agreements*

"Democratic theory has little to gain from talking the language of representation," wrote H. B. Mayo. "There is no need to confuse democratic politics by a theory that makes the difficulties appear to be metaphysical or logical within the concept of representation."[5] The concept of political representation undoubtedly seems vague, and is certainly so if we, like Mayo, are used to talking the languages of fact and norm. It is true that opinions vary greatly when it comes to the meaning of the concept and that it is even difficult to give "representative" examples of it.

What is significant in this connection is that representation is relatively indifferent to the various political systems that mankind has known or devised in the course of its history. It can be claimed that the Egyptian pharaohs represented their people in the contact with other rulers and countries, or that the Soviet Russian government at least to some extent represented the Russian people before its ultimate collapse. This state of affairs, though, should not be interpreted as a veiled plea for a representation positivism that would take for granted representation as soon as or in any circumstance that anyone might like to use the term; the positivist proposal to talk about representation as soon as a political order is accepted in fact would be just as strange as the artist proposing to view with perfect equanimity every past and present style, including his or her own. There is a difference between the undecidability referred to above and an indifferent acceptance of all possible alternatives. Again, as was suggested above, debate is what separates undecidability and acceptance. And more or less the same is true of the normative alternative: What artist could reasonably demand that his or her style and artistic intuition will henceforth be the norm for every future artist? Independence of the world of fact and norm is undoubtedly the explanation for this indifference of representation to concrete political institutions, which has been observed by several writers.[6] And it is precisely this fact about the notion of representation that makes it, in a way other than Mayo suggested but, paradoxically, on account of identical considerations, such a useful concept in political philosophy. Everything can be said or expressed in it, without the representation vocabulary compelling one to accept a particular content. Representation is, perhaps, the most neutral concept one can think of in political philosophy, and for that very reason arguably of central importance in that discipline.

Nevertheless, I will approach political representation here exclusively from the perspective customary since the beginning of the eighteenth century. Since that time the problem of representation has, broadly speaking, been concerned with the question of when and under what circumstances governments, as far as composition and decision-making go, are a reflection of the mind of the people. For that reason the concept of representation has since that time been associated in particular with what we have come to understand by democracy and democratic government by consent (of the people).

From now on I will accordingly take "the person represented" to mean the individual voter and "the representative" to mean the individual representative of the people. Furthermore, I will assume that representation is always partial, that is to say, one is represented insofar as one is a citizen of a particular country, or insofar as one belongs to a group within a particular nation, or because one wishes to promote certain interests, or because one entertains particular political ideas, and so on. I mean by this that the person represented is never represented *in toto*. Representation is metaphorical and always concerns only one aspect of the person represented. In accordance with this I will subscribe to the current opinion that only human beings can be represented and not abstractions such as "Reason" (Guizot),[7] or a "transcendent truth" (Voegelin),[8] or, to mention a few more prosaic examples, party manifestos, interests, or political ideals.[9] For a significant asymmetry can be observed here. If the individual voter is only partially represented, for instance as the citizen of a nation, this in itself is insufficient occasion for doubt or worry since we all agree that the individual is always more than just the citizen of a certain nation. That we are only partially represented can even be seen as mirroring the fact that the individual always transcends his or her political denomination(s); hence this fact of partial representation can be conceived of as one more guarantee of his or her (negative) freedom. The individual is never completely politicized, at least not in liberal representative democracies. However, mere partial representation of, for instance, an interest or a political idea could not be seen as anything other than an inadequate representation of that interest or idea. This does not mean that one would not be allowed to speak of the representation of interests or ideas. It is merely to say that we should only do so in an indirect way, that is, via individual people. Thus, the interest of the person represented could be defined as the political desire(s) that person has, or will develop, if he or she incorporates in desire all the data relevant to him or her over a sufficiently long period of time. In this way, a connection could be made between abstractions such as interests or political ideas, on the one hand, and the desires of the individual voter on the other. In this circuitous way no political idea or desire of the voter is in principle excluded from the possibility of being politically represented.

Acceptance of the idea that only voters and not interests or ideas and so on can be represented also leads, surprisingly enough, to the obligation to accept universal suffrage. The only argument against universal suffrage that has any chance of success is the argument that the interests of those without franchise can indeed be looked after even without their effectively having the vote (in this case the term "virtual representation" is often used).[10] The rejection of the representation of interests—as advocated by Edmund Burke, for instance—consequently compels us to accept universal suffrage.

Furthermore, especially in the German literature on representation, often a third party is required, in addition to the person represented and the representative: a body before whom, or with regard to whom, the representative represents the person represented. Hans Wolff in particular leaves a variety of possibilities open for this "addressee," (as this third body is usually called): "This third party need not be an individual person, nor a certain group of persons, for it can be any indeterminate collectivity, as, for example, the whole of contemporary or future humanity. It can be any collectivity that is competent to have a well-considered opinion. It can even be 'public opinion,' or even the historian and his audience writing and reading in a later age [Dieser 'Dritte' kann nicht etwa nur ein Einzelner, können nicht nur bestimmte Einzelne oder bestimmte Gruppen, sondern kann auch eine unbestimmte Vielheit, die gesamte Mitwelt oder Nachwelt und jede andere in Zeit und Raum verstreute urteilsfähige Menge, kann die 'öffentliche Meinung' oder sogar nur ein einzelner rückschauender Forscher und seine Leser oder Hörer sein]."[11] In this postulate of a third body there are reminiscences of the Middle Ages, when the representative represented the person represented before the monarch. In a situation such as this, however, just as in those mentioned by Wolff, it indeed is not so much a question of representation *by* a government but rather *before* one. Seeing that these days representation is usually studied from the perspective of "representation by," there is every reason to eliminate this third body from the phenomenon of representation.[12]

Thus whenever we are talking about representation by the government, no distinction will be made between the representative of the people, the legislator, and the government in the proper sense of the word. It is interesting that these distinctions are not very meaningful from the point of view of representation and are consequently seldom made in the literature on representation. Even more so, the fact that these distinctions are less pertinent in this context has led some theorists to see civil servants who have been appointed by the executive also as representatives in the proper sense of the word. Sartori objects to this propensity to make the term "representation" cover the whole of the government, countering that representatives are always elected and not appointed and that for that reason such an extension of the concept of representative is not permissible.[13] The objection seems reasonable. On the other hand, an ambassador can properly be said to "represent" a country, yet this official is appointed and not elected. More or less the same applies to the judge or the police officer in the execution of their duties. We may conclude that it will be not easy to say precisely where the realm of the representative ends and that of the mere executive of the representative begins. There is a tendency, however, in contemporary theory on representation to see the state in its totality as the *representative* of the totality of the citizens that it represents. In this way one can avoid the undesirable situation that parts of the government can theoretically escape political responsibility, though this political responsibility can, for practical reasons, be denied to individual civil servants and restricted to persons elected by the electorate only.

Finally, it is to be expected that the problems surrounding representation will become complicated due to party formation within the representative body. Nevertheless, I will not deal with party formation in the following because, from the point of view of representation, party formation is the solution to a practical problem rather than a theoretical one. I am referring here to the practical problem that a representative body without parties so much more readily rejects proposals than accepts them that it would consequently be doomed to impotence.[14] Parties mainly serve the practical purpose of creating workable majorities in parliament. It must be conceded though, that theoretical problems can certainly be raised with regard to political parties. For example, is the electorate represented by the parliament as a whole, the parties present in parliament, or by the individual members of the parties? But this question can only be dealt with if one takes into account the different electoral systems obtaining in different countries. This would oblige me to renounce the theoretical level of the present discussion. A more essential complication is that the answer to this question depends on the perspective of the questioner: undoubtedly, the citizen of a foreign country will say that the parliament of another country represents its electorate, whereas a voter in that country will feel himself or herself represented by a party in parliament rather than by parliament as a whole. Nevertheless, this chapter will end with a short excursus on political parties, mainly because of the role that will be assigned to parties in the conclusion of this study.

2. *The Debate on Political Representation*

In the debate on representation there are two opposing views. According to what I will call the *mimetic* theory of representation, the representation of the people should reflect the people represented as accurately as possible. In the words of John Adams: the representation "should be an exact portrait, in miniature, of the people at large, as it should think, feel, reason and act like them." [15] Within this mimetic theory of representation, the *identity* of the representative and the person represented is, of course, the ideal of all political representation.[16] As opposed to this, we have what I will call, for reasons that will become clear in the course of my argument, the *aesthetic* theory of representation. According to this theory, the difference between the representative and the person represented, the absence of identity of the representative and the person represented, is as unavoidable in political representation as the unavoidable difference between a painted portrait and the person portrayed.

Generally speaking, it could be said that up until about 1800 the mimetic theory of representation seemed to be the more plausible of the two, whereas after that the aesthetic theory of representation became the most authoritative. Rousseau can be considered to provide us with the transition from the former theory to the latter—a statement with which Rousseau himself, however, would have disagreed very strongly. Rousseau, with his customary merciless radicalism, rejected all representation: "The people's will does not permit representation: it is what is, or something different, there is no other possibility. The people's deputies therefore are not, and could not be, its representatives; they are merely the people's agents; and they cannot take any decision outside the people itself. [La volonté ne se représente point: elle est la-même, ou elle est autre; il n'y a point de milieu. Les deputés du peuple ne sont donc ni ne peuvent être ses représentants, ils ne sont que ses commissaires; ils ne peuvent rien conclure définitivement]."[17] In other words, representation is for Rousseau the identity of the representative and the person represented. Seeing that this could not be realized, he recommends that his readers reject all political representation. Hence Rousseau gives us first an uncompromisingly consistent definition of what mimetic representation is; next, decides against representation if defined in this way; and precisely by his uncompromising and radical rejection of representation he in practice invites us to consider alternative forms of (aesthetic) representation. Others, such as Sieyès, whom I will discuss later, are in complete agreement with Rousseau that this identity of the person represented and the representative is not possible, but see precisely here the decisive argument in favor of an aesthetic theory of representation.

That does not alter the fact that the mimetic theory of representation does still have its adherents. Whereas aesthetic representation has been defended in the Anglo-Saxon world since the time of Burke or perhaps even as early as Algernon Sidney's *Discourses on Government* of 1698, in Germany there has until the present day always been much sympathy for mimetic representation. One of the most important and influential advocates of mimetic representation was the Nazi ideologist Carl Schmitt[18]— the idea is, roughly, that there is ideally a relationship of identity between the "Führer" (the representative) on the one hand and the people (the persons represented) on the other. Schmitt was an ardent disciple of Hobbes, and if we recall that Hobbes defined the representatives as having "their words and actions owned by those whom they represent,"[19] thus effecting identity between the representative and the person represented, we can plausibly see Schmitt as radicalizing Hobbes's argument into a recommendation of a twentieth-century Leviathan. One may surmise from this that mimetic representation is in practice less attractive than its theory initially seems to be. It is therefore all the more amazing that someone like Gerhard Leibholz, an eminent constitutional law scholar who was in the recent past a highly esteemed member of the Bundesverfassungsgericht in Germany (and to whose conceptions I shall return in the excursus to this chapter) actually did little more than transpose Schmitt's mimetic theory of representation from the state to political parties.[20] Jürgen Habermas remained even closer than Leibholz to Schmitt in a work which perhaps we should regard as an error committed in his youth—though it certainly is no coincidence that his former Marxism moved him close to theories such as Schmitt's.[21] It goes without saying, however, that there is a world of difference between the early modern mimetic theories of representation and the

Nazi theories. The "intellectual soil" of the twentieth century is so different from that of the seventeenth and eighteenth centuries that the same
intellectual seed causes entirely different plants to flourish.[22]

I would like to look at these differences in "intellectual soil" more
closely, because only this sort of analysis can deepen our insight into
the course of the debate on representation. Since the works of Gierke,
Griffiths,[23] and many others, hardly anyone will challenge the fact that
the origins of modern representation are to be found in the Middle Ages.
These origins are complex and have been interpreted differently by various writers. In spite of my wish to avoid an exposition of these interpretive
problems, one aspect of the medieval conception of representation cannot
be left unmentioned here. In an ambitious essay comparing medieval and
modern representation, H. C. Mansfield writes:

> The English king *faced* the people's representatives because he was not a mem-
> ber of the people himself. He was a member of the realm. In his private capacity
> he was a member of the realm whose head he was in his public capacity; and in
> this public capacity he represented a community that included a king. . . . In
> the analogy between the human body and the realm the king was head or heart.
> (italics mine) [24]

This is also why representation in the Middle Ages, as we have seen, is not
representation *by*, but representation *before*. The idea here is that there is a
broader, profounder, or more fundamental order or structure encompassing both the representative and the represented and that all representation
takes place against the background of this all-encompassing order or structure. Only against the background of "the realm," which embodies this
encompassing order, can the representative, the person represented, and
the monarch play their roles. Without the background of the realm as an
encompassing order they would be like travelers without a map, incapable
of ever meeting one another. It is therefore crucial that all parties—the
representative, the person represented, and the addressee—are functions
of this all-embracing background. As a result, there is no room for the
introduction of an essentially new element in the transition from the person represented to the representative. In this lies the explanation for the
mimetic nature of medieval representation: the medieval representative is
the delegate of his principals; the presence of the all-encompassing background ensures that he can function in this way.

The classical period was essentially hostile to the idea of political representation. If one associates this period with the political Cartesianism of

absolute monarchy—not an unreasonable thing to do, since in both cases a sovereign creator of order forms an initial chaos, either as absolute monarch or as transcendental subject—then one may be surprised that political representation survived the seventeenth and eighteenth centuries at all. (In the next two chapters the anti-representationalism and anti-aestheticism of the Cartesian tradition will be more fully elaborated.) Cartesian epistemology seemed to rob the represented of the rights they still possessed in the medieval conception of political representation. The survival of political representation in the classical period can probably be explained by the peculiar coincidence that the medieval idea of an order encompassing simultaneously the person represented and the representative remained acceptable to the later period as well. The acceptance of this idea left some room for a variant of political representation founded on the intuition that both the ruled (the represented) and the ruler (the representative) can be seen as the cognate emanations of that order.

This brings me to a crucial stage in my argument. If we wish to know what constitutes the link between medieval and early modern conceptions of representation, let us look at the Stoa. Seventeenth-century rationalism and the natural law theories of the classical period were so closely and so intimately related to it that one can best describe them as forms of neo-Stoicism. Most of the central concepts of Stoicism return in seventeenth- and eighteenth-century rationalism, and it has been argued by many intellectual historians since Dilthey that rationalism and rationalist natural law philosophy could best be seen as modern variants of Stoicism. The Stoic notion that is of specific interest in this connection is that of the so-called *logoi spermatikoi*. These logoi spermatikoi were considered to control, as the principles of rationality, both reality itself and our thinking about that reality, and the fact that they were operative on both these levels guaranteed conformity between thought (or representation) and the reality represented in our thought. Because of the logoi spermatikoi the pre-Kantian period did not know an "an sich," so that the logoi spermatikoi sustained an order encompassing simultaneously the representation and the represented—an order that secured the correspondence between these two (which is also, as will become clear, why Stoicism never developed an interesting theory of aesthetic representation). In this way, though by means of a fundamentally different ontology, the medieval conception of an order encompassing the representative and the person represented unexpectedly acquired its epistemological counterpart in the neo-Stoicism of the classical period.

In his authoritative study of Descartes, Bernard Williams speaks in this connection of Descartes's "absolute concept of reality," in principle accessible to thought, which is the touchstone for all our representations of reality—"the object of any representation which is knowledge"[25]—and the arbiter in all our differences of opinion concerning the nature of reality. Within Cartesianism a *tertium comparationis* thus came into being, which besides the representation and the person represented offered a background common to these two and of which they both were functions.[26] Nowhere was this idea of a tertium comparationis expressed more strikingly than in Leibniz's "harmonie préétablie." This harmony guarantees a perfect accord between the infinite number of representations of all the separate windowless monads constituting Leibniz's monadological universe. Leibniz expressed this as follows in his *Monadologie*: the monads "agree with each other by virtue of the harmony preestablished between all substances [monads] since they are all representations of one and the same universe."[27] There is one universe, and the "harmonie préétablie" takes care of the harmony between this universe and all our correct representations of it. In sum, just as there is, in terms of the notion of "correspondence," a background that is shared by both the true statement and the reality described by the true statement and which explains and justifies our use of the notion "true," so there is in the neo-Stoic order of the classical period an encompassing order in terms of which the representative and the represented can always meaningfully be compared to one another.

The objection will undoubtedly be raised that I have played here upon the ambiguity of the word "representation" and that in the above it should be taken in the epistemological and not the political sense. However, a second peculiarity of the Stoa and the neo-Stoicism of the classical period is the parallelism and sometimes even identity of the order of thought and that of practical or ethical action. Natural law philosophy can be seen as the most impressive effort ever undertaken in the history of Western philosophy to derive the "ought" of the good ethical or political order from the "is" of human nature or the nature of society. Remembering this we will recognize how in the neo-Stoicism of seventeenth- and eighteenth-century natural law philosophy epistemological representation could become the model for political representation. But let me add a further clarification. The Stoa required of human beings a "logical life," as Diogenes Laertius so nicely put it.[28] For the Stoics, as for the rationalists and natural law theorists, there was no thought, no *theooria*, which did not have an immediate parallel in action. To quote Lobkowicz:

but as the emphasis was on the practical, the *theooria* of the Stoics was little more than the knowledge for the "kata phusin zēn," the life according to nature; it was reasonable thinking rather than either contemplation or "theory." In fact, except for logic and the study of nature the Stoics were no longer interested in the intelligible order and even their study of nature was not an end in itself—it was only pursued insofar as it was relevant to living a life according to nature.[29]

In passing, I would like to add how surprising it actually is that in all present-day theorizing about so-called practical philosophy, Aristotle always gets all the attention. Practical philosophy, emphasizing the unity of thought and action, is nowhere so firmly embedded as in the Stoa and the neo-Stoic natural law theories of the classical period.

Seventeenth-century rationalism and the natural law of the classical period also saw ethics and politics as a whole comprising guidelines for the "kata phusin zēn." From the "phusis"—from the nature of Man and that of a hypothetical state of nature—norms can be deduced for our actions and for the establishment of the rational society. In principle, ethics and political philosophy are exact sciences like physics and are capable of the same precision as mathematics, provided one proceeds "more geometrico." Even in Kant, who in many respects already belonged to another world, we still find a clear reminder of this political arithmetic, of these classical attempts to establish political philosophy as a social science. We recall how Kant formulated the categorical imperative in his *Grundlegung zur Metaphysik der Sitten*: "Always act as if the maxim of your action were to become, because of your will, a universal law of nature [Handle so, als ob der Maxime deiner Handlung durch deinen Willen zum allgemeinen Naturgesetze werden sollte]." [30] We can observe here how the logical nature of the laws obtaining in physical reality, that domain of the "is" par excellence, still provided the model for legislation in the realm of ethics and politics.

In short, it was of great importance to the Stoa and the neo-Stoicism of the classical period to avoid the introduction of any new element in the transition from thought to action. The parallel between representation as depiction in thought and political representation as the basis for political action is therefore of fundamental importance for the rationalism and the natural law thought of the classical period. Political representation thus took on the nature of a "parousia," a political revelation of what essentially already was and always had been in human nature and that of society, or in the order embracing both the individual and the domain of politics. Political representation is the means we must use to achieve this parousia and to let Reason or the nature of things actually express itself.[31]

For political representation this meant that it was first indispensable; next, static; and last, mimetic. Political representation was indispensable because it is the only instrument with which to accomplish the parousia of political truth. It is static because it aims at the representation of a static natural order. Before 1800, political representation was therefore oriented more toward constitutional law and constitutional matters than toward everyday political problems—in which, for that matter, pre-nineteenth-century political philosophy did not have the slightest interest. Representation finds its expression in the constitutional form of the state rather than in the political decisions that are enacted by the state. It is mimetic because here too, as in the Middle Ages, the representative as well as the person represented belong to an order encompassing them both, within which they both function. In terms of this order they are mutually comparable—or commensurable, to use the most suitable word here—and reducible to each other. To put it briefly, in terms of this background one can reason from the person represented to the representative without anywhere coming across an element that is essentially new.

The reasons for acceptance of an encompassing order (either the medieval realm of which the king and his subjects are both part, or the Stoic order of natural law philosophy) have been sketched above in some detail in order to show that the assumption of such an order (which is questionable, as we will see in a moment), has always been the condition for and will always lead to mimetic theories of representation. Whether this encompassing order is understood as it was in the Middle Ages or as it was during the classical period; whether this order is simply postulated, as in modern political science research, as the common background shared by both the representative and the person represented—whatever the case, always we encounter this presupposition of the presence of a universally shared background. It is a tertium comparationis, by which everything can be meaningfully compared to everything else and in terms of which one can safely reason from the one to the other. It is very difficult for us to bid farewell to this sort of mimetic concept. This is evident from the fact that in practice we all readily enough accept the aesthetic theory of representation to be discussed below and feel quite comfortable seeing the representative as a trustee and not as a delegate. As soon as we begin to think about representation, however, we immediately fall back on some variant of the tertia that are common to the representative and the person represented and in terms of which both would be comparable or commensurable. We cannot escape the temptation of these tertia comparationis until we have learned to recognize them for what they are.

In the period from 1800 up until the present day, this encompassing reality has gradually disintegrated in almost every imaginable place. Kant's critical philosophy made the gap between thought and reality "an sich" unbridgeable for good. After Hume and Kant, the symbiosis of fact and norm, *Sein* and *Sollen*, came to an end. Since Hegel and eighteenth- and nineteenth-century speculative philosophy of history one has become aware of the unintended consequences of intentional human action.[32] The political order in which one was confronted with these unintended consequences thus became independent with respect to ethics. History and the social sciences introduced a way of talking about social reality as if it were a sort of object that could be shown to an interested outsider, thus suggesting a dissociation between object and subject that would have been unthinkable within the classical conception of order. Utilitarianism introduced an element of subjectivity, as a result of which, as MacIntyre complained in his *After Virtue*, this order splintered to the level of separate individuals. All this culminated in the present, when the last remainders of the concept of this encompassing order and of all tertia comparationis were to be cleared away—remainders which, precisely because they were the remainders, were probably also the most fundamental parts of it.[33] And the joyful embrace of fragmentation by contemporary postmodernism gave the death blow to the last Stoic reminiscences lingering on in the philosophy and culture of the late twentieth century.

This evolution since 1800 has had its consequences for theorizing about representation. I will mention the four most important. First, thought and action can no longer form the unity they did before 1800. At least, this unity can no longer be postulated a priori, but will have to be "narrated" separately each time, a posteriori. What we associate with the tertia is a *terminus ad quem* to be achieved by (narrative) organization of knowledge and no longer a *terminus a quo*.[34] Due to the loss of this unity, separate theories were also developed for the representation of the thought of the person represented and for that of his actions. If we consider, for instance, Pitkin's book—which after thirty years is still by far the best study on political representation—it strikes us to what extent, in her book too, the two kinds of theories, focusing on either thought or action, have become independent with respect to each other.[35] Representation is first the representation of the thought and the opinions of the person represented, and next that of his actions, but the relation between them remains strangely obscure, as if we had to do with a being whose thoughts and whose actions belong to entirely different worlds. Mimetic representation, apart from its affinities with Cartesian rationalism discussed above, also seems to have a strange elective affinity with Cartesian dualism, insofar as this dualism tends to dodge the issue of the relationship between thought and action. In general, it can be said that in the case of the representative the element of action stands out the most (normally, only the representative has the capacity to translate political ideas and proposals into political action), while the element of thought, of having opinions, tends to be associated most closely with the person represented. The body politic becomes, hence, a kind of inverted human body in the sense that here the body thinks and the head (or mind) is the agent. Many of the problems of (mimetic) political representation can be identified and presented in the language of this paradoxical metaphor.

It is only in the revolutionary situation that thought and action are temporarily united again and it is only during a revolution that the paradoxes of Stoic, mimetic representation are effectively avoided. It need not surprise us, therefore, that the end of the reign of (neo-)Stoicism was marked by a period of revolutions. In any case, having no opinion on the relation between thought and action as it can be observed in present-day theorizing about representation implies that one cannot have an opinion on the relation between the representative (action) and the person represented (thought)—and this relation is what ought to be the main issue of the debate on the nature of political representation. Here we find the impasse into which mimetic representation will inevitably lead us.

My second point follows: in order to push this embarrassing question about the relation between thought and action into the background, theorists consistently talk about the *individual* representative of the people as opposed to the representative body as *a whole*. For in the case of the individual representative of the people, the divergence between thought and action will never be able to exceed certain limits. This means that representation retains at least a certain minimum credibility. I should add that it is here that political parties play a role that is of interest for the theory of representation and not merely for its practice. For the party, at least to a certain extent, still embodies the unity of thought and action that we primarily associate with the relationship between the *individual* representative and the voter. Moreover, the remnants of this unity are also reflected by the profound observation that for the politically educated ear the word "party" will always have a peculiar Jacobinist, revolutionary ring to it. Pre-revolutionary Europe feared parties as "factions" aiming to overthrow the state, and these fears, though unjustified, are not difficult to understand. Indeed, parties can well be seen as the fossilized and politically neutralized remains of Europe's revolutionary past.

In any case the represented can still identify with the party of his or her choice, recognizing there at least a significant remnant of the unity of thought and political action. But on the level of the parliament as a whole the represented can only feel himself or herself represented by it, to the extent that the unity of thought (the electorate) and action (the state) is ir-revocably broken up. The problems of the vertical relationship between the represented and the representative thus take on the more radical form of a horizontal caesura between the electorate and the state—a caesura that obviously is at odds with the whole essence of mimetic representation.

A further aggravation, from the perspective of the represented, is the loss of cohesion that we may observe in all political parties in Western democracies since the eighties and the beginning of the nineties of this cen-tury. Until then ideology guaranteed a sufficient degree of identity of voter and party. It is here that the anti-ideological tendencies of the contempo-rary, postmodern world further undermine (ideals of) mimetic political representation. The end of ideology also brings about the end of mimetic representation (and this is how it ought to be from the perspective of the present account of political representation). The result of all this is that contemporary political thought presents us with a sort of halved theory of representation. For authors go on to theorize about how the individual rep-resentative can and should do justice to the diversity of opinion that exists in the electorate, but they never wonder under what circumstances the individual representative can still recognize him- or herself in what the rep-resentative body *as a whole* thinks, wants, and does. And, needless to say, this problem concerns the heart of all political representation. We would have little reason to have confidence in political representation if there were only a single representative in the representative body who acts more or less as we think or wish, whereas the behavior of parliament as a whole is arbitrary, incomprehensible, or inexplicable from the point of view of con-temporary theory of representation.

The issue is further complicated by the fact that the presence of different parties in parliament is not a sign of the political imperfection of a nation (as the Stoic would have to interpret this fact) but precisely the raison d'être of the institution of parliament or of political representation. For we have a parliament that represents the electorate in order to settle existing differences of opinion. It is therefore the essence of the representative body to be divided. A representative body that is *not* divided is a contradiction in terms, is useless and superfluous, because it will make decisions that could just as well have been reached without it. In this way the political conflicts parties represent and express on the one hand, and the separation of thought and political action that parties instantiate on the other, mutually tend to reinforce each other, and the result will be a political machinery whose workings are an unfathomable mystery to us. Put differently, due to the necessity of making decisions in this discord (which is the essence and raison d'être of all politics), the existing theories on representation fall short because they do not explain why, despite the consistent discrepancy between the represented and parliament resulting from this discord, the person represented can still consider himself or herself represented by parliament at all.

To come to my third point: without the neo-Stoic encompassing order, in whatever way this order is understood or defined, without the tertia comparationis, without the postulate of the reducibility of the representation to the person represented, the mimetic theory of representation loses its basis and justification. This conclusion has been reached by most. Few political theorists will nowadays defend Stoic mimetic representation and be prepared to deny the representative a degree of autonomy and independence with regard to whom he or she represents. From a theoretical perspective mimetic representation on the level of political ideology is rejected because that would deprive parliamentary work of any purpose: Why deliberate different political proposals if in the final analysis one remains bound by the opinions of the people represented?[36] Next, mimetic representation requires that the opinion of the representative and that of the person represented coincide. If this is to mean anything, we must assume that both are known. If the opinion of the person represented is already known, however, it is precisely within the assumptions of mimetic representation that representation is superfluous.

At this stage it will undoubtedly be objected that opinion polls can provide us with exact information about the opinions of the electorate. For do opinion polls not give us information about the "objective nature" of "political reality"? Similarly, politicians have a tendency to speak about the desires of "the voter," suggesting that there is an objective, given reality corresponding to this fiction of "the voter." And, certainly, the seductions of Stoic political theory invite us to believe that there is and must be such an objective political reality. Mimesis presupposes the presence of a reality that is represented. But from the undeniable fact that polls do undoubtedly measure *something* we cannot infer that this something can be equated with objective political reality. Measuring, as in the case of opinion polls, is one of the most suggestive "reality effects" for the modern mind, but it is just as much of a "myth" as the Barthesian myth of an objective social reality that was supposed to be copied in the realistic or naturalist novel. It is here that the nature of aesthetic representation provides us, for the first time in this essay on political representation, with an important insight. For, similarly, the kind of "objective" measurements of depicted reality that have been developed by artists like Alberti or Dürer are undoubtedly an ingredient in aesthetic representation but are never the entire artistic representation of reality.

What is missing in such "objectivist" simplifications is an insufficient account of the relationship between the represented and its representation. What ensues is the failure properly to recognize the priority of the representation to the represented. Whereas we can argue that what the true statement is true of has priority to the statement, in the sense that the rose's redness precedes the statement "the rose is red," this is different with representation. In the case of the true statement this priority announces itself in that the true statement defines a specific state of affairs preexisting itself and independent of itself that may make the statement true or false. This is different with the representation and the represented. The representation is selective: it proposes that we see the world from a certain perspective and that we arrange what can be seen in a specific way. As a landscape cannot determine from what perspective it is seen, so the representation always contains an element that is essential to its representationality and that can never be reduced to aspects of the world *itself* and to what is true or false. Representation always raises the question of what set of true statements we might prefer to other sets of true statements; obviously, such preferences cannot be decided in terms of truth and falsity. This is not a failure or a shortcoming of representation (as those people might believe who are still bewitched by the true statement) but is just what we have representations for: representations *organize* knowledge (that is, true statements) without being knowledge themselves. It is thanks to their capacity to organize knowledge that we can orient ourselves in reality and entertain a meaningful relationship with it. It would therefore be wrongheaded to regret the priority of the representation to the represented as some lamentable or incurable imperfection of representation and as proof of its sad incapacity to live up to the pure and demanding standards of the true statement. For this priority is precisely why we need representation, and why it is for us an indispensable instrument for finding our way about in reality. A "true representation" of reality would be just as useless to us as the facsimile of a text that is handed to us in answer to our question how to interpret that text.[37] This may teach us that we should not assume that there is somewhere or somehow in the electorate a dimension that corresponds or ought to correspond to its representation (either by the politician, the political party, or by the state) *in the way* that the true statement can properly be said to correspond to a dimension of reality. This is true despite the fact that such similarities of representation are suggested by our mistaken belief in opinion polls as determinative or indicative of all legitimate political action.

The argument against opinion polls as a substitute for the interaction between the represented (the electorate) and its representative (the politician and the state) does not at all imply that the represented and its representation should be entirely unrelated: obviously there *is* a relationship between the represented and its representation that may sometimes be more "intense" and more "intimate" than that between the true statement and reality. Similarly, paintings often represent reality in a way that gives us access to "deeper" levels of reality than the true statement would ever be capable of. I only claim that truth and falsity, and the admittedly "objective truth" of opinion polls, are not the proper criteria for assessing the nature of that relationship and that the criteria that we should appeal to here are essentially aesthetic. Artistic representation may sometimes even require a certain amount of deliberate distortion of "objective truth." Thus Gombrich quotes the seventeenth-century aesthetician Roland Fréart de Chambray as follows:

> Whenever the painter claims that he imitates things as he sees them he is sure to see them wrongly. . . . Before taking up his pencil or brush he must therefore adjust his eye to reasoning according to the principles of art which teach how to see things not only how they are in themselves but also how they should be represented. For it would be a grave mistake to paint them exactly as the eye sees them, however much this may look like a paradox.[38]

To mention a more telling example, historical theorists have been at pains in the last three decades to point out the Stoic illusion of measuring the exact dimensions of past reality and of the "translation rules" that allegedly would enable the historian to achieve an objective representation of the past.[39] But there are no such "translation rules," and each attempt to define the nature of such rules and to provide the candidates, proposed to that effect, for a convincing epistemological legitimation have proved futile. Or, to be more precise, such "translation rules" are never given to us in either historical or artistic representation. Rather, they are what historical discussion and the history of pictorial style are all *about*. Hence the assumption that there are such "translation rules" for historical representation would automatically mean the end of all that is at stake in historical debate. It would also invite the philistine decree that henceforward one specific style should be obligatory to all pictorial representation of reality and that those painters who would stubbornly refuse to adopt that style should never, under no circumstance, be considered to be true artists anymore. All the interest both of historical writing and of art lies in the fact that we always can (and even more so, we always ought to) discuss the adequacy of any such suggested translation rules; these translation rules are never a given in either historical writing or in art (as is surely the case with the true statement) but are always the really interesting problem.

And it is the same with political representation: the desire for fixed rules that would be binding for both the voter and the politician, which would have their origins in our alleged certainties with regard to the nature of an "objective political reality," would automatically mean the elimination of all that politics, political discussion, and political struggle is about. We must therefore resist the temptation to reduce political representation to fixed rules and matrices we associate with a "correct measurement" of the "objective nature" of "political reality" by opinion polls, or, to mention a theoretically more interesting alternative, by direct democracy.

Finally, mimetic representation theorists "sound as though everyone [that is, every voter] has opinions ready on every possible question, and hence the only political problem is to get accurate information about a national opinion which already exists."[40] That is, of course, unrealistic: the electorate does not have an opinion on many of the issues that the representative nevertheless has to deal with. Moreover, what is of real importance about the voter are not so much his or her political principles or preferences but how the voter conceives of the relationship of these principles and pref-

erences to those of his or her fellow voters. Not principles and political preferences but how to *negotiate* with these principles and preferences is what
truly counts in democratic politics. That will determine its outcome, the
quality of democratic decision-making, and the voter's assessment of it. For
democracy and democratic decision-making only begin after we have left
the sphere of the constitution of the individual voter's principles and opinions and after we have reached the level where some kind of compromise
can be negotiated between competing sets of principles and preferences.

Political principles and preferences themselves are *sui generis* still predemocratic. And, certainly, for this negotiation of principles and preferences which is the essence of democracy, no solid basis can be found in
the mind of the individual voter nor even in that of the collectivity of the
voters. The voter's opinion about the negotiation of such a compromise can
only be established with any degree of precision and reliability *after* actual
negotiation has resulted in a certain compromise. For it is only then that
the voter can have a realistic appraisal of what his or her options actually
were when the procedure of the negotiation of principles and preferences
was entered upon. As deconstructivists would say, democratic decision-
making is essentially "intertextual" and resists "the metaphysics of presence" that is suggested by taking the opinions of the voter as the only solid
foundation of democracy and democratic decision-making. It is this "intertextuality" of political principles and opinions, it is this *interrelationship*
between principles and preferences rather than these principles and preferences themselves, that is at stake at the occasion of an election. That is
why the only real opinion poll is and always will be an election; this is also
why opinion polls, or even the kind of "electronic voting" that is now envisaged by some political scientists, will never replace real elections.

However, this does not mean that they could never and under no circumstances do so. The crucial datum is, rather, that in our contemporary
democracies the kind of election that we have is decisive for what should
count as a representation of the electorate. This is how *for us* political representation is realized, and to consider then whether opinion polls or electronic voting would not be better is much like saying to Titian that instead
of his own portrait of Charles V he might consider the one that was painted
by Bernard van Orley or the one that might have achieved the photographical precision of a portrait by Ingres or Delaroche. But under the specific
circumstances—because Charles V was Titian's sitter, and because of the
way that Titian succeeded, at that specific moment, in penetrating into

the Emperor's mind and character—his portrait was *for him* how Charles ought to be represented. But, needless to say, however much we might agree with Titian's own preference of his painting of the Emperor to that of Van Orley, this surely could never be a decisive argument in favor of that particular representation.

And so it is with political representation. There certainly is a great deal of arbitrariness and sheer historical contingency in how we constitute our representative bodies. If, for example, electronic science would have been as advanced as it presently is in the days in which representative democracy came into being, it might well be that we would have conferred the constitutional accolade on some electronic voting system and then we would have considered our current elections as a peculiarly crude and antediluvian way of representing the will and preferences of the electorate. There is nothing intrinsically wrong with replacing elections with opinion polls or electronic voting, or with some combination of all these systems (if one wishes to make things complicated for the citizen). But now that we have, for whatever historical reason, chosen elections, elections are why we are doing representation "our way," to quote Frank Sinatra, and why we could not say that electronic voting would better measure the will of the electorate than a regular election. For there simply is nothing to be measured beyond or behind what elections measure: we accept them because they measure what they measure and only they can measure this thing. In any case, and that is my main point here, one should avoid the temptation to predict, correct, or check one system of representation by another; for that would be like saying that now that we have photography painting has become obsolete. We are tempted to say this kind of thing because we always like to believe that there is some "objective" essence or core of represented reality hidden in reality itself and some set of "translation rules" that would enable us to truthfully get hold of that core or essence. But the conclusive argument against all such intuitions is that representation (think of painting) always happens, so to speak, *between* the represented and its representation; it always needs the presence of this distance and the ensuing interaction between the represented and its representation. Consequently, we could never identify a set of features of represented reality itself that would be sufficient for determining the nature of its representation.

The mistaken belief in this essence or core of the represented, and in the existence of translation rules, is the heart of mimetic representation. Mimetic representation has its origins in our intuitive belief that, ideally, the representation is, or ought to be, a perfect "mimesis" or copy of represented reality, a copy so accurate that we could no longer tell the representation and the represented apart from each other. And it is here that we may discover the crucial fallacy behind all these mimetic intuitions. For if the representation has to be the represented's indiscernible twin, we could just as well do with represented reality alone and abandon representation as a dangerous and useless detour. Put differently, the mimetic theory of (political) representation is, in fact, not a theory of representation at all, but a theory *against* representation. It need not surprise us therefore that, in addition to the theoretical arguments against mimetic representation expounded just now, we may find a number of more practical objections against mimetic illusions. Mimetic representation with respect to actions, according to which the representative is no more than the delegate of the voter, is rejected these days because this theory, inconsistent with the parliamentary practice we all know, would reduce the representative to a mailbox. Another objection is that the voters are so often divided that they would not be able to give a mandate to a representative; finally, political issues are often so complex that they cannot be formulated in a clear question to the electorate with regard to what action should be taken.[41] The danger that the representative, once chosen, would no longer take any notice of the voters is met by pointing out that the representative is accountable to voters,[42] who require that the representative will be responsive to those who chose him or her.[43] This last suggestion on the part of H. F. Pitkin was received with particularly great enthusiasm by American political scientists.[44] The reason is probably the spongy nature of the word "responsive": a great deal can be absorbed by this concept without it visibly changing shape. It is the ideal passe-partout conception under which we may plausibly hide all our unsolved problems concerning the nature of political representation.

To move on to my fourth point: the arguments enumerated above in support of aesthetic representation are not particularly impressive. Apart from the shortcomings that they identify in its opponent, the mimetic theory of representation, they are mostly of a practical nature. As such they are undoubtedly correct. A more theoretical basis for aesthetic representation is desirable, however, for two reasons. In the first place, the temptations offered by mimetic representation will always remain strong as long as no theoretical alternative is presented to the Stoic concept of an encompassing order from which mimetic representation always drew its plausibility and justification. Without a convincing, autonomous theory of aesthetic representation we shall always feel tempted to fall back on the mimetic theory. In the second place, as we shall see, it proves possible to derive a number of interesting conclusions from the theoretical justification of aesthetic representation.

3. Aesthetic Representation

(Political) representation, it is often said, is making something present that is absent. The thought and actions of the people not present are made present by the representative body. In the political representation process, a depiction of a political will that exists in one medium (the people) is made visible and present in another medium (the representative body). Hence, representation is essentially a process of depiction. The depiction or representation of reality is the activity of the visual artist. For that reason, what aesthetics has to say about artistic representation will permit us to deepen our insight into political representation. In particular, aesthetics will be able to make our insight into aesthetic political representation more precise, seeing that (modern) aesthetics abandoned mimetic representation too. Gombrich rejected *expressis verbis* the idea of a tertium comparationis—the idea of an order or background encompassing simultaneously a depicted reality and artistic representation.[45] Speaking about Egyptian art or primitive art, both of which we are inclined to condemn because they do not accurately reflect reality, Gombrich writes:

> But recently we have been made aware how thoroughly we misunderstand primitive or Egyptian art whenever we make the assumption that the artist "distorts" his motif or that he even wants us to see in his work the record of any concrete experience. . . . In many cases these images "represent" in the sense of "substitution." [46]

The crucial insight is that artistic representation does not offer a mimetic likeness of what is represented, but a substitute for it. The artist does not set himself the goal of bringing about purely trompe l'oeil effects, of producing works of art that we would not even notice because they fit into and are absorbed into reality itself without being clearly distinguishable from it. If this were the case, precious few artists would have accomplished their goals, as no one will confuse a painting of a landscape with a real landscape. What the visual arts offer is a substitute for reality, a substitute that admittedly evokes an "illusion" of reality,[47] but which nevertheless remains distinguishable from reality itself. It is precisely this distinction, this difference between representation and what is represented, which is the source of and condition for all aesthetic pleasure: "This sort of pleasure," writes Arthur Danto, "is available only to those who have a concept of reality which contrasts with fantasy—or imitation."[48] Aesthetic pleasure is not possible until we have learned to accept the radical rift between the real world and the world of artistic representation; mimetic representation's aim is precisely the removal of that rift.

This has meaning for political representation. We have to reject mimetic political representation not so much because it shows certain theoretical shortcomings, but (as we observed in the previous section) simply because it is not a theory of political representation at all. We can only talk about representation when there is a difference—and *not* an identity—between the representative and the person represented. The representative cannot be a substitute for the person represented if the latter is supposed to be identical to the representative (as the identity theorists of political representation always required). As in the visual arts the work of art is essentially different from its subject and essentially more than a trompe l'oeil effect, the wish inspired by the mimetic conception for a likeness as nearly perfect as possible between the representative and the person represented conflicts with the nature of aesthetic representation and therefore also of political representation. The same dividing line runs between person represented and representative as between the real world and the world of art. Moreover, we should not look for fixed rules for the relations between the representative and the person represented. If the world has broken up into the world of the representative and the world of the person represented and if there is no tertium comparationis common to them both, such rules are no longer possible. Just as there are countless styles in the history of art and every artist to some extent develops his or her own style, and just as admiration for or acceptance of one of these styles need not imply the rejection of all of the others, there are no exclusive rules for how the relation between the representative and the person represented should be defined. The representative therefore has the autonomy with respect to the person represented that the proponents of aesthetic political representation have been advocating ever since Edmund Burke and Emmanuel Sieyès.

This comparison of artistic representation and political representation does give rise to a problem. In the case of artistic representation, we know simultaneously reality itself and the artistic representation of it created by the artist—despite there being no tertium comparationis. We can still observe them both independently of each other. In the case of the electorate or the persons to be represented in political representation, reality is, as we observed in the previous section, not a reality that is objectively given to us in one way or another. But we may argue that precisely this is what representation is for: because there is no objectively given proposal for political action on the part of the people represented, and because it would be a category mistake to expect the existence of such an objectively given proposal, we need representation in order to be able to define such proposals at all. Representation finds its purpose and meaning in the indeterminate and interpretable character of the "reality" that is to be represented. It is here that political representation strongly resembles historical representation: as the constructivist argument in historical theory emphasizes, we cannot properly speak of a historical reality outside or apart from its representation by the historian. Historical reality is always a reality that is given to us in and by representation—which does not in the least imply, I hasten to add, the idealist conclusion that historical reality is a mere *product* of historical representation. The existence of a historical reality that is the object of historical representation is an undeniable fact that no sane person should wish to doubt.

This state of affairs in (historical, aesthetic, and political) representation brings me to the essence of my argument. The thesis I wish to defend is that political reality is not first given to us and subsequently represented; political reality only comes into being after and due to representation. I will invoke here Danto's view of artistic representation. According to Danto, we do not have only the trivial truth that all representation is a representation of reality. He also urges us to accept the more interesting view that "something is 'real'" when it satisfies a representation of itself, just as something only becomes a "bearer of a name" when it is named by a name.[49] In other words, reality does not exist as such until there is a representation of that reality. The idea is that reality does not exist in the proper sense of the word until we have placed it, so to speak, before us at a distance, and it is this which is effected in and by representation. In order to correctly appreciate the nature of this claim, it is worthwhile to point out where representation, as conceived in this way, differs from the kind of knowledge offered by the sciences. In science "reality" is a superfluous notion that does not refer to anything other than what true statements are true of. It is these true statements and what they are true of that do all the work and no job is performed by the notion of "reality" apart from that. Science can do without the notion of "reality." In the case of representation, however, that notion is indispensable as the counterpart of its representation, as that of which a representation is a representation of. "Reality" is only a philosophically active and nonredundant concept in the context of representation (either aesthetic or political). It is only in the distance and difference and the mutual independence of a representation and what it represents that we encounter "reality" and that reality comes into being. Other forms of reality knowledge, such as cognitive scientific knowledge of reality, do not give rise to this distance and therefore do not bring about a genesis of reality (though, once again, I immediately add that this should not be taken to mean that representation *creates* reality. The insight is better captured by considering what takes place when we encircle a certain territory on the map and call it "France" or "Germany").[50] It is in this way that we may say with Danto that it is only by creating a substitute for reality (that is, a representation) that we place ourselves at a distance from reality and thus bring it into being. Only in representation are our representations and reality separated by the dividing line that assigns to each of them their proper domain.

The significance that this insight has for political representation is easy to guess. It is not a case, as the mimetic line of thought suggests, of there first being a reality of individuals to be represented—the voters of a later phase—while this primary reality is subsequently represented in the representation of the people. This was the way one reasoned within the mimetic natural law theories, and up to the present day we do all feel a strong tendency to revert to this intuitive reasoning. Political reality, however, is not a reflection of a natural reality of people represented that exists first; political reality does not exist *before* political representation but only exists *through* it. Political reality is not something we come across as if it has always existed; it is not found or discovered, but made, in and by the procedures of political representation. The cliché about the creation of a new fact can be taken literally here. In contrast to physical reality, which we have to take as it is—and which can therefore also be studied without ever using the word "reality," because the use of this word does not signify any gain for the physicist—we are dealing here with a reality that, with respect to form, magnitude, extent, and the laws valid in it, is as changeable and varied as the styles in the history of art. Just as art has no tertium comparationis that as an arbiter on the factual or the normative level has power of decision concerning the adequacy of the various styles in the representation of reality, political representation does not have any facts or norms that can prescribe which forms of political reality we should strive for. The aesthetic reality of the work of art does not arise from the artistic rules the artist learned and neither does political reality originate from the acceptance of certain facts or normative rules.

As has repeatedly been stressed, all this is not a form of idealism; idealism is a philosophical reflection on the nature of reality and that is not the issue here. Here, however, we are dealing with the quite different issue of the *genesis* of political reality instead of the proper philosophical interpretation of the ontological status of an already existing reality. And, obviously, not until we have reached an explanation of its genesis can we ask the subsidiary ontological question.

The nature of the reality that comes into being in political representation, however, can be further specified. As we have seen, there is no identity of the representative and the person represented in political representation. Hence there is no identity either of the political will of the representative and that of the person represented; yet the former is binding for the latter. The political reality created by aesthetic representation is therefore essentially political *power*. The aesthetic difference or gap between the represented and his or her representative is the origin of (legitimate) political power, and we are therefore justified in assigning to political power an *aesthetic* rather than an *ethical* nature. If this sounds unduly bold and crude, I propose to take into account the following two considerations. First, the fact that the political will of the representative and that of the person represented are not identical does not necessarily imply that the two are conflicting (although that certainly may be the case as well). The seductions of mimetic representation immediately make us think — just like Rousseau — of a conflict in such a case. But a moment's thought will reveal to us the weakness or even the absurdity of the mimetic theory. For the mimetic theory permits of two situations only: either the representative is a correct representation of the represented (but is in that case superfluous), or he or she is not (and in that case the representative's power is, according to the logic of the mimetic theory, illegitimate). Such was, as we have seen, the impeccable logic of Rousseau's argument, and it follows that adherents of the mimetic theory will be forced either to deny the existence of political power or to declare *all* political power intrinsically illegitimate. If we return to the aesthetic paradigm, however, we will recognize that the painting the artist makes of a landscape is not identical to the landscape painted, and still we do not speak of a conflict. The difference between the landscape itself and its artistic representation is not a mere mistake in or a shortcoming of the painting—on the contrary, precisely in this difference originates all that might aesthetically please us. Hence political "reality," the legitimate political power I mentioned just now, comes into being in the hollow or the lee, so to speak, which political aesthetic representation generates between the representative and the person represented. In other words, while in mimetic representation the domains of the representative and the person represented in principle always coincide or are congruous, with the result that every difference in political will on the part of the representative and the person represented would imply a harsh exercise of power by the former against the latter, aesthetic representation creates an opening between the two, which allows both the representative and the person represented their own space to move in without coming into conflict with each other.

Second, the claim that the power arising from representation is legitimate power can be amplified in two ways. First, the power used legitimately by the representative can just as easily be taken from him again by the voter. Obviously, this is how power is constitutionally legitimized. But more important is a second consideration. It immediately follows from my account of the aesthetic nature of political power that though it can be *used* by the representative (or the state) it is *in possession* of neither the represented (or the people) or the representative (or the state). For, as we have seen, power originates neither in the people (as the theorists of popular sovereignty have argued) nor in the ruler (as was argued by theorists of the absolutist state), but *between* the people and the state. Or, in order to avoid the suggestion of a quasi-mystical origin of legitimate political power, one might say that power originates in the decision of the people to allow the body of the people to be divided into representatives and persons represented. The constitutional rules between voters and the person elected are the rules of play for the control of something that does not belong to either of them— for the simple reason that political power *could* never belong to either one of the two. If political power were to be given to either one of the two parties, this would inevitably lead to a renaissance of mimetic concepts.

Much of this was already to be found in the speeches and pamphlets written by Emmanuel Joseph Sieyès on the eve and during the first years of the French Revolution. In my opinion, Sieyès penetrated deeper into the secrets of representation than any other theorist before or after him. For Sieyès, too, political philosophy is not a science like physics, not a form of ethics, but an *art*. Political philosophy is not restricted, as is physics, to a theoretical connection between facts; it is an *ars combinatoria* and resembles the work of the architect, who first has to create an image, a "representation" of a building, before this representation can become reality.[51] Next, ethics gives guidelines for the actions of the individual. "The art of the social," on the other hand, is, according to Sieyès, "the art of assuring and augmenting the happiness of nations," and for this art it is true that "because it is truly creative, it cannot rely upon already existing models in either nature or history; it must exceed mere reference to history or nature."[52] For Sieyès, too, political representation was aesthetic, as understood here, and the source of all legitimate political power. "All power originates in representation,"[53] not because representation legitimates power, but because all legitimate power arises exclusively in and through political representation.

4. Some Conclusions

"For Alexander Hamilton, John Jay and particularly James Madison in the Federalist Papers," writes Pitkin, "representative government is a device adopted instead of direct democracy, because of the impossibility of assembling large meetings of people in a single place, a substitute for the meeting of the citizens in person."[54] Justifications of political representation like these should be cast aside completely. Representation is not a device for solving the practical problem of getting all citizens together somewhere, not a *faute de mieux* for direct democracy, but the indispensable and the only constitutional procedure for generating the political power needed to solve our most difficult political and social problems. Even if a direct democracy were realizable (*quod non*), aesthetic representation would *still* be preferable by far. Without aesthetic representation, our society degenerates into a chaos in which we are both helpless and powerless. The boundaries of representative democracy are consequently situated where differences of opinion do not exist and mimetic representation would thus be possible. Beyond these boundaries lies the domain of mimetic representation, where state and society have become inseparable and where political power is inevitably illegitimate.

Legitimate political power presupposes the (aesthetic) distinction or separation of state and society. Surely many of the problems of late twentieth-century parliamentary democracy originate in this gradual disappearance of the boundaries between state and society. One cannot doubt that this blurring of the distinction between state and society—this gradual depletion of the immensely valuable political inheritance that was bestowed on us by the ancien régime—has, at least partly, been stimulated by the seductions of the mimetic theory. We have (unwittingly) been living for two centuries on this inheritance, and it is only because of the exhaustion of this political capital in our present time that we can now become aware of its value and importance for the proper functioning of the machinery of the public domain. The result of our exploitation and careless dissipation of this political inheritance has been that *both* society *and* the state became the (double) emanation of one (still unnamed) substance. And this achieved what totalitarianism had also striven for: the subsumption of state and society under one principle.

It is, from this perspective, imaginable that the violence and barbarism that we are used to associate with totalitarianism are not its most essential properties. Especially if we think of Carl Schmitt's defense of Nazism, it is possible that this violence and barbarism should rather be seen as merely the means to achieve the union of state and society that is promised by the mimetic theory of representation. And that would imply that we should see totalitarianism not as totally alien and different from the general line of the development of Western democracy but rather as its most dreadful and terrifying phase. What most Western democracies had achieved in a relatively peaceful and gradual way—the identification of state and society—was radically, brutally, and ruthlessly striven for in totalitarianism. That would also explain why totalitarianism had so much affinity with politically less developed countries: countries where the identification of the citizen with the state was only partially realized, or not realized at all. Consequently, the immense differences between contemporary liberal democracies and totalitarianism have less to do with the intrinsic nature of these two kinds of political systems than with the question whether the mutual identification of state and citizen came about in a gradual and controlled way or was a matter of political coercion. As a matter of political principle there is a far from reassuring family likeness between totalitarianism and the typical, present-day Western democracy. It is only the practice of political representation that separates the two: all the more the political theorist is required to develop a satisfactory theory of the practice of political representation. As Tocqueville already predicted one and a half centuries ago, we have become the citizens of a benevolent, totalitarian society without being aware of the process. Only such a satisfactory theory will in good time caution us against renascent proto-totalitarian tendencies in our democracies.

More specifically, it has been the seductions of the mimetic theory — our misguided belief that an identification of state and society and of the representative and the represented really is the best we can politically hope for — that have generated the amount of illegitimate political power that is presently circulating in Western democracies. For as legitimate power can arise solely in a situation where the distinction between the state and society, between the representative and the represented, is as clear as possible, *illegitimate* power, in its turn, is generated by their being fused together, by the disappearance of the gap between the represented and the representative and by the wish of the representative to identify as far as possible with the represented (and vice versa). This is also where the views that have been expounded in this chapter differ from the tradition of aesthetic political philosophy whose history has recently been described by Chytry[55] and that found its clearest expression in Schiller. Within this tradition aesthetics is used for a unification of the individual and the state. Commenting on Schiller, Chytry writes: "By promoting empathy and an awareness of others, aesthetic sensibility gives rise to the development of a society in which the individual becomes, as it were, the state itself."[56] In opposition to this, the kind of aesthetic political philosophy that has been defended in this chapter presents us with an irrevocably broken world, a world without tertia, a world whose components are as irreducible to each other as a painting and what it depicts. And against the background of my argument it need no longer surprise us that the tradition of aesthetic political philosophy studied by Chytry became a powerful ally of totalitarianism.

Next, as has been suggested above, the idea of popular sovereignty will have to be rejected. For popular sovereignty aims at the legitimation of political power by placing its origin with the people, that is to say, the people represented. The peculiar lack of logic in the concept of popular sovereignty was already mercilessly denounced by Guizot one and a half centuries ago: What sort of theory is this, according to which "il y a un souverain qui, non seulement, ne gouverne pas, mais obéit; et un gouvernement qui commande, mais n'est point souverain [there is a sovereign who does not rule, but obeys; and a government that rules but is not the sovereign]?"[57] Political power has its origin neither in the people represented nor in the representative, but in the representation process itself. Political power is a quasi-natural phenomenon that comes into being in the relation between the representative and the person represented and cannot be claimed by either one of the two parties. Political power is not the possession of anyone, though its *use* can be entrusted (if certain conditions are met) by the represented to his or her representative.

It also follows that the referendum, that most obvious instrument for operationalizing popular sovereignty, is not the appropriate solution for reestablishing a satisfactory relationship between the represented and the representative when this relationship has become strained or, as in many Western democracies today, is characterized by a mutual indifference. To return once again to the aesthetic metaphor that supports this chapter, if we do not like a certain picture or a certain style of painting only the philistine will conclude that we should now return to the ideal of photography. Not photographic precision, but a new style of painting is what is called for in this circumstance. And so it is in politics: when asking himself or herself how best to represent the represented, the representative should ask what political style would best suit the electorate. And this question really requires an essentially *creative* answer on the part of the representative, in the sense that there exists no style in the electorate itself that is quietly waiting to be copied; neither does the landscape itself suggest the style in which it shall be depicted by the artist. I do not wish to imply that the notion of popular sovereignty has not been a most useful conceptual asset in the struggle since the seventeenth century against absolutist political theories. Certainly the notion has been a most valuable and effective fiction in this struggle—but we should never forget that it is and will always remain a fiction.

If mimetic representation and misguided democratic ideals effected an increasing unification of state and society, this process had its natural counterpart in the development of government bureaucracy. In order to merge into society, the state attempts to become as close a copy of society as possible (in the way that a chameleon takes on the colors of its surroundings). The state as well as government decision-making strive for a maximal identification with all the nuances existing in society. Every ripple on the surface of society is now required to have its counterpart in the decision-making process of the state. What follows is that most peculiar mixture of absolutism and conservatism typical of the modern democratic state. The state is absolute in the sense that it attempts to eliminate all possible sources of (aesthetic) friction between itself and society and thus to realize the total domination of society that absolutism saw as the proper aim of the state. The state is conservative in the sense that it does not attempt to achieve this domination by organizing society from a standpoint clearly outside society itself (as was the case in absolutism). Rather the state attempts to do so by hiding itself as much as possible behind what it considers to be the most conspicuous features of society. Bureaucracy is the state's instrument for obscuring as much as possible the (aesthetic) differences between itself and society: bureaucratic rules aim at the identification of state and society in the same way that we believe that certain projection rules can define the relationship between a painting and what it depicts. If mimetic representation is the illusion in terms of which the represented hopes for an identity of state and society (believing that this would be the ultimate realization of political freedom), so the state hopes to achieve the same identity with the help of bureaucracy and bureaucratic rules. Bureaucracy and mimetic representation are branches of the same tree—and it need not surprise us that the tree in question found its most fertile soil in the totalitarian state.

But if one wants to put an end to suffocation by bureaucracy and to prevent the state from sinking ever further into the social morass, the representative nature of the state should be enhanced. Where once was bureaucracy, there should be representation—to paraphrase Freud—while the distance between the representative and the person represented should be clearly marked again. Only if this difference or distance is accentuated can political power be made visible again. We should recognize that, from the perspective of the state, the great merit of the mimetic theory is that it helps the state to make itself invisible, to obscure the nature and the extent of political power as much as possible and to assume without opposition the Leviathanistic dimensions that it has acquired in the course of the last two centuries. Mimetic political power tends to become invisible, and therefore uncontrolled, power; aesthetic power, on the other hand, is clearly visible, recognized as such. In this way it keeps alive at all levels, from the mind of the individual citizen to the collective "mind" of representative institutions, the desire to control and to check collective power. Mimetic representation paralyzes political control, aesthetic representation stimulates it while at the same time creating political power. Hence only aesthetic representation enables us to avoid the Scylla and Charybdis of tyranny and impotence. Mimetic representation, on the other hand, invites these unseemly allies. And the fact that the most characteristic feature of contemporary Western democracies (if compared to previous forms of gov-

ernment) is this paradoxical combination of tyranny and impotence demonstrates both the extent of the victory of the mimetic conception of the
state and the necessity to return to its aesthetic interpretation.

A final conclusion: the individual only becomes a citizen through aesthetic representation. The individual living in a political order without representation or with mimetic representation need never step outside him-
or herself, need never see the world from an other point of view, and can
therefore afford to remain a stranger in the political order. Mimetic representation stimulates the creation of a political order where nobody really
encounters anybody else, because all believe that they live in a mimetic harmony with the collectivity. Only because of aesthetic representation does
the individual become a microcosm of the whole political order whose self
reflects this; not until then does he or she truly become a *zoon politikon*.
Contrary to our intuitions—and to a powerful republican tradition—direct
democracy stifles the citizen's readiness to recognize the presence of this
political macrocosm. Again, contrary to what has become an almost universally accepted topos in political philosophy, the citizen who votes for a
representative is potentially a better and more responsible citizen than the
citizen in a direct democracy who can afford to remain a one-person political party. There is thus no reason to agree with Hannah Arendt's admiration for the Greek polis, which, as the historical facts sufficiently demonstrate, rarely rose above what Schiller saw as the "dynamic state," where
political disagreement never furthers the cause of political creativity and
only saps the strength of the body politic. Only aesthetic representation
truly civilizes and socializes.

Excursus: On Political Parties

Neumann observed in 1954 that the political party has always remained "a
stepchild of political theory" and the situation has not much improved over
the last forty years.[58] As Ware has emphasized, all the dramatic metamorphoses that the political party has undergone since its emergence one and a
half centuries ago have eagerly been studied and commented on by political scientists, but these metamorphoses never attracted even the slightest
interest on the part of the political philosopher.[59] Characteristically, in the
books written by such influential political philosophers as Rawls, Robert
Nozick, William Connolly, Robert Bellah, and so on, the issue of the political party is never addressed. Brian Barry's *Democracy, Power and Justice*

is a rare exception, even though in this bulky and authoritative volume a mere two pages are devoted to the political party.[60]

It is not difficult to explain this striking deficiency of contemporary political theory. We should recognize, first of all, that the two obvious and natural principal actors on the political scene will necessarily be the citizen and the state. We therefore conceive of the political party as a mere intermediary between these two and we will conclude that whatever we might wish to say on the political party can only be said after complete clarity has been achieved in the relationship between the citizen and the state. Hence the party does not seem to confront us with a political problem of primary importance, and the problems posed by it can only be answered after a number of deeper and more fundamental problems have been solved.

At this stage of my argument I do not wish to challenge this (tacit) assumption in contemporary political philosophy; it may even be true. It is sufficient, in this context, to observe that this tacit assumption already suggests an interesting question. If the political party is an intermediary between the citizen and the state, should we then relate the party to the citizen, or should the party rather be seen as part of the state? At first sight, it might seem that a democrat can only choose the first option: for does democracy not require that state and citizen be as close to each other as possible, and is an intimate relationship between the citizen and the state not an obvious instrument for realizing this praiseworthy goal? But this conclusion would be too hasty. We should not forget that democratic decision-making requires us to consider the *whole* trajectory between the citizen and the state. From this perspective, it might well be that strengthening the ties between the citizen and the political party on one part of the trajectory will inevitably entail a loss of control of the state by the party at the other part. The closer the party is to the citizen, the further it may thereby become from the state and the political decisions that can only be reached at that level. Similarly, we distinguish between governmental parties and parties that are content to voice their ideological convictions (and by doing so remain closest to their voters), knowing that the latter rarely influence political decision-making. The implication is that within a well-functioning democracy parties will be ready to operate at a relatively large distance from their voters by coming as close as possible to the state.

But there is a more interesting problem, suggested in the writings of one of the few political philosophers who have discussed the political party in contemporary democracy. Gerhard Leibholz (whom we have already met before in this chapter) recognizes the indispensability of the political party in contemporary democracy: without the party the electorate would lack an effective instrument for influencing public decision-making.[61] The distance between the individual citizen and the state is too large for the former to have any effective influence on the latter; without parties democracy would quickly degenerate into autocracy. One may doubt whether Leibholz's fears are historically justified, since political parties were formed largely to overcome the state's inertia and weakness: without parties the government will only rarely succeed in getting parliament's approval for any of its plans. So paralysis rather than despotism is what we really have to fear from a political system without political parties. But leaving this aside, we observe how Leibholz's argument forces him to assign to the party the role that one might initially have given to the citizen: it is only thanks to the political party and not thanks to the individual citizen that the will of the people can express itself at all. Or, as Leibholz writes: "The democratic party-state is both formally and essentially nothing but a rationalized variant of plebiscitary democracy—a surrogate of direct democracy adapted to the needs of the modern state."[62]

In other words, Leibholz's party-state is a surrogate for direct democracy in the sense that the role that the citizen is supposed to play in direct democracy is given by Leibholz to the party. This also implies that in Leibholz's party-state public debate in parliament will lose much of its significance. If democratic decision-making is modeled after plebiscitary democracy, as demanded by Leibholz, parliamentary debate will make no sense anymore, since there is no legitimate political institution for implementing its results. We have only parties; it is they that dictate to the state what it has to decide; and this is why Leibholz concludes that in his democracy political parties are "the true lords of the legislation [die eigentliche Herren der Gesetzgebung]."[63] Leibholz is thus forced to ignore the fact that parliamentary debate often results in compromise, that compromise may sometimes give a whole new complexion to a political issue, and that the amazing capacity of democratic decision-making to solve otherwise intractable social and political problems and its unparalleled talent for defusing dangerous political conflict originate in what happens in the interaction between parties, and hence beyond the party itself. One may completely agree with the important role assigned by Leibholz to the political party, only to disagree with him no less completely because of his lack of insight into what makes democracy so far superior to other political systems. Indeed, what must strike us most in Leibholz's account of the democratic state is his blindness to the paradox that our main political principles can only be safeguarded by our readiness to negotiate them. He who does not wish to negotiate his highest political principles will for that very reason betray them within the admittedly peculiar logic of democracy.[64]

This brings me to another feature of Leibholz's conceptions, namely, his "identity thesis," that is, his view that ideally an "identity" of voter, party, and state is achieved in democracy. Two aspects may be discerned in this thesis. In the first place the thesis requires a maximum of "continuity" between the citizen and the state (as we may find this continuity optimally realized in direct democracy) and that every "unevennness" that could threaten this continuity be smoothed out as completely as possible. That naturally leads to a second aspect of the identity thesis. The political party is the most obvious candidate for effecting this smoothing out of any twists in the line connecting the citizen to the state, for it is the party that covers most of this long trajectory. The inevitable result is that both the citizen and the state will lose much of their significance to the political party (an implication of his thesis that was welcomed by Leibholz). The state now becomes only an extension of the party while the citizen is wholly absorbed by the party. The party as an intermediary between the citizen and the state thus calls into being a party posing as the new Leviathan in political reality. After the Leviathan of the Hobbesian state, after the Leviathan of the individual voter in Rousseau's direct democracy, we now also have the Leibholzian Leviathan of the political party.

From the perspective of this chapter's analysis of political representation, it will not be hard to identify the weaknesses of Leibholz's account of the political party and of its role in the democratic state. We observed that notions like those of Leibholz and Rousseau ignore the aesthetic gap existing between the electorate on the one hand and the political party or the state on the other, and thus in both theories the only origin of legitimate political power is eliminated. And this already suggests how we should answer the question that was raised at the beginning of this excursus: Where should we situate the political party on the trajectory between the citizen and the state? As the question was reformulated: Should the political party be seen as an extension of the citizen or, rather, as being to some extent part of the state?

It will be clear, then, that if we exchange Leibholz's identity thesis concerning the relationship between the citizen and the political party for the difference thesis advocated and justified by an aesthetic interpretation of the nature of political representation, the aesthetic gap must be located between the citizen and the party, and not between the party and the state. The party *is* not the citizen but *represents* the citizen; and it is not true that the state represents political parties. Moreover, we cannot fail to notice the totalitarian seductions implied by Leibholz's account of the relationship between the citizen and the party.[65] It is only thanks to the aesthetic gap between the citizen and the party that the citizen can "keep both hands free" in a relationship with the political party, and that the citizen's political and civil freedom will be guaranteed. Looking for unity and identity in places where we should not discover them has always been the most important stimulus to totalitarian patterns of thought and to political systems intent on endangering the citizen's freedom. Finally, we may infer from these considerations that in contrast to Leibholz's conceptions, the political party is closer to the state than to the citizen. The political party is therefore to a certain extent already part of the state and could be rightly seen as an embryonic or a proto state and not as a kind of civil organization with political aims. The political party is more than a generally recognized and successful pressure group.

I shall immediately concede that this way of situating the political party in the public domain is sometimes problematic. For if the party is considered an embryonic or proto state, the danger obviously exists that the party will start to behave accordingly and will thus threaten the unity of the state. These fears were already expressed by the politicians and theorists of the period in which the party system gradually had emerged in West European countries since the eighteenth century. Beyme characterized this youth of the political party as follows: "In early theories of the political party, they were accused of being 'factions' promoting the narrow interests of certain social groups [In der frühen Parteitheorie wurden Parteien als Interessengruppen, als 'Faktionen' negativ bewertet]."[66] And, in the good company of Hobbes, theorists did not doubt that "factions" belong to "those things that weaken, or tend to the dissolution of the commonwealth."[67] There was fear that the "faction" would pervert the unity of the body politic or would parasitize on it (elsewhere Hobbes expressively described factions as "worms in the entrails of the state") because an opposition of interest between the faction or party and the state was believed to be inevitable.[68] Factions — and what we now refer to as parties — were conceived of as being essentially conspiracies against the nation or the state. For any assessment of the state's interest will always be distorted when it is perceived from the perspective of the interest of a faction or party—which is where one faction or party may differ from another. According to this view, therefore, the width of the spectrum of differences existing between parties is a good measure of the extent to which they will be prepared to pervert the state's interest. The faction or party can perceive the state only from the perspective of its own interest, and so can only "decenter" the state and make it subservient to its own perspective and interests. It need not surprise us, then, that in the first hesitating defenses of the political party it was always emphasized that there is a crucial difference between factions and parties. Thus Voltaire in the *Encyclopédie*: "This term [*faction*] primarily signifies a seditious party in a state; the term *party*, on the other hand, never has unpleasant associations, while the term *faction* always has these suspect associations [La principale acceptation de ce terme signifie une partie séditieuse dans un état, le terme *parti* par lui même n'a rien d'odieux, celui de faction l'est toujours]." [69] And Ball has shown that parties only became acceptable to many people after the offensive term "faction" had effectively been banned from political discourse and replaced by the more neutral term "party": the latter term was borrowed from the unexceptionable and venerable practice of jurisdiction, where the "party" of the defendant is opposed by the "party" of the plaintiff. [70]

A different nomenclature does not alter the thing itself, however, and one may also doubt whether the political party sufficiently resembles a party in the juridical sense of the word to justify this transposition. Borrowing the word "party" from jurisdiction is indeed most misleading, since the relationship between the state and political parties is quite unlike that between the judge and the parties in court: one need only think of what would happen if jurisdiction were to be modeled on parliamentary decision-making. Next, after Jacobinism and the rule of communist parties in Soviet-dominated Eastern Europe, the term "party" will retain a somewhat nasty ring. Certainly these former communist countries offer us the best and most convincing illustration of how dangerous parties can be, and of how apparently justified our ancestors were when they expressed their doubts with regard to political parties. But precisely this fact demonstrates under what circumstances such fears are and are not justified, and when the party may indeed become a threat to the unity of the state. Of course, I am referring here to the fact that the difference between having either one or two (or more) parties is decisive. And I am not primarily thinking of the

trivial insight that the presence of (at least) two (or more) parties is a necessary though not sufficient condition for the possibility of an effective protection of the citizen's freedom and civil rights, but rather of the more interesting and far less obvious fact that the presence of two (or more) parties is,
strangely enough, a stronger support to the unity of the state than the presence of only one party. On the face of it, the opposite would be the more
plausible intuition. Does not the conflict between parties promise greater
dangers for the state's unity than if the state had its reliable support in one
strong party only? And, in fact, this is how politicians like Lenin argued for
the usurpation of the state by the party during the transitional phase between capitalism and socialism that was recommended by them. Thus we
may well ask ourselves by what apparently so counterintuitive mechanism
party conflict supports rather than weakens the unity of the state.

Beyme shows us how to answer this question:

> The very word for parties, derived from the Latin word *pars*, suggests that a
> democratic party could never pretend to represent the whole, however much
> its propaganda emphasizes the public interest or even develops the tendency to
> behave as a natural party in office [Der blosse Name der Parteien, abgeleitet
> vom lateinischen Wort *pars* (Teil), deutet darauf hin, dass eine demokratische
> Partei niemals beanspruchen kann, das Ganze zu repräsentieren, so sehr sie
> auch in ihrer Propaganda das Gemeinwohl herausstellt oder sogar die Tendenz
> entwickelt, sich als natürliche Regierungspartei zu gerieren].[71]

The crucial suggestion here is that the party is *always* partial or partisan
and therefore can *never* be seen as a completely adequate expression or,
rather, representation, of "the whole." In other words, the paradox is that
the party, precisely because of its being merely "partial," precisely because
of its always needing (in the terminology of Derrida) a "supplement" in the
form of other parties, best legitimizes the notion of the whole and of the
state's unity, by obliquely referring to or by tacitly presupposing the presence of other parties. Just as in Derrida's way of reading texts, the notion
of the whole of the text (or of its meaning) can only be thought in terms of
the partiality and the bias of several individual interpretations of the text,
so the party is the best argument in favor of the unity of the state precisely
because of its own imperfection in representing the whole. When seen from
this perspective democracy *sui generis* is "postmodernist" in the sense that
the unity of the state can only properly be thought in terms of differences.

This brings me to the conclusion of this excursus. It is now possible to see that political parties are not an accidental ingredient in the democratic state, justified only by the requirements of political practice, but an essential condition for its unity. In other words, the party is not a mere intermediary between the citizen and the state but, no less than the citizen and the state, one of the indispensable political *dramatis personae*. Without it the game of politics could not be played at all. As has been observed by Thomassen, the political theorist who neglects the significance of the political party, or who considers it to be of merely derivative importance, thus is robbed of the possibility of obtaining an adequate insight into the nature of the democratic state.[72] Seeing that political parties belong to the very core of democratic government, one might even venture the argument that as long as no parties have effectively been formed, the individual voter should be seen as a personal union of the voter that he or she is and the political one-person party that he or she is voting for (and here we have the moment where direct democracy and representative democracy begin to diverge). Another conclusion that can be derived from the necessity of competing political parties would be that democracy can only function because of lively political debate and the conflicts between *several* political parties. Monistic tendencies that might obscure potential political conflict do not promote but threaten the unity of the state. Not "concordia" but "*dis*cordia res parvae crescunt," to paraphrase the device of the Dutch Republic prior to 1795. As Machiavelli already saw, union requires conflict and *dis*union.

2. Stoa, Aesthetics, and Democracy

1. *Introduction*

One of the most characteristic features of contemporary political philosophy is its apparent inability to define the domain of politics and the nature of the political object. We no longer seem to be able to demarcate politics from what lies before or beyond it. A striking example is the following statement by Fred Dallmayr in his *Polis and Praxis*: "I would prefer to describe politics as a human practice, namely as the ongoing institution of the practice of friendship."[1] This is, on the face of it, quite an attractive statement and many will tend to agree with Dallmayr. However, if we link the domains of politics, human practice, and friendship in this way, the result will inevitably be that political philosophy is no longer distinguishable from philosophy of practice, nor from an encompassing philosophy of life that purports to deal with even the strictly private world of our relations with our friends (one is reminded of the Jacobinist's demand that the "citoyen" should publicly testify concerning friendships at least once a year). An even more convincing example of the present difficulty in setting politics apart from other aspects of the "condition humaine" is provided by the Freudian notion of the super-ego and by Foucault's thesis on the relationship between power and discourse, resulting in both cases in the introduction of the dimension of politics into even the most private and intimate aspects of the individual's daily life.

Politics now seems to be simply everywhere. But what is everywhere is in practice nowhere. We recognize that seventeenth-century theologians were quite justified in mistrusting Spinoza's pantheistic "Deus sive natura." If God is an aspect of nature, we may at first seem to honor Him beyond all measure, but the net effect of the claim will be, in the end, that God will have become a redundancy and that we will be content with nature only — all the more since nature is so much more reliable and consistent than God in our transactions with either of them. And so it is with politics: if we say that friendship and most of our discourse is politics already, politics will become a useless notion. So it may seem that we have every reason to agree with Kossmann when he argued:

> As soon as we accept that the state or the political factor has become a natural part of our daily life, we no longer see them as problematic, we even no longer notice them. Our existence is then politicized to such a degree that we can no longer isolate the political factor and we feel no need to study it as a specific object of our attention.[2]

Thus, according to Kossmann, we may witness today the evanescence or the evaporation of the political object, precisely because of its omnipresence. One might wonder, therefore, whether politics in our time has withdrawn behind the screen of metaphysics precisely because of its metaphysical omnipresence — a development that would certainly be baffling for political scientists who pretend to have a quasi-positivist certainty as to where the object of their research is and where it is not. But political philosophers would not be in a more fortunate position, in spite of their professional affinity with metaphysics. For it would mean that their field of action is now reduced to that of metaphysical speculation, that is, to a political philosophy from which no practical inferences can be deduced that might change political reality in any important respect. For this is how things are with metaphysics: if it would invite us to change existing reality, it is either no metaphysics at all or a deficient metaphysics (whose incentive to action results from its deficient understanding of that part of reality on which it requires us to act). Metaphysics and creative political thought and action therefore mutually exclude each other, as Tocqueville, with his usual acumen, has observed: in politics "nothing is more unproductive to the mind than an abstract idea."[3] And so it is in history. In both politics and history there are, admittedly, some trajectories where one may safely argue from position A to position B by means of logic, deduction, theory, causal infer-ence, or metaphysical argument, but these are always disappointingly short and the going most insecure.

Nevertheless, considering the present state of political philosophy, we must unfortunately observe that it has only too easily and too gladly yielded to the seductions of idle metaphysical speculation, thereby inevitably reducing itself to practical irrelevance. It has therefore, in practice, served the cause of a mindless conservatism. For this is the fate of all political analysis that does not succeed in—or, as in current political philosophy, does not even *aim* at—"cutting the world at its joints." But political metaphysics is not only conservative in practice, by being simply irrelevant to all meaningful political action. From a theoretical perspective metaphysics is no less essentially conservative, and we should not forget that even the metaphysics of Hegel and Marx has been conservative in the sense of firmly enclosing historical and political reality within the narrow confines of dialectical metaphysics. Admittedly, this must sound most counterintuitive. But we need only compare Soviet-style communism with antimetaphysical Western parliamentary democracy—so infinitely more hospitable to historical change—to become aware of the profound conservatism of these apparently revolutionary political systems.

Metaphysics is an intellectual device to eliminate those surprises with which history likes to confront us. This is why history is the most antimetaphysical of all intellectual disciplines and why metaphysicians have always discovered in history what they recognized as their ultimate and most interesting challenge. A metaphysics of history is the analogue in the humanities of that "theory of everything" that contemporary theoretical physicists are so arduously looking for. What inspires the pursuit of both the theoretical physicist and the metaphysician is the idea of a system that will give us the final and decisive grasp of all that goes on in reality. That is, both cases display the paradigmatically conservative dislike of being surprised by the unpredictable contingencies of reality. Hence, nothing could be more conservative than a historical or political system that boasts of being able to account for all historical change.

Paradoxically, the revolutionary pretensions of such systems are precisely where we may discover the causes of their lack of understanding of the sociopolitical world: if put into practice they may, admittedly, change the world in a revolutionary way—but not because of their understanding of the world. On the contrary, these changes will occur in the world precisely because of their lack of understanding of it. What is, or has been, historically effective in such metaphysical systems is not what these systems explicitly state, but their holes and absences. Their effectiveness stems from where they fall short of their own metaphysical pretensions and where we are at the mercy of their unpredictable and random blindnesses. Because of this we can be sure that metaphysics will in politics inevitably be either stultifying or, even worse, an implicit invitation to disastrous political adventures. History (and politics) is always where we think it is not—and this is why each "system of history" inevitably is a *contradictio in terminis*. This may also indicate and explain in what respect history is so tremendously important to us all, and why both the politician and the political philosopher (both operating in the realm of history) should always concentrate on what transcends our apparently most legitimate and justified expectations. It is at these places that we shall discover both the grave of metaphysics and the birthplace of history and politics.

We can react in two ways to the contemporary disappearance of the political object in a metaphysical mist. In the first place we might acquiesce in or even applaud this evolution and observe with deep contentment that, though in a way quite different from what we had been made to expect, Marx's prediction of the "withering away" of the state and of politics has become a reality after all. Indeed, Saint Simon's venerable ideal of exchanging "le gouvernement des hommes" for "l'administration des choses" seems finally to have been realized. However, such an optimistic interpretation of the present state of affairs with regard to the political object will make us realize how shortsighted such a reaction would in fact be. For many disputable things can be said about the state, but certainly not that it has withered away. Though democratic states attempt to make themselves as invisible as possible (and have actually been miraculously successful in blinding Anglo-Saxon political philosophers to its existence), we need only be aware of their huge budgets, their continuous presence in our lives, and the way they interfere with even the smallest and the most intimate aspects of our existence, to recognize that the state is far from absent. Even more, the dysfunctioning of democracy that is the major theme of this book can, to a large extent, be related to a dysfunctioning of the democratic state. The democratic state is no longer the mere instrument for solving our political problems that it was intended to be, but has become itself an important part of our political worries: it is as if hammer and saw have become part of the problems involved in the production of a chair or a table. More specifically, as we shall see in the next chapter, there is a category of problems—problems that do not divide society against itself but affect us all in a more or less similar way—that democracy is unable to solve and that, if democracy attempts to deal with them, will turn it into a political machinery that is as huge as it is ineffectual. In sum, the state as a collective problem-solving instrument has gradually transformed itself into a screen that is blinding us to our most urgent political problems instead of giving us a clear view of them. Hence, if a situation has arisen in which we find it hard to identify "the political object," a situation in which political problems tended to become metaphysical problems, we may surmise that this reflects the inability of contemporary political philosophy to properly grasp the nature of what are our most urgent political problems, rather than their actual absence or disappearance in contemporary Western democracies.

The alternative, obviously, would be to start the search for the political object all over again. This is the strategy proposed by John Gunnell in an article appropriately entitled "In Search of the Political Object." Gunnell admonishes us not to define politics in terms of the leftovers of epistemology or philosophy of science, as is so often done in the relatively helpless political philosophy of our time, and to avoid the perennial seduction of seeing in the labyrinth of Habermasian metaphysics the royal road to political insight. For him there are no *intrinsic* political objects: "There are political objects, but the fact that they are political is predicational. It is a property, an attribute, or quality attached to certain instances of conventional objects."[4] In other words, it is convention that makes an object into a political object; something is a political object simply because we decide to see it in this way. This proposal has an immense plausibility if we bear in mind the variety of topics that have been politicized in the course of two and a half thousand years. But, in spite of its plausibility, the proposal will offer us little help in our present predicament. If present-day "convention" is such that we find it hard to define the political object, then an appeal to convention cannot contribute to a more accurate definition of what a political problem is. "Convention" can only result here in a restatement of our original difficulty and we could explain the failure of this initially promising definition of the political object with the observation that it is just one other example of political metaphysics.

In this chapter I shall try to offer an explanation of why the political object has gradually lost its contours over the last three centuries. Next, we shall see how this same insight can lead to a resurrection of the political object in aesthetic political philosophy. In the last sections of this chapter I shall investigate the nature of this new political object and of the aesthetic political philosophy that has to deal with it.

2. *Stoic Political Philosophy and Its Discontents*

The gradual disappearance of the political object can be explained if we first resort to the Stoic character of modern political philosophy since the seventeenth century. In fact, it will be the major topic of this chapter to elaborate this insight, briefly given in the previous chapter, into the essentially Stoic character of the greater part of Western political philosophy. The Stoicism of the seventeenth and eighteenth centuries has been demonstrated by several intellectual historians—thus already Dilthey: "The influence of the Roman Stoa penetrates deeply into the psychology and the political theory of Hobbes and Spinoza, and into Spinoza's and Shaftesbury's pantheism [Die Abhängigkeit von der römischen Stoa reicht tief in die Psychologie und Politik von Hobbes und Spinoza, in den Pantheismus von Spinoza und Shaftesbury]." [5] And more recently Spanneut has spoken of a "permanence du Stoicisme." [6] In spite of these assertions, however, the Stoic character of seventeenth- and eighteenth-century (political) philosophy has rarely been emphasized in intellectual history. The explanation may be that Stoic patterns of thought even determine much of contemporary philosophy and are therefore very difficult to recognize for the same reason that it is hard to single out a red object from a background having exactly the same color (though, of course, it would be more appropriate to say that the redness of an object is less conspicuous if placed against a red background). More specifically, it will be only from a consistently anti-Stoic position—and I shall argue that aesthetics offers such a position—that the Stoicism of Western philosophy, not only of the seventeenth and eighteenth centuries but also of our own time, can properly be appreciated.

When we think of the monism, the realism, or the rationalism of Stoicism, or of its profound interest in logical and epistemological questions, when we consider its sympathy for a rationalist ethics or political philosophy (as in Cicero), we find the same mood that has inspired most of modern Western thought about knowledge, science, and the sociopolitical order since the end of the sixteenth century. Whether we think of the Stoic intellectual faculties of "sunkatathesis" and "dianoia," our inner forum where true ideas are admitted to the mind, so obviously similar to Descartes's "idées claires et distinctes"; whether we think of the Stoic "aisthèton," that which is empirically perceived by the senses; whether we think of the Stoicist "heimarmenè," the equivalent of the modern idea of causality; whether we are reminded of the functionalism and the nominalism of the Stoics— everywhere we look we find ample evidence that Western rationalism and empiricism since the seventeenth century have largely been a reenactment and elaboration of Stoic conceptions.[7] No author has been more effective in reminding us of the reintroduction of Stoic ideas by the humanists at the end of the sixteenth century than Gerhard Oestreich.[8]

Of course, I do not wish to imply that modern philosophers in the rationalist and empiricist traditions have unwittingly been Stoics. My thesis is that Stoicism can be seen as a kind of master code that will enable us to take a new look at much of the history of Western (political) philosophy and may explain most of the reflexes and the "instinctual reactions" of Western philosophers to developments in their discipline. This thesis can be elucidated if we devote some attention to the two closely related Stoic notions of "oikeioosis" and the "logoi spermatikoi." "Oikeioosis" (with its root "oikos," meaning house) denotes the capacity of the human individual to identify the self both epistemically and morally with the intrinsically rational or logical order of the universe. "Oikeioosis" can describe the effort to domesticate and appropriate reality that is so characteristic of the wish to understand and explain, the basis of the rationalist mentality of Western philosophy. Within this mentality understanding and explanation are always reductive, a reduction to what is already familiar to us and part of our intellectual "oikos." Everything is explained by reducing it to what has already been explained and what is already an accepted part of the furniture of our cognitive house. Its movement is a pulling toward oneself, rather than a reaching for the object of investigation. Explanation is "oikeioosis": it aims at the domestication of the world.

As we already observed in the previous chapter, it is crucial in the Stoic argument that the identification effected by oikeioosis becomes possible thanks to the metaphysical assumption that the logoi spermatikoi rule over two domains: according to Stoic panlogism, reason rules both the world *and* the thought of rational man. The idea is, roughly, as follows. Reason is an active principle that is operative on two levels. In the first place the logoi spermatikoi—that is, these logical or rational "seeds"—inhere in reality itself, in the things contained by reality, and in this way they determine the behavior of these things. Because of this we can say that reality is, essentially, rational. And if we think of, for example, the reality that is investigated by the physicist, do we not have every reason to be confident that this reality always behaves in an orderly, predictable, and hence "rational" way? But secondly, these same logical or rational seeds are also operative in our minds and thus enable us to think rationally. Decisive, then, is the apparently undeniable fact that the *same* principle, Reason or the logoi spermatikoi, structures *both* reality and thought; and it is only thanks to this happy state of affairs that reality is accessible to thought and that reality will have no impenetrable secrets for us. The laws of reality are also the laws of thought, and this guarantees the possibility of knowledge of reality.

Or, to rephrase the same argument in a different terminology, Reason or the logoi spermatikoi function as the common background of both reality and knowledge; Reason or the logoi spermatikoi are the *tertia comparationis* in terms of which reality and thought can be compared and the truth and falsity of our beliefs can be established. There are, then, not just two things, knowledge and the world, but three things: knowledge, the world, and a tertium comparationis, a hidden but ever-present background to both. Bearing this Stoic model in mind, one could say that most of Western philosophy since Descartes has been a continuous effort to offer a satisfactory definition of the tertia. There have been metaphysical definitions of the tertia, such as "idea", "matter," or "Reason" (the candidate proposed by Stoicism itself and by seventeenth-century rationalism); there have been epistemological definitions, such as "truth," "reference," or "correspondence"; but what all these notions, which have been so hotly discussed by so many generations of Western philosophers, all had in common is that they attempted to bridge in one way or another the gap between the world and knowledge of the world. And if they were to be successful in this we would effectively have solved the problem of the nature of the tertia that the Stoics had put on the philosopher's agenda more than two millennia ago. This is, by the way, also an appropriate vantage point for properly assessing the truly revolutionary character of pragmatism from James via Dewey to Rorty.[9] For pragmatists see in the Stoic's tertia nothing but a useless intellectual overhead: according to the pragmatist we have the world and true (or false) belief, and there is no such third thing as a common background to both. Pragmatists argue that it is a typical philosopher's illusion to believe that the tertia, or some definition of the tertia, is an indispensable ingredient in our intellectual effort to penetrate the secrets of the world. If anything, these tertia are like Wittgenstein's wheel in the machine that is turned by the machine but without moving anything itself. They are a useless redundancy that complicates rather than facilitates our understanding of understanding.

But instead of continuing with a closer investigation of the pragmatist argument, I now wish to focus on a far more obvious enemy of Stoic patterns of argument — aestheticism. Or, to put it differently, pragmatism should be seen as a mere soldier in the army of this enemy rather than as its ally: it is the strategy of this enemy that will also dictate the movements of that soldier. This enemy's intentions are therefore one's best guide in the struggle against the many-headed Hydra of Stoicism. It may well be that in the contemporary intellectual world pragmatism is Stoicism's main enemy, but even this recognition would not yet show us how we should operationalize anti-Stoicism for specific areas of philosophical investigation (such as political philosophy). We often encounter this perplexity in the history of philosophy: quite often we will find that the battle of philosophical traditions tends to obscure our view of the far more important battle over the objects of philosophical investigation, since the latter can always be constructed as a mere derivative of the former. And as soon as such an opportunity presents itself philosophers rarely succeed in resisting the temptation to make an optimal use of it, since a discussion of philosophical traditions is always much easier and far less hazardous than a discussion of philosophical objects themselves. Turning, then, to specific areas of philosophical investigation, it will demand little intellectual effort to recognize that aestheticism will enable us to successfully transcend Stoicism and to avoid Stoic seductions (even insofar as these may still be discerned in pragmatism).[10] This is how aestheticism will function, and how it will be presented, throughout this chapter and this book.

The fact that aestheticism rejects the tertia comparationis of Stoic philosophy, whatever their nature may be, is absolutely crucial here. It is so obvious as to be trivial that a rejection of such tertia is constitutive of the world of art. Art knows neither tertia nor a common background for comparing the work of art with what it represents; what makes art interesting, "new," and aesthetically pleasing is that it successfully resists all attempts to reduce the work of art to reality by means of Stoic tertia. The difference between style and mere mannerism may be illuminating here. When contrasting the two Arthur Danto, in a subtle comment, writes: "It seems to me that what we mean by style are those qualities of representations which are the man himself, seen from the outside, physiognomically. And the reason that there cannot be knowledge or art for style, though there can be for manner, is that the outward aspects of representations are not commonly given to the man whose representations they are: he views the world through them, but not them."[11] The upshot of Danto's argument is that style in representation cannot be objectified without ceasing to be style and thus becoming mere mannerism. The artist who represents reality with style does not apply a certain a prioristically given schematism for how to relate represented reality to its representation. His relationship to the world as expressed in his work of art is not mediated or determined by the tertia that define such a schematism: he represents reality as it *is* to him. Nevertheless, one may try to discover such a scheme or system for relating reality to its representation and if one is successful in doing this one has a set of tertia whose application to artistic representation will result in the mannerism corresponding to the artist's style. But, as we all know, mannerism is merely an imitation of great art and never great art itself: hence, when confronted with the work of art we will predominantly see its aesthetic merit precisely in the manner and extent to which it challenges (an appeal to) tertia. Thus Stoic philosophy should primarily be contrasted with aesthetic philosophy. Because of the way this contrast has been formulated, there can be no doubt that, formally and theoretically, these forms of philosophy are mutually exclusive.

A further clarification of the opposition between the Stoic notion of the tertia and aestheticism can be given if we ask how the two relate to metaphysics and to epistemology. Reason, the "recta ratio," provides Stoicism with an answer to the question about the metaphysical nature of reality as well as to the epistemological question of how we can know it. But aestheticism is indifferent to both. Let us suppose, for the sake of argument, that one may say of the work of art (or of the style of an artist) that it expresses a metaphysical conception of a part or an aspect of reality (in order to reduce aestheticism to Stoic metaphysics). Indeed, we often say of a portrait that the artist has succeeded in presenting to us the "essence" of the personality of the sitter. But then the following difficulty presents itself. If we wish to contrast the relevant metaphysical conceptions as expressed by different works of art in different styles, these works of art only present us with *evidence* for such differences — evidence, that is, for how these differences can be described (in language) — and not with these different metaphysical conceptions themselves. The works of art and their styles only give us arguments for how to formulate metaphysical disagreement. That means that raising the issue of metaphysics with regard to the work of art inevitably results in a pushing back of the work of art into the world of things, shifting the artwork from the conceptual level where we speak *about* the world of things and its metaphysical properties to the world itself. And as soon as that has happened, the work of art (or its style) is just one more part of the world whose metaphysical character is at stake. But at this level there will be no metaphysical difference between the painting and what it represents; after this maneuver the work of art (or its style) has become as indifferent to metaphysical argument as reality itself. Thus the most influential contemporary theory of the nature of aesthetic representation—Gombrich's and Danto's view that the work of art is a substitute or a replacement for what it represents—primarily results in granting to the work of art the same metaphysical status as its referent, or what it represents.

Characteristically, much the same argument can be given for epistemology. For whether one (and this is no less true of the artist him- or herself!) is looking at a landscape itself or at the painting (that he or she) made of it, exactly the same epistemological account must be given of how experience and knowledge of either the landscape or the painting can come into being. Hence epistemology can never begin to tell us what takes place in the aesthetic representation of reality; epistemology is necessarily blind to what separates the work of art from what it represents and to what happens in the transition from the latter to the former, since epistemology is unable to discern a categorial difference between representation and what it represents. It need therefore not surprise us that Stoicism, from which so much of Western philosophy down to the present day derives and that has been so decisive in giving form to modern metaphysics and modern epistemology, has never cared to develop an aesthetics of its own. Not only are Stoicism and aesthetics fundamentally at odds with each other, Stoicism can only be completely indifferent to the kind of philosophical issues raised by aesthetics. The very notion of a Stoic aesthetics is a contradiction in terms.

Because of its pronounced rationalism we are inclined to associate Stoicism primarily with epistemology and philosophy of science, and with the sciences themselves. However, most of our thinking about politics and the sociohistorical order (and its nature) is governed even more by the Stoic Weltanschauung. This should not surprise us. We all tend to agree with Vico's thoroughly Stoic insight that we can understand the sociohistorical world because we have made that world ourselves, whereas the physical world is not of our own making and is thus less accessible to our understanding. That the sociohistorical world should contain something radically alien, something radically in- or unhuman certainly is most counterintuitive. Consequently, the Stoic notion of a tertium comparationis behind the individual human being or citizen and the sociohistorical world of the State and political order has always seemed so self-evident that it has hardly been noticed. But its ubiquitous presence in much philosophical thought cannot be doubted. Take, for instance, the twentieth-century phenomenological tradition that did always strive for an unbroken continuum between the world of the individual and the social order: "Lebenswelt" or "interpretation" (both reflecting and structuring the social world) form their common background. Even more telling is the fact that ethics still is the main philosophical instrument for thinking about politics and the good state and that this honor is denied both theoretically and practically to history. Ethics only makes sense on the assumption of a (Stoic) continuity between our intentions, our actions, and their results in the sociopolitical world, whereas history originates in an awareness of the (anti-Stoic) gaps and *dis*-continuities between them.

The most impressive proof of Stoicism's contemporary triumph over aestheticism is that it even succeeded in conquering the domain of its main enemy, that is, the world of history. We may think here of the kind of philosophy of action that was originally proposed by Robin G. Collingwood and subsequently developed by William Dray, Georg Henrik Von Wright, and many other proponents of intentional explanation or of the so-called logical connection argument. Surely, "social Stoicism" never found a clearer expression than in Collingwood's reenactment theory.[12] The suggestion that we can only understand the past by "reenacting" the thoughts of the historical agent in our own minds is the most perfect parallel of the Stoic tertia in historical and social theory that one could think of. As in Hegel, (practical) Reason is here the (Stoic) tertium that rules both the object and the subject.

Yet this Stoicism of so much of contemporary historical and social theory is all the more disappointing if we recognize that historical writing has been perhaps the only discipline dealing with the sociohistorical world in a way that invites us to resist Stoic seductions. How much of what interests us in history concerns the unintended results of intentional human actions! They make us aware of the presence in history of a dimension that is *not* reducible to human intentions. As I have argued elsewhere, this dimension of the unintended results of intentional human action should not be explained by or reduced to the inventory of the past. It originates instead in historical language, and in the essentially aesthetic *representation* that the historian gives of the past.[13] The unintended results of human action only present themselves to us after we have permitted ourselves to see the actions of the agent from a point of view different from that of the agent himself when performing the action in question. Point of view, however, does not lie in the past itself. It has a certain autonomy from the past itself, and this autonomy imparts itself to the historian's language, in which such points of view are articulated. What historical representation shares with aestheticism is the fact that there are no fixed rules or algorithms that would permit us to argue safely and under all circumstances from represented reality to its representation in thought or in writing—and vice versa. It is therefore most satisfactory that since the seminal work of Hayden White there is a small yet growing number of historical theorists ready to appreciate this fact about the aesthetic character of the historian's language and to recognize that the absence of such rules is not a sad defect of history but precisely its greatest virtue. It is why we need history at all. A Stoic copy of historical reality could never give us that *organization* of historical reality that is effected in and by historical (aesthetic) *representation*.

Furthermore, the anti-Stoic character of historical writing becomes no less clear if we recognize that modern historical writing was (re-)born from the rejection of two prestigious showpieces of modern Stoicism: Stoic natural law theory and Stoic speculative philosophies of history.[14] Historism rejected Stoic natural law because of its conviction that we can never see a historically given social and political order as the expression (or representation) of some matrix to be found either in the human individual or in a hypothetical state of nature (what is represented). Hence, there can be no Stoic tertia underlying *both*. Next, what Leopold von Ranke, Jacob Burckhardt, and so many other historians found repulsive in the Hegelian system (and in other speculative systems) was the assumption that history is an essentially rational process in which Reason, in its subjective form, ultimately recognizes itself in objective Reason, thus resulting in absolute Reason—in short, the typically Stoic idea "that Reason rules the world and that, therefore, world-history is an essentially rational process [dass die Vernunft die Welt beherrscht, dass es also in der Weltgeschichte vernünftig zugegangen ist]."[15] As Croce already noticed, what Hegel did was in practice a historicization of the Stoicism of classical natural law philosophy, while at the same time he carefully preserved for Reason its traditional role of the Stoic tertium.[16] Historical writing, on the other hand, is born from a rejection of Stoicism and is arguably, outside art, the only domain in the contemporary intellectual world where anti-Stoic aestheticism could develop and flourish.

Let us pay some extra attention to historical theory: being a philosophical reflection on that sole anti-Stoic discipline that we still possess in our contemporary world, its fate may be instructive in the present context. Indeed, whether it drew its inspiration from Hegelian or Marxist, from Collingwoodian or from socioscientific ideals, historical theory (here, obviously, at odds with historical practice) has ordinarily been Stoic in nature and intent. Even historism, which at first courageously attacked the Stoic God, as we saw a moment ago, and thus seemed destined to become an anti-Stoic bastion of aestheticism in contemporary culture, also yielded finally to the seductions of Stoicism—as was amply demonstrated by Hans Gadamer. For in his *Truth and Method* Gadamer convincingly expounded how historism could not prevent itself from falling into the trap of (Stoic) epistemology. It ended up making common cause with Kantian and nineteenth-century ideals of science, and it therefore only too gladly abandoned its initial anti-Stoicism for a search for the epistemological conditions for the possibility of true historical knowledge. And (Dilthey-type) hermeneutics was appealed to in order to fit the (Stoic) epistemological neo-Kantian bill. We can discern a similar pattern in most nineteenth- and twentieth-century reflections on the nature of historical writing. Most of historical theory, with the exception of the aestheticist narrativism inaugurated by Hayden White, is a debate that carefully respects the limits prescribed by Stoicism. I mention two further illustrations. When Popper launched his attack on Hegel and Marx and, generally speaking, on speculative philosophies of history and on historicism (not to be confused with its near-opposite, Rankean historism) he exchanged one variant of Stoicism for another, scientist variant.[17] For it was in the name of science that Popper (correctly) criticized historicism's scientistic pretensions. Nevertheless, despite Popper's politically praiseworthy motives, his argument read as if one should criticize a bad painting not because of its being a bad painting but because of its not having photographic accuracy. Admittedly, the criticism was salutary in the time that it was made but it was developed from the wrong point of view. If one is in a somewhat paranoïac mood, one might even argue that its effectiveness tended to confirm, in practice, the value of this mistaken (scientist or Stoic) point of view, one shared by Popper and his pseudo-scientific opponents. Lastly, a no less illustrative example is Gadamer himself, whose Heideggerian "Being that can be understood is language [Sein das verstanden werden kann ist Sprache]" presented us with "language" as our historical and social tertium. So even his pronounced aestheticism did not, in the end, allow Gadamer to escape from the Stoic master code. Finally, though White did more than any other single theorist to contest Stoicism in historical theory, even in his writings traces of Stoicism turn up.[18]

But what, then, of political philosophy? Having seen just now how even historical theory, despite being a philosophical reflection on a fundamentally anti-Stoic discipline, rarely succeeded in wrestling itself free from Stoicism's embrace, we will expect much the same for political philosophy. We will not be surprised to find that the political theorists of the seventeenth and eighteenth centuries, operating within the assumptions of natural law philosophy because of the latter's obvious Stoic inspirations, can all be considered Stoic epigones. Indeed, because of the Stoicism that Dilthey (as we saw above) already ascribed to the natural law theorists of that period, these theorists always sought Stoic tertia that would enable the political philosopher to explain, justify, or legitimate the State by deriving it from the (nature of the) individual citizen, the social order, the state of nature, or from whatever other tertium one might prefer.

For example, let us consider Hobbes and Rousseau. In that most memorable chapter on representation in the *Leviathan* Hobbes writes with respect to the representative (whom he designates as a "person artificiall") that his actions are "owned" by those whom he represents.[19] Postulating an extremely close relationship such as ownership between a person and the actions performed by him firmly ties together the citizen and the Hobbesian sovereign State. All the provocativeness of Hobbes's theory surely lies in his effort to make this link as strong as possible. Next, when Rousseau writes the famous words, "In the end, since one surrenders oneself to all the others, one does not give oneself to anybody; and since there is not a fellow-citizen on whom one does not acquire the same rights as one cedes to him, one gains the equivalent of what one loses [Enfin, chacun se donnant à tous ne se donne à personne; et comme il n'y a pas un associé sur lequel on n'acquière le même droit qu'on lui cède sur soi, on gagne l'équivalent de tout ce qu'on perd]," the political order is presented to us as nothing but a convenient rearrangement of what was potentially already present in the prepolitical, natural order.[20] And nowhere have the Stoic tertia found clearer and more influential expression than in the idea of popular sovereignty. This notion of popular sovereignty is a metaphor suggesting an idealized background against which we can move freely from the citizen to the State and vice versa.

For all their rhetoric against ahistorical natural law theories, nineteenth-
and twentieth-century ideologies did not abandon the Stoic tertia, which
here took the form of "history" or "sociology," in whatever way these words
were to be understood. When Hegel saw in the Absolute Mind the ultimate
recognition of Reason in its subjective form in Reason in its objective form,
the political order corresponding to it was the realization of the Stoic "right
reason" through history. Consider further Marx's idea that the proletariat
in our time is the designated maker of a new social order for no other reason than that the proletariat today is the substance of world history. Here
the makers make themselves, they are their own actions and what is effected
by them. This reads exactly like a historicized version of Hobbes's theory
that the person represented "owns" the actions of the sovereign State. In
both cases it is reliance upon a Stoic tertium that underlies the ideological
short cut.

In still another way the Hegelian and the Marxist systems may further
our insight into the nature of Stoic political theory. We should observe that
both Hegel and Marx attempted to offer an *explanation* of the mechanisms
that create our political world. It was their interest in history, where they
both differed from the preceding natural law theories, that gave them, in
their view, the best perspective for satisfying these requirements of explanation—which was for them an essential dimension of all political theory.
History gave them the explanation of the existing political order, of its
shortcomings and of how these would be dealt with or would have to be
dealt with in the future. At the same time this historical perspective gave
them a *legitimation* of (their conception of) the future more satisfactory and
more just political order. Their writings may therefore illustrate to what
extent explanation and legitimation go together in the Stoic tradition of
political theory. Obviously the natural law systems that were constructed
in the seventeenth and eighteenth centuries had always hoped to do the
same. Thus to Hobbes the individual desire for self-preservation primarily
explains why the state came into existence, but on the other hand this very
same desire is also the legitimation of "that mortall God" that the Leviathan is. And, if we think of Althusius, to take another example, it was his
conviction that the human striving for symbiosis resulted in both the explanation and the legitimation of yet another kind of state. In all these cases
the suggestion is that only the state that we can explain and understand
could be a legitimate state.

We are well advised to take this peculiarity of Stoic political theory into account, since it is not in the least self-evident that only that state which presents itself with explicatory transparency can be the legitimate state. Explication and legitimation are by no means coextensive: obviously injustice, too, can be explained without thereby deserving to be legitimized. Furthermore, we are here presented with a curious paradox that may already make us skeptical of this Stoic endeavor to legitimate by explanation. When Stoic systems (whether originating in natural law theories or in a historicization of some Stoic logos spermatikos) developed into the social sciences or into a form of historical writing, legitimation of a specific political order soon came to an end. Obviously we would have expected the opposite: namely, that a strengthening of the "explicatio" will also lead to strengthening of the "legitimatio." If, however, we look for example at Adam Smith's development from his *Theory of Moral Sentiments*, based on natural law, to the (proto-)social-scientific *Wealth of Nations*, we will observe that Stoic legitimation has indeed completely disappeared in the latter work—but not without something else making its entrée as its substitute. For econometric expertise can, admittedly, now no longer serve as the (de-)legitimation of a certain political order (in its totality) as was always the aim of Stoic natural law philosophy, but it may serve instead as the legitimation of a particular economic policy while avoiding prescriptions for all other aspects of society. Of special interest, in this context, is how this transition came about in the intellectual career of Adam Smith, which is exemplary for how the social sciences developed from Stoic natural law conceptions. As was demonstrated by Schumpeter in his not very sympathetic account of Smith's economic thought, the latter, when teaching his courses on ethics and morality (the "sciences morales" of the eighteenth century), gradually found it increasingly difficult to integrate his material successfully within one coherent and all-encompassing survey. Thus simply for practical (or, rather, for didactic and rhetorical) reasons he now decided that it would henceforward be best to detach economics from ethics in his survey. This actually is how *The Wealth of Nations* came into being—and, thereby, modern economics.[21] Hence the transition from Stoic natural law philosophy to economics (and the social sciences), and the transition from a teleological to a merely instrumental Stoic reason (which has determined the nature of the social sciences down to the present day) is the consequence of a falling apart of the Stoic natural order. In this way a refinement of explanation undermined the perennial Stoic attempt to legitimate in terms of explanation.

On the other hand, it is the entirely undramatic way in which this happened in the development of Smith's intellectual career, and its conspicuous lack of support in any well-considered (anti-)Stoic argument, that may make us realize how much the modern social sciences can still be considered the true heirs of seventeenth- and eighteenth-century Stoic natural law philosophy. This circumstance makes evident how very appropriate the eighteenth-century notion of the sciences morales actually still is. The social sciences never really abandoned Stoicism, but for simple convenience (as in the case of Smith) they restricted their epistemological matrix to the individual areas of research in the different social sciences. They thereby carefully avoided the problems that Stoicism will inevitably run into when asked how these individual social sciences, their respective areas of research, their results, and so on might fit together after the breakup of the self-consistent Stoic social or political order. These nasty problems were carefully hidden from view in the intellectual minefield of the relationships between the different social sciences, where the dangers facing the researcher are far greater than the fruits that one may expect from one's investigation. The intrinsic aesthetic dimension of sociopolitical reality now hid itself in these relationships between the individual social sciences and, to all practical purposes, managed to successfully occlude itself there. It is illustrative that those who actually ventured into this minefield have always been philosophers (discussing, for example, methodological holism and individualism or rational choice theories) rather than social scientists. Contrast this with the sciences, where the interrelationships between, for example, physics and chemistry, or between medical science and biochemistry, are eagerly explored by scientists themselves. One might surmise that the social sciences can only subsist as long as they remain embedded (and separated from each other) within a tacit Stoic order that is forgotten and rejected as obsolete metaphysics but is still very much the presupposition of the very possibility of the social sciences.

Moreover, the social sciences combine an anti-Stoic awareness of the impossibility of reasoning by means of (some) tertia from the details of the sociopolitical order to its totality, with a Stoic readiness to do precisely that for those dimensions of that order in which they happen to be interested. Whereas Stoic natural law philosophy both explained and legitimized a certain political order in its totality, the social sciences explain and legitimate a certain political strategy in their specific area of research. And this transition is of far less importance than claimed by the alarmed polemics of Habermasian theorists against instrumental reason, all the more so since these Habermasians, because of their neo-Marxist inheritance or because of their infatuation with such an utterly inane ideal as Habermas's "herrschaftsfreier Dialog" (ideal speech situation) are no less Stoics than their opponents. More specifically, the crucial distinction is not that between "good" teleological reason and "bad" instrumental reason, but between the Stoicism that is shared by both and, opposite to it, an aesthetic conception of the political order. And a corollary, of course, is that political science, being just one of the social sciences, will be a poor and unsatisfactory substitute for the understanding of our political order as presented in the aesthetic tradition since Machiavelli and developed in this book.

Next, to return to my criticism of the Stoic pretension to legitimate in terms of explanation, it is by no means evident that by cutting through these ties between explanation and legitimation, we would thereby have robbed the term "political legitimation" of all meaning and significance, as Stoics might wish to suggest: less pretentious but more practical alternatives, such as efficiency, common sense, tolerance, and sheer decency can easily do the job and have actually always done the job in the eyes of the ordinary citizen who has not acquired Stoic reflexes. And, more generally, it is quite dangerous to theorize too much on the notion of legitimacy and on what constitutes the legitimate political order, for the more this notion disappears behind theoretical clouds, the easier it will be for less well-meaning politicians to misuse it for their own advantages. The ideologies that were used by totalitarian leaders for legitimating their politics are an example in point. From this perspective it is reassuring that most people will never bother to learn to speak the language of political philosophy, so that in contemporary Western democracies the obfuscation of the notion of "political (il-)legitimacy" can take place mostly in the fortunately rather harmless writings of Rawls and Habermas and their many disciples.

This alliance between *explicatio* and *legitimatio* so characteristic of political Stoicism produces another effect that deserves our attention. Both notions stimulate a dichotomy between explanation and what is explained or between legitimation and what is legitimated. That is to say, the existing political order is divided into, on the one hand, its concrete and historically contingent manifestation and, on the other, what is conceived to be its (Stoic) essence that provides the Stoic political philosopher with the model in terms of which he may explain or legitimate the former (or attack its legitimacy). Stoic political philosophy exists by virtue of this essentialism, and by virtue of this modernist distinction between appearance and being, or between foundation and what is to be erected on that foundation. This may explain the innate resistance of Stoic political philosophy to history as the domain of the historically contingent. This is also why it will necessarily see history as the domain where the political order will begin to deviate from its pure, uncontaminated, ahistorical essence. Rousseau offers a perfect example: for him all that was initially clear, well-defined, and in agreement with its nature tends to become confused, blurred, and deteriorated in the course of history. It is no less characteristic that when history is accepted within Stoic political philosophy, history will immediately take here the form, not of the kind of academic history that we have been acquainted with since the days of Ranke, but of speculative systems like those of Hegel and Marx, where, as we saw above, the historically contingent has been neatly boxed and accounted for by the overall Stoic rationality of the historical process.

Since the defects of a political order preferably develop in the margins of that system, however, there are few territories where Stoic essentialism is as counterproductive as in politics (and in history). Stoic essentialism will only rarely develop a positive interest for this myriad of minor and apparently insignificant changes that constitute the development (or the deterioration) of a political system. And if it notices these (historical) changes at all, it will, as was the case with Rousseau, be content to dismiss them all with one wholesale, all-encompassing condemnation. So here as well, there is a reason for exchanging the Stoic notion of "legitimacy" for the more practical alternatives of efficiency, decency, and so on that were enumerated above, which focus on just this myriad of minor details instead of on whether a political system correctly reflects some ideal model or abstraction. Even more so, precisely because of its essentialist reduction, Stoic political philosophy will tend to ignore the proper domain of politics that must, self-evidently, be situated in the sphere of the historical and the contingent. To put it differently, ignoring this dimension of political practice will, in the case of Stoic political philosophy, amount to the suggestion that political philosophy must *put an end* to political practice. Political practice —history—is considered within the Stoic tradition as a kind of prepolitical phase. We will only find politics in the true sense of that word in the realization of the Stoic order as defined by the tertia, while at the same time this realization of the Stoic tertia is the death of all politics. Stoic political philosophy is therefore a philosophy of how to *end* politics instead of a philosophy of how to *deal* with politics. Stoic political philosophy is, in fact, a profoundly *anti*-political philosophy attempting to show us how to do away with politics forever and how to reduce it to a merely propaedeutical phase we unfortunately have to pass through on our way to a future postpolitical society.

3. Why Politics Has Evaporated in Our Time

Before entering upon a closer investigation of the tertia in Stoic political philosophy, we shall first proceed with the solution that can now be given for our initial problem: the disappearance of the political object. It should be observed here that it is the purpose and logic inherent in the political tertia that they should obliterate in the end the political object and the clarity with which the political object stands out against the background of the tertia. For it is the task of these tertia to make everything in the political universe as comparable or commensurable as possible with everything else in it. In other words, the tertia will naturally tend to suppress the generic differences between the citizen, the social order, and the State—in short, exactly that which is at stake in, and the presupposition of, all politics. And this tendency has been reinforced by the ideological debate that has been taking place over the last two centuries. For most of this debate took, and had to take, the form of a debate about the nature of the tertia—about how the citizen, the sociohistorical order, and the State could be understood in terms of one another, and thus tended to hide from view all that might resist the pressure of the tertia.

Thus (and this is essential) ideological debate invited the tertia to surrender their previously modest though influential role in the background and to place themselves ever more firmly in the foreground. It is this gradual movement from the background to the foreground on the part of the tertia that caused the political object's loss of identity and clear contours, and that gave us a political reality consisting only of a background, while eliminating all that could be placed against that background. This process was further stimulated by more prosaic factors, such as the growth and the alphabetization of the population, the increase in the state's power and the intensification of interhuman contact, growth in the use of money (arguably, with language, the paradigmatic and most successful tertium, to which we shall return in the next section), and, last but certainly not least, the revolution in the nineteenth and twentieth centuries in means of communication. This communication revolution in particular effected a melting away of the purely physical boundaries between ruler and ruled, between the state and the public, and so of the political object. In sum, it has been the victory of the Stoic tertia that has been responsible for the disappearance of the political object. This victory has made it disappear, not by reducing these elements to each other—the key notion of Stoicism is commensurability rather than reductionism—but by erasing the contours and limits of these elements.

This gradual evaporation of the political domain has had some peculiar consequences. It has resulted in a depoliticization of politics and of the state. To be more precise, politics and the state in its anti-Stoic, aesthetic or Machiavellianist form have gradually been forced into a quasi-transcendental position—in a position that, like the transcendental ego, it can never be aware of itself. It is like the transcendental ego of which Kant wrote that it accompanies all our thought but can never be an *object* of our thought. The political object has become a negative presence; that is to say, politics has henceforward tended to manifest itself in a depoliticized way, as if all the decisions that are made by the state and that may profoundly influence our lives were not political decisions at all but rather the actions of some anonymous and unknown person or entity that we can only accept in the way we accept the caprices of the weather. Instead of government, we have bureaucracy—for it is in the cloak of bureaucracy that this transcendentalized and antipolitical politics ordinarily prefers to manifest itself. In bureaucracy the visibility of aestheticist, Machiavellian politics has been transcendentalized and exchanged for the invisibility of a bureaucratic anonymity and of a general transcendental political subjectivity. Jean Cohen and Andrew Arato summarize Hannah Arendt's thoughts about bureaucracy:

> If tyranny is "government that is not held to give account of itself," then bureaucracy, as "rule by Nobody," goes so far as to hide the agents who might be held accountable. Such, according to Arendt, is the case in modern welfare states, where the idea of democracy is converted from that of public participation to the achievement, through the most efficient administrative means possible, of the goals of public welfare.[22]

It is this transition from government to bureaucracy that has transcendentalized politics and thus brought it outside our grasp. As a result of the process, we may now discuss, vote, and write about politics; we may well have our complaints and wishes that are even quite universally shared; but nevertheless politics enacts itself with the same imperturbability and indifference to these complaints and wishes as a thunderstorm. Moreover, we should not accuse any specific category or group in contemporary democracy of having caused or wished this death of politics. We are all the creators and the victims of the process. Voters, citizens, politicians, civil servants, and the bureaucrats themselves are all the victims of the process; we are all like ants creeping over a large piece of rock, and even our united efforts will not move that rock a fraction of an inch.

What a difference, then, from the state of the nineteenth century and the beginning of the twentieth: though one may now disagree with its aims and many of its individual decisions, one must jealously recognize that this state still had the capability "to cut the world at its joints." The transcendentalization of politics has given us a world of Kafkaesque features, a world in which everybody is ruled, where even the tiniest details of one's life are concerned, and yet nobody seems to rule. It is no coincidence that I compared the present depoliticized politics with our utter powerlessness with regard to the whims of nature: by transcendentalizing itself Stoic political philosophy had always taken its model in nature. If, as was argued above, Stoic politics saw its "natural" goal in putting an end to politics, we need not be surprised that this would result in a kind of politics that confronts us with the same inexorability that we associate with natural processes. The absence of an agent that is the primary property of such processes characterizes this sort of politics as well. Obviously, a political philosophy (or science of politics) taking nature as its model can only end with the naturalization—that is, with the depoliticization—of politics. The metaphor of nature has become a literal reality, and has proven to be politics' nemesis rather than the condition of its existence.

The social sciences, modeling the historical, social, and political world on the world of nature, presents to us the realm of politics as ruled by inexorable social laws that we can at most use within the narrow confines of instrumental reason. This tendency has an affinity with the transcendentalization of politics and the disappearance of the political object. Our tendency to conceive of sociopolitical reality in terms of social science and to see in its prescripts the most reliable guide for political action has further contributed to this "naturalization" of that reality. There is a lesson for the political philosopher in this. For if the social sciences in general and political science in particular are, in fact, the socioscientific expression or reflection of Stoic political philosophy, we may expect them to be our best guides if we want to know what practical effects the latter has. What can be a better clue to the labyrinth of our contemporary political reality without a political object than that which has so powerfully contributed to building it?

Indeed, contemporary political science clearly and candidly announces what the practical implications are of accepting Stoic political philosophy and what our political world will be like if we allow ourselves to be guided by the (mentality of the) social sciences and of political science in particular. In his authoritative *Political Theories of Modern Government*, Peter Self concentrates on two such implications that he considers to be of primary importance: the fact that we can no longer distinguish between the state and society; and the growth of government bureaucracies. "It may pay both government and interest-group," Self writes, "to cooperate closely in policy-making and enforcement." [23] This close cooperation between the state and interest groups led, in the eyes of political scientists like Self, to a blurring of the contours of the state. They therefore proposed the notions of the corporatist and the interventionist state in order to account for this gradual dissolution of the state in the social order. [24]

Of course, I am not implying here that the insights presented by political science have caused rather than contributed to the disappearance of the political object (though the Foucauldian contemporary social and political order is, perhaps, the result rather of the application of socioscientific models than of political decision). I am content here to indicate the complicity existing between the social sciences on the one hand and Stoic political conceptions on the other. For we should note that the thesis of the dissolution of the state—which is the primary political agent in the public domain—pointed out so fondly and with so much satisfaction by political scientists like Self, only makes sense against the background of Hobbesian or Rousseauist conceptions of the sovereign state. To put it bluntly, political science owes its existence to our unwitting attachment to the Stoic state and it owes its field of investigation to the admittedly quite real gap existing between the Stoic state and the actual state. As in psychoanalytic therapy the exploration of this gap tended to push the actual state in the direction of its Stoic model. Thus Stoicism produced a state that gradually dissolved into society and a political science that is in the best position to give us a detailed account of this evolution, since it is based on the same Stoic assumptions that have brought about the disappearance of the state—an achievement that is all the more impressive since, as the state became more and more invisible, it grew into a size compared with which even Hobbes's Leviathan pales into insignificance.

Turning to Self's second implication—the growth of government bureaucracy—a further consideration may be added to the thesis of the complicity between the social sciences and the disappearance of the political object. When criticizing older theories on bureaucracy, such as those of Max Weber and Woodrow Wilson, in which bureaucracy is still seen as an instrument under the control of a centralized power, modern political scientists like Self primarily focus on the weakened capacity of political leadership to direct and control bureaucracy from the top down.[25] Bureaucracy is a morbid growth, which could attain its present proportions and complexity because of the characteristic Stoic unwillingness to acquiesce in the aesthetic rifts between the state on the one hand and the citizen and society on the other. Stoicism always strives for continuity, smoothness, linearity, for a blurring of contours; it always experiences discontinuity, rifts, frictions, or interstices as challenges to itself. Obviously, this must strongly stimulate the growth of government bureaucracy. For it is bureaucracy that we will find in the void between the represented (the voter) and the representative (the state), and which must regulate the contacts (with the sole exception of voting itself) between them to the minutest (Stoic) detail. Bureaucracy is the concrete, institutional form of the Stoic tertia, and where the tertia materialize and institutionalize. Once again, we may observe here the striking elective affinity between bureaucracy's attack on discontinuity and the scientism of the social sciences in which truth—the correspondence between the true statement and what the statement is about—is the cognitive counterpart of bureaucracy's desire for continuity. In both cases rifts, oppositions, conflict—all that is precisely at stake in politics—is marginalized. That is why Stoicism is the common background of both political science and of the bureaucratization of what used once to be politics.

The result of Stoic political philosophy and its political practice has been succinctly summed up by Michael Walzer as follows: "In contemporary Western societies power is dispersed, but not as democrats hoped to disperse it; not to citizens who argue and vote and so determine the politics of the central government. Citizenship and government alike have been superseded."[26] Stoic political philosophy has always aimed at putting an end to politics by means of its tertia, at "superseding" politics, and in a way it has succeeded. Political power, political issues, the political object have dissolved in the Stoic order like a drop of ink in a glass of water.

How can this development be reversed? That is the question that will concern us in the next two sections.

4. On the Nature of the Stoic Tertia and Their Effects

Up till now I have refrained from saying anything specific about the nature of the tertia. We have seen that they can take many forms: the individual's need to live in symbiosis with his fellow human beings that was proposed by Althusius, the Hobbesian instinct for self-preservation, Spinoza's similar "conatus sese perseverandi," pity in the case of Rousseau, practical reason in the case of Kant, history with Hegel and Marx, and so on. And today we may witness a remarkable renaissance of utilitarianism — that quantum theory of moral and political matter.

But however variegated these tertia may be, it is nevertheless possible to detect a certain logic in their evolution over the last centuries. The nature of that logic follows from the task that the tertia were supposed to perform. As we have seen, it is their role to effect the commensurability of all the different elements that constitute the political order, and they therefore gradually developed into an increasingly intricate and refined web behind the elements contained within the political order. And indeed, since Hobbes's and Spinoza's "conatus sese perseverandi," via the enlightened self-interest of Mandeville's *Fable of the Bees*, via the utilitarian maximalization of utility, through the moral rules of Rousseau and Kant, down to the historicized tertia of Hegel (reason) and Marx (the class struggle), we can indeed observe such an evolution. One hopes that the history of the tertia will one day be written; I am convinced that a more detailed characterization of that history would be most enlightening. Certainly such a history could deepen our insight into our present political predicament.

More intricate than all these tertia from the past, however, are those with which Stoic political theory managed to achieve its *nec plus ultra* in our own days. I am thinking of money and language. The former functions as tertium for our political practice, which has been reduced almost completely to economic issues. Money has proven to be the most successful tertium and the next-to-ideal common background of each conceivable political object in our time; moreover, money provides the politician with the best instru-

ment for calculating the implementation of each successful effort to reconcile the political divisions existing in society. Democracy's main task has
always been to reconcile such political divisions.[27] Also, in conformity with
the process described in the previous section, the tertia will tend to assert
themselves at the expense of the political object. Here is the explanation for
why, in our Western democracies, politics has been reduced almost completely to the discussion of economic policies, and why so much of political
theory prefers to deal with issues of income distribution (as in the case of
the Anglo-Saxon political philosophy that we associate with the name of
Rawls). Money provides the political theorist with the *language* that enables free movement through all the areas of political reality, and is the
language that can render commensurable all the objects encountered there.

This may deepen our insight into the nature of the relationship between
contemporary Anglo-Saxon and continental political philosophy. For where
Anglo-Saxon political philosophy was looking for a *language* as defined just
now, continental political philosophy, in agreement with its traditional transcendental leanings, preferred to focus on that language itself. More precisely, for Anglo-Saxon political philosophy political reality itself retained
its natural priority—and philosophers now started to look for a language
that would be best suited for doing optimal justice to it. In the end, this
turned out to be the language of economics. Continental political philosophy, in its turn, being aware that language is the transcendental condition
for the possibility of political "knowledge," now started to investigate language—though not necessarily the language of economics. To simplify, I
would say that whereas in Anglo-Saxon political philosophy an empiricist
definition of the tertia was preferred, continental political philosophy was
more interested in a transcendentalist determination of them. In this way
language has proven to be the tertium that is *money*'s obvious counterpart
in continental political philosophy—and that may explain why political
philosophy's tendency to become absorbed by the tertia gave us two tertia
instead of either just one or more than two, and why these two tertia happen
to be money and language. When thinking of language as a tertium comparationis, the paradigmatic example is how Foucault presents language,
"discourse," as a kind of Freudian social norm that is internalized into our
superegos and that has thus woven the finest web up till now for the trans-
mission of political power. And it is Foucault's main point that "discourse"
has succeeded in becoming this most powerful political agent because it is
never perceived as such by us. That is, we think it to be a mere tertium,

whereas in fact this tertium has become the supreme political agent by having gradually absorbed since the Enlightenment the political into itself.

Nevertheless, the linguistic model of politics is far from being a latter-day twentieth-century (French) invention. Hobbes had already seen the significance of language for politics,[28] and one hundred years later, at the end of the eighteenth century, Herder made an ingenious suggestion that legislation should take language as its model. Language has a universalist dimension because it enables people to communicate with one another; but language is also congenial to the individual since it allows the individual to express his or her individuality. Thus the miracle wrought by language is that it reconciles the general with the individual; in language the general and the individual coexist in perfect harmony. If the law and the state are like language, according to Herder, our most urgent political problems must have been solved.[29] And though he does not mention Herder, a very similar idea has also been put forward by Michael Oakeshott.[30] Nevertheless, when I present language here as one of the two ultimate tertia, I am thinking only of its role in contemporary politics and political theory. More specifically, when discussing language in the present context, I particularly have in mind any of the following specifications: "speech" as in the case of Hannah Arendt, "moral and political language" as meant by Oakeshott, "writing" if we wish to attribute to Derrida a political philosophy, "discourse" or even "truth" in the case of Foucault's speculations on power, "political vocabularies" as investigated by Pocock, the "speech acts" discussed by Quentin Skinner, Habermas's "communicative action" and "ideal speech situation," "figurative language" as discussed by Hayden White, and, lastly, language as it has been operationalized for the purposes of political philosophy by a host of less well-known authors such as Schapiro, Harvey Brown, Lemert or Dallmayr.[31]

There is, incidentally, a remarkable paradox here. For whereas at first sight the traditional issues of political philosophy, state and political power, seem to have more affinity with money than with language as the alternative tertium, we will be surprised to find that, on the contrary, the practitioners of a *linguistic* political philosophy have always remained most sensitive to questions pertaining to the state and political power. By contrast, political philosophers concentrating on "money matters" like the question of a just income distribution ordinarily tend to ignore the presence of the state and the issue of political power. The differences between Foucault (language) and Rawls (money) are paradigmatic in this regard. I find it difficult to explain this improbable state of affairs in contemporary political philosophy. The only explanation that I can now think of is that Anglo-Saxon political philosophy tends to share the liberal disregard of the state, whereas continental philosophy with its Hegelian and Marxist traditions has always been much more aware of the state's role in society. And obviously the continental obsession with the transcendentalization of philosophical issues (as was discussed a moment ago) must have further contributed to this paradoxical state of affairs. It is a permanent feature of continental political philosophy to speak in the most abstract and unpractical way about the most concrete and urgent political issues, whereas Anglo-Saxon political philosophy has a no less inveterate propensity to do the reverse, and to reduce political abstractions to the simplest level, thus effecting a trivialization of the complexities of government. Political philosophers would be well-advised to look for the *juste milieu* between these two traditions and to speak concretely about complex and abstract issues (as historians may teach them to do).

I must emphasize that it follows from the foregoing that we should not see the contemporary infatuation of politics and political theory with money and with language as expressive of an objectionable "materialism" (in the case of the money option) or of an unpractical "idealism" (in that of the language option). How characteristic it is that we tend to associate money and language with these two traditionally opposite extremes of materialism and idealism! For money and language have acquired this place in contemporary politics and political philosophy for no other reason than that their role as our contemporary tertia has been the necessary final result of a long historical evolution of the tertia. Neither need we be surprised, then, by the central place of money and language in the contemporary world and in contemporary political theory, nor by the all-pervasive conviction of contemporary political philosophers that economics and rhetoric are our last resort in our attempt to get hold of political reality. Because they are so excellently suited to play the role of the most refined tertia, there obviously must be a profound "elective affinity" (whose nature was suggested a moment ago) between the two. The existence of this affinity was ingeniously hinted at by David Lodge in his amusing novel *Nice Work*, when one of its protagonists (who had given up literary theory for speculation) offers the following thought-provoking observation: " 'This isn't business,' said Charles, 'it's not about selling and buying real commodities. It's all on paper, or computer screens. It's abstract. It has its own rather seductive jargon—arbitrageur, deferred futures, floating rate. It's like literary theory.' "[32] Indeed, the paradoxes of the deconstructivist conception of language and meaning seem to have their counterpart in the paradoxes of value in contemporary economic reality. There is a deep truth in Lodge's suggestion that philosophy of language or literary theory and economics have, in our days, become each other's natural counterpart—and it is an evolution in the political object that may account for the amazing fact that these two apparently so different disciplines suddenly appear to have so much in common. The famous "il n'y a pas dehors texte" of the deconstructivists has its financial counterpart in the immense capital flows that, separate from the real economy, move across the world in a way that seems to rule out any prediction based on what is happening in the real economy and that may, at times, overthrow whole national economies the size of that of Great Britain.[33]

As will be argued in the next section, the mechanism behind these capital flows is always that money has become self-referential in a peculiar way (that may remind us of the self-referentiality that deconstructivists always like to attribute to language or to the text) and can now create an opposition within itself that may be a source of capital gain for the investor. But this development is not without its ironies. For the gains that can be made depend on the amount of money invested, on where it is invested, and on whether the investor is sufficiently quick in reacting to the opportunities that the market offers. Taking these three factors together, we will understand why the computerization of the financial markets and the increased accessibility of all markets have resulted in ever greater amounts of money, traveling at an ever greater speed, with ever less chance of profit, in a global financial economy with ever less contact with the real world of industry and commerce. This will also explain why the behavior of these capital flows is fundamentally unpredictable. For the chances of profit that could be created by correct prediction are immediately exploited and thus annihilated in agreement with the well-known mechanism that if everybody knows that a certain investment will offer chances for profitmaking, these chances will decrease accordingly. Hence computerization and the enormous amounts of money involved in these global capital flows will automatically tend to undo any economic analysis of its causes.

That is why, as was recently explained by Millman, participation in these capital flows handled by the financial network is inspired by hedging rather than by speculation. Companies make use of this financial network not for speculation but, on the contrary, for buying there the certainty that they can sell or buy a certain currency at a certain price at a certain date. And, as Millman goes on to say, "the company that did *nothing* to manage its financial risks was the most flagrant speculator, because it retained every risk." [34] Hence these immense capital flows, exceeding by far the total amount of money involved in transactions all over the globe in goods and services, are, to speak metaphorically, rather an umbrella to protect us against the rain than a bucket for collecting it. Economic analysis will here be (self-)defeated by the immediate exploitation of the knowledge gained by economic analysis.

Economics is no longer the science that we can correctly describe as the systematic attempt to understand a certain aspect of socioeconomic reality with the help of or in terms of certain tertia, for now these tertia have become objects for themselves. And that means the end of economics as the empirical social science that may guide us in our actions. Or, to put it in the form of the "catch 22" paradigm characteristic of so much in contemporary democracies: either we closely follow the recommendations of economists—but then we will face a situation that is the reverse of what Adam Smith had in mind with his "invisible hand" metaphor—or we do not follow these recommendations—and in that case our not following them will be punished in the way the textbooks predict. The textbooks are only correct if they can, so to speak, "be used against us." Contemporary economic realities seem to present us with a world that is fundamentally beyond our grasp and closely resembling the medieval world of "Fortuna imperatrix mundi" that will be our point of departure in Chapter 4. And certainly, "hedging" as a protection against currency risks closely resembles Machiavelli's political discovery that we are not, as medieval people still believed, completely helpless against the whims of the Goddess Fortuna.[35]

Furthermore, as was already suggested by the quotation from Lodge: if we think of the way in which Derrida reads his texts, then we can notice a similar unpredictable distribution of flows of meaning over the surfaces of language and the text. In both cases these ultimate tertia of the Stoic period, money and language, seem to want to produce a new tertium—or at least we feel compelled to look for one—whereas it appears that this new tertium can no longer emancipate itself from the old one, unlike before. There is nothing *behind* or *beyond* money and language. Here the search for ever more refined tertia seems finally to have come to an end. With this the political object has disappeared or, rather, been absorbed by its own background. For, contrary to what one might initially have expected, these most refined tertia do not permit the most accurate articulation of the political object, but instead express its ultimate *loss* of contours. In a similar way clouds lose their clear contours as we move closer to them and so we see them *less*, precisely because we see them *better*. Put differently, these ultimate tertia may well look ideal to us, as now everything has been made commensurable with everything else, but for that same reason we have now become blind to all the differentiations and frictions that constitute the political realm. Here we have another illustration of the old truth that what looks ideal often turns out, in the domain of politics, to be exactly the reverse. This familiar but thought-compelling insight was once formulated in terms of a suggestive metaphor by Wittgenstein: "We have got onto the slippery ice where there is no friction and so in a certain sense the conditions are ideal, but also, just because of that we are unable to walk. We want to walk: so we need friction. Back to the rough ground!"[36]

So friction is what we need—only friction can give us a reality we can refer to and that is no longer purely self-referential. Moreover, friction is what politics has always been and will always be about; for it is in friction that the political object stands out against the background of the tertia, it is friction (as Wittgenstein's metaphor suggests) that gives us a point of application in politics and makes meaningful political action possible at all. Without friction we may make all the movements that would enable us to move forward while inevitably we are condemned to remaining in one place forever. Political action requires friction, and the opposite is true as well. For "friction" in politics always has its origin in political *action*. It is only political action that truly "makes a difference" (and thus creates friction) in political reality, that differentiates the situation prior to political action from the one that comes into being as a consequence of it. It is in politics the analogue of walking in Wittgenstein's metaphor.

So let us now ask the question "Who acts?" or, rather, "To whom or to what must we ascribe the kind of political action 'that makes a difference' in politics?" On the face of it, this is not a difficult question, and many plausible answers suggest themselves. For example, according to liberalism individual citizens or politicians should be seen as the paramount political agents; according to Marxism, economic groups or interests fill this role. We should note that, in both cases, we are still dealing with entities existing *outside* (political) language. Language and reality are still clearly separated in these two examples, and it is political reality (and not some fact about language) that will be decisive in the debate between liberals and Marxists. The transition from the liberal proposal to the Marxist one was made mainly because the latter was supposed by its adherents to be more in accordance with what political reality itself showed to be the case—or, more specifically, with how this political reality had to be explained. For according to the Marxists explaining what goes on in political reality in terms of the intentions and actions of human individuals will provide us with a far less satisfactory explanation of politics than explanations adopting the phraseology of the class struggle. Thus the perspective of explanation (and of what we identified at the end of section 2 as its closest political cognate, the notion of "legitimacy") stimulated a process of decentering that moved the real political agent ever further away from the liberal, Enlightened individual who could still believe that he was in complete control of his actions. Explanation and legitimacy functioned as a *vis a tergo*, a backwards force that pushed the political agent deeper and deeper into (explanatory) language. So we may observe with regard to the notion of political action an evolution that is an exact parallel of the story told above about the absorption of the political object by the tertia against which it used to articulate and define itself. In this way the Stoic interest in the explanation (and legitimation) of political action effected an absorption of the political agent and political action into language no less total than we had already observed for the political object.

It follows from this that the Stoic tertia, because of their elimination of friction and this dimension of "making a difference," tended to undermine the possibility of political action. The regime of frictions and of "making a difference" had demonstrated a fairly even, entropological scatter of frictions over the whole of the political domain in the Western democracies of half a century ago, and until quite recently it had guaranteed the possibility of meaningful political action. To be more precise, as a rolling pin may flatten the dough in the center and leave there unevennesses only insofar as they succeed in escaping the rolling pin, while, precisely by doing so, creating rims at the edges, so the tertia succeeded in driving out frictions from the center of the political domain, that is, from politics as a going concern, while they now tended to gather again at the edges of the political domain. The frictions now coagulated at these edges into extremes of the most severe and far-reaching interventions in the social order. Interventions of this scale would at last place us again beyond the range of the Stoic tertia simply because they would completely break up the whole political order, the tertia and everything else that is glued together by them, thus creating some huge new rifts and frictions. Or, to take the other possibility that is suggested by the metaphor of the rolling pin, we could also focus on the microscopic frictions that have hitherto escaped the rolling pin of the tertia and, in this way, opt for an exclusive fixation on matters of such a small administrative scale that they still could remain unnoticed by politics and by political philosophy. Thus the tertia effected a polarization in the political domain between, on the one hand, total revolution, and, on the other hand, Foucauldian micropolitics (in fact, these two extremes are combined in Foucault's deeply ambiguous political philosophy—and that is also why Foucault can be seen as the most conservative among conservatives and as the most revolutionary among revolutionaries at the same time). Revolution and bureaucracy thus are seen to be the only alternatives that are left to us to implement the idea of true and meaningful political action.

With political action goes the capacity of the state to learn from its mistakes. For when, owing to the effectiveness of the tertia, everything becomes comparable with everything else and the contours of each political issue are lost in those of others, we will no longer be able to tell political problems apart from either our strategies of dealing with them or from the results of our political actions. Problems, solutions, and political action now all dissolve in one inextricable chaos and it has become impossible to learn lessons from past political experience, simply because such lessons can no longer be detached from their historical context. And if people now complain that the state apparently "is not a learning system" and tends to repeat endlessly the same kind of mistakes, this testifies to the extent to which the state has lost its way in the hopeless labyrinth that is built out of the most refined tertia. With the loss of political action we have also lost the possibility of learning from it.

So the final stages in this endless refinement of the tertia had to be that money and language are designated as the ultimate tertia and that we find in them our true political agents, seeing their nature and behavior as the most important determinants of political reality. And indeed, whether we think of how the laws discovered by economists determine government policy and function as the highest arbiter of political wisdom; whether we think of Freudian psychoanalysis as interpreted by Lacan; or of Gadamer's, Foucault's or Derrida's speculations about who the author of the text is; in all cases what is outside money and language (the individual, the social or historical group, and political ideology as the latest victim of the tertia)

has had to give way to money and language as the true emperor and em-
press of the contemporary political world. More specifically, the traditional
tertia of ideological political philosophy, which were still referentially defined and which, by their relative imperfection, still left a certain distance
between the tertia as background and what was defined against that background (that is, the political agent and the political object), now gave way
to the most perfect tertia of money and language, which absorbed this referential distance into themselves and thus drove both the political agent
and the political object into a completely marginal position insofar as they
could still properly be said to exist at all.

This must be the end of the evolution in question, for precisely because
of its nonreferentiality the linguistic tertium can no longer be replaced by
an even more perfect one. The referential nature of the older tertia always
evoked, and made us look for, the idea of an even more fundamental tertium situated somewhere between itself and the level of language. This is
why explanation (and legitimacy) naturally tended to absorb sociopolitical
reality into economics and language. With money and language, however,
this three-centuries-long development has come to an end: *economic politics*
and *linguistic political philosophy* truly represent the last and the highest
stage of Stoic politics.

5. *Aesthetic Politics and Democracy*

Economics and linguistic political philosophy as the logical outcome of
three hundred years of Stoicism must awaken in the political philosopher
an intense feeling of despair and hopelessness. For does this outcome not
imply that political philosophy has now, like its object, dissolved into economics and into literary theory (that is, into deconstructivism)? Moreover,
money and language are so ubiquitous, have such a protean nature, know
so infinitely many usages, are such elusive cultural phenomena, permeate
so much all aspects of human life, are both so strong and so weak, so hard
and so pliable, that political philosophers must feel at a loss regarding both
their goals and their instruments (it was precisely these characteristics of
money and language that assured their success as tertia). What can they
expect from a political philosophy that has been swallowed by the tertia
and therefore no longer recognizes an economic reality outside economic
politics and a "dehors texte" outside language, that is no longer interested
in leaving room for the existence of individual human beings and of social

groups, on their own terms? What perspective or point of view is left to us if we wish to objectify the reigning tertia? We feel as if we had been asked to produce the transcendental conditions of the possibility of transcendental philosophy itself.

What seems to be left but the unpalatable choice between a quietist acceptance of the existing political language and institutions and a self-destructive disregard of the recommendations of economists or Orwellian attempts to tamper with this language? It may seem that we witness here the death of political philosophy. Or, at least, we may suppose that political philosophy now finds itself forced to choose between explaining the inevitability of the contemporary self-elimination of politics or making proposals with regard to economics and the use of language, insofar as the latter affects power relations, that can only result in the kind of catastrophe depicted in Orwell's *1984*. Has, then, Marcuse's "one-dimensional man," who constitutes a society without realistic alternatives, finally come into being just when we all thought that we might safely forget about neo-Marxist paranoias and the historical dialectics in which neo-Marxism had always looked for its shaky foundations? Are we now reduced to the alternative of simply going on to endlessly vary the principles tying us to an eternal present [37] or to throw ourselves headlong into a revolution whose outcome nobody can predict, except that it will cause a chaos unparalleled in the whole history of mankind? [38]

In order to address these urgent questions, let us first return to the global capital flows referred to at the end of the previous section. What determines the course of these capital flows is what we can best capture in the strange phrase "the value of money": money is attracted to where it has its highest value. If we realize that money exists to express the value of something, that this is what we have money for, then it will be clear that this phrase "the value of money" (and the fact that economic realities are partially determined by what this curious phrase refers to) betrays the need for a tertium that could be located *behind* or *beyond* money, but which we are apparently unable to discover there, thus forcing us to make use of this impossible notion. We are thus led to the doubling of the notion "money" that we find in the phrase "the value of money." It is striking that in the realm of language we encounter a development similar to that of money. This can be illustrated with the help of Roland Barthes's notion of myth, which is, in many ways, paradigmatic for how contemporary literary theory explains the production of textual meaning. Barthes's argument on myth, as expressed in *Mythologies*, comes down to the following: Barthes discerns two semiological levels in language or in the text, the first of which is the observable surface level to which intentionalist literary criticism always restricted its gaze. As Barthes argues, anything said at that level always parasitizes on the "doxai" or tacit assumptions concerning reality that lie on a deeper semiological level of language or the text. Language "speaks" itself, though it would be more accurate to say that language articulates itself in relation to itself. In sum, textual meaning is produced by textual meaning.

Naturally what we find here reminds us strongly of our conclusions concerning the phrase "the value of money." In both cases the tertia become tertia for themselves without potential for further refinement. This reinforces the argument of the previous sections that at the end of Stoic politics we find economics and literary theory, and that both these studies will permanently replace former Stoic political theory. Besides, I emphatically speak here of the study of literature and not, for instance, of linguistics or philology. The explanation is that literary theory investigates the phenomenon of textual *meaning* and it presents us, in this respect, with the rightful equivalent in the field of language of the economic notion of *value*. We now understand that current discussions concerning the political content of the study of literature, discussions involving writers such as Frank Lentricchia, Stanley Fish, and Fredric Jameson, are by no means trivial: their studies focus on the last variant of Stoic political philosophy and are, from the point of view of practical politics, just as relevant as economics.

This ultimate version of Stoicism requires us to return to aesthetics and to an aesthetic political philosophy. The following arguments support this claim. First, the supreme effort to effect as a tertium a maximal continuity between money or language and the world meets a point beyond which it cannot go, folding money and language around themselves, creating the movement of doubling we noticed earlier. Put differently, the concepts of money and language now begin to form within themselves small anti-Stoic rifts or tensions that seem to imitate the familiar rifts between the concepts and the world, which typified a previous political dispensation. Stoic (political) philosophy had always tried to eliminate these rifts, but they now lie entirely within the domains of money and language themselves. Money and language now create within themselves "the rough ground" that Wittgenstein referred to and that will give us the "friction" that will enable us to walk again in political reality.

This necessarily places us in the domain of aesthetics. For, as we observed in section 2, aesthetics differs from Stoicism (as defined here) in that the domain of the representation and that of the represented can never be defined in terms of each other with the help of Stoic tertia. There are no fixed rules, as suggested or defined by the tertia, that tell painters how to move from landscape itself to their pictures of it. On the contrary, it is the permanent newness of how each artist, or each particular style, effects the transition from the represented to its representation that is of interest. This is also why there is a "world of art," in the sense that all works of art belong to a new or extra world that cannot be reduced by means of tertia to the world that is given to us in experience.

Characteristically, within this new or extra world meaning is created, not by repeating differentiations in represented reality, but by frictions and oppositions within the world of art itself. One might say that each individual work of art is the proposal of a certain tertium comparationis and that all these different proposals as embodied in individual works of art make the art world into a world of frictions. Here, then, we may discover the structural similarities between aesthetics and of the work of art and the tertia of a certain political philosophy. This philosophy, forced into using the phrase "the value of money," recognizes that language creates meaning by its own internal oppositions and frictions—by the kind of frictions of which the deconstructivists, as well as Barthes's notion of myth, have made us aware. In sum, at the end of the route suggested by the nature of the Stoic tertia themselves, we find how Stoicism turns against itself, and erects an insurmountable barrier between money and language as opposed to reality that is both exemplified and explained by the work of art. Value and linguistic meaning are produced without a proper counterpart in reality itself. The highest stage of Stoic political philosophy is also the birth of aesthetic political philosophy.

When asking ourselves how we should translate these abstract and methodological considerations concerning the differences between Stoic and aesthetic political philosophy into actual political practice, we are well advised to begin with a remark on political indifference and its role in the domain of politics. The previous discussion of the absorption of politics into the background of the tertia naturally invites us to consider political indifference—indifference being the counterpart in the voter's mind of the absence of frictions in the political domain. Since Schumpeter's cynical comments on the voter and a famous essay by Converse, it is often pointed out that the average voter invests less intellectual energy in his or her political choices than in a game of bridge, and that many of the voter's political desiderata are inconsistent with each other (I shall return to this topic in the conclusion of this book).[39] Now, political indifference confronts the Stoic political philosophers with an unpleasant dilemma. On the one hand the Stoic, and especially the *republican* Stoic, will argue that the political order has its only legitimate support in the willingness of the citizen to identify with the state or the common interest. Indifference suggests nothing of the kind: indifference expresses a resistance to identify with whatever political institution one might think of. Indifference will thus inevitably, within this Stoic conception, effect an atrophy of the body politic and finally result in its falling apart. That is why Stoic political philosophers often seem to consider political indifference as the worst thing that may happen to a democracy. On the other hand, one may *also* argue that no single factor will be more effective in smoothing the political domain in the way that is always required by the Stoic tertia than political indifference. An indifferent electorate is like the dough that has been completely flattened, to use once again the metaphor proposed in the previous section. So Stoics should also applaud indifference as the ultimate triumph of their political conceptions. When trying to evade this unpleasant dilemma, Stoics might point out that political indifference, in practice, is the result of a (defective) democratic political order rather than its legitimating origin. But since social and political reality always is so conspicuous for the complicity of causes and effects, this way out seems decidedly hopeless. Stoic political philosophers are thus left with the necessity of hating what is, to all practical purposes, their highest political ideal.

The aesthetic political philosopher, however, is not confronted with such a hopeless dilemma. Discussing political indifference, Walter Bagehot made the cynical but worldly-wise comment that "stupidity is essential to political freedom" and that the revolutionary-minded French (of his generation) were "too clever to be free." And he continued with the no less cynical observation that "the mass of the English people yield a deference rather to something else than to their rulers. They defer to what we may call the *theatrical show* of society. . . . Courts and aristocracies have the great quality which rules the multitude, though philosophers can see nothing in it — visibility."[40] These two observations by Bagehot, if taken together, may help us to further our insight into the nature of aesthetic politics and aesthetic political philosophy. Bagehot makes us aware of the fact that indifference and stupidity are not necessarily the sand in the political machine but rather the indispensable oil for making it function. It is only because we do not personally care about every problem confronting society and are indifferent to a large number of issues that political compromise is possible at all. If each citizen were always fully aware of the political issues at stake and correctly figured out to the last detail what these issues might mean for him- or herself and if, next, each citizen never tired of being heard in political society, even a small country would immediately be paralyzed politically. But, as Bagehot points out, this is not even what the population desires itself. What it wants instead is "visibility": that is, political power and its representatives are left great political freedom on the single but crucial condition that power should be *visible*. In other words, indifference creates a distance or an alienation of people and its rulers that allows the latter the kind of autonomy that is the political analogue of the autonomy of money and language that we ascertained for post-Stoic politics above. And it is precisely this distance or this alienation of the represented from the representative (and vice versa) that makes power "visible," in the same way that we can only interpret a painting if we dissociate ourselves, so to speak, from its surface and look at it from an appropriate distance. Hence, for successful political machinery we need these two things, indifference and the visibility of power, and these two things cannot exist without each other. Political representation only makes sense on the assumption of the presence of a certain amount of political indifference and only political indifference can create the distance from which the voter can get a grasp of the political domain and of the (in)adequacy of how politicians propose to deal with it.

This brings us back to the topic discussed in the previous chapter, that of representation. We observed in Chapter 1 that the aesthetic interpretation of political representation created between the representative and the represented an essentially aesthetic gap, which we may now conceive of in two ways. In the first place we can see the gap as embodying the void that is created by indifference. It is the citizen's often most reasonable and understandable indifference to much of what its representatives do that is the very raison d'être of an assembly of representatives, which attends to all kinds of matters beyond the citizen's direct interest and control. As Sieyès noted, it is only this that makes civil life in a socially and economically complex society like ours possible at all. Nevertheless, indifference has to be checked in order to prevent tyranny and arbitrary government. And it is this combination of requirements that is ideally satisfied by what was called "aesthetic representation" in the previous chapter. Aesthetic political representation accounts for an acceptable degree of indifference on behalf of the citizen for what is transacted in the public sphere; at the same time it creates the distance between the represented and the representative in which legitimate political power originates, becomes visible, and, most important, can be controlled by the electorate. We can only control what we can "see." That is why the elimination of the aesthetic gap between the voter and the representative is not the realization of democracy, but an invitation to tyranny. This gap prevents both the totalitarian identification of the voter with the politician and our contemporary "negative" totalitarianism that requires the politician to identify with the voter.

6. Representative Democracy and Aesthetic Representation

I want to conclude this chapter by focusing on those aspects of contemporary capitalist democracy that are suggestive of a countermovement against the tendencies of Stoic political philosophy that have been discussed above. This countermovement might prove to be a point of departure for a further development of the rifts and tensions announcing the end of Stoic political practice and the necessity for an anti-Stoic, aesthetic political philosophy. As we have seen, it is the difference, or aesthetic gap, between the represented and its representation that is responsible for these rifts and tensions. These rifts and tensions should not, however, be predicated of the aesthetic gap itself. Their domain is exclusively that of the representation and not of what makes the representation different from what is represented. Nevertheless, one might say that they are the echoes in the domain of representation of that insurmountable aesthetic barrier existing between the represented and its representation. It follows that this aesthetic gap is truly the heart of representative democracy: here the power is generated that keeps its machinery going. If this power is weakened, either by implementing notions of direct democracy that delegitimate the aesthetic gap or because the aesthetic gap begins to be filled by social and quasi-political institutions that are no longer tied either to the represented or to the representative, the machinery comes to a standstill, bureaucracy takes over, and administration is then where politics was.

It is here, by the way, that one may discover an important difference between the notion of the aesthetic gap or void discussed here and the void that was postulated by Claude Lefort to explain the workings of democracy:

in the case of Lefort this void or empty place lies outside the aesthetic relationship between the state (the representative) and the citizen (the represented) and functions in his conception of democracy merely as a passive
screen onto which the symbolics Lefort feels to be essential for democracy
can be projected.[41] In aesthetic representation, however, the void lies between the elector and the person elected, or between the citizen and the
state, and it really forms the heart of the democracy. Lefort's (theologically
inspired) search for a symbolic political meaning outside of or transcending the political machinery itself is replaced here by a consistent immanence. Though neither Lefort nor the aesthetic political philosopher wishes
to attribute legitimate political power to either the ruler or the ruled (or to
both, for that matter), Lefort situates its origin in a sphere beyond both the
ruler and the ruled, whereas the aesthetic political philosopher discovers
this origin between them.

So let us see what role is fulfilled by the aesthetic gap or void in a properly functioning democracy. First of all we should note that both in the
field of economics and in that of language—those two fields in which Stoic
politics seemed to culminate—we find something that will strongly remind
us of what has been said about this aesthetic void. In the world of economics and of business—unlike what the term "market" suggests—everything takes place in silence. When using the word "silence" I am primarily
thinking of what Sennett understood by the silence of the contemporary
public domain: after the development of the first Western democracies the
individual abandoned the public order in order to retreat into the private
domain.[42] Silence now took the place of the noisy and theatrical presentation of the self still characteristic of eighteenth-century society. Henceforward silence and indifference are the main features of how the public
sphere manifests itself. But democratic silence and indifference should certainly not be associated with absence, negativity, or lack of productivity. On
the contrary, silence and indifference may well be seen as the most powerful historical and sociological forces that ever determined the course of the
world's history. It is precisely in silence and indifference that political and
interhuman contacts transcended the zero-sum model of the Stoic social
order and that productivity and creativity were freed of all the restrictions
of the Stoic order. This has always been a characteristic of the world of art
and thought, where success never could be converted into the failure of
others and vice versa. It was this model that now also conquered the world

of economics and politics, and is surely one of the few features of the contemporary world that might justifiably stimulate some optimism about its future.

How the metaphor of silence can be implemented for the domain of economics can be illustrated as follows. A product that is substandard or too expensive is not attacked or challenged, and does not become the subject of a noisy debate, legal or otherwise, that might bring it to anybody's attention and thereby, by a perverse effect, perhaps even reinforce its position on the market. It is simply ignored and dies in silence because of the indifference of the public. It is the void of potential indifference between producer and consumer that is the most powerful stimulus to economic growth and that determines its direction in individual cases. Enthusiasm and feigned or sincere admiration of the consumer for producers and their products create, at best, a Soviet-style kind of economic system. If the capitalist market functions so much better than planned economies, that is mainly because the former is ruled by indifference and the latter by enthusiasm. Just as there is an aesthetic incommensurability between representation and what is represented, so there also is an incommensurability between supply and sales in the sense that the rejected product fails to have its counterpart in sales of that product: there can be no "negative" sales, only their absence. As far as this absence of sales is a factor in the market economy, it takes the form of a void. One can say that this void is a most powerful causal determinant in the economic process, since each producer so strenuously attempts to avoid it.

Here representative democracy and the market economy are in line. For something similar can be observed in the field of language—and of course I am thinking here of language as used in political debate. One of the most successful strategies in such debate is not the direct challenge of the opinion of one's political opponent, but avoiding a confrontation with that opinion by convincingly pointing out, or merely suggesting, its irrelevance. Political debate in democracy is positively antidialectic: it does not attempt to retain the best out of two opposing opinions, but to put displeasing opinions in quarantine, so to speak. It is here that political debate is quite unlike the kind of debate that one may find in the sciences. In the latter kind of debate it is of the greatest importance that one should recognize and address the cognitive heart of the position of one's opponent. Without this one will not be taken seriously in the intellectual contest. In political debate, by contrast, the argument of one's opponent has to be encapsulated, rendered innocuous, shown as not deserving serious consideration. Such a strategy entails that one should avoid the cognitive heart of the position of one's opponent as much as possible. Getting entangled in it is admitting his or her point. This can only serve one's purpose in the relatively rare case that one has all the facts and arguments on one's side and is set on the road to a complete victory by graciously granting to the opponent his or her point. Hence, generally speaking, it is unwise to try to refute one's opponent's opinion (at least in the way this is done in the sciences), all the more since, political issues being what they are, one can only be successful with the direct, "scientific" strategy in a few quite exceptional cases. One should hope rather to isolate the opinions of the opponent, to declare them irrelevant, to create a vacuum, or, to use the most appropriate term, to create a void around them.

It must immediately be added, however, that only good arguments can guarantee the success of this strategy of putting one's opponents' political position in quarantine. One can only hope to succeed in avoiding the cognitive heart of the position of one's opponent if one is able first to identify it and then to invent the kind of arguments that might render it innocuous. In fact, this requires that the politician be able to transcend disagreement with an opponent. This is not at all an easy task. Political rhetoric is not necessarily irrational; on the contrary, it is both rational and something more than that—and this "extra" can properly be explained and defended by the aesthetic gap or void accompanying all the major moves that can be made in democracy. Needless to say, these facts about political debate in democracies strongly suggest the silliness of Habermas's speculations about the so-called ideal speech situation. Such a situation could only come into being after the successful elimination of all that democratic politics is about, all that makes it interesting and valuable to voters and to politicians themselves. Habermas wants the kind of politics that we can only expect after the death of politics, and his political and social philosophy is therefore just one more chapter in the book of German attempts to put an end to politics, which has always been profoundly distrusted in the German tradition.

Taking a closer look at this strategy of isolation in democratic political debate, two phases or elements can be discerned. First, the suggestion that one's opponent's opinion is not so much mistaken but irrelevant (thus creating the aesthetic void around it) does not fail to give to the person making that suggestion an aura of impartiality. For the implication is that maybe there is something to be said for the view challenged and that certainly the good intentions of its adherents are not in doubt—just as the same could,

perhaps, be said of the opposite view—but that *both* views, the view itself
and its opposite, simply do not further a good understanding of the question under consideration. It is one of the most persistent urges of democracy to cover up partiality with impartiality:[43] the best thing that can happen to a democratic politician is to see his or her political views confirmed
by quasi-objective evidence, as for instance by socioscientific research or by
objectively verifiable facts. This may account for the community of interests of democratic politics and the social sciences; a community of interests
to which the social sciences can be argued to owe their coming into being,
if we recall the German eighteenth-century tradition of "Statistik." The
practitioners of this discipline gathered all kinds of data with regard to the
wealth of the country in the conviction that this knowledge might further
the interests of the state (hence the term "Statistik") by suggesting how its
economic prosperity could best be served. This embryonic social science
had no other aim than to further the interests of the state.

The second element, dependent on the one expounded just now, is no
less important. By confirming the irrelevance of both the view in question
and its opposite (for neither is challenged), the fact that the political views
in question are not representative is underlined (in the sense that they do
not adequately represent anything in the aspect of the public domain that
is under discussion). As a result a situation arises that within the Stoic
order must be experienced as a minor cognitive impasse: for within that
order, where thanks to the Stoic tertia a representation is always connected
to what is represented, it is inconceivable that both p and non-p (that is,
the irrelevant opinion and its opposite) could be placed *outside* that order.
The Stoic political world is ruled by Aristotle's principle of "tertium non
datur": either the tertia connect a representation to a represente, or they
don't, but the condemnation of *both* possibilities as irrelevant is at odds
with the logic of the tertia. Obviously there is no problem here from the
perspective of aesthetic representation: what the painter considers irrelevant will neither be confirmed nor challenged in a painting. The painter
simply does not portray it.

We have just seen how even in areas where Stoic politics has celebrated
its greatest triumphs—those of money and language—small frictions, im-
balances, and asymmetries develop, infringing on the continuity and the
commensurability typically desired by the Stoic political order. Even here
voids may occur, even here incommensurabilities arise that enable aesthetic
politics to escape from the grip of the Stoic tertia. The question presents
itself whether it is possible to discern a certain system in the production of

these aesthetic voids in present-day democracy. If we wish to prevent a continuation of the political standstill of a Stoic politics that remains frozen in its last and ultimate phase, and if we are not content with the limited aims of a Foucauldian "micropolitics," it will be of the greatest importance that we shall be able to identify such a system in the workings of aesthetic politics.

To answer that question, we can turn to the writings of Tocqueville, whose insights into the peculiarities of democracy are, in my opinion, still unsurpassed.[44] In the second part of his study Tocqueville gives a characteristic of public debate in democracy that is very similar to what has just been said on that topic:

> Time, events, or the unaided individual action of mind will sometimes undermine or destroy an opinion, without any outward sign of change. It has not been openly assailed, no conspiracy has been formed to make war on it, but its followers noiselessly secede; day by day few of them abandon it, until at last it is only professed by a minority. In this state it will continue to prevail. As its enemies remain mute or only interchange their thoughts by stealth, they are themselves unaware for a long period that a great revolution has actually been effected; and in this state of uncertainty they take no steps; they observe one another and are silent.[45]

Tocqueville here describes how public debate in democracy refutes the old saying "du choc des opinions la vérité jaillit": opinions do not directly confront each other in democracy, and the evolution of public opinion is not to be seen as the result of a debate in which the whole nation participates, but rather as what takes place at the stock market. One does not argue with the board of an unsuccessful company; one simply sells its shares. And as Tocqueville's own words abundantly suggest, it is here, too, that silence, the creation of a void, and avoidance rather than conflict are the decisive factors in the progress of public debate.

It is of the greatest interest that Tocqueville discerns something similar in the relationship between the state and the citizen. In the fourth book of the second part of *Democracy in America* Tocqueville describes this relationship in democracy. In this context he points to the fact that the most serious threat to the citizen's freedom or independence lies in the democratic state's ambition to establish contact with the citizen *not* in big and important things, but especially in small things and administrative details:

> I admit that, by this means, room is left for the intervention of individuals in the more important affairs; but it is not the less suppressed in the smaller and more private ones. It must not be forgotten that it is especially dangerous to en-

slave men in the minor details of life. For my own part, I should be inclined to think freedom less necessary in great things than in little ones, if it were possible to be secure of the one without possessing the other.[46]

A century and a half of experience with representative democracy has confirmed Tocqueville's expectation that in its contact with the citizen the state always much preferred the small administrative detail while leaving to the citizen the freedom to discuss and decide on the larger issues. As was the case with the progress of public debate in democracy, so it is here as well: the state's choice in favor of details arises from its wish to avoid conflict with the citizen as much as possible.

The actions of the state should not be seen as the enactment or expression of a consensus achieved in public debate, but rather as the outcome of a role play between the state and the most prominent and powerful agents in society. It is profoundly mistaken to conceive of the democratic state and its actions as the expression of "the will of the people," in whatever way this confused notion is understood. For the state, the representative, is an autonomous factor in public decision making; it has its own interests and its own reflexes. And its most cherished strategy is and will always be the avoidance of conflicts with society, for it never has anything to gain from such a conflict. That is why the state fragmented the political domain (not to be identified, of course, with civil society itself) into a myriad of small, individual, preferably merely bureaucratic issues; for it is at the level of the details that conflicts with society are least likely and can most easily be avoided. And if they arise despite this, the state has secured for itself the most advantageous position in its conflict with society. We are used to seeing the state as a busybody, constantly interfering with everything we do — and to some extent that is certainly a correct observation. But if we remember the extreme pretensions of the ancien régime state, in areas such as religion, ethics, and social hierarchy, then this teaches us to put the nature of state intervention into the correct Tocquevillian perspective. The state no longer attempts to prescribe our religion, or what social class we shall belong to or what classes society should possess; the state has come to realize that here is a potential of resistance in society that, if activated, can only result in the gravest dangers for itself. This is why, as Tocqueville so clairvoyantly saw, the state sought and discovered a far safer support for its autonomy and position in details. Hence the represented and the representative are like ships that pass in the night: both maximally attempt to avoid collisions that are fatal to all concerned by carefully respecting the aesthetic void between them.

Nevertheless, though these voids that were created by the state's strategy of avoidance and that are so essential to the machinery of representative democracy concern the trivial and banal aspects of existence, we should not underestimate the role they play in modern democracy. The state, having thrown itself on these details with all its weight, thereby succeeded in effecting a kind of transfiguration of those details that would transform them into major political issues. We should also appreciate to what extent the modern state is the product of these strategies of avoidance. The state does not like contrasting impulses, since the complicated administrative systems produced by democracy during the last century would be unable to survive a continuous political tug-of-war between them. We should not picture the state, then, as a neutral area in which the political and social conflict is fought out. On the contrary, the state is itself involved in that conflict and has its own interests there, and as soon as we realize that, we will understand that the state will always try to divert to areas where conflict is least to be expected. Should the state now seem to be closer to the citizens than fifty or a hundred years ago, this is not due to the fact that the state, thanks to democracy and an ongoing effort to perfect that political system, now acts more in accordance with the wish of the electorate than before. Rather this is due to the fact that the state has managed to maneuver itself into a position with regard to society where the pursuit of its own traditional aspirations will least occasion conflicts with society that are counterproductive for all actors in the theater of politics. Democracy is not, as we all like to think, a political system for executing that mysterious entity to which we refer by the phrase "the will of the people." To minimize the potential conflicts between the complex society and the powerful and ambitious state we need both that society and that state. Without a complex and supremely sophisticated civil society or a powerful state, democracy would be without its appropriate biotope and would degenerate into a useless construction.

7. Conclusion

It is now possible to say something about the significance of an aesthetic political philosophy and also to demonstrate why it is superior to Stoic political philosophy. To begin with the latter claim, from the perspective of aesthetic political philosophy we can explain the origins, the nature, the shortcomings and the inevitable fiascoes of Stoic political philosophy, whereas the opposite does not hold. We may conclude from this that aesthetic political philosophy has a wider scope than its Stoic rival. The following comment should be taken into account here: Stoic political philosophy will be unable to explain (in the way this can be done from the perspective of an aesthetic political philosophy) why the relationship between the democratic state and society will tend to restrict itself to those Tocquevillian administrative details discussed in the last section, and why because of the same mechanisms of avoidance operative there, the democratic state will do what it can to get political debate into the area of economic and financial affairs. In fact, there is more than a mere elective affinity between economic politics and the democratic state's love for the administrative detail.

The word "economics," as Hannah Arendt never tired of pointing out, is derived from the Greek word "oikos," and must be associated with the puny details of the household. It has been the great service rendered by economics to the democratic state to demonstrate that, surprisingly enough, a social "science" could be developed to account for the details of this private and therefore apparently so unpredictable domain of human existence. It was a rare stroke of luck for the democratic state, as welcome as it was unexpected, that these puny details constituted a large potential domain of political action, both less contested and far more influential than the kind of issues that previous political systems preferred to focus on. The coming about of Stoic politics, so much informed by economics, is therefore a movement that is completely understandable within a theoretical universe defined by aesthetic political philosophy. Hence, in any discussion with Stoic colleagues, the aestheticist political theorist will feel as confident as the aesthetic philosopher when asked to answer the simple question of why the naive aesthetics of the layman will always force him to privilege the photograph over a Titian—even when this same layman would actually by far prefer the latter to the former. Surely all aesthetics begins by showing what is wrong with this naive intuition and what the arguments against it are: Gombrich developed them some three decades ago in his *Art and Illusion*. For the same reason aesthetic political philosophy is far better equipped than its Stoic counterpart for teaching us how to place the democratic state in a wider perspective, one that will enable us to see traditional political problems in a new way.

In this context I am primarily thinking of the following. Science has always served to help us to conquer social and natural reality; Stoic political philosophy linked up with that ambition easily enough and, to a certain extent, even originated in the effort to do so. The high expectations we have had in our recent positivist past of this essentially Stoic program have become considerably more modest over the last few decades, and a concomitant awareness of the limitations of politics is stronger than ever. Within the Stoic political and philosophical program the awareness of these regrettable limitations is difficult to conceptualize. Attempts to that effect will often lead to strange paradoxes: for instance, one gets *more* of a grip on political reality precisely by *releasing* one's grip. An aesthetic political philosophy, with its awareness of how the mechanisms of avoidance and withdrawal may generate political power, will be able to explain and therefore avoid such paradoxes. In short, the now often recommended programs of deregularization, of denationalization, or of debureaucratization (bureaucracy being the Stoic institution par excellence!) have a natural affinity with aesthetic political philosophy while at the same time enlarging our capacity for dealing with our most urgent political problems. By getting rid of former and by now obsolete objects of political concern, the state will be able to wield more power for dealing with the new kind of political problem that challenges the politician of this and the next generations.[47] Knowing when to exchange old problems for new ones is, indeed, one of the primary conditions of the efficacy of the state's actions. The state that continues to devote much of its energy to issues that have lost the interest of the citizen or, worse still, which endows a social political problem with near-permanence because of its all-too-apparent incapacity to effectively deal with it, will lose all credibility in the eyes of the voter.

One must realize that political problems are not like the objects that an archaeologist may discover in a burial chamber: there is such a thing as an "economy (or aesthetics) of political problems," in the sense that certain subsets of political problems either belong together or mutually exclude each other. Similarly, there is such an "economy" in the representation of reality: "the spirit of a painting" automatically rules out the representation of those aspects of reality whose inclusion in the painting would destabilize this "spirit"—even when the objective importance of these aspects would be doubted by nobody. Similarly, this "economy of political problems" must always precede and determine the politician's assessment of the more or less objective importance of the problems in question. The politician (or the state) who disregards or forgets this economy will contaminate any solution of the right problems with an inadequate focus on the wrong set of problems. The wise author of *The Spirit of the Laws* (to whom I already referred, of course, when speaking of "the spirit of a painting") already knew as much when he wrote that unnecessary laws will have the counterproductive effect of weakening the necessary ones, or, as he put it, "les loix inutiles affaiblissent les loix nécessaires."

Aesthetic political philosophy can cast a new light on how power functions. We associate power primarily with order, command, or with the power of Foucault's "discourse." Aesthetic political philosophy draws our attention to the fact that a form of power that is no less interesting and no less prominent than those others is generated in and by the strategies of avoidance current in present-day democracies. Where weakness is expected —in the avoidance of conflict—an important source of power exists instead. But most important of all, aesthetic political philosophy reestablishes the state in the center of the political philosopher's attention. Due to the tertia, which tend to blur all the contours of the various elements in the political universe, it gradually became common wisdom in contemporary political theory to present the distinction between state and society as an outmoded and obsolete naïveté. The state now became, undoubtedly much to its own satisfaction, the "empty place" or void in debate in political philosophy, and its tremendous growth over the last decades remained strangely unaccompanied by the political philosopher's critical reflection.[48] However, that meant the creation of an empty place or a void precisely where it should not be. For due to the aesthetic gap or void between the represented and the representative, between the state and society, which aesthetic political theory makes us aware of, the state ought to regain in political theory its prominent role, and to become, once again, the main issue in our effort for a better understanding of contemporary democratic politics.

3. Romanticism, Postmodernism, and Democracy

---

1. Introduction

In this chapter I shall defend two theses. The first is that we can only understand democracy properly if we realize that it came into being during the Romantic movement in the period of the so-called Restoration—that is, the period between 1815 and 1848—and consequently that democracy is in essence Romantic. My second thesis will be that postmodernism can be seen as a specification of the relevant aspects of Romanticism and that therefore postmodernism can help us to become aware of certain peculiarities of democracy in our contemporary world, and can thus help us to deal with these peculiarities and to react to them in an appropriate way wherever necessary.

2. "Metaphysical" and "Aesthetic" Political Theory

I shall begin with some theoretical reflections on the nature of my investigation. In Chapters 1 and 2, these general reflections were predominantly epistemological: they argued against an application of the Stoic conception of (ethical) knowledge to the domain of politics and in favor of allowing aesthetics to do for politics the job that was traditionally assigned to epistemology. Here my introductory remarks belong to the domain of metaphysics. In the next chapter epistemological questions will be raised again:

Can we know political reality? Under what circumstances? What may we expect here from the point of view of irony? In that sense this chapter could be seen as a mere *trait d'union* between the previous chapter and the next.

The metaphysical consideration of specific interest in the present context could best be introduced in the following way. In the seventeenth chapter of his *Leviathan*, which appeared in 1651, Thomas Hobbes presents to his readers an explanation of his ideas on the origin of the state and of civil society. He does so in the following words: "the finall Cause, End, or Designe of Men, (who naturally love Liberty, and Dominion over others,) is the introduction of that restraint upon themselves, (in which we see them live in a Commonwealth,) is the foresight of their own preservation."[1] Hobbes's thesis here is that the origin of the political order, of (in his terminology) the state or the "Commonwealth," lies in our permanent striving for self-preservation. As was demonstrated in the previous chapter, it is this principle that is for Hobbes (as it would be for Spinoza) the analogue in the domain of politics of the principle of inertia determining the nature of the reality that is investigated in the sciences. And it is in this principle that Hobbes discovers the foundations of the state. For it is only the political institution that we call the state that offers us the possibility to guarantee the personal safety of the citizen, of order and peace and the self-preservation of the individual. As Hobbes continues, it is also "the only way to erect such Common Power, as may be able to defend them [that is, the citizens] from the invasion of Forraigners, and the injuries of others . . . is to conferre all their power and strength upon one Man, or upon one Assembly of Men, that may reduce all their Wills, by plurality of voices, unto one Will."[2]

To sum up, there is a clearly identifiable foundation of the state, of politics, of the "Commonwealth" or "civitas," all terms used by Hobbes to refer to the state. And this solid and well-defined foundation is the innate striving for self-preservation of all the individuals who unite themselves in political society or in the state. Furthermore, taking into account the foundations of the state as described just now, we can give the following definition of the essential nature of the state. It can be best characterized in terms of Hobbes's construction of the Leviathan, of "that mortall God" to which the citizen has handed over his pre-political autonomy and independence. "I authorize and give up my right of Governing myselfe, to this Man, or Assembly of Men, on the condition, that thou give up thy Right to him, and authorize all his Actions in like Manner"[3]—it is in this renunciation of self-government of pre-political man that we may discern both the foundation and the nature of the state. This renunciation marks the transition from pre-political to political society.

If Hobbes is often seen as the father of modern political theory, we have every reason to agree. Admittedly, it is true that the conclusions of later political theorists such as Locke, Rousseau, and Kant, and generally the seventeenth- and eighteenth-century natural law theorists, sometimes differed dramatically from the position argued by Hobbes. This is even more true of the historically and sociologically inspired political theory of the nineteenth century as developed by Hegel, Marx, or Spencer. Nevertheless there always remains an essential point of agreement. And this agreement is that all these political theorists, at some stage in their argument, express an opinion on the origins and nature of the unity and coherence of the political order and of the state. The same can even be said of contemporary political theory. As has been stated in the Introduction, it has become customary to discern in mainstream contemporary political theory the following three traditions: liberalism, the republicans, and the communitarian tradition. These traditions can be defined as follows. Liberals (such as Rawls) attempt to discover the principles for distributive justice that ought to obtain in the just society and have remained closest to the ideas of natural law theorists from Hobbes to Kant; the republicans (such as Pocock) require from the citizen a patriotic identification with the public interest, while the communitarians (such as MacIntyre or Taylor) employ various arguments to show that it is only in a social and political order that the individual can fully realize him- or herself. But what all of these three traditions and their many adherents share with Hobbes is that they all have an opinion on the foundations of the political order, an opinion on how this order can or ought to be legitimized metaphysically and on how the unity and coherence of the political order comes into being or ought to have come into being, taking into account its metaphysical foundations.

Thus one might well characterize all these political traditions as "metaphysical." I understand by metaphysics here the philosophical subdiscipline that aims at giving a definition of the foundations and the essence of reality (or aspects of it), and thus pretends to be able to discover a unity in the multiplicity and multiformity of the phenomena the world presents to us. And indeed, just as Hobbes offered a political metaphysics with his statement that the foundation of the political order lies in the human striving for self-preservation, so all the political theorists of the three traditions just mentioned have, each in their own way, given an answer to the question concerning the foundations and the unity of the political order. To be more specific, in each of these three traditions a principle is discerned (principles of distributive justice, the common good, or the social nature of the human individual) in terms of which one can freely move from the individual or the citizen to the state or society and that therefore embodies the metaphysical heart of the political order as a whole. Of course, this translates the argument of the previous chapter on the epistemological role played by the tertia into metaphysics.

The persistence of this political metaphysics into our own days (as exemplified by the three traditions in contemporary political theory) may surprise us because our century has generally been so hostile toward metaphysics. Perhaps someone might now say that this hostility to metaphysics has resulted in an abandoning of political theory for political science and that contemporary political theory is an increasingly obsolete remnant of a scientifically less sophisticated age. Certainly this is how political science often likes to present itself. Contrary to the pretensions of political science, however, and contrary to its confident and clamorous rejection of political theory as a metaphysical enterprise that is unable to further our insights into the nature of political reality, political science can be shown to possess the same foundationalist aspirations as its adversary. Admittedly, just as physicists have, since the seventeenth century, rarely been looking for certain metaphysical principles underlying the way nature presents itself to us, so political scientists openly disavow interest in the ultimate, fundamental principles of political reality that have always attracted the attention of political theorists; they content themselves with a description—as accurate as possible—of what political reality in fact looks like. But we should observe that, even in doing so, they still embrace the notion of fundamentals or basic principles that had always inspired the metaphysical tradition of political theory. Summarizing this in one sentence: foundation and unity are now no longer sought in the *object*, in reality, as was and is the case in political theory, but in the knowing *subject*, in the researcher and in the cognitive instruments that enable him or her to deal with political reality. The starting point for all political science is, in the words of David Easton, who was one of its most illustrious students, that it aims to develop a "systematic theoretical structure of its own," especially on the basis of an "integration of the methods of science" through which, leading on from that, "the fundamental coherence of its subject matter" can be effected.[4] Hence, in political science, as opposed to the metaphysics of political theory, fundamentals and coherence are no longer sought in the object, but now receive an epistemological justification. Within this new epistemological and antimetaphysical socioscientific approach, too, however, fundamentals and coherence remain the starting point and aim of the investigation in question, as was stated *expressis verbis* in Easton's declaration of the aims of political science quoted just now. And we may conclude that political science remains firmly within the Stoic tradition no less than do liberalism, republicanism, and communitarianism. Just like these, it will preclude our access to aesthetic political philosophy.

In short, it is only for the tradition of aesthetic political philosophy that we may claim immunity from all those metaphysical and epistemological reflexes described in the previous chapter and in the present one. We may add that from the perspective of aesthetic political philosophy, metaphysical or epistemological political theory and political science have more similarities than differences. Hence, it is its anti-Stoicism that effectively separates aesthetic political philosophy from all its rivals.

If we wish to understand the nature of this alternative aesthetic tradition in political theory, then the dedication to Lorenzo de Medici with which Machiavelli opened *The Prince* offers good guidance. In this dedication Machiavelli apologizes for the fact that he, a simple private citizen, dares to give advice to monarchs. "But," he continues, "just as painters sketching a landscape study mountains and high areas from a valley, but study low country from the mountains, just so one has to be a prince in order to understand completely the nature of the people, but a simple citizen to comprehend fully the nature of princes."[5] This surprising statement contains at least three interesting elements. First, the political domain no longer has here the unity we always find in the metaphysical tradition, but is essentially a *broken* world. There is the political world of the prince and, next to this world, that of the people, and to Machiavelli's mind these worlds are essentially different and cannot be reduced to each other. Where the metaphysics of political theory and the epistemology of political science always presupposed the presence of one or more principle(s) enabling us to argue from the citizen to the state (or the prince), Machiavelli resists the seduction of these presuppositions. And we need only remember Machiavelli's rejection of ethics (belonging to the domain of the individual) for the prince (belonging to the domain of state and politics) to realize that this is surely no accidental feature of Machiavelli's conception of the political domain but was decisive for his whole enterprise.

His rejection of ethics for political action is the logical result of this perspectivist (or representational, or aestheticist) incommensurability of the world of the prince and that of the citizen. We are equally justified in discerning here Machiavelli's revolutionary break with the unity of the medieval conception of the world in which he was born and lived. Second, this broken world owes its brokenness to the different *perspectives* from which the political actors operate; the perspective from which the prince acts cannot be reduced to that of the simple citizen and consequently they live to some extent in different political worlds. And third, in the world of politics we apparently move around gropingly; certainties hardly exist and others usually see better what we are doing than we ourselves do. Even more so, neither prince nor citizen is completely "at home" with himself; there always is in him something that is alien to himself and that can only properly be recognized by the other. The people understand the prince better than he understands himself, and vice versa.

In order to distinguish Machiavelli's approach from metaphysical political theory as characterized above, two options recommend themselves. In the first place the Machiavellian approach could well be called "practical" political philosophy. This label could be defended with the following argument. The brokenness of the political domain and the absence of one single foundation for the entire building of politics was related by Machiavelli to the perspective from which, respectively, the prince and the people *act*; this brokenness therefore has its basis in political *practice*. And, surely, as is well known, it is political action that is the subject of *The Prince*. But for much the same reason we could have recourse to the term "aesthetic" political philosophy, which we have been using already throughout this book to refer to the antimetaphysical tradition. For it is a perspectivist difference, and therefore an essentially aesthetic divide, that separates the prince and the people from each other, a separation as decisive as that of a painting and what is represented by the painting. The prince is always a representation in the minds of the people (like Machiavelli himself), whereas the people can only present themselves to the prince's mind as a representation—and there is no medium, neutral, or common ground where these two representations meet or could be matched. In both cases it is essential that we realize that it is only via representation, and not thanks to self-awareness, that the transition from insight to meaningful political action can be made at all. To put it dramatically, alienation is where all politics begins. Since my argument in this chapter, as in the preceding ones, mainly relies on aesthetic arguments, I shall use the term "aesthetic" instead of "practical" for characterizing it.

Although this aesthetic political theory has always remained a background voice in the history of political theory, the metaphysical tradition has never succeeded in silencing it completely.[6] We hear its voice in seventeenth-century *raison d'état* thinking, which indeed is a *trait d'union* between political theory, history (or, better, historism), and politicology;[7] in Montesquieu's pragmatics concerning the balance between legislative, executive, and judiciary powers;[8] it expresses itself in the work of Alexis de Tocqueville (with a clarity never surpassed since then), which, not coincidentally, has democracy as its main issue; it is found in the clearheaded if not outright cynical writings of authors like Bagehot or Schumpeter; and, finally, coming to our own days, it is best exemplified by Foucault's discussions on power and discourse. In contrast to the appetite for systematic exposition that we always find in political theory and in political science, aesthetic political theory ordinarily has the character of a series of aphoristic observations concerned with the practice of politics, which cannot be systematized. It is neither metaphysics nor science; it does not shun the fragmentary and is, in its pretensions, closest to the study of history, though without sharing the latter's desire for coherence and synthesis. It can perhaps best be put on a par with the great art of fictional writing, with its independent insights into the contingencies of human existence. The value of such writing also is directly proportional to its resistance to systematization. Insofar as postmodernism generally is skeptical about systems, with their pretensions to universal validity in the understanding of foundations, metaphysics, and unity, there is certainly much to be said for calling this aesthetic political theory "postmodern."

3. French Versus German Political Romanticism

Let us now look at democracy from the perspective of both these political theoretical traditions. There is no question as to the contribution of the metaphysical tradition and the great importance of that contribution to the coming into being of democracy. A great and extremely successful democracy such as the United States is essentially a product of this metaphysical tradition (and this is where this democracy so conspicuously differs from the democracies of continental Western Europe, "les démocraties Rhénanes" as Michel Albert recently called them, which will be the main subject of this chapter). Like Hobbes, his seventeenth- and eighteenth-century heirs attempted to base the state on certain aspects of human nature in its social functioning, such as self-preservation and self-perfection. In this context theorists spoke without reservation of the nature of *the* human being and his relevant characteristics. For a correct assessment of the significance of the origins of democracy we should pay close attention to the figure of speech "the" citizen or "the" individual human being. We may see in this stylistic peculiarity of the natural law tradition a more crucial contribution to democracy than what is explicitly argued for in this tradition. The undoubtedly unintentional effect of discussing the human being in such general terms was the suggestion of the essential equality of all human beings: there is indeed something inherently egalitarian and "democratic" in metaphysics. For whoever speaks of "*the* human being," of "man," "*the* state," or of "society" avails himself of a figure of speech inevitably implying the (metaphysical) equality of human beings, men, women, states, or societies. This is where metaphysics differs from science. Whereas science carefully takes into account all the contingencies of the real world, metaphysics pretends to express truths that are valid for all the individual instances belonging to a certain category, such as the human being, man, the state, and so on. Hence metaphysical political theory was — again unintentionally — an important preliminary exercise for democracy insofar as the latter has the essential equality of all citizens as one of its fundamental premises. Furthermore, since in the tradition of the metaphysical political theory the state and the political order are always founded on certain properties that were considered to embody the metaphysical political or social nature of the individual, it was, as a logical consequence, out of the question that the good state should do injustice to these properties. For the justification and the raison d'être of the state was precisely to protect and to assure the unimpeded development in the citizen of these properties (such as the love of liberty, the right to property, and the pursuit of happiness).

As a result metaphysical political theory was inclined to determine certain limits to the state's legitimate interference with the citizen. The basic rights of the individual and the notion of the constitutional state were the result of this. And, as with the equality of all citizens, this principle of respect for certain basic human rights obviously presents us with another essential principle that we ordinarily associate with democracy. Surely, one may discern here the main contribution of the metaphysical tradition to what we all value in democracy: though the notions of equality (political and social) are discussed far beyond the point that these discussions can still be said to serve a concrete political purpose in contemporary political theory, one cannot doubt for a moment that it is every generation's task to supply these (and derivative) notions with a new content. Next, since the state, within the metaphysical tradition, is constructed out of "material" originating in the citizen, this tradition will tend to disregard the state's inclination to begin to lead a life of its own and to develop autonomy with regard to the citizen. A striking illustration is that the eighteen-page index to Rawls's *A Theory of Justice* does not even mention the notion of "state." The belief in the transparency of the state in relation to the political will of the citizen testifies to the laudable love of freedom characteristic of the metaphysical tradition, but has deprived it of the instruments necessary for conceptualizing in a meaningful way the threat to freedom that is always potentially present in the state. We may discern here the paradox of the democratic state as defined within the metaphysical tradition: love of freedom may inspire a political theory that has unintentionally blinded itself to what may effectively threaten it.[9]

Though we may rightly praise the metaphysical tradition for having made an absolutely indispensable contribution to the coming into being of democracy, however, we should not lose sight of its shortcomings. It is always dangerous to build a good thing (like democracy) on shaky foundations. For, to use a venerable Burkean metaphor, just as a company or a club cannot be reduced to its charter or its articles of association, so the democratic state cannot be restricted to how the metaphysical tradition conceives of it as a covenant of individual citizens who decided to unite within a body politic. As is well known, this is the upshot of the critique that was leveled at natural law philosophies, in many different ways, by nineteenth-century political thinkers. But instead of repeating this rejection of the metaphysical tradition on the basis of historical (or historist), sociological, or economic arguments (though I believe it to be fundamentally correct and indispensable), I want to give to this criticism a more precise and workable form that cuts right through the distinction between democracies based on metaphysical foundations and those having other origins.

This brings me to the essence of my argument in this chapter. It will be my heuristic point of departure here that we must always realize that each political system is, above all, a system for conflict control, and that the nature of a political system is therefore determined to a large degree by the kind of social and political conflicts for which it pretends to offer a successful solution. Thus feudalism was the answer—not unreasonable, and fairly effective given the political means available then—to the challenges facing the Christian Western world after the collapse of the Carolingian Empire and the raids of the Norsemen. By delegating political and military power to the level of the individual baron, count, or bishop, a more or less adequate solution was found for the problems of public safety facing Europe in that period. The feudal world is a world that is symbolized by the gate, separating the safety of the city or the castle behind the gate from the unsafety of the world outside. Each gate therefore gives us a fragment of the feudal political mosaic. Similarly, the royal absolutism of early modern Europe was the political answer to the challenges of the religious civil wars of the sixteenth and seventeenth centuries that came so very close to destroying Europe. If we think of its major theorists, such as Bodin or Hobbes, it will become clear that it was not in the metaphysical political argument expounded in their great works that we must look for the true motivation of their political theories. This real motivation rather lay in their understandable fear that the religious civil theory and what resulted from it might well prove to be the end of European civilization. And each historian even superficially acquainted with the cynicism, the all-pervasive pessimism of the seventeenth-century mind (so well depicted by Paul Hazard) and with the desperate effort of its leading intellectuals to develop some kind of political device to prevent a repetition of horrors like the English Civil War or the Thirty Years' War, horrors that would traumatize Western Europe for almost a century, will comprehend that these great theorists attempted to find a political solution to a problem of great urgency, an urgency recognized by all their contemporaries. If seventeenth-century political thought demonstrates an originality and a vigor that has rarely been surpassed in the history of political thought, that has, arguably, much to do with the fact that political theorists seldom faced a greater challenge (and were, unlike ourselves in our own age, aware of the nature of that challenge).

I do not wish to claim any originality for this heuristic principle. It has often been adopted and defended (for example, by Quentin Skinner in several publications) as a condition for the possibility of reliable insights into the history of political theory; nevertheless, it is striking that this seemingly so useful and innocuous principle has rarely, if ever, been applied to our own political system—that is, to democracy. The explanation is, perhaps, that while we consider feudalism and absolute monarchy as the slightly weird and timebound political systems antedating the rediscovery of democracy in the last two centuries, we think that democracy is a kind of political theorem of Pythagoras that is, in principle, valid for all times and an answer to each conceivable kind of political problem that might confront humanity. Perhaps, precisely because we all love democracy so much, and have every reason to do so, we cannot bring ourselves to recognize that democracy is no less an answer to a quite specific political problem than were feudalism and royal absolutism, and that the nature, the reflexes and the workings, of that political system down to the present day are to a large extent determined by the nature of that problem.

So let us now ask ourselves: What was the nature of the political problem that democracy as we presently still know it was intended to solve? When posing this question, I am specifically thinking of how that political problem presented itself in continental Europe after the French Revolution and after the fall of Napoleon. Formulating our question in this way, we may expect a most elucidating insight into the origins and the nature of democracy from that supremely brilliant but controversial German scholar on constitutional law, Carl Schmitt (1888–1985). Concerning Schmitt many good as well as bad things can be said.[10] As for the good things, during his exceptionally long life Schmitt wrote an impressive and highly original oeuvre demonstrating an analytic accuracy that has rarely been paralleled in this century. This certainly has a great deal to do with the fact that his Machiavellian cynicism kept him clear of the sandbank of noble intentions on which so many political analyses have run aground through the centuries (and which at least partly explains the insufficiency of all political theory taking ethics as its point of departure). Furthermore, perhaps it is precisely "outsiders" to democracy, like Schmitt or Tocqueville, who can tell us things about democracy that would never occur to sincere and devoted democrats. Similarly, a fish may only become aware of the water in which it was swimming after having been put on the dry land. As for Schmitt's worse sides, his cynicism tempted him to demonize politics, and to be so ruthlessly consistent in this that in his political philosophy room is left only for the negative realities of the political domain like conflict, polarization, and enmity, while it reduces the positive realities of deliberation, consensus, and cooperation to zero importance. This may at least partly explain why Schmitt, though he had at first shown neither a sign of interest in nor sympathy for Nazism, suddenly came to realize after Hitler's Machtübernahme in 1933 how much his political theory of confrontation and polarization was in fact in agreement with the political atmosphere in which the

Nazis liked to operate—and it was only then that he joined the NSDAP. Three years later he came into conflict with the Nazis, who typically could not feel really at ease with this highly original and brilliant mind, but that did not stop Schmitt from writing a number of abject articles in the next years with which he forever disgraced himself.

It is of interest to note that Schmitt's demonization of politics was in fact a radicalization of Hobbes. Hobbes's "bellum omnium contra omnes" was also Schmitt's fundamental political datum; but whereas Hobbes's *Leviathan* aimed at finding a way out of this war of all against all, for Schmitt this war is still latently present in civil society and it remains for him the final and decisive criterion for deciding the origins and nature of political power and sovereignty. For what takes place in the most extreme cases and under the most extreme circumstances, when society is confronted with its gravest dangers and the most extreme measures are called for, is for Schmitt the heuristic principle for finding out what regime of power is, in the end, decisive in the public domain. The not unreasonable intuition behind this heuristic principle is that we will only find out how a political system *really* works when the worst comes to the worst; it is only then that you see what finally gives way and what proves in the end to be of decisive significance in that system. Extreme circumstances momentarily draw "the veil of ignorance" that ordinarily hides the political machinery from inspection aside. It need not surprise us, however, that the adoption of this heuristic principle, and the resulting complete disregard of what makes a political system function as a going concern, had to result in a political theory ready to embrace the *nec plus ultra* of political extremism. Put differently, whereas for Hobbes the state is a kind of transfiguration of the war of all against all, Schmitt sees in it the heuristic principle for discovering and defining the nature of power and sovereignty.

What is for Hobbes a mere *primum movens* is for Schmitt a permanent matrix for assessing political realities. What both share is the reduction, so typical of all metaphysical political theory, of the nature and the workings of politics to a first principle. And this may suggest the correctness of the statement, defended by, among others, Karl Popper, Jakob Talmon, and Berel Lang, that the political Enlightenment (of which Hobbes definitely is a part and whose argument was carried by Schmitt to its ultimate logical extreme) [11] has not only given us the metaphysics of democracy but also the totalitarianism of Hitler's Germany and of Stalin's Soviet Union. [12] And what effectively separates these two offshoots (both so very different) of the same stem of the Enlightenment belongs less to the field of political metaphysics than to that of the political practice of democracy. As Rousseau's political philosophy shows, in modernist enlightened political theory ideals of freedom and proto-totalitarianism were surprisingly comfortable bedfellows. And the actual direction taken by democracy at the moment of separation of these two conceptions of democracy depended much more on political practice than on political metaphysical concepts—which may give an impression of how to assess the relative importance of both traditions.

It will be obvious from the foregoing that my appeal to Schmitt in this context is not justified by his being a critic of the metaphysical tradition. On the contrary, it is precisely because Schmitt can be seen as the most consistent adherent of the metaphysical tradition that his position almost becomes a dialectical invitation to its opposite, that is, to aesthetic political theory. As is often the case in intellectual history, it is the most radical and implacable formulation of a tradition that may shade off into its theoretical antipode. The fact that there are undoubtedly some striking similarities between Schmitt and Machiavelli, especially if we think of the cynicism that they share, already demonstrates that here "les extrêmes se touchent." But just here as well we may find the clue to what separates them: where Machiavelli shows how to cope with the enmities and the brokenness of political reality, these enmities and brokenness had become a foundational principle for Schmitt. And this is a crucial difference. For where Machiavelli's position invites us to think how best to *deal* in a practical way with these unpleasant but inevitable aspects of political reality, Schmitt's Hobbesianism requires him to construct a political reality that is effectively *founded* on enmity and brokenness, thereby transforming enmity and brokenness into metaphysical principles. It is as if marital quarrels were seen not as an unavoidable aspect of living together, but as its very basis.

Perhaps, within the framework of this study on aesthetic political theory, their difference could best be formulated as follows. Machiavelli, if we think of the remark in his introduction to *The Prince* quoted above, which demonstrates how and why in his opinion there is an unbridgeable gap between how the prince (or the people) represents himself and how the people (or the prince) represents him, is like the aesthetician being aware of the deep and unbridgeable gap between a landscape and its aesthetic representation. Schmitt, on the other hand, by elevating this essentially aesthetic gap into a matter of metaphysical principle, is thereby reduced to the absurd position that this aesthetic gap should be a feature of reality itself, thereby importing that gap either into the landscape itself or into its painting (if we decide to say that there is a "reality" of the works of art next to that of represented reality itself). It is here that we must discern the crucial difference between a metaphysical political theory founded on the brokenness of the political world and an aesthetic or practical political theory that merely sees here the primary challenge of all meaningful political theory. Schmitt tends to demonize and to absurdly radicalize what Machiavelli only tries to divest of its potential dangers.

But Schmitt's position with regard to enmity and the brokenness of political reality can best be demonstrated not by abstract arguments, but by considering his assessment of democracy. This we find in a work he wrote at a surprisingly early age, his magnificent *Politische Romantik* dating from 1919—undoubtedly one of the greatest political texts written in this century. The title of the book already indicates what statement concerning the democracy Schmitt intended to defend: namely, the statement that liberal, parliamentary democracy as we know it until the present day is not a product of the Enlightenment but of Romanticism, and that the practical political theorist can only obtain a grasp of the nature of democracy when he has recognized the essentially Romantic character of democracy and has properly thought through all the consequences of this absolutely crucial insight.

When Schmitt made us aware of the Romantic character of democracy, however, it certainly was not his intention to see in this an occasion to praise democracy; on the contrary, all the flaws that he liked to discover in democracy can be traced back, in his view, to democracy's Romantic origins. What Schmitt found utterly objectionable in both Romanticism and democracy was the fact that both seem to have so strikingly little respect for the clarity and lucidity so much desired by the Enlightenment— as the very name of the period expresses. Romanticism did not have any clear and well-defined principles, did not look for Cartesian indubitable certainties, for definite and calculable results, nor for axiomatic starting points or clearly defined aims. It is with utter distaste for Romanticism's vagueness that Schmitt quotes Novalis: "Everything is the beginning of a never-ending novel." [13] As a result of this all-pervasive vagueness Romanticism had, according to Schmitt, a curious "rootlessness" and a universal "inability to retain any important political idea." [14] Contrary to the consistent rationalism of Hobbes's political theory,[15] which was founded on clear and well-defined fixed principles, the Romantic rejected any political foundation for politics because "each foundation is false, since with a basis also a limit is given." [16] And Romantics had an instinctive distaste for clear-cut definitions and restrictions of principles—"here anything can change place with anything else," as Schmitt observes with disgust and contempt.[17] Ideas are here like clouds: for a little while they keep their contours only to lose them a little later, or they let them melt into those of other clouds, or even evaporate into nothing. And all this lack of intellectual solidity and precision seems to serve no other purpose in practice than to avoid all conflict. "The Romantic avoids reality, but with irony and with the disposition of an intriguer." [18] No wonder that Romantic politics gave Schmitt "the impression of a lie." [19]

We are still all sufficiently children of the Enlightenment to consider Schmitt's harsh critique of political Romanticism as initially convincing. With such a judgment, however, we would lose sight of the fact that the curious lack of principles observed by Schmitt pertains to the essence of democracy, and, even more so, that paradoxically it is exactly in this chaos devoid of principles that the unparalleled creative political power of democracy is to be found. It is precisely thanks to his attachment to the principles and the ideals of the Enlightenment, an attachment unequaled by any other twentieth-century political theorist, that Schmitt could discover the "aesthetic" (as defined above) characteristics of democracy behind the "metaphysical" principles that it had inherited from the Enlightenment— which, strikingly enough, Schmitt did *not* criticize in his book. Schmitt's advocacy of direct democracy, which was discussed in Chapter 1, clearly illustrates Schmitt's indebtedness to these less attractive aspects of the Enlightenment's "metaphysical" defense of democracy.

In short, it will be my thesis that the political mentality of democracy is correctly related by Schmitt to the relevant aspects of political Romanticism, but with the all-important proviso that what Schmitt found so repugnant in democracy is its very power. Now, before proceeding further, another proviso will have to be made: by concentrating on people like Schlegel and Müller, Schmitt availed himself of a very easy target. These two North-German Protestants, who turned Catholic in the first decade of the new century and chose of their own free will exile in the reactionary Austria of Metternich after lending their considerable literary talents and their reputations to several abject political purposes, are surely not the kind of theorists that any political system would like to claim as intellectual ancestors. Add to this that in the whole history of political theory probably no theorists have been more totally and completely devoid of any practical sense than these two literary theorists; that their writings were formless, incoherent, and ridiculously abstract; and that this incoherence and abstraction has been the reason why their abstruse political meditations could be used to vindicate the most divergent and hostile political doctrines.[20] One will then agree that Schmitt could not possibly have found more appropriate candidates in his devilish search for a compromising intellectual ancestry of democracy.

However, there is a group of theorists who have been immensely more influential, whose theories were inspired by the profoundest practical sense and who have more than any other group of theorists contributed to the construction of parliamentary democracy as we find it on the European continent down to the present day. And yet they share with Schlegel and Müller precisely those features that were the target of Schmitt's vicious attack on the latter. These are the so-called doctrinary liberals who were politically active in the France of Louis-Philippe and in the decade preceding the birth of the July monarchy. The best known and most influential doctrinary liberal has undoubtedly been François Pierre Guillaume Guizot (1787–1874), historian, statesman, and prime minister under Louis-Philippe from 1840 to the revolution of 1848.[21]

Unlike what their name suggests, the doctrinary liberals were anything but doctrinarians. They owed this misleading label, in all likelihood, to the school of the Père de la Doctrine de l'Oratoire, where the unofficial leader of the group, Pierre Paul Royer-Collard (1763–1845) was educated. In fact, their political philosophy was the very opposite of doctrinaire; it found its philosophical articulation in Victor Cousin's eclecticism, the philosophical tradition with least affinity with any variant of doctrinary dogmatism, and one that could be best seen as a nineteenth-century predecessor of contemporary Rortyism (no less a philosophy of democracy, for that matter). The doctrinary liberals shared with Schlegel and Müller a profound dislike of the perky moral and political systems that were constructed by the *terribles simplificateurs* of the Enlightenment; no less than Schlegel and Müller, they were deeply aware of the complexity of social and political reality, and that this awareness ought to restrain the ambitions of political action. To put it in the terms proposed in Chapter 2, they no less than Machiavelli were aware of the "brokenness" of political reality. They recognized that no (transcendental or Stoic) point of view is possible from where we could see it within one all-encompassing survey and that therefore a firm and certain grip of political reality—that domain of the Goddess of Fortune—is forever unrealizable. The political mentality of this Restoration (and proto-democratic) variant of Machiavellism has been aptly summarized in Koss-mann's characteristic of Royer-Collard's political position:

> Royer-Collard never developed some closed political or philosophical system. It is true that he has been one of the few sincere and honest legitimist liberal thinkers of the Restoration, but it is no less true that his theory never takes on the outlines of a philosophy of the Restoration because his views were always in-spired by the different fronts against which they were directed. His speeches are always polemical, even though they seem to have been inspired by the profound-est principles. They always have to be interpreted in the light of the obtaining parliamentary situation.[22]

This feature of the political theory of the doctrinary liberals may explain why its representatives were accused, no less than Schlegel and Müller, both in their own time and by almost all later historians of all political convic-tions, of muddle-headedness and of a mindless and egoist conservatism.[23] Illustrative here is Tocqueville's epitaph of the July monarchy as the incor-poration of doctrinary liberalism (from *Souvenirs*):

> In 1830 the triumph of the middle class was decisive and so complete that the narrow limits of the bourgeoisie now encompassed all political powers, fran-chises, prerogatives, indeed the whole government, to the exclusion, in law, of all beneath it and, in fact, of all that had once been above it. . . . No sooner had this occurred than a marked lull ensued in every political passion, a sort of uni-versal shrinkage,[24] and at the same time a rapid growth in wealth. . . . Posterity, which sees only striking crimes and generally fails to notice smaller vices, will perhaps never know how far the government of this time towards the end took on the features of a trading company whose every operation is directed to the benefit that its members may derive therefrom.[25]

For once Tocqueville's predictions proved incorrect, since history has, with a consistency only rarely encountered in that most uncertain discipline, always underwritten Tocqueville's condemnation of the July monarchy. What so much struck and disgusted Tocqueville (no less than a politician of quite different convictions such as Lamartine),[26] was the unprecedented banalization of politics that had taken place during the Restoration and received its consecration during the July monarchy. For one or two genera-tions politics had been the sublime fight over the principles of the Revo-lution and over the future of Europe—and now nothing seemed to matter except the trade balance and the question of how best to further public and private material interest. I emphasize this change during the July monarchy, since the exchange of a politics of national *grandeur* for the sordid details of public and private interest may to a large extent explain the unreasonably negative reputation that the July monarchy has always had down to the present day. The egoism attributed to the July monarchy and associated with Guizot's notorious "enrichissez-vous"[27] had its origins in this shift from a politics in the revolutionary and the Napoleonic style toward a national politics merely attempting to make life as comfortable as possible for its citizens. This was a shift little understood at the time—not even by such a supremely acute observer as Tocqueville—and it therefore all too easily lent itself to the association with narrow egoism. And if we wish to avoid being hypocritical we should recognize that what Tocqueville, Lamartine, and so many others condemned in Guizot and the July monarchy was exactly what we most recommend to the attention of our own politicians. We are more the heirs of the political mentality of the July monarchy than we often like to believe.

It need not surprise us, then, that the verdict of muddle-headed and egoist conservatism, pronounced against Schlegel and Müller by later theorists such as Schmitt, was also leveled at Guizot and the July monarchy. In both cases shallow opportunism seemed to have been the only constant in their aimless political theory and practice. And this brings me to my main point in this phase of my argument. For though the accusation may well be to the point in the case of Schlegel and Müller, it misses all that doctrinary liberalism was about, all that makes it so interesting from the perspective of democracy's history (and that of liberalism, I should add). In order to adequately assess this difference between German and French political Romanticism, we should note that perhaps no political theory—including Hegelianism or Marxism and its many later variants—took history more seriously than doctrinary liberalism. Surely Müller sincerely admired Edmund Burke's proto-historism, surely both Schlegel and Müller opposed history to the timelessly true systems that the Enlightenment had set such great store by, but what all these German historist attacks on the Enlightenment had in common is that for them history became just as much a source of truth as Reason, Experience, or the Idea had been before. History was no less the source of incontrovertible truths for Hegel and Marx as it would be for the later nationalist historists of the Prussian School, such as Sybel or Treitschke. Much (though not all) of German historism did not result from an opposition of Reason and History but rather from a historicization of Enlightened Reason. For the doctrinary liberals, however, history was not a source of incontrovertible truth but rather like Oedipus's Sphinx—we must be able to solve her riddles, but even if we succeed in that supremely difficult task, this merely means that we shall not be devoured by the Sphinx of History. For the Germans knowledge of history was a sufficient condition of political success; for the doctrinary liberals it was merely a necessary condition—but as such ignorance of history and of historical context was, for them, politically absolutely suicidal.

In order to grasp this very crucial difference between the Faustian German attitude toward history and the "existentialist" or Machiavellian one of the doctrinary liberals, we should take into account the historical context within which the doctrinary liberals developed their conceptions of the relationship between history and politics. We should realize that for the French of the Restoration the Revolution and all that sprang from it had been no less traumatic than 1494 had been for historians such as Machiavelli and Guicciardini. If trauma can be defined as a past that cannot or should not be remembered, because remembrance is simply unbearable, but that at the same time cannot be forgotten, both Guicciardini's attitude toward 1494 and 1527 and the French reaction to 1789 can properly be called traumatic. After twenty-five years of revolutionary pathos, after the collapse of a thousand-year-old monarchy, after the enthusiasm about the advent of a new era and new world order, after having run through the *corsi e recorsi* of expectation and disillusion so many times, after having used up in a quarter of a century a greater number of political régimes than more modest countries in a millennium, after this continuous staccato of the most dramatic events, the country was utterly exhausted, at the end of its forces, and, above all, sick of all political experiments. The misery of the situation after Napoleon's "Hundred Days" was, however, that one more political régime had now come to its final and irreversible end and that one more new experiment was therefore inevitable, however much everybody hated the thought of it.

Add to this the following unique fact: though France had gone through so many different régimes in this short span of time, none of them had completely discredited itself in the eyes of all the Frenchmen. The nobility and the higher bourgeoisie still felt an understandable nostalgia for the ancien régime, the lower classes hoped for a continuation from where the Revolution had so abruptly (been) stopped in 1794, and almost all the French still felt a patriotic warmth about the conquests of the little man from Corsica.

This is where France in 1815 so completely differed from, for example, Germany in 1945: France had a history that nobody needed to forget (unlike Germans who after 1945 had excellent reasons for wishing to forget about Hitler and Nazism), but that, at the same time, nobody wanted to remember or revive—and it was the utterly impossible task of the politicians of the Restoration to build a new and sufficiently solid political edifice on this most shaky and self-contradictory foundation.

It is against this complicated background that we must place the effort of the doctrinary liberals, the constitutional experiments inspired by them in which the democracies of continental Europe originated. And, in order to specify the nature of the challenge as they perceived it, we must realize that they were aware that all these recent and mutually exclusive "pasts" had to be incorporated in one way or another in the political system to be developed, since any system that failed to do so would be crushed immediately by the strong existing political forces of these pasts persisting in post-Napoleonic France. One had to retain something of the ancien régime but one should also do justice to the inspiration of the Revolution and to Napoleon's reforms. In short, the impossible task was to find a new political matrix, which inevitably had to be, once again, a new experiment, while at the same time avoiding all that might make it look like another experiment—it had to be something new, and yet should not seem like something new. The impasse or paradox of the situation was made perfectly clear by Guizot himself when he explained what ideas had inspired the doctrinary liberals after the Restoration:

> There has in the Revolution been nothing but error and crime, said some; the ancien régime was right against it; —the Revolution only sinned by her excesses, others said; its principles were good, but it pushed them too far; the Revolution has abused its rights. The doctrinary liberals rejected both these assertions; they resisted both a return to the principles of the ancien régime and the adhesion, if only speculative, to the revolutionary principles. . . . It was to this mixture of philosophical elevation and of political moderation, of a rationalist respect of rights and of historical facts, of doctrines both novel and conservative, antirevolutionary without being retrograde that the doctrinary liberals owed both their importance and their name.[28]

Here lies the secret of the *juste milieu* politics, from which continental parliamentary democracy originated. Here it showed the same urge to reconcile the irreconcilable that Schmitt found so utterly repulsive in Schlegel and Müller. It is from this desperate effort to square the political circle that continental European democracies originated; this has determined their political mentality down to the present day—though the French situation, because of all these incompatible pasts existing next to each other, was so much more critical than the German that we may well understand that French Restoration theorists could not afford the idle political speculation characteristic of German political Romanticism.

We should recognize, next, that Anglo-Saxon democracy, neither in Britain nor in the United States, was ever required to meet a challenge of such proportions. In these countries there never was such a complete and dangerous political impasse as the one in Restoration France (and in several other European countries whose fate had been tied to that of revolutionary and Napoleonic France)—an impasse created by the deathly polarization between those who wanted a return to the ancien régime and those who wanted to continue the Revolution. A remnant of this difference between Anglo-Saxon and continental democracy can be found in the two-party systems of the Anglo-Saxon countries, whereas the countries on the European continent that were once dominated by Napoleon ordinarily have coalition governments even now. This difference is more telling and significant than it may seem at first sight. For we should recognize that a political system in which one party rules while the other is in opposition does not require a negotiation of political principles. Admittedly, the party in power will be well advised to carefully heed the political position of its rival, but, in the end, it is free to decide for itself to what extent it will adapt its own political position to that of its opponent. A coalition government, on the contrary, requires the politician to be, to a certain extent, above the opposition between him- or herself and the opponent in order to observe from that quasi-historical point of view what might seem a sensible reconciliation of their mutually exclusive positions. Hence the term *juste milieu* is, in fact, not wholly correct—to quote an eminent practitioner of *juste milieu* politics: "Whoever wishes to exercise practical influence, should not place himself between, but above the parties." [29] And this is not mere word-play, since the politically creative potential of the *juste milieu* politics adopted by continental European democracies must be situated in this necessity of creating an essentially new political position above the existing ones, from which existing oppositions can be objectified first and then reconciled. It must be added, though, that this system will be weaker than the Anglo-Saxon one when, for whatever reason, "above" is reduced to "between" and politicians start to move around in a political morass in which nobody knows the way about any more. Accordingly, the political history of the Anglo-Saxon countries could best be written in terms of political solutions that have proven to be expedient or not, and that of the countries of continental Europe in terms of political creativity versus political inertia. Considering this contrast, one might conclude that continental European democracy potentially possesses both greater advantages and greater dangers than its Anglo-Saxon counterpart. Anglo-Saxon democracy will always function reasonably well, though never excellently, whereas continental European democracy may sometimes get completely paralyzed by the contradictions that have arisen either in society or in the democratic state itself. Anglo-Saxon democracies can function somewhat better or somewhat less satisfactorily, depending on the circumstances; whereas the democracies of continental Europe can function excellently, but can also end in utter disaster.

4. How and Why Democracy Came Into Being

Returning, then, to the heuristic principle expounded in the previous section, according to which each political system ought primarily to be understood against the background of the kind of political problem that it was created to solve, the foregoing can be summarized as follows.

We must bear in mind that when parliamentary democracy as a political system was constructed in the Romantic period, during the Restoration that followed the fall of Napoleon, it was the system's specific aim to control the conflict between the principles of the ancien régime and the Revolution of 1789, and, where possible, to settle this conflict. This resulted, especially in France, in a flourishing political theory that would find its equal in originality and profundity only in seventeenth-century England. Most of continental Europe, which had undergone the French Revolution and the political upheavals provoked by it, was completely traumatized by the events of the Revolution and by the Napoleonic wars of the first decade and a half of the new century. It was widely believed by all the ruling elites that at any moment a repetition of all these political disasters could be expected. And the political instability of the 1820s and the revolutions of 1830 and 1848 proved that these generally shared fears were anything but unfounded. Nevertheless—or, rather, precisely because of this—the most responsible rulers and statesmen realized that a return to the world before 1789 was impossible and that therefore—and this is crucial—some *reconciliation* between the old and the new was the only real and sensible option.

To say it all in one sentence, the practice of parliamentary democracy that was first tested and developed in the course of these years was the political instrument chosen to control the apocalyptic conflict between tradition and revolution that dominated politic reality after 1815 and that threatened to throw Europe into a new era of civil wars.

In spite of an apparent similarity, this was a conflict completely different from that of the religious wars of the sixteenth and seventeenth centuries. Certainly, just like the religious civil war, this conflict also placed one category of citizens in a mortal opposition to another. But the nature of the two conflicts was very different. There had been two workable solutions to the religious conflict. It could be solved geographically by placing Catholics or Protestants under a Catholic or Protestant government in conformity with the principle of "cuius regio, eius religio" that was accepted by the warring parties in Augsburg in 1555, but that would not suffice to bring the religious conflict to a final end. The other possibility—and from a political point of view the far more interesting and fruitful solution—was, as Koselleck argues in his impressive *Kritik und Krise*, to neutralize the conflict in a political way.[30] In this neutralization, the state distanced itself from the warring parties in order to create a reconciliation between them and to be a believable arbiter in the conflict. What made this second solution so attractive to the state and the monarchs of early modern Europe is that it invested the state with an amount of power and political goodwill that it had never before possessed. It was now possible both to increase considerably the authority of the state and to guarantee a minimum of religious freedom, because the latter required the former. The state declared itself religiously neutral and could now tower high above the ugly and disastrous religious conflicts existing since the Reformation and the Counter-Reformation. The almost innate confidence that we still have in the state is undoubtedly to a large extent an atavism recollecting the eagerness with which people in early modern Europe accepted the authority and the sovereignty of the state if it was used to put an end to the collective suicide of religious civil war. One may even surmise that the early modern state, thanks to its adroit exploitation of the religious issue, succeeded in securing for itself some of the respect that was traditionally granted to the church and its representatives. Indeed, the strongest and most healthy states developed where the religious civil war had been worst and where its citizens were in the best position to appreciate properly the advantages of a strong state. Furthermore, this enabled the absolute monarchs of the ancien régime to present themselves as secular gods. For the first time we see the curious paradox that the state, by careful abstention, avoidance, and neutrality, managed to increase and legitimize its power.

But—and this is crucial to my comparison of the two kinds of political conflict discussed here—the political conflict presenting itself during the Restoration was *not* of such a nature that it could be avoided by raising oneself above it in a superior and sovereign way. This comfortable solution, for which the absolute monarchy could still opt two to three centuries before, was no longer open in Restoration politics, since now the state *itself* had become the main issue of the conflict. The struggle between the principles of the Revolution and those of the ancien régime concerned who would possess the political power accumulated by the state during the ancien régime. In that sense the democratic state cannot be called "absolute," however much it may be seen as the heir to the absolute monarchy, as was argued by Tocqueville and, in our own time, by Furet. The political power of the absolute monarch was "legibus absolutum," and, as Kossman argued, was best symbolized by Louis XIV's decision to leave Paris for Versailles in order to express his detachment from society. And it is no less significant, as he goes on to say, that Louis XVI was brought back to the Tuileries as early as October 1789 and that, immediately upon his arrival there, he became, as the physical embodiment of the state, the plaything devoid of will in the hands of the political forces fighting for control of the state. In a way this situation has continued down to the present day, though the political theorists of the Restoration were miraculously successful in transforming this apparently suicidal conflict into the best political system that has ever been devised. Parliamentary democracy can best be seen as the institutionalization of revolution (thereby transforming it into a conservative force rather than a "revolutionary" one).

Indeed, what is new in the situation arising after and because of the French Revolution is that the state itself now became involved in, and was pulled back into, the web of political forces existing in society all desperately trying to take possession of the state now that the absolute monarch had lost control of it. "Left" and "right" in politics—this terminology, still so familiar to us, came into fashion in these years—were divided as to the state's legitimation, position, purpose, and task. When properly taking into account the main issue of this conflict, we must conclude that the state no longer had the freedom to look down upon this with superior indifference. At the level of the state itself a solution had to be found for the problem of whose authority it embodied. And if this problem already had all the features of a logical contradiction, matters became even worse after constitutional monarchy had more or less been accepted and different political parties struggled for control of the state's power. The paradox of impartial partiality became the squaring of the political circle, and politics now saw itself confronted with it. On the one hand the state ought to be the state of all citizens and to be recognized by the citizens as such, but on the other hand it should also correctly represent all the dissensions existing among the citizens in society. Surely, on the face of it, the problem seemed to permit of no rational solution.

At the time no one was more aware of the scope and the nature of the problem than Benjamin Constant (1767–1830); more than anyone else he has contributed to the subtle and well-balanced political instrument we now know by the name of constitutional parliamentary democracy. And if in contemporary political theory relatively little attention is paid to Constant this is, I fear, only too good a measure of our present incapacity to adequately understand the nature of the political system in which we all live and all so much believe in. In a brochure from 1816 Constant compared the political situation of post-Napoleonic Europe to a shipwreck. The wreckage of former political systems was floating around in a hopeless chaos; it was the politician's task to collect those pieces that could serve not renewed polarization, but reconciliation and future cooperation.[31] A return to the ancien régime he considered as fatal as the wish to take up again the work of the Revolution. Under the existing circumstances political principles did not have their value in their abstract purity, but in their mutual interweaving; and the parliamentary democracy for which Constant made his constitutional proposals would be the stage upon which this interweaving of political principles was to be realized and enacted.

To us all this may seem trivially obvious, but one should realize that this playing around with the most fundamental and sacred political principles—into which the state itself, in conformity with Constant's suggestions, should also be drawn—violated everything people were used to in politicis in those days. What now is the practice of everyday politics, to which we have all become so much accustomed and that we now consider so much a matter of course that we could not even conceive how politics could possibly be done otherwise, was in Constant's time perhaps no less revolutionary than the Great Revolution itself. So much may already become clear from the fact that even such an astute and supremely intelligent observer of democracy as Tocqueville never quite succeeded in making his peace with what he saw as an utterly repellent feature of democratic politics.[32] Moreover, Constant believed that not only was this principled lack of principles a necessity (as was already suspected by Spinoza and was to be explained later by a disgruntled Tocqueville),[33] it was also the way to transform the destructive potentialities of the political conflict of the Restoration into political creativity. Contrary to what Enlighteners like Schmitt (and Rawls, for that matter)[34] would have believed to be possible, it is in compromise and in a playing around with principles that we may discover the most formidable resources of democracy.

To Constant the state was, in Dodge's words, "a *juste milieu* between the *ancien régime* and the Revolution or, to put it another way, between royal absolutism and popular despotism."[35] By opting for this position of the "juste milieu," the democratic state opted for what I called a moment ago the partial impartiality and the principled lack of principles at the basis of all democracy. Or, as Fontana phrases it, "in Constant's reconstruction one of the most distinctive features of post-revolutionary society was that in it no authority and no truth could any longer claim to be absolute."[36] Now the state itself no longer had any absolute foundations and could at best be merely the place where the debate on the consequences of these absolute foundations could be fought out. It was not theological, philosophical, or ethical foundations that now held the state and the political order together, but "discussion" and a striving for "balance and equilibrium"—typically the kind of preoccupations of political Romanticism for which Schmitt, as an epigone if not the *nec plus ultra* of the Enlightenment, felt such utter contempt;[37] the uncertainty and the absence of absolute foundations thus acquired a positive, creative, and political aura. That which first causes dissension later unites—paradoxically.

Constant's brave submersion of the state in the political conflict is expressed in his definition of the nature of the king's power, which he describes as a neutral power ("pouvoir neutre"). Constant saw the monarch's authority as a fourth power, above the three distinguished by Montesquieu. And in his eyes it was the task of the monarch to maintain the balance and equilibrium between these three powers,[38] but besides that he accorded to the monarch neither real power nor political responsibility. "Le roi règne, mais ne gouverne pas," as the expression goes. Hence, at the center of the state, where people used to imagine the heart and the foundation of the political order, Constant created an emptiness or a void—and this center could only function as such in Constant's construction thanks to its being such a void. This void was, as it were, the neutral background against which the political debate could articulate itself and against which the political balance could establish itself.[39] Within the whole of Constant's pronouncedly Romantic political thought the monarch therefore has a position comparable to that "point of undecidability" which postmodern authors such as Jacques Derrida or Paul de Man always look for in their reading of texts.[40] In both cases one is concerned with a central, empty space around which political power and textual meaning respectively organize themselves.

5. Romantic and Postmodernist Political Theory

And this similarity of political Romanticism and postmodernist proposals for reading texts brings me to the essence of my argument. In his discussion of political Romanticism Schmitt concentrates mostly on two authors — Friedrich Schlegel and Adam Müller — who were actually connected by an intimate personal and intellectual friendship. Friedrich Schlegel (1771–1829) is generally considered one of the most important representatives of Early Romanticism (the "Frühromantik") and was certainly its main theorist. Adam Müller (1779–1829) shared Schlegel's great interest in literature, but managed (as is often done nowadays as well)[41] to attach certain political conclusions to literary-theoretical perceptions. There are certain striking parallels between both these Romantics and present-day postmodernism, which is, after all, not so surprising since both have a common starting point in their critique of the Enlightenment. And the relationship between Romanticism and postmodernism could best be expressed by saying that postmodernism is more consistent in its criticism of the Enlightenment than Romanticism and avoids the halfway houses in which the latter was content to live[42] — anyway, the two are sufficiently close to make for a useful comparison. Moreover, where postmodernism goes a step further than Romanticism it enables us to further specify the above-mentioned thesis of the Romantic character of parliamentary democracy.

I will proceed by comparing (political) Romanticism and postmodernism from three different perspectives, concentrating on what that comparison can tell us about democracy. The three perspectives are Romantic irony, the notion of the fragment, and variation. I will start with Romantic irony.

Romantic irony as developed by Schlegel differs from what we usually mean by irony. If we hear someone speaking ironically about "the clarity and transparency" of Derrida's writings, then we know that we should *replace* that clarity and transparency by their opposites. In Romantic irony, however, the opposition is *retained*. Thus Schlegel writes with regard to Romantic irony: "It contains and causes a feeling of the insoluble conflict between the conditional and the unconditional, of both the impossibility and the necessity of a complete statement." [43] Romantic irony expresses the awareness of the paradoxes and contradictions of the world in which we live, and knowledge of the fact that these contradictions inevitably will recur in the area of the statements ("Mittheilungen") we make. Similarly, at the age of 25 Müller devoted his *Lehre vom Gegensatz* to a political interpretation of Romantic irony: "opposition," and how a "mediation" between opposing principles could be achieved while respecting the nature of these principles, was the main theme in this infuriatingly vague and ill-organized piece of writing. Nevertheless, Müller's main intentions are clear enough. For like Constant, Müller saw his own time as torn between the principles of the ancien régime and those of the Revolution and, like Constant, he put all his confidence in "mediation" in order to "keep both these worlds, so unhappily separated, in equal balance." [44] In short, in the area of language and in that of politics Romantic irony consists of balancing contrasts, of searching for a *coincidentia oppositorum*, to speak with Cusanus while at the same time retaining the opposition.

A similar line of thought is found in postmodernism. I am thinking here primarily of deconstructivism, to which especially the names of Derrida and Paul de Man are connected and which is often considered to be the philosophical heart of postmodernism. Now it is dangerous and perhaps impossible to summarize what deconstructivism is. The explanation for this is, as Richard Rorty once wrote in an essay that possibly is still the best introduction to deconstructivism, that deconstructivism cannot be reduced to a statement, theory, or philosophical position with regard to language or interpretation. He sees the impossibility of doing so as an essential part of deconstructivism's intellectual message. Derrida does not take up a philosophical standpoint, unless this would be the standpoint of not having a standpoint—and even this oxymoron he would already consider too much of a standpoint. [45] Deconstruction is a practice of reading, and as a practice it is averse to all metaphysics and epistemology, just as aesthetic political theory is averse to traditional, metaphysical politics. But the following may serve to give an impression of what deconstructivism is. In 1778 the German poet Johann Ludwig Gleim wrote a poem in praise of the German Emperor Joseph II of Austria; some ten years later Mozart was to put it to music, with the charm and originality that only he could bring to such texts (KV 539). The poem's final stanza runs as follows:

> Ich möchte wohl der Kaiser sein,
> Aber weil Joseph meinen Willen
> Bei seinem Leben will erfüllen,
> Und sich darauf die Weisen freu'n
> So mag er immer Kaiser sein![46]

Of course this primarily was an elegant compliment to Joseph II and no doubt it was meant and understood as such. But we should pay attention to the "but while . . . , so let him . . ." phrase in the poem. For the disquieting implication of this phrase is that Joseph ought *no longer* to remain emperor as soon as he no longer fulfills the poet's wishes—that is, of course, the wishes of his subjects. Hence this stanza is in the poem the locus of an "undecidability"—in Paul de Man's terminology—from which the poem points in two different, even opposite, directions. It can therefore be compared with the "juste milieu" that Romantic politics is always looking for. It is in fact the textual equivalent of that political concept, for on the one hand the poem suggests an acceptance of traditional imperial authority, but on the other hand a proto-revolutionary, Rousseauistic undermining of that same authority. As deconstructivists always emphasize, however, we should not suppress or eliminate one meaning in favor of the other. For the interesting thing about this little poem is precisely the fact that the compliment to Joseph II is formulated here in such a curious and ambiguous way. Now, then, if this is deconstruction, it goes without saying that as a way of reading deconstruction is very closely related to Romantic irony. (There is, however, a difference between Romantic irony and deconstructivism. The deconstructivist situates oppositions, as meant here, in reading, where within Romantic irony they are considered to be characteristics of the text itself.)

What does this mean *in politicis*? It does mean, above all, that democracy is a political system that can only function in a satisfactory way if society is divided against itself (in the way that deconstructivism shows us how a text is divided against itself). Democracy will not work in a society or in a political reality that has no deep cleavages or in which these can insufficiently articulate themselves—or perhaps one should rather say, where they can *no longer* sufficiently articulate themselves, since it is the very purpose of democracy to achieve by a reconciliation of all relevant oppositions the kind of political order in which it will have condemned itself as a useless political construction. Democracy strives for the creation of a political biotope in which it can itself no longer survive. And democracy cannot be rescued in such a situation by a deliberate attempt at polarization undertaken by, for example, political parties. For what democracy reconciles lies outside the state or political parties themselves. Moreover, such attempts at polarization will effect a renaissance of metaphysical politics. Deliberate political polarization will tend to force all political relationships within the friend-versus-enemy opposition that Schmitt had derived from Hobbes's conceptions of the origins of the state and of political society. In this way democracy would stifle itself, or what remained of it, by contradicting its own principles.[47]

But political Romanticism and postmodern deconstructivism instruct us that this is not how things work in democracy. Romantic irony and deconstructivism teach us that the political debate cannot be thought of as part of the polarizing friend-versus-enemy matrix, since each political view *itself*, and its own "ideological text," so to speak, is already divided within and against itself. We should not locate Müller's contrast ("Gegensatz") that determines the nature of democracy merely *between* political standpoints but also *within* them (though of course the former is trivially true as well). One is guilty of what Derrida called "the metaphysics of presence"— that is, of an unfulfillable desire for self-understanding and for being transparent to oneself—when one believes that one is able to capture one's own political view, or someone else's, within a consistent and coherent system. As is the case with looking through a microscope or through binoculars, to focus on one spot inevitably leads to a blurred view elsewhere. Since Gödel, we know that such clarity and transparency are impossible to realize even in mathematics. How could we then wish them to be realizable for politics?

Tocqueville, that political postmodernist *avant la lettre*, gave a striking example of this division of the political standpoint against itself with his "deconstruction" of the ideology of the Revolution. It was one of the major insights of his *De la démocratie en Amérique* that the two political ideals of the French Revolution, freedom and equality, are intrinsically opposed to each other: the attempt to realize equality will mean coercion, and if we give rein to freedom, inequality will be the result. In his other major book, his *L'Ancien Régime et la Révolution*, Tocqueville was no less successful in deconstructing that other great ideology of the Restoration: that of the ancien régime. Tocqueville showed there that the centralization by which the ancien régime tried to confirm its authority turned out, in practice, to be the overture for the Revolution.[48] Without centralization there would have been nothing at the center to grasp for the revolutionaries; revolutions are impossible in states without centers. In this way the ancien régime may be considered to have been, paradoxically, the principal cause of its own downfall.

And this is the way it is with political positions: they are divided against themselves and therefore necessarily inclined to ironize themselves. In each political position there is always a "point of undecidability" from which uncertainty and vagueness spread over that political position and on account of which it generates unintended consequences that are different from or sometimes even in opposition to that position's overt and manifest intentions. I would like to add to this that as the network of democracy becomes more subtle, the failure of the political position to appreciate this dissension against itself will put an ever heavier burden on the functioning of democracy. This is where the hidden "modernistic" potency of postmodern democracy could perhaps be discerned: the initial "dissemination" of the political position has to be thought through with so much consistency and with so much quasi-modernistic rigor that the emphasis automatically shifts to the modernist latter at the expense of initial postmodern dissemination.

But rather than lamenting this Machiavellian brokenness of the political domain up to the level of each individual, it is here that we should locate the strength of democracy. Friedrich Schlegel wrote: "He is liberal who is free from all sides and in all directions, and who realizes his entire humanity."[49] One is "liberal," that is to say, one is a democrat, if one is aware of the multipolarity of each political position, if one succeeds in mobilizing that multipolarity for the "entire humanity." For only then are we able to recognize someone else's view as part of our own view (and vice versa), and only then does it become possible to have this voluntary agreement between different views for which democracy is always striving. This intertextuality of political positions—the fact that political positions can only articulate themselves in and by means of each other—is more than a simple expression of the desire for consensus. It expresses the acknowledgment that the realization of one's own position is partly also the realization of the other's position and vice versa. The most striking evidence for the correctness of all this is given by the rhetoric of political debate in democracy: if we closely follow a political debate we will notice that the strongest argument in such an exchange is where one knows how to graft one's own position onto that of one's political opponent, and how to demonstrate that if the opponent consistently adheres to his or her own position he or she will recognize that that position and one's own are ultimately the same. In politics it is self-destructive to entrench oneself in one's own position; one should instead always attempt to base one's own conclusion on the premises of one's opponent. The best political argument is the one that can live and sustain itself as a kind of parasite on the argument of one's opponent—or, to use a less unpleasant biological metaphor, that can live in symbiosis with it.

This brings me to my second parallel between political Romanticism and postmodernism: the notion of the fragment. As would later, not coincidentally, be the case with Nietzsche, Schlegel's most influential writings have the nature of aphorisms and fragments. As is so often the case, the form expresses the content: Schlegel's writings defend and exemplify an aesthetics of the fragment. The idea behind this is that art is not bound to the ideal of a representable and unified entity, and that a work of art always possesses an aesthetic "surplus" on account of which it cannot be considered the reflection or representation of a historically defined totality.[50] Romantic poetry is fragmented poetry—albeit the totality still remains present as an object of criticism and as a poetic form that has to be transcended. In the person of Derrida, postmodernism again goes one step further than Romanticism, in that for Derrida the fragment is not merely a fragment against the background of an admittedly unattainable larger unity. For him the text can never be said to constitute an entity or unity because of the text's own self-division.

The political implications of this were explained by Jean-François Lyotard in his *La condition postmoderne*, which is often seen as the more or less official manifesto of postmodernism. Lyotard defines postmodernism as "the disbelief in meta-narratives."[51] Meta-narratives usually have the character of comprehensive historical stories (and as such they are paradigmatic of the postmodern striving for unity and coherence) with the aid of which certain social and political ideals can be legitimized. One could think of Marxism as the ideology of the now collapsed Soviet Union; or of the idea of progression of the Enlightenment as legitimizing the insatiable desire of capitalist societies for ever more, better, faster, and bigger. Nationalism is another obvious example. Lyotard observes—without, however, feeling challenged to give an explanation for this—that nowadays these meta-narratives have all disintegrated and dissolved themselves in clouds of local narratives which only have meaning within certain restricted contexts. Each of us lives at the intersection of some of those micro-narratives, and there no longer is a totality, of whatever nature, into which they can be integrated.[52] Society and the political order have thus been fragmented up to the level of the separate individuals—which means, in a certain sense, a return to Hobbes's prepolitical natural state.[53] Ironically, it seems as if, at the "end of history" as imagined by Fukuyama, we find ourselves once again at the beginning of history as this beginning was conceived two hundred years ago by the theorists of natural law. It is as if, underneath the well-ordered society of our nineteenth- and twentieth-century Leviathans, a new state of nature gradually came into being, with which these tired old Leviathans are unable to cope. So what should one conclude? Have our Leviathans failed? Should they be replaced by new and more effective ones? Or should we interpret their failure as a proof of the permanence of the state of nature, even in civil society? Can Leviathan then only give us some more or less effective rules for fighting, in civil society, the war of all against all, instead of ending the state of nature by effectively replacing it by something entirely different (as natural law theorists themselves believed)?

At first sight one could suspect in this return to the matrix of the state of nature a consistent individualism, now pushed to its ultimate extremes. And to some extent such a view would be correct: the postmodern political aesthetic of the fragment offers a stronger argument in favor of individualism than can be found even in liberalism or anarchism. From that point of view postmodernism is the culmination of democracy and liberalism. But such a diagnosis would be only part of the whole story, for this movement of fragmentation does not stop when we have arrived at the level of the separate individual. The Romantic Schlegel already realized this. Thus in 1789 he wrote the following in a letter to his brother: "From my entire 'I' I cannot give a specimen other than a system of fragments, since I am myself like that."[54] The aesthetic of the fragment here becomes a philosophical anthropology, a view of the self, and it shows us the self as an incoherent series of fragments that cannot be put together within a definite story of the self, nor within a totality or a personal essence. And it need no longer surprise us that Richard Rorty, the American philosopher who once liked to describe himself as a "postmodernist bourgeois liberal,"[55] similarly characterized the self as "centerless, as a historical contingency all the way through, as a network of beliefs, desires and emotions with nothing behind it."[56]

To Rorty, as to Schlegel, the self is a collage, an incoherent hodgepodge of more or less autonomous fragments. Rorty links this acknowledgement of the fragmented nature of the self with Freud, for Freud taught us that the self is nothing apart from being the place where a conflict is fought out, the conflict between a number of libidinous urges and a host of social and ethical norms which we have gradually internalized and which thus became part of our personalities. In the terminology of this chapter one might describe the ego as the place where a "democratic reconciliation" of the conflict between libido and superego is achieved (if all goes well). We are made of imported material, of material from outside the ego that we mistakenly consider to be our individual essence. And if we can be said to possess a personality, then it merely consists of a number of vaguely recurring patterns in the way in which that conflict between libidinous urges and internalized norms is fought out. Or, in other words, the self is, if anything, the *style* with which the internal conflict is controlled—and I will come back to the subject of style later on. "Le style c'est l'homme même," as Buffon said, and from a Freudian point of view we can only agree with him. The Romantic and postmodern aesthetics of the fragment therefore teach us that the individual person and what we have come to associate with this entity is no more fundamental and final than the social or historical group socialists and nationalists had in mind. And this means that the debate between liberal individualism on the one hand and holism or collectivism in any of its many manifestations on the other is a pointless debate, which we should not embark on again. The first task of a political theory adjusted to the demands of today is not to be tempted back to the endless swing between individualism and collectivism.[57] There is no intelligent way of (re-)formulating this old opposition since what we associate with individuality and with the collective is as much a part of the collective as of the individual (as Freud already observed at the beginning of his study devoted to mass psychology).

I now come to my third topic: that of variation. In his *De la démocratie en Amérique*, a work that cannot be praised enough, Tocqueville describes the mentality of democracy as follows: "The human spirit would like to change position but since nothing urges it forward nor leads it, the spirit oscillates around itself and does not move."[58] Tocqueville's metaphor suggests that even though in democracy everything is continuously in motion, this motion takes place around a static center. In other words, the center is of interest only because of its *in*activity and by its ultimate absence. We are reminded here of the "pouvoir neutre" (discussed in the previous section) that Constant ascribed to the king. And Tocqueville emphasizes that this is not an accidental curiosity of democracy; we are here dealing with one of the most important characteristics of that political system. For shortly before, he had noticed (and this must have been an amazing discovery to Tocqueville's readers in Restoration France) that democracy is in fact conservative and counter-revolutionary. And this is not the case, Tocqueville continues, because in democracy the human spirit is inactive — on the contrary — "but it is rather directed toward an endless varying of certain known principles and a looking permanently for new consequences, rather than toward discovering new principles."[59]

Now, there is something curious about variations, which Kundera pointed to in *The Book of Laughter and Forgetting* and which we should take into account here. In this book he wonders why in old age at the climax of his musical achievement Beethoven could have become so fascinated by the variation, that seemingly "most superficial of musical forms."[60] Kundera's answer is twofold. First, variation means to break open — and hence to fragment — the unity that the theme, the "principle," so to speak, at first seems to have. Thus the path of variation leads "to the endless inner variety that lies hidden in each thing."[61] Here variation is obviously akin to the aesthetic of the fragment, discussed above. But second, and more important, variation dissolves the theme in its variations; the theme becomes both irrelevant and incomprehensible, as much divided against itself as the variations among themselves, and it thereby eventually loses even its presence in the variation. Indeed, whoever listens to Bach's Goldberg variations or Beethoven's Diabelli variations will realize that eventually the theme is here robbed of its reality and "originality" (in the proper sense of being an *origin*): the theme amounts to nothing more than the eventually almost forgotten and incidental occasion for the variations. The variation, and the style of the variation, obtain a priority above what is varied. The theme is, in a variation on one of Carl Schmitt's themes, merely the "*occasio* [in the sense of Malebranche's occasionalism] for the creative capability of the romantic subject to produce the work of art, a mere occasion for poetry, for the novel or for a merely romantic atmosphere."[62]

This insight into the nature of the democracy expressed by Tocqueville in 1839 also has its parallel in postmodernism. I am referring here to the notion of the "simulacrum" developed by Jean Baudrillard. The image of the deity, in sculpture or in painting, serves as a model for the notion of the simulacrum. Such an image is a representation of the deity itself, in which, as the word "re-presentation" indicates, the deity is made present again. That may explain why the representation of the deity can establish a stronger presence than the deity itself and make the believer forget about the deity in favor of its representation. Just as a theme can be robbed of its logical priority by its variations, so representations made of the deity gradually displace the deity from the believers' minds. Judaism and eighth-century Byzantine iconoclasts were well aware of this feature of the psychology of the believer. The religious bond the believer felt with the deity is now transferred onto the representation, so that the representation becomes more real than divine reality itself. For this representation by a reality that has become more real than represented reality itself Baudrillard used the word "hyper-reality." He points to the functioning of the media in democracy: media representation is often more real than that which is being represented; the news does not exist until it has been represented.[63] Surprisingly enough we can also find this idea of the hyper-reality of the simulacra in Tocqueville, namely, where he asserts that in democracy imitations of (for instance) diamonds cause the originals to lose their special quality and "aura" (to use Benjamin's terminology),[64] so that in the end the authentic diamond has no more value than the glittering stones imitating it.[65]

An important conclusion can be attached to Tocqueville's and Baudrillard's insights into democracy's inclination to replace reality by a hyper-reality. The logical result of that inclination is that democracy will only be effective as an instrument for conflict control in relation to problems arising in the area of that hyper-reality. For that is the world democracy has created for itself, which it can understand and change, and with which it feels a natural affinity. Like any other political system democracy much prefers to live in its own self-representations and to absorb all that is outside into them. Consequently, problems relating to a reality having its origin and autonomy outside democracy and outside the reality generated by democracy itself will be hard to solve by means of democracy. This may make us skeptical of democracy's ability to deal with ecological problems—arguably the most important challenge for the present and the future of our Western societies. This kind of problem can only be introduced into the machinery of democratic decision-making after having been translated into the language of democratic self-representation—and we can expect that much will be lost in this translation process.

This can be elucidated. We have seen that democracy is indeed the very best instrument for solving the kinds of problems that divide society against itself. It was to solve this sort of problem that democracy was called into being during the Restoration, and one can only be deeply impressed by the way in which democracy has managed to neutralize the enormous social and political conflicts arising from the industrialization and modernization of society in the nineteenth and twentieth centuries. But for a problem that does *not* divide society against itself because it more or less equally concerns all citizens—in short, for a typically "modernistic" problem like that of ecology, of energy shortages, of pollution, of crime, and most of all, of overpopulation—democracy is not the appropriate political instrument. And though one may certainly argue that such problems are a *consequence* of the functioning of democracy—though they present themselves no less to nondemocratic societies—these problems cannot be situated in the hyper-reality of democracy, since democracy resists the discussion of them as being contrary to its nature. Therefore democracy will not produce these problems as its hyper-reality. Paradoxically, democracy is little suited to initiate the political decision process needed for this "democratic" type of problem, which one might describe as problems we all confront in more or less the same way and of which we are just as much causes as victims (getting stuck in a traffic jam is the paradigmatic example). Here the political instrument of democracy is helpless for two reasons. First, this type of problem is structurally similar to the public safety problems for which feudalism and absolutism proved to be an adequate response. Hence, solving these problems forces democracy to perform a task that goes against its very nature, and the ineluctability of this new kind of problem might even jeopardize our democracies by inviting an infatuation with modern forms of feudalism or autocracy.

Indeed, one may observe tendencies suggesting a development in this direction if we realize that the social welfare state, insuring us against unemployment, illness, old age, and so on can be seen as a modern successor of feudalism and autocracy, protecting us against our more modern forms of unsafety. The bureaucratic rigidity characteristic of the public institutions that were created for dealing with these new forms of public unsafety can certainly be felt to be a mixture of feudalism and autocracy. Most states in continental Europe have come to deplore the quasi-feudal independence that these institutions have obtained in their relationship with the state;[66] while the citizens, in their turn, having to deal with these institutions have ample opportunity to find out about their autocratic tendencies. It need not surprise us that the book in which recently the blessings of the social welfare state were used in order to distinguish between the "Rhine model" (as represented by countries like Germany, France, and the Netherlands) and the Anglo-Saxon model and to extol the former variant of capitalism above the latter, was written by the chairman of the Assurances Générales de France.[67] There undoubtedly is an intrinsic relationship between the erosion of the democratic state and the recent feudalization of the public realm on the one hand, and our tendency to cast all political problems into the mold of social security on the other. The democratic state acts as an insurance company, discussing the costs of policies against all kinds of uncertainties and how these costs shall be distributed over the population, rather than serving as an institution for solving the political problems causing these uncertainties. Both the erosion of the democratic state and the refeudalization of the public domain have their origins in the kind of security problems that now demand, so much more than ever before, the democratic state's attention. Here, then, we have another argument in favor of Alain Minc's thought-provoking thesis of the refeudalization that we may observe in several areas of the contemporary social and political world.

The general malaise that seems to pervade most contemporary democracies at the end of the century, the all too understandable tendency of democratic states to cling desperately to the kind of political problem that it knew how to deal with and to fit the new type of problem within the matrix of the traditional ones, suggest that fears of the erosion of the democratic state are far from unfounded. Surely our greatest political challenge for the future will be how to deal with this kind of problem without falling back into new forms of feudalism or autocracy, as we are invited to do by the nature of these problems.

The second handicap of democracy with regard to the new type of problem is that democracy is by its nature reactive: it awaits the way in which the division of society will manifest itself. Reconciliation, by its very nature, can only take place after some conflict has arisen. Hence democracy cannot anticipate the future insofar as this is a future that will be shared by all of us, and may not be expected to oppose one part of the electorate to another. And, unfortunately, that is most likely to become the truth of our global village, whose future seems to have developed into a common future. One solution, which is suggested by the nature of the problem, would be to make sure that the environmental issue (to take a paradigmatic example) will divide society against itself again by means of a carefully elaborated system of taxes and subsidies, the "eco-tax"—in which case the machinery of the democracy could bring about a solution in the form of the kind of reconciliation that has always been the natural outcome of democratic decision-making. But first creating oppositions of the required scale in society in order to reconcile them in a later phase would certainly require a democracy quite different from the one we presently have; it would require a variant of democracy capable of a quite undemocratic and Machiavellian awareness of its own nature. Unfortunately, one of the main weaknesses in a democracy is that its Machiavellianism can only remain effective so long as it does not rise to political self-consciousness.

And this leads me to another remark that can be made following on the insight into the Romantic and postmodern nature of democracy developed above. People often complain that modern democracies are "better at variants than at vision"—that is to say, democracies will only be prepared to consider the introduction of new principles after having varied all existing principles in all conceivable ways in order to meet adequately the problems facing democracy. For the introduction of new principles can, in democracies, only take place in a natural way if they reflect new divisions in society. That is why a democracy will be very reluctant to introduce new principles of its own accord as long as this condition is not satisfied. Self-evidently, this places some grave restrictions on democracy's capacity to solve its problems: because of its natural tendency to conservatism in defining political problems, certain new problems are only recognized as such after a failure to address them has had the most appalling and disastrous consequences, more especially if these consequences have occasioned some new and dramatic divisions in society. But ordinarily democracies will always attempt to solve social problems in such a way that, whatever the merits of the solution may be, the solution chosen will not tend to create new oppositions. This has, arguably, been the rationale of the development of the welfare state, and has regulated how democracies deal with the dialectics of the welfare state (and thus sadly demonstrates the vicious circle in which modern democracies are caught up). More specifically, we may discern in most contemporary democracies (especially European ones) a propensity to obscure as much as possible the intrinsic conflict of interests between those who are marginalized and those who are part of the existing political and economic system. Thus democracy will not hesitate to demand substantial sacrifices from the active population for the unemployed, the unfit, or for ethnic minorities, and will present the problems these marginal groups pose in terms of the old and reassuringly familiar oppositions, such as that between capital and labor.[68] Such oppositions, and even the deliberate cultivation or exaggeration of such oppositions, are most congenial to democracy.

Perhaps, then, a political order that is better at varying principles than at principles itself is the kind of political order to be expected from a society that no longer has any serious social and political divisions[69] and that therefore has created for itself an "Umwelt" that is fundamentally at odds with its own nature. The previous argument suggests that democracy will, in the end, see itself confronted with the kind of problems that it is not properly equipped to solve, problems best exemplified by environmental damage and the traffic jam. So the dilemma democracy has to face is that it must choose between creating, once again, a society with political divisions, or adapting itself to new kinds of problems.

The questions occasioned by this dilemma can be reduced to the question of democracy's possibilities of existence in a society devoid of ideologies, a society in which political principles and ideologies can no longer serve as a compass, or rather, can no longer generate the conflicts that were the traditional fuel for democracy. In answer to this we are well advised to remember that the word "politics" is not derived from the Latin "polire," meaning "to civilize"—which would certainly have been a most satisfactory etymology—but from the Greek word for "city": the word "polis." And it was no coincidence that the first political theorist, Hippodamus of Milete, was a town planner. We may therefore expect the town to be a suitable metaphor for politics. And if we decide to use this metaphor, we can compare the modernistic, ideological politics antedating our present postmodern society with the logical and transparent urban development projects of which Pierre L'Enfant's Washington is such a striking example.

American constitutional relations are mirrored in L'Enfant's design. Thanks to their clear logic, their obvious center, cities built thus are even to strangers cities in which it is easy to find one's way, and with which it is easy to identify oneself. This conception of the city is closely related to the old Stoic notion of the cosmic city, which has its origin in Diogenes the Cynic's description of himself as a "kosmopolitès": a "citizen of the kosmos," thereby implying that he was nowhere at home, except in the universe itself. As is argued by Schofield, there can be little doubt that the Stoic doctrine of the cosmic city was developed as an explanation of this dictum.[70] Both in the case of the logical city of eighteenth-century architecture and in the case of the Stoic's cosmic city, it is Reason, the logos, that enables us to identify with either city and to "dissolve" in it in the way that the political object has gradually dissolved into the Stoic *tertia*.

If we were to think of a contemporary analogue to Hippodamus of Milete, Richard Sennett certainly would be our best candidate. For no sociologist or philosopher—not even Fredric Jameson in his voluminous study devoted to "the cultural logic of late capitalism"—has been so subtle and acute an observer of changes in the city and the public place since the eighteenth century. And nobody gave us a more profound and convincing account of what these changes must mean for political philosophers who wish to identify those aspects of contemporary society that their theories must be grafted onto (after having discovered these aspects the political philosopher has performed the better part of his or her task). A large part of the political evolution of the West since the eighteenth century can be read from Sennett's fascinating account of the metamorphosis of the public place, the city, and the presentation of the everyday self in the street, the coffee house, and so on (*The Fall of Public Man*, 1978). In addition, in his *Uses of Disorder* Sennett added a psychological background to this metamorphosis, explaining why this love of the Stoic, "cosmopolitan" city could be such a permanent source of inspiration for so many architects and politicians since the days of Hippodamus to those of modernists like Le Corbusier. The crucial insight here is that the Stoic tertia may achieve our identification with a (social) reality that is initially felt to be strange and alien. In one word, the logical, cosmopolitan city satisfies a psychological need. And it is adolescence in which this psychological need is most strongly felt.

Adolescence is for Sennett the phase in which the individual first conceives of intervening in reality, without having sufficient expertise to do so. One possible reaction to this stage in human growth, "in which the time scales of growth are not in harmony,"[71] is to look for some "scheme" within which the initial and feared incommensurabilities between the self and what is not the self become commensurable. Thanks to such a scheme, the individual can develop a set of "purifying identity relations" that will enable him or her to identify with the outer world. It is the Stoic notion of the "logoi spermatikoi" that will transform the adolescent personality into Diogenes the Cynic's "kosmopolitès." In it we may discover the psychological motivation of the "logical or cosmic city."[72]

But the urban development parallel to postmodern politics is no longer the "logical" Stoic town of the seventeenth and eighteenth centuries and of Baron Haussmann, who, characteristically, rebuilt Paris in such a way as to render it an inappropriate locus for beginning revolutions. What arose instead was the modern metropolis, as described in a number of "large-city novels" (*Gross-stadtromane*) as written by Alfred Döblin and John Dos Passos, or as shown in a typical postmodern film such as *Blade Runner*.[73] Los Angeles, where *Blade Runner* is situated, is the ideal model for the typically postmodern city: it is a huge urban conglomerate, without a center and devoid of internal logic. Life seems to take place in a periphery of suburbs and shopping malls rather than around an urban heart, and the social and political complexity of the city eludes any attempt at conceptualization. The paradox expressed again and again by the authors of the Gross-stadtromane is that one can only be an insider in the metropolis by being an outsider to it. (Stoic) identification now can only emphasize the impossibilities of identification. That is to say, one is no longer the citizen of the metropolis in the way that one is the citizen of a village or of a small town (being interested in its fate and even sharing it—as the republicans want to have it). The metropolis is a background, an environment (*Umwelt*) against which one can organize or narrativize one's own life, but the narrative is composed without any identification with this metropolis. The identification of citizen with place that is still possible with a village or a small town is not an option with the metropolis.[74] On the stage of the metropolis one no longer aspires to have a part, but to be a spectator. And thus it is with the postmodern state and politics. We no longer feel the contact that used to be established by participation in or identification with an ideology or party program—such internalization of politics belongs to the past; this contact has now taken the form of a large, indeed a very large, number of important or less important events without any clear coherence. Despite the alienation which undoubtedly is the basis of how we experience the Gross-stadt and the kind of politics associated with it, there is no reason to worry about this. For exactly this is what political representation was invented for: representation is not identification, and it allows politics to dispense with the latter.

On the other hand, one might argue that this metropolitan politics must undoubtedly be a source of despondency for the political theorist. For if postmodern politics can indeed be metaphorized by the image of the metropolis, and if the political domain is subject to the process of fragmentation and marginalization just described, then what is left to enable to us to regain a grip on the political domain? But there is an obvious instrument that can help us to theorize about this postmodern political reality and how to deal with it: the notion of *political style*—my argument is therefore primarily a plea for a theory on political style and for adding the notion of style to the repertoire of the aesthetic political theory that is defended in this book. Let me expand on that. A painter's or sculptor's style is to a large extent independent of content: one recognizes a painter by style and not by the subjects chosen for his or her paintings. Similarly, we can speak meaningfully about political style without involving ideological or party-programmatic considerations, or considerations of a politically fundamental nature. Style differs from meaning and does not have its locus in the semantic center of the work of art, but in the semantic periphery or margin. The style of a work of art is shown in its contingent details rather than in an overall conception or in what the work of art represents—these are aspects that works of art may share even when they differ dramatically from a stylistic point of view—and it is for this reason that style is a suitable instrument for conceptualizing the contact between the state and the citizen in postmodern political practice.[75]

Most important, style should be distinguished from manner. Manner is the repertoire of forms that an artist has deliberately and consciously chosen: an artist is mannerist if he or she seeks to imitate or paraphrase others (or sometimes even the artist's former self of a more creative period). Style, on the other hand, is a characteristic *assigned* to an artist, sometimes many centuries after his or her death; style is how the artist sees the world and the artist cannot objectify that because to the artist the world *is* as he or she *sees* it.[76] Contrary to the "modernist" mannerism of ideological politics, which leaves open to politics and the politician every possibility of manipulating the citizen, the notion of political style therefore gives the citizen the same authority of judgment as the connoisseur possesses with relation to the works of art he or she examines. Political mannerism forced citizens into trying to assume as well as they could the point of view of the politician in order to be able to say anything meaningful, which gave politics and the politician a considerable advantage over citizens—an advantage that finds in elections its only (and hardly effective) limits. The notion of political style, however, guarantees citizens much the same autonomy with regard to politics as connoisseurs have in their stylistic judgments with regard to works of art. Thanks to the concept of political style, the technical side of mannerist politics, with which citizens can feel little affinity, simply because they do not possess the required expertise (and thus where democratic politics always sought to hide itself from the judgment of the citizens), can be reduced to the mere "inside" of politics, which is as irrelevant to citizens as are the merely technical aspects of the work of art to connoisseurs.

Furthermore, and following naturally from the foregoing, both on the side of politics and on that of the citizen the loss of the participating identification of citizens with politics is often lamented. Now that politics has so much withdrawn into this "inside" of technicalities a different situation can hardly be expected. The result is a yawning gap between politics and citizens that is deplored by both citizens and politicians. Political style, however, is clearly recognizable even for the citizen only marginally interested in politics, and is moreover a *reality* to that citizen, who cannot pass a well-founded judgment on that interior world of technicalities. Political style therefore is the concept by means of which citizens can regain their grip on a complex political reality. In short, the dimension of *experience* —which should be the starting point for all meaningful contact with reality, including political reality—this experience of politics can only be reintroduced into the practice of democracy by way of the notion of political style. It is in this way that the aesthetic experience of the connoisseur will effectively have its counterpart in our relationship to politics. I therefore wholeheartedly agree with John Nelson's statement that, "at a minimum, it seems to follow for the historical moment that political theory and political interpretation should concentrate on politics as style and style as politics."[77] And we should not forget to what extent the stylization of politics is in fact a reality. For eight years the most powerful country in the world was ruled by a former film actor, and whatever one may think of Ronald Reagan, it cannot reasonably be doubted that in his stylization of politics he was supremely successful.

Finally, political style is by no means an irrelevancy, and regard for it is by no means a license for irresponsible political practice where charisma, appearance, and show replace the seriousness of politics. The following reasons for this can be put forward. Style in politics is concerned with the question whether the state, bureaucracy, and jurisdiction should be strict or lenient, active or reserved, moralizing or liberal, modest or dominating, generous or economical, and so on. To the average citizen these are far more important questions than the question of how, in the ideological conflict, the financial implications of the latest political compromise should be specified up to three decimals. That which pleases or irritates citizens in the state's behavior —and, indeed, the quasi-anthropomorphic notion of "the state's behavior" will be of much help in the future—is much more a matter of political *style* than of a barely recognizable (to most people) ideological *policy*. Next, theorists such as Nelson Goodman, Donald Davidson, and Hayden White have used different arguments to point out that style and content cannot be strictly separated. In art, says Goodman, style is to a large degree also a matter of preference for a certain content. Much of traditional, ideological politics can therefore be translated into terms of style, and hence into a language that is more accessible to the citizen than the one that is presently in use. And, once again, (the writing of) history may provide us with useful and illuminating examples of this still insufficiently recognized continuity between the style or form of politics and its content. To take one example, in his *Formation of the British Liberal Party 1857–1868*,[78] Vincent does not restrict his attention to the parliamentary situation, as is customarily the case in books like these, nor even to the emergence of the Liberal Party as the political expression of new socioeconomic realities. He also considers changes in the relationship between political leadership and the rank and file, the discovery by politicians of the press as a new and powerful instrument in the political struggle, changes in the public behavior of politicians—in short, changes in political style. We should observe, then, that such changes almost automatically entailed a political interest for new topics. Doing politics now meant, before anything else, focusing on the kind of issues that are optimally suited for reaching the newspaper-reading public. Esoteric details of government not reducible to an interesting and accessible report in the newspapers now lost their political significance. Similarly, the increased interest of the leadership in the desires of the rank and file might often suggest to that leadership to put items on the political agenda that would have seemed irrelevant and trivial to a previous generation of politicians (and there certainly is a most intimate relationship between the notion of political style and the dimension of the important versus the trivial and the irrelevant). In this way political content and new issues on the political agenda were, in point of fact, a spin-off from changes in political style. Here political style can even be said to have a priority to political content.[79]

6. Conclusion

In this chapter we have come to see democracy as a product of Romanticism. We also observed that democracy's Romantic potentialities were able to develop to their furthest degree in our postmodern world. Postmodernism—and in particular, deconstructivism—can therefore really contribute to a better understanding of democracy. This insight into democracy offered by postmodernism can be summarized in the conclusion that ideological foundations of politics are no longer functional and that as a result our political world and political practice has fragmented and moved away from its former center. Postmodernism shows us a world with centrifugal tendencies manifesting themselves on all levels in the present-day political reality. Solid alliances and even centuries-old national states break apart into their ethnic components. And in national politics the state seems barely interested in what traditionally was considered its proper tasks, those tasks that the state had been founded for in the seventeenth and eighteenth centuries. Order, peace, and the safety of citizens' lives and property are low on the state's list of priorities—if the state still thinks a list of priorities to be at all desirable—and these traditional goals have had to move from their former central position to the periphery of an inextricable and very complex network of quasi-feudal public institutions into which the state has gradually dissolved itself since the establishment of the welfare state.

In our postmodern democracy fragmentation and decentralization have occasioned a political practice no longer based in natural law theory or its modern (and modernist) epigones such as Rawls—the theory that has been since the Restoration the ideological starting point for political affairs. In one of his most interesting political essays Richard Rorty argued that this need not be a reason for despairing of the future of (liberal) democracy. His argument is that speaking about absolute political foundations has never been more than a rhetorical move in the political debate: "The idea that moral and political controversies should always be 'brought back to first principles' is reasonable if it means merely that we should seek common ground in the hope of attaining agreement. But it is misleading if it is taken as the claim that there is a natural order of premises from which moral and political conclusions are to be inferred."[80] In the practice of democracy the main issue was always the striving for "whatever intersubjective equilibrium may be attainable."[81]

I emphasize the fact that Rorty's word "equilibrium" evokes reminiscences of the political Romanticism and the notion of the *juste milieu* that were discussed in this chapter, and from that perspective absolute foundations are at best a pointless redundancy, often misleading and at worst even dangerous. In practice only the debate directed at "equilibrium" and balance was effective; the philosophical foundation of political principles was not. Hence Rorty could most appropriately title his essay "The Priority of Democracy to Philosophy." In political theory we would therefore do well to replace the idea of "political foundation" by that of political style. This idea fits in best with the present-day postmodern, democratic practice and gives back to citizens in their relation to the state the priority that is rightfully theirs in democracy. The notion of political style suggested by Romantic and postmodern aesthetics proves that aesthetics will provide us with a most fruitful point of departure if we desire to improve our political self-knowledge. We should therefore replace the "truth" of ideological politics by the "beauty" of a postmodern aesthetic political theory.

4. Politics and Irony

1. Introduction

It is a somewhat precarious undertaking to write about the relationship between two concepts, as I shall attempt to do in this chapter. This is because there are no two things in our universe that do not have anything in common, and it is therefore always possible, should one wish to do so, to establish certain connections. And that not only applies to things but equally to concepts, such as irony and politics. Ironically, even when it proves impossible to find a common denominator for two things or concepts, this already constitutes an interesting fact about the two things or concepts and that unites them in a certain sense; for now we shall desire to know how these two things or concepts could have been so remarkably successful in completely freeing themselves from the conceptual web with which we have covered our world. How can these things or concepts escape even the finest *tertia* at our disposal—in the sense given to this notion in the preceding chapters? So we will begin to wonder what might be the interesting features of these two things or concepts that apparently do not permit us to conceive of some *tertium* or scheme within which they can be meaningfully related. Phrasing our bafflement in this way already suggests in what direction we will now start to look. More specifically, we will now abandon our interest in the delinquent things or concepts themselves and turn to an investigation of our conceptual apparatus (where such *tertia* and "schemes" are developed), and the problem caused by the things or concepts in question now becomes a problem not of objects of the intellect but of the nature of the intellect itself. And then one might in the end conclude that there must be, nevertheless, a scheme that will fit the two things or objects together in a meaningful relationship: namely, the meta-scheme that will explain why the scheme in question cannot be conceived by our intellect. So, after all, either directly or by some cumbrous detour through (a reflection on) the intellect, we may argue that there are no two things or concepts in our universe that have nothing in common with each other. At the end of our search, then, we may expect to find at a meta-level a scheme (or tertium) explaining why no such scheme or tertium could possibly be found at the object-level—and then the two refractory concepts *have* been united, albeit at a meta-level.

This being so, the danger obviously exists that writing about the relationship between politics and irony will result in an attempt to impress one's readers by one's ingenuity in linking together two more or less arbitrarily chosen concepts. Nevertheless, I believe that such a danger can be avoided. The attempt to do so will require one to demonstrate a connection between the concepts of irony and politics that is neither trivial nor merely clever or contrived, but truly interesting. And the connection actually becomes interesting when it is not merely some conceptual common denominator between both concepts that is indicated, not merely some perspective demonstrated from which the two can be argued to have some affinity (which will always be possible), but when the perspective of one concept actually changes the meaning of the other concept and vice versa. In other words, the connection can become interesting when in the course of the argument an *interaction* between both concepts can be effected, an interaction by means of which both concepts take a position somewhat outside their original centers. Or, to put it differently, the comparison is interesting insofar as one succeeds in metaphorizing both concepts in relation to each other; for the metaphor is the figure of speech within which such an interaction takes place.[1] If such mutual metaphorization and decentering appear to be possible, this means that the two concepts can be seen as necessary "supplements" (in a Derridian sense) to each other, and that they actually *need* each other when we desire to fully understand them. An idea of what I have in mind here can be found in the work of the sociologist Pierre Bourdieu. Often he projects the concepts of one vocabulary onto those of another (see his notion of "intellectual capital"), and sometimes, though not always, this leads to surprising results. This suggests the necessity or fruitfulness of clarifying a concept in terms of another concept that would, at first sight, seem completely alien and unrelated to the original one.

Naturally our first question will therefore be whether the concepts of irony and politics leave enough room for achieving such an interaction. Opinions differ on this. Japp apparently thinks that there is not when he observes: "Thus, for instance, the domains of labour, politics and love are undeniably anti-ironic."[2] Labor, love, and politics are preeminently serious; "happiness is no laughing matter," as the old saying goes. And is there not much truth in these observations? For is not politics often concerned with matters that may mean life or death to numerous people, and would we therefore not demonstrate a painful lack of political responsibility if we were to try to ironize politics? A radically opposed view is found in Thomas Mann—in whose works irony occupies an extremely important place.[3] In the last essay of his *Betrachtungen eines Unpolitischen* Mann contrasts irony and radicalism with respect to their political implications in the following way: "The intellectual has the choice (insofar as he can properly be said to actually have this choice at all) whether to be a man of irony or of radicalism; a third option is not possible within the bounds of reason." For Mann this means, in the end, a choice between radicalism and conservatism. For "radicalism is nihilism. The ironist is conservative."[4] The ironic conservative is prepared to ironize himself, his views and his actions, and is prepared to accept the inconsistencies that result from such self-ironizing because he knows that life requires us to do so. But to the nonironic radical "life" is no argument: "Fiat *iustitia* or *veritas* or *libertas*, fiat *spiritus*, pereat mundus et vita"; let justice, truth, freedom or spirit be realized, even though the world and life would have to perish for them. To Mann the radical's weakness is above all his radical impurity (however odd that reproach perhaps may seem after the worldly-wise acceptance of inconsistencies that Mann praises in the ironist). This impurity lies in the fact that in his urge to act, the radical has forgotten that by nature he is merely predestined to contemplation. For Mann the conservative must be considered to be the man of action, who lives the *vita activa*, whereas the radical represents the *vita contemplativa*.

Mann proposes here, in fact, a remarkable inversion of how sixteenth-century humanists conceived of both forms of life. According to the humanists the *vita contemplativa*, the life of the truth-seeker, whether philosopher, theologian or scientist, is devoted to the discovery of eternal truths (whatever their nature). They would have objected strongly to Mann's claim of the "radicalism" of the *vita contemplativa* (supposing that the meaning of

the term had been explained to them). They would have pointed out to
Mann that the truth-seeker looks for eternal truths and that these truths
reflect an immutable and intrinsically conservative order rather than the
essentially creative and therefore potentially radical world of the *vita activa*. And they would even have gone on to express their doubts with regard
to the value of the kind of truths that we might expect from the *vita contemplativa*. For them, as for such diverse contemporary philosophers of
language as Austin or Foucault, truth is a matter of the use of speech, of
communication, of *oratio* rather than of *ratio* (as Lorenzo Valla put it five
centuries ago), because truth is not discovered in the silence and depth of
the solitary individual living *domestice ac privatim*, but only in the public
domain, feeding on freedom and political rhetoric.[5] So they would see conservatism where Mann expected radicalism, and vice versa. But for Mann
the rejection of the *vita contemplativa* and the essentially private search for
scientific truth is, on the contrary, an insight that we owe to the conservative. It might be argued that Burke's attack on the ideals that inspired the
French Revolution, an attack that was more influential in Germany than in
Burke's own England, was the decisive landmark in this "renversement des
alliances"—rhetoric and Mann's irony now moved from the radical, republican left to the conservative right, leaving the republican tradition little
more than an empty shell.

   In any case, the results of this lack of self-insight and ironic self-
awareness that Mann ascribes to the radical can only be disastrous: "The
actions of one who is born for contemplation can only be an unnatural, an
ugly, a distorted and self-destructive activity, that is, the 'action directe'
can only be an abortive action."[6] Unlike the ironic conservative, the serious radical has no instinct for the inconsistencies and complexities of life
and of the sociohistorical world; he therefore can only vandalize it. Creative
politics is conservative and ironical. Thus Thomas Mann in the revolution
year 1918.

2. *Irony, History, and Politics*

Mann's argument offers the prospect of a truly interesting relation between
politics and irony, while at the same time suggesting in what direction
this interesting relation can best be looked for. In the sociohistorical world
the ironist discerns a complexity to which the radical is blind, and consequently we will be well advised to inquire in what this complexity con-

sists—such seems to be Mann's suggestion. The most obvious answer is the notion of "Weltironie," "irony of events," "cosmic irony," or simply the "irony of fate."[7] It means that the results of (political) action often differ dramatically from their intended results. Our actions are aimed at achieving a certain goal, but instead, or at the same time, we achieve something different. The classic formulation was given by Hegel: "This connection implies that in world history, thanks to the actions of individuals, something more is achieved than what they aimed at, and what they brought about is more than they knew and wished to achieve. They realize what their interest is, but something further is achieved as well that was inherent in it, but that was not recognized by them and not part of their aim."[8] For example, the "serious," radical French revolutionaries were striving for a society free of injustice and brute violence, but achieved the very opposite of these lofty ideals in the September murders, the guillotine, and the Kafkaesque law of 22 Prairial (on the basis of which one could be sent to the scaffold simply because one was "soupçonné d'être suspect," as Fouquier-Tinville once put it). Just as in the ironic utterance the opposite of what is literally said is meant, so here, too, there is an ironic contrast between intention and effect—hence the term "Weltironie." It should be noted, however, that as the quote from Hegel already makes clear, there is as yet no reason to assume that the unintended result is not merely different, but also in outright opposition to or conflict with what was intended (as is suggested by the word "irony"). The politician who in his striving for full employment increases inflation achieves something *different* from what can properly be said to be the *opposite* of what he originally aimed at. Since "metaphor" refers to deviant use of language that is not necessarily the precise opposite of what is literally said, the notion "the metaphor of the events, or of fate" might, after all, have been more appropriate. But it is certainly true that in the case of actual conflict unintended consequences must make the profoundest impression on us, and this may account for the fact that we prefer to speak of the irony of fate rather than of the metaphor of fate. But whatever term we use to refer to it, it cannot be doubted that the notion of "Weltironie" makes us aware of the limitations of our adequate grasp of reality and makes us realize that social and political reality will consistently escape our attempt to conform it to our wishes and desires. Hence in "Weltironie" we encounter the inconsistencies and complexities of political reality that Thomas Mann had in mind in their most dramatic and persistent manifestation.

One might argue that our contemporary notion of "Weltironie" actually is a later variant of the Goddess Fortuna, who is within the medieval conception of the world the Imperatrix Mundi. Or, to quote from the *Carmina Burana*:

> Fortunae rota volvitur,
> Descendo minoratus,
> Alter in altum tollitur
> Nimis exaltatus.

> The wheel of Fortune turns,
> I go down to humiliation,
> and beyond all reason and measure
> another is extolled.

Pocock has given a most intriguing account of why, for medieval man, Fortuna ruled the world.[9] He reminds us of the Augustinian conception of the world in which there was room only for the vertical relationship between the individual believer and God or the *civitas Dei*; as a consequence of this fixation on the vertical relation, seeing in this the only source of meaning, medieval man lacked the conceptual means to make sense of the horizontal relationships within the *civitas terrena*. Because of this, medieval man lacked historical consciousness, in the sense that he was not equipped with the intellectual means to relate historical events in a meaningful way. That is why for medieval man the sociopolitical world was, essentially, a chaos, and in a permanent state of decay; why the medieval historian wrote chronicles, since simply enumerating chronologically one event after another on the scale of the Christian chronology of the life of Christ (the only real contact between the two *civitates*) was the only device available. And that is also why medieval man had to conclude with Boethius's *De consolatione philosophiae* that the completely unpredictable whims of the Goddess Fortuna ultimately decide our fate, and, last, why medieval man was unable to develop a conceptual matrix for understanding practical politics.

And when speaking of "practical politics" I am not thinking of the king's *jurisdictio*, for this department of his prerogative had been charted reasonably well by natural law, the fundamental laws of the kingdom, and by precedent. Here the king's power was clearly circumscribed; here the king could not do anything really "new," without justification in the already existing rules constituting a kind of political *civitas Dei*. Here his subjects therefore might feel justified in calling the king to order if he ignored these sources of just law. But apart from *jurisdictio*, the king also had the power to declare war, to make peace, and to act in this enigmatic realm of the *civitas terrena* and its unfathomable and unnameable horizontal relations. It will not surprise us, then, that this part of the king's power was referred to as the *arcanum imperii*: the impenetrable "secret of government." It had to be such, since medieval philosophy and medieval jurisprudence lacked the means for adequately conceptualizing it. One might even go so far as to construe this into a kind of epistemological defense or legitimation of the king's worldly power: it was recognized that, in the end, these strange and intractable problems had to be dealt with in one way or another, so what could be better than to box them all together and leave the problematic content of this box to the king, who is supposed to know how to deal with it? The person of the king was thus the solution to an otherwise insoluble epistemological problem.

All this changed with the introduction, mainly by Machiavelli, of the notion of *virtù* in political theory. Whereas its medieval predecessor, *prouesse*, always required the application of preexisting codes for chivalrous behavior, no such application takes place in the case of *virtù*. *Virtù* is a complex concept; it stands for the properties that may make a prince successful, such as power, authority, a natural preponderance, and, above all, an instinct for the right moment. Unlike *prouesse*, it cannot be learned in the sense that there is a code formulating its rules. It is rather a matter of one's personality, rather a matter of political education, edification, or Bildung, and more a question of "knowing how" than of "knowing that," to use Ryle's terminology. But however hard to define, its significance cannot possibly be overestimated. For *virtù* enabled the Machiavellian politician to engage in the struggle with the Goddess Fortuna and to conquer both intellectually and politically, at least partly, that enigmatic realm of the medieval *arcanum imperii* and to bring at least some order to the horizontal relationship within the *civitas terrena*. All the instruments we presently (hope to) possess to structure social and political reality are merely the modern variants of the notion of *virtù* that was born from the crude and bloody realities of Renaissance politics.

And if even contemporary politics is still little more than such a modern variant of the struggle between our *virtù* and the forces of chaos, which fate has entrusted to the Goddess Fortuna, we have every reason to be interested in how Machiavelli describes our chances in our struggle against the actions of this goddess:

I am not unaware that many have held and hold the opinion that events are controlled by Fortune and by God in such a way that the prudence of men cannot modify them, indeed, that men have no influence whatsoever. Because of this, they would conclude that there is no point in sweating over things, but that one should submit to the rulings of chance. . . . Nonetheless, so as not to rule out our free will, I believe that it is probably true that Fortune is the arbiter of half the things we do, leaving the other half or so to be controlled by ourselves. I compare Fortune to one of those violent rivers which, when they are enraged, flood the plains, tear down trees and buildings, wash soil from one place to deposit it in another. Everyone flees before them, everybody yields to their impetus, there is no possibility of resistance. Yet although such is their nature, it does not follow that when they are flowing quietly one cannot take precautions, constructing dykes and embankments so that when the river is in flood they would keep to one channel or their impetus be less wild and dangerous. So it is with Fortune. She shows her potency where there is no well-regulated power to resist her, and her impetus is felt where she knows there are no embankments and dykes to restrict her.[10]

One important consequence of Machiavelli's colonization of that hitherto inaccessible domain of the *civitas terrena* should be mentioned here. This secularization of the Augustinian conception of man and the world involved two movements: first, the vertical bonds with the *civitas dei* were now cut through and, second, *virtù* was strongly centered upon the individual. Obviously, this second movement was near to inevitable, given the intellectual means that Machiavelli had at his disposal: there were as yet no intellectual instruments for structuring the *civitas terrena* and it was therefore only natural that Machiavelli should begin to do so by appealing to the individual's *virtù*. What had to be the immediate result of this secularization of the Augustinian conception of the world was a community of individuals wholly reduced to their own capacity for structuring their world (by making use of their *virtù*) in the absence of any social or political matrix.

This may explain under what strange circumstances Western individualism came into being, and why Renaissance anthropology was naturally inclined to such an amazingly cynical, pessimistic, and egoistic conception of the human individual. With regard to the former, individualism and human freedom should not be seen as the triumphant heralds of Western man's victory over the medieval order but rather the only instruments, however inadequate and unreliable, with which Western man entered a new, alien, and frightening political reality, and where the pursuit of his own

personal safety was the only meaningful source of inspiration for all his actions. If this incomprehensibly negative image of the individual persisted
for such a long time after Machiavelli's and Guicciardini's time, until in
the days of seventeenth-century authors like La Rochefoucauld or the Cardinal de Retz, this has nothing to do with a perverse interest in the less
redeeming features of the human individual, but rather with the lack of instruments for structuring social and political reality. There was simply no
means to express a symbiosis between the individual and the social order.
It was, therefore, only when in the eighteenth century the old *civitas terrena*
gradually became covered and structured by all kinds of social and ethical
inter-individual connections that a more optimistic view of the human individual was possible. And it is illustrative that this more positive view of the
individual was developed out of a prior recognition of such an individual's
intrinsic egoism: Adam Smith's "invisible hand" metaphor and Hegel's
closely related notion of the "cunning of Reason" are paradigmatic. Here,
then, we have another chapter from the book of the history of the ironies of
Western political thought.

Politics is the struggle of *virtù* with the Goddess Fortune. What is of particular interest in Machiavelli's account is that this struggle is presented
by him as a fight between ourselves and an order that is radically alien
and beyond our grasp. It is here that the medieval Goddess Fortune retains
much of her power, but at the same time we are not entirely helpless, insofar as Machiavelli (and that is where Machiavelli is so much superior to
previous and later political theorists) makes us aware that politics must be
situated at the meeting point of *virtù* and Fortune. Not everything is Fortune, as medieval man believed, nor is everything within the grasp of *virtù*,
as ethical political theory and the social sciences suppose with their optimism inherited from the Enlightenment. It is Machiavelli's main intention
to remind us of this brokenness of political reality and of the fact that all
meaningful political action can only originate in our encounters with Fortune, resembling a game of chess, which both parties can win or lose. This
brokenness would be lost from sight on the assumption that it is up to
us to decide whether to leave everything to her or to create for ourselves
a political domain where only we can be the masters. For similar reasons
Machiavelli should not be interpreted as attacking ethics and morality (examples of domains in which we think our dominance is unchallenged by
Fortune); he shows, rather, where the limits are to the Stoic conception of
the public domain that is always presupposed by ethics—to put it in the

terminology proposed in the previous chapters. His position is not anti-ethical, but is a transcendence of ethics. Certainly, he could only take this surprising position thanks to the historical circumstances of his time, in which both the strengths and the weaknesses of the individual's interaction with his *Umwelt* were more strongly polarized than ever before or after. More specifically, what makes Machiavelli so interesting within the frame-work of this book is that Machiavelli antedates the restoration of the Stoic order in the seventeenth and eighteenth centuries, whereas aesthetic politi-cal philosophy explores our contemporary predicament, in which the Stoic order is gradually disintegrating again, and in which, therefore, the Renais-sance political mentality is reborn. Our present situation must therefore stimulate a deep interest in how these sixteenth-century humanist politi-cal theorists conceptualized a pre-Stoic political order (or dis-order). The conceptual instruments for structuring the *civitas terrena* that Machiavelli lacked and that were developed during the centuries that separate us from him are now found wanting again, so in a certain sense we seem to return to a sixteenth-century Machiavellian political *Umwelt*.

We should observe, next, that Machiavelli's acceptance of the broken-ness of political reality necessarily implied a positive assessment of the presence of political conflict in a society. A society without conflict and in which harmony and tranquillity are ideals that have actually been realized is at odds with the Machiavellian assumption of its brokenness: here the political and sociological facts would be at odds with the intrinsic nature of political society. Brokenness is conflict. As Pitkin remarks, for Machiavelli "republican authority must be exercised in a way that further politicizes people rather than rendering them quiescent." Similarly, Machiavelli is so much interested in Roman history because, in opposition to Florentine his-tory, it shows how and why political conflict can be creative rather than de-structive: "The entire *Florentine Histories*, one might say is a meditation on this topic, why did internal conflict in Rome serve to strengthen the state and enlarge liberty, while in Florence it produced only factional dissension, destructiveness and weakness?"[11] For Machiavelli, either enforced or volun-tary altruism (or "solidarity," as we nowadays would say), instead of being the oil in the political mechanism, will obfuscate a society's real problems and contribute to its ultimate destruction, since it will weaken our aware-ness of the essential brokenness of political reality. A contemporary illus-tration of this insight into the wholesome effects of conflict might be the readiness with which the English of the pre-Thatcher period identified with the wishes of strikers and trade unions regardless of the inconveniences caused by strikes, which hurt Britain rather than helping it. Therefore, only a certain propensity to irritation, egoism, dissension, and conflict can guarantee that all the forces in political society that can potentially further the cause of freedom and public welfare are mobilized as much as possible. A society of purely altruistic individual human beings is just as impossible as one that is exclusively ruled by egoism: the very idea of society presupposes individuals that are a mixture of both. It would be a society without the inexorable objectivity distinguishing reality from idle imagination. Here we discover one of the ironies that determine, according to Machiavelli, the welfare of the successful republic: what seems to threaten their unity, cohesion, and mutual cooperation — conflict and political dissension — is in fact the condition for their cohesion and existence.

Not only did *virtù* inspire the first attempts of Western man to conceptualize his efforts to get hold on social and political reality, *virtù* also gave us history. Creative politics and history are branches of one and the same tree — the tree of the struggle between Fortune and *virtù*. In order to see this we should consider how Fortune, politics, history, and the unintended consequences of intentional action are linked together in the work of Machiavelli's friend Francesco Guicciardini. Living and writing some twenty years after Machiavelli, Guicciardini was in a better position to assess the disasters brought to Italy by Lodovico il Moro's invitation to Charles VIII of France in 1494 to invade Italy:

> Lodovico was not sure he had found adequate support for his security. Doubting . . . that therefore his affairs might for various reasons meet with many difficulties, he applied his mind more to curing from the roots the first ill which appeared than to those which might in consequence arise later. He forgot how dangerous it may be to use a medicine more powerful than the nature of the disease and the constitution of the patient warranted. . . . The King [Charles VIII] entered Asti on September 9, 1494, bringing with him the seeds of innumerable disasters, terrible events and change in almost everything. His invasion was not only the origin of changes in government, subversion of kingdoms, devastation of the countryside, slaughter of cities, cruel murders, but also of new habits, new customs, new and bloody methods of warfare, diseases unknown until that day; and the instruments of peace and harmony in Italy were thrown into such confusion that they have never since been able to be reconstituted, so that other foreign nations and barbarian armies have been able to devastate and trample wretchedly upon her.[12]

In short, where the French Revolution was for the Europeans of the Restoration a Pandora's box of unintended consequences, so the year 1494 was for Guicciardini and his contemporaries the paradigm of *Weltironie*. But whereas a previous generation would have seen here the hand of the Goddess Fortuna, Guicciardini tried to discover a historical explanation for the discrepancy between intentions and consequences. And the immense achievement of Guicciardini was therefore to make the domain of the unintended consequences, of the Goddess Fortune and of *Weltironie*, accessible to historical Reason. It was history, it was historical writing as exemplified by Guicciardini's *History of Italy*, that gave Western man the conceptual means to explore for the first time the horizontal relationships in the *civitas terrena*. The implication is (and that is why I discuss Guicciardini here) that it is history, the methods and the conceptual instruments of history, that will provide us with far better instruments for understanding politics and political reality than the (Stoic) social sciences that have willfully blinded themselves to the workings of the Goddess Fortune.

One last comment must be added to this. As I have argued elsewhere, *Weltironie* and the Hegelian thesis of unintended consequences should not be interpreted as if now a new category of historical phenomena had been discovered, the kind of phenomena to which medieval man had remained blind.[13] The discovery of this domain of unintended consequences should rather be seen as the discovery that our view of the past need not be restricted to that of the historical agent. Hence the nature of this discovery is epistemological rather than metaphysical. It is, essentially, the recognition that we may well see the past from a different perspective than did the historical agent living in that past, and that a wholly new historical world will be revealed to us as soon as we do. And we should observe that this new historical world only became visible through a new mobility of the historian's point of view and not through the discovery of some new set of historical objects. The (metaphysical) "inventory" of the past remained exactly the same as it had always been. Only this new mobility of the historian's eye enabled him or her to see new and other aspects of it. If anywhere, we may discern here the birth of history as an autonomous discipline, as a discipline that is defined by the (counterintuitive) freedom of the historian to see the past from ever new points of view.

Within the framework of this book this is a most satisfactory fact, as I would like to emphasize: for we will now agree that the brokenness of our historical and political world—a brokenness initially symbolized by the struggle between *virtù* and the Goddess Fortuna, and which would create the logical space for the writing of history—is to be defined in terms of perspective or point of view. I would like to recall here how Machiavelli defined the brokenness of our political and historical world in the dedication of *The Prince* (discussed in Chapter 3) and how he ironized there the self-awareness of both the Prince and the people. It is only in the *representation* that they have of each other that true insight may arise. This is where the irony that must necessarily pervade the historian's work strongly recalls how Rorty mutually related irony and "redescription." One might argue that the shifts in perspective in which originate the object and content of historical writing both exemplify and explain Rorty's claim of how language ironizes itself by "redescription": the term by which he describes the operation he considers to be the heart of all intellectual debate and progress.[14] In short, irony and "redescription" have their ultimate sources in how the politician (as in the case of Machiavelli) or the historian (as in the case of Guicciardini) *represents* sociopolitical reality. This suggests how much the Machiavellian thesis of the radical brokenness of the sociopolitical world is essentially an *aesthetic* insight, for which aesthetic representation offers the only appropriate model. It also suggests why we may discern in the foregoing an extra support for the case against Stoicism and in favor of the aestheticism that was defended in Chapter 2.

3. The Irony of Liberal Individualism

The later bourgeois theorists of the eighteenth and nineteenth centuries would not be satisfied with a mere historical explanation of man's struggle with the Goddess Fortune à la Guicciardini. They attempted to discover certain philosophical, economic, or sociological patterns in this never-ending contest. We owe to this effort Mandeville's *Fable of the Bees*, Smith's "invisible hand," Hegel's "cunning of reason," and Marx's dialectical logic of the historical process that would give us the victory of proletarian society over its capitalist predecessor. There even is a poetic version of Hegel's and Marx's confidence in the successful outcome of this contest to be found in Goethe's *Faust*, when Mephistopheles described himself as being "a part of that force of evil which unwittingly always brings about what is good" ("Ich bin ein Teil von jener Kraft, / die stets das Böse will und stets das Gute schafft"). In short, according to these and like-minded theorists the struggle between the individual with his egoist impulses and his historical *Umwelt* should be considered from the point of view of world history, and if we were to place ourselves at that sublime vantage point, we would, as these theorists assured their intrigued readers, observe in each phase of history a necessary stage in an all-encompassing, majestic historical evolution that would ultimately result in the victory of bourgeois capitalism or that of the industrial proletariat.

Renaissance *virtù* now became the villain that, just like Goethe's Mephistopheles, in spite of itself was always the creator of a better, more just and more rational world. Put differently, these theorists shared with Machiavelli the conviction that the Goddess Fortune rules the world, but they changed the lady into the Goddess of Reason who would, in the end, comply with all the reasonable wishes of the human individual. In this way *virtù* could be reduced to the passion of Hegel's world-historical individual for conquering the world, the egoist interest of the capitalist industrialist in his bank account, or the hopes for a better future of the proletariat, and all would be well, in the sense that now the Goddess of Fortune and *virtù* were supposed to have the same aims in world history, however much their means for achieving those aims might differ at first sight.

Though this link between *virtù* on the one hand and the bourgeois's worries about his bank account on the other are certainly part of the truth, they are not the whole truth. For *virtù* had a more variegated offspring. Let us recall that these theorists from the seventeenth down to the nineteenth centuries all liked to emphasize to what extent that majestic historical evolution investigated by them surpasses what each individual thinks or wishes, and to contrast the historical agent's limited knowledge of his or her own situation with the supreme insights in the workings of history that were put forward by these theorists themselves. So if Machiavelli's *virtù*, and the complete subjection of Fortune by *virtù*, finally found its incorporation in a certain class of human individuals, we should not primarily think of Hegel's kings or statesmen, nor even of the bourgeois capitalist or Marx's individual worker, but rather of these theorists themselves. For they claimed to be able to decipher the ironical workings of world history and to be, therefore, our natural guides on our difficult path to the future. Not statesmen but these theorists were the true heirs of Renaissance *virtù*: they insisted that they were best informed about what to do when (which is where the Renaissance *condottiere* always followed the inspiration of his *virtù*), and they tended to reduce statesmen to the status of their mere executives. These theorists presented themselves as the prophets of a new world, enjoining their readers to listen if they sincerely wished to enter that better, more just, and more rational world. Neither Machiavelli nor Guicciardini (nor the historist historians since Ranke, for that matter) ever had such far-flung pretensions. They were content to describe the world and its workings as they saw them. Because this modest goal was sufficient for them, they could be the supreme analysts of human action that they were.

These later theorists had to pay a high—and an interesting—price for their prophetic pretensions, however. For in contrast to Machiavelli's teachings and Machiavelli's *historia magistra vitae*, the majestic historic panoramas of these theorists were of surprisingly little practical value. For if their insights into the workings of world history could actually be applied and thus effectively alter the course of world history, they can necessarily no longer be considered true insights into the course and workings of world history; if, on the other hand, they could *not* alter that course of history, what could then possibly be the practical value of these insights? It is as if the constructors of these Stoic historic systems had, in one supreme and gigantic effort, swept all the aesthetic rifts (symbolized by Machiavelli's and the modest historian's practical insights into the brokenness of political reality) onto one last huge and insurmountable barrier: the logical impossibility of jumping over world history. By doing so they had unwittingly erected a no less insurmountable barrier between the practical and the impractical. Their insights into the realm of practical politics were *sui generis* inapplicable and were therefore entirely unpractical. And the irony is that our deepest and most valuable insights into the workings of the social world in which we live happen to be exactly those that are necessarily completely devoid of any practical significance. Or to put the same point differently, even if (Stoic) Reason actually rules world history, it is only the Goddess Fortuna who has the authority to decree that this is how world history shall be. It will therefore be she who, in the end, proves to be the real arbiter in the struggle between the practical and the impractical. And with that we would be back again in the Renaissance, or even in the Middle Ages (since these profoundly impractical modern theorists, in spite of their pretensions, did not really possess the *virtù* that might assist us in our struggle with the Goddess Fortuna).

But this is not the only irony in the history of Stoic Reason and in its relationship with Renaissance political theory. Let us listen to Hegel:

> At a certain time there has been much talk about the opposition between morals and politics and about the requirement that, after all, the second ought to be de-

rived from the former. What is of relevance in this context is that we must note that the well-being of a state has a justification completely different from that of the individual. . . . The claim that it will always be politics that is guilty of injustice and illegitimacy in such alleged conflicts has its origin in the shallowness of ideas of morality, of the nature of the state and of its relation to moral viewpoints.[15]

At first sight, this is the kind of statement that one might have expected to find in *The Prince*. In the same vein one might properly speak of the "Machiavellianism" of a Mandeville or of an Adam Smith. In all cases it is suggested that the individual, contrary to what the ethical paradigm requires, has desperately few resources at his disposal for determining the world he is living in. And in all these cases, their observations will never fail to give an unpleasant jolt to our moral consciousness. Similarly, for both Machiavelli and Hegel the *raison d'état* thesis demonstrated the necessity of the subjection of the individual's welfare to that of the state—thus suggesting the fundamental incompatibility between the two. Even Hegel's world-historical individuals, rulers like Alexander the Great, Caesar, or Napoleon; philosophers like Socrates (or Hegel himself, for that matter); and the founders of religions (such as Christ)—individuals who changed the course of world history beyond measure—had the experience of being mere instruments in the hands of Reason striving for self-realization. History needs these individuals (just as Machiavelli's conception of politics requires the powerful individual ruler possessing *virtù*), and this is why we should never interpret (as is done so often) either Hegel's or Machiavelli's argument as an expression of collectivism. Their argument is meant to show the strength of the forces that these individuals have to struggle with. They therefore add to rather than diminish the individual's *grandeur*. From this perspective there is even a striking similarity between Machiavelli's and Hegel's arguments; this similarity could be best summarized by saying that for both individualism is not something that is automatically granted to each human being. It has to be conquered in a struggle with the brute and unyielding inertia of social and political reality. They recognize that the actual facts in social and political reality always tend to favor the collectivity and that we should love individualism all the more because of that. For both of them, the facts of human history prove that the collectivity ordinarily is the primary term in the relationship between individualism and collectivism (perhaps some mechanism in the psychology of the human being is responsible for this surprising and disappointing asymmetry). Individualism is therefore artificial and collectivism is natural, and that is why we should so much cherish the former because as soon as we forget to do so, collectivism will naturally take over again. And that is also why both Machiavelli and Hegel can be said to be better individualists than many of their liberal opponents, for whom individualism is reduced to the mere status of a passport that each person can obtain without any real effort.

However, we should add an important qualification to these similarities of Machiavelli and Hegel that may make clear in what way Renaissance individualism crucially differs from that of Hegel. For though there may be a *material* identity of Hegel's statement and similar statements that one may find in *The Prince*, they differ completely with regard to *the point of view* from which they have been formulated. Machiavelli's book is a high point in the tradition of books that were written to advise the ruler — and we should therefore never forget that the book requires its readers to place themselves at the vantage point from which the ruler will see the world. And that is the point of view of the person who has to deal with actual people, with actual states of affairs, with nasty surprises such as betrayal by friends and allies, in short with that whole host of ordinarily unforeseen and unforeseeable events playing havoc with how we had hoped to organize our lives and social or political reality. Hegel, on the other hand, is undoubtedly the philosopher with the most remarkable knack for the eighteenth-century strategy of placing oneself at a vantage point far above that of simple mortal beings (including kings, emperors, or statesmen). And this difference in vantage point is essential for their respective definitions of individualism. Machiavelli's definition puts us squarely and unconditionally in the place of the individual human being of flesh and blood, with all the hesitations, natural likes and dislikes, inclinations and disinclinations that the human individual typically has, and shows us then, first, what an unexpected range of resistances will always stand in the way of the realization of that individual's will and next, how, to a certain extent at least, the individual might nevertheless succeed in overcoming these resistances. The whole book of *The Prince* could therefore be said to be an expatiation on the *incommensurabilities* obtaining between human beings and the government of their interactions: it truly is a book about incommensurability.

Now, if we recall the quote from Hegel given a moment ago, and consider what the world must look like from the God-like point of view adopted there, we will observe exactly the reverse. For Hegel wants to make clear that there is, from that elevated point of view, in the end a commensurability of all human individuals and of all individual human action, in the sense that they unwittingly realize the aims of world history. What may seem incommensurable at first sight becomes commensurable when seen from that Hegelian God's-eye point of view. This is, therefore, a philosophy of commensurability—and this is where Hegel's philosophy of history can, after all, be seen as a perfect exemplification of (historicized) Stoic liberal individualism—though, needless to say, liberal individualism would reject out of hand Hegel's embarrassing speculations about the world-historical individual. But what both Hegel and liberal individualism share—and what opposes the two of them to Machiavelli—is their Stoic conviction of the fundamental commensurability of all the ingredients of the social and political order.

Let us recall here, furthermore, the origins that Machiavelli's Renaissance individualism had as the severing of the vertical link between the individual and the "civitas dei." As we have seen when discussing Guicciardini, this resulted in a peculiarly cynical and bitter individualism: the individualism of the person who finds himself completely left to his own devices, without any real support in an alien world. A desperate effort will be required of him to achieve even a minimum of mastery of this world. In a way the Renaissance individual truly was alone in the world, and that awareness gave unparalleled vigor to Renaissance individualism. It was this extremely strong, deeply and existentially felt individualism that also lent to the notion of *virtù* its unique and characteristic color. It will require little effort to see that this made Renaissance individualism into an individualism completely different from the one that came into being after the theorists of the modern period domesticated the Goddess Fortuna into the Goddess of Reason, of History, of Distributive Justice (or any of her other many later metamorphoses).

This new, liberal individualism was an individualism well adapted to, and commensurable with, the social and political order. We need only think here of those Stoic theorists of natural law and of the social contract who always tried to base (political) society on the relevant properties of the individual, and who by doing so effected, explained, and justified this commensurability of the individual and the (political) order. The Renaissance individual, however, is (still) outside the social and political order, or rather beyond that order, since the notion of such an order did not yet exist in the Renaissance.

We modern individuals are the heirs not of Renaissance individualism but of the liberal variant that is based on the assumption of the (Stoic) continuity between the individual and society. This is not the right place for enumerating all the pros and cons of these two kinds of individualism. For my purposes here the following will have to suffice. In the first place, we should stop seeing, with Burckhardt (and with those many later historians attempting to translate Burckhardt's views into a chapter in the history of liberal individualism), the announcement of our modern brand of individualism in that of the Renaissance. These two individualisms are really quite different, and they originated in quite different (intellectual) historical contexts—a difference that could theoretically be best articulated in terms of the difference between aesthetic (Machiavelli) and Stoic (Hobbes, Hegel, Rawls) political philosophy. From a practical point of view, the essential difference is that our weaker liberal individualism sees no ineradicable incommensurabilities between the individual and the social order. Because of this the individual's liberties are, within the modern(ist) liberal tradition, in principle always politically negotiable (for there is no insurmountable barrier to such negotiations). We will never come accross a barrier that would resist all attempts to find some new and more attractive equilibrium between the requirements proper to the individual and those of the encompassing political order. This is why liberal individualism in practice so often proved to be the slide moving us almost automatically from the most principled individualism to the most principled collectivism; and why, even in our contemporary Western democracies, we welcome interventions in the private sphere that would immediately have incited our medieval and Renaissance ancestors to a spontaneous revolution.

This, then, is the irony of liberal individualism: by taking the individual as its sole point of departure, from which everything else—the social order, the body politic with its balance of freedoms and obligations—can be derived, precisely because we recognize nothing but the individual as the exclusive legitimate basis for all these later constructions, the individual's freedom will under the conditions of (Stoic) liberalism always be vulnerable, because fundamentally negotiable. Liberalism has extolled individualism to such a degree that, ironically, it cannot fail to fatally undermine itself. Individualism and the individual's freedom can only be secure when something is recognized outside the individual, something having a political autonomy of its own and against which (as a potential source of resistance to individualism) the cause of individualism can be defended. And obviously, this is the essence of Machiavelli's conception of political reality as the continuously changing balance between *virtù* and the whims of the Goddess of Fortune. In sum, while Machiavelli can be said to focus on individualism as incompatible with collectivism, Hegel and bourgeois liberalism focus on the compatibility of individualism and collectivism—or, at least, on a variant of individualism trying to eliminate as much as possible the potential frictions between individualism and collectivism. (From this perspective Rawls can be seen as the contemporary guru of liberal bourgeois individualism and as Hegel's present-day solicitor.)

Obviously, Renaissance individualism could never provide the political philosopher and the politician with this comfortable liberal (Stoic) slide. So if one regrets the extent to which we have proved willing to exchange our freedom, personal honor, and dignity for social gains (whose immense value surely no reasonable person would wish to contest), one would be well advised to exchange the weak individualism of liberalism for that of the Renaissance. If one truly loves liberty, one should distrust liberalism, since it has proven to be one of the supreme ironies of liberal individualism to clear the way for both weaker and stronger variants of il-liberalism. Liberalism has been the main agent in the process of the political domestication and emasculation of the individual, and has changed us into the nice and malleable people that we have become.

But, last, we should realize how difficult it will be to actually surrender liberal individualism and exchange it again for Renaissance individualism, since the former always goes together with the possibility or accessibility of the God-like point of view adopted by the Enlightenment philosophers, which became the customary starting point for each philosophical journey undertaken in German idealism. And finally, the God-like point of view has become thoroughly democratized in what Heidegger called our contemporary "Age of the World Picture," in which each individual who respects himself intellectually has his own worldview as a basis for making all individuals commensurable. And it is not likely that we will be prepared to abandon these joys of the construction of worldviews. Nowadays nothing is more popular and easier to do than to place oneself outside and above the whole of human history; the capacity to do so is now almost a regular part of growing up. And food for thought is provided by realizing that the reduction of the human individual to the status of "the men without chests" that Nietzsche and Fukuyama discussed was compensated for by the individual's infatuation with these points of view from which the whole of mankind and its history can be objectified. The smaller we became the more sublime became the perspectives from which we like to see our world and ourselves.

So, on the one hand, one might argue that as soon as the possibility of the God-like point of view was introduced in Western civilization and every-body became his own Hegel, it became just as hard to give it up as to give up extramarital escapades after having discovered how pleasant and exciting these can be. That might well mean the ultimate triumph of Stoicism. On the other hand, it may be that this "democratization of the worldview," and the resulting incommensurability of all these different worldviews, will re-constitute at least part of the mental world of Renaissance individualism. Perhaps that is what postmodernism, in the end, has been all about.

4. The Irony of Liberal Ethics

We may further specify these ironies of the liberal defense of individualism, individual freedom, and of the regime of the practical and the impractical with the help of Reinhardt Koselleck's brilliant *Kritik and Krise*. Koselleck begins his argument with the Machiavellian observation that the absolute state effected a dichotomy between politics and ethics. As we observed in Chapter 3, the absolute state was, after all, the "political" answer to the religious and ethical wars that tore Europe apart in the sixteenth and seven-teenth centuries. This should remind us of the fact that religion and ethics can just as well produce (civil) war as peace—ethics has its less pleasant episodes, no less than does Machiavellianism; so the reign of ethics will not mean the end to all our social and political troubles, as many people naively believe. Only by taking up a "political" standpoint, a standpoint beyond those of the conflicting religious parties (as did in sixteenth-century France the partisans of a *juste milieu* politics *avant la lettre* who called themselves, like L'Hôpital, "les politiques"), the absolute state could fulfill the role that so many were ready to grant it. As we saw in Chapter 3, more than anything else in Western history this conjunction of circumstances has contributed to the coming into being of the modern nation-state.

But, as Koselleck goes on to show, the very fact that the absolute state had created this chasm between politics and ethics (or religion) made it an obvious object of ethical (and political philosophical) criticism:

> But to the extent to which the now politically powerless individuals outgrew the bonds of religion, they entered into a conflict with the state; with a state which has indeed given them their moral freedom, but which at the same time denied them any responsibility by firmly locking them into the sphere of the private. Inevitably the citizen came into a conflict with a state which, by the subordina-tion of morals to politics, interpreted politics in a formal way, and thus did not

reckon with the confidence that its subjects owed to their (religious) emancipation.[16]

And, as is suggested by Koselleck's argument, the liberal philosophers of the eighteenth-century French Enlightenment did indeed develop an essentially *moral* critique of the absolutist state—and of this critique Koselleck observes that it had its *target* in the public sphere while having its *origin* and proper domain of application in the private sphere of the drawing room (or of the Parisian eighteenth-century salon). But perhaps because of their painful awareness that the moral convictions of a number of philosophers, however rational and sincere these convictions might be, would not be sufficient to change the face of history, these philosophers attempted to present history now as evidence for the correctness of their moral convictions. If one looked at history, as was done by Fichte, Hegel, or the liberal philosophers of progress, from the elevated God's-eye point of view that was discussed a moment ago, one would discover that fortunately history itself had the good sense to aim at the realization of these moral convictions. It was these majestic hypostases of history that they therefore decided to present to their awed audience as the historical justifications of their "moralities of the drawing room."

History was now presented as an essentially "trans-political, moral process,"[17] to use Koselleck's words. The liberal theorists opted for these sublime systems because only systems with such eschatological pretensions might elevate them far above the world of politics in a way reminiscent of how, in the seventeenth century, the absolute state had been able to look down from such a safe and elevated position and with a profound *air de dédain* on the zeal of fanatic and "enthusiast" priests and clergymen. Having learned this useful strategic lesson from the absolutist kings, the bourgeois philosophers of history now arrogated to themselves the right to look down from their drawing room or, rather, from their study, on the fussing around of puny politicians. It was this vantage point that, they believed, enabled them to penetrate into the secrets of the *arcanum imperii* and to discover the solution to these secrets in their conviction that there was a perhaps surprising but all the more certain alliance between world history and the silence of the study (think of Hegel's famous statement, when looking down upon Napoleon from the window of his study in Jena in 1806: "*I* know what *he* is doing").

The wise lessons of the fifteenth-century humanists were now scornfully pushed aside. There was supposed to be an intrinsic relationship between the truth about world history and the life that is lived *domestice ac privatim*. This position was all the more comfortable since philosophers could now formulate insights without for one moment having to risk their own historico-philosophical discourse either politically or morally. This is where the hypocrisy of the Enlightenment and of the liberal bourgeois philosophers of history is to be found, according to Koselleck: they wanted to be involved in politics (by attempting to overthrow the absolute state), but without at the same time having to abandon the sphere of private morality within which they had been locked up since the birth of the absolute state. As Koselleck observes, "Hypocrisy was the veil, ever woven anew, which the Enlightenment carried before it and which it never succeeded in tearing apart." [18]

And hypocrisy it was, for, admittedly with the wisdom of hindsight, we know that this pathetic appeal to the lessons of world history was of course only meant to justify their moral convictions. The same undoubtedly well-intentioned hypocritical pattern of argument can be found a century later in ethical justifications of colonialism. In both cases there is a self-serving mixture of ethics and historical argument that openly reveals its hypocrisy to a later generation not sharing either these ethical or historical arguments. When pretending to speak the language of world history, these liberal Enlightened philosophers (and their idealist successors) were, in fact, still speaking the language of the morals of the drawing room—from which their moral language and moral convictions had originated. The enormous distance between their moral systems and actual political reality was not interpreted by them as an indication of the potential weakness of these ethical systems but, instead, of the utter depravity of actual politics and the urgent necessity to completely reform it. Thus the intellectual climate came into being in which Marx could formulate his eleventh thesis on Feuerbach according to which it is more important to change the world than to correctly interpret it. Morality thus effected, down to the present day, an alienation between politics and itself, as Koselleck correctly points out: "Due to the separation of politics and morals, moral principles must necessarily estrange themselves from political reality." [19] And, in conformity with the foregoing, this alienation had its origins less in the alleged moral depravity of politics than in the lack of motivation, so characteristic of all ethics, to try to understand politics and to appreciate what dilemmas the politician ordinarily has to deal with. We see here another illustration of the old and familiar truth that historical explanation, focusing on precisely this issue, is always ethics' greatest adversary.

The result had to be that state and citizen now began to speak and to address each other in their own political idioms, while each of these idioms made sense only within its own proper sphere. This led to a fruitless and pointless *dialogue des sourds* between the state and the most vociferous advocates of society that was only interrupted by revolutions. As in a bad marriage, the two did not really communicate but could only fight each other. The oppositions between politics and morals and between the public and the private now mutually reinforced each other and thus produced and perpetuated this pointless dialogue. And no real effort was ever made to change this situation. We gradually discovered that the "discussion" between the citizen and the state is quite unlike what we normally expect discussions to be, but have apparently acquiesced in the existence next to each other of these two conflicting political idioms. Disabused by previous attempts, we have now lost our appetite for revolutions that try to make states speak our language, and we now wearily allow the state to continue addressing us in its reprehensible and incomprehensible lingo.

Perhaps all this is reasonable and understandable enough after the disappointments caused by the tragedies of revolutions, but the strange fact remains that never, not even in a more orderly and peaceful way, was any attempt made to develop a new political idiom that might enable both the state and the citizen to speak the same language and to address each other in that shared language. In a curious way we are still all so liberal and still so much the children of the Enlightenment that we never felt challenged to exchange the relationship between the citizen and the state for a new relationship better adapted to existing political realities; we still now take for granted the relationship that was the unintended result of the singularly inept intervention of the liberal eighteenth-century Enlightened political theorists. We happily continued the *dialogue des sourds* initiated by eighteenth-century liberalism. Little has actually changed since then in our ideals with regard to how the transactions and the relationship between the citizen and the state ought to be—even if this "ought" is almost daily refuted by the actual facts of this relationship. We continue to see only the unclear and untidy interaction of state and civil society while we never feel challenged to explain or clarify the facts of this interaction by a recognition of the presence of the two poles of state and civil society that is its explanation (or, even worse, we allow ourselves to be blinded to the presence of the state by Anglo-Saxon political philosophy).

It is as if in psychology Freud's topological model of the human self, with its division of the self into a supego, a self, and a subconscious, never really succeeded in structuring our interpretation of human behavior and as if we always immediately forgot about it as soon as an appropriate occasion presented itself for seeing the behavior of our fellow human beings in terms of it. More specifically, up till now we never really succeeded in properly reconciling the political idiom of the public sphere with that of the private sphere, though there has been a continuous effort to translate the one in terms of the other and to address each other in the terms of these inept (and often infantile) translations (which is, of course, something different from a conciliation).

5. The Ironies of State and Civil Society in Democracy

But, paradoxically, this is precisely what one ought to have expected from the point of view of an aesthetic political philosophy. Perhaps there is, after all, some unsuspected method in the apparent madness of this *dialogue des sourds*; perhaps this persistent practice of representative democracy really is the right one after all, whereas the (Stoic) reasons we might have for denouncing it are wrong. In any case, if a practice can subsist for so long despite its apparently having all the good arguments against it, we are well advised to consider the possibility that reality might be wiser than apparently rational abstract argument. So perhaps we had better look for a satisfactory explanation of our universal practical acquiescence in this existence of a double political idiom—a practice so utterly different from what (Stoic) theory would require us to accept. Our question therefore has to be whether, in opposition to what Stoic tidiness and order would suggest, it might not be better to have these two political languages, instead of just one that is spoken by all. And, indeed, if we give the matter some thought, we shall see that there are good reasons for upholding this peculiar anomaly.

For does one not irresponsibly risk abandoning one's own position by declaring oneself ready to speak somebody else's political idiom? Are not our vocabularies our ultimate refuge against our most dangerous political enemies (the state, for example)? And is that continuous change of vocabularies that we may observe in all aspects of human history, so much discussed by Richard Rorty, not inspired by a Darwinian struggle for survival and by our continuous effort to stay ahead of our rivals as much as possible? Certainly, vocabularies are our most effective weapons in our struggle for (political) survival—one need only think here of the attachment of a conquered nation to its language—and each of the important evolutions in the political history of Europe can be explained in terms of the discovery of a new vocabulary by either the state or by civil society, giving each in turn a temporary advantage over the other. It was, for example, the vocabulary of liberalism that meant the end of absolutism, while that of the welfare state brought about the death of economic liberalism.

Perhaps, then, the *dialogue des sourds* between citizen and state really is, from the point of view of each, the best matrix for their transactions. Or, if one is in a cynical mood, one might say that the immense and incomparable contribution of (Stoic) liberalism to the cause of freedom and representative democracy has been its complete lack of understanding of it, and its decision to persist in this stubborn incomprehension. For by precluding an understanding of representative democracy, liberalism has ensured that the two political idioms have always remained in use and that neither one was sacrificed to the other, nor both of them to a (later) third candidate. Perhaps we ought to come to the ironic conclusion that the practice of liberal democracy is excellent, whereas the official liberal theory of representative democracy is a disaster, and that it is to this state of affairs that we owe our political freedom.

And, indeed, it is not difficult to see that the continuation of the *dialogue des sourds* must have contributed in important ways to this cause of freedom and democracy. For, as we saw a moment ago, if one succeeds in forcing the other to speak one's own idiom, or to the extent that one is successful in this, an important initial victory over one's adversary has been won. This is at least partly confirmed by an impartial assessment of the results of this war of political idioms that began somewhere in the eighteenth century. For the result of this *dialogue des sourds* of the state and the citizen has been that the idiom of each could win where the other was relatively weak; and this gain was ordinarily accompanied by a loss elsewhere. And if each of the two parties was weak in a certain area, this was mainly because it lacked interest in that specific area. Its willingness to make concessions there was on the condition that these concessions would, in one way or another, be compensated for elsewhere. It is essential that we should realize that this war of the idioms fought between state and society was by no means a zero-sum game, and that the game could be played (or the war be fought) in such a way that both parties ended in a better position than before. When seen from that perspective, both absolutism and its eighteenth-century critics were right after all, so that one might plausibly defend the thesis that our contemporary and highly successful democracies owe their existence to the fact that both Louis XV and Voltaire could somehow continue their political life into our world, and further, that this world was born from a reconciliation of the two, rather than from the ultimate victory of the one over the other.

Indeed, few dialogues have been politically more creative than this *dialogue des sourds*. Thus the citizen succeeded in robbing the state of all the majesty with which absolutism had always liked to display itself. The citizen has thus won some decisive victories in the attempt to reduce the state to the level of the drawing room, and to force it to present itself to the citizen in proportions appropriate to the drawing room (and especially its television). The state as a secular God became the state as an insurance company; and since God's gifts are free but customarily of a most doubtful status, we ordinarily have every reason to prefer the gifts of the insurance company, though unfortunately we have to pay our insurance premiums in order to be entitled to them. The state, in its turn, by transforming almost all politics into economic politics, succeeded in achieving a "transfiguration" of the problems of this same drawing room (of the "oikos"), giving to them proportions of a truly world-historical significance and making them worthy of the state's attention. By shifting the center of gravity of these details of the household away from the citizen to itself, the state also managed to estrange the citizen from his or her own proper sphere and to confront that citizen, in the process, with a number of unpleasant paradoxes that weaken (perhaps fatally) the citizen's position with regard to the state. For if there is one specific area where the struggle between state and civil society gave one of the two the means for permanently blackmailing the other, this surely has been the state's adroit strategy to obtain such a preponderant position over the affairs of the household.

So, to summarize, this struggle between state and civil society, and the deals originating in it, have benefited both parties: the citizen could now enjoy material prosperity and believe in the fiction, carefully upheld by the state's most cherished ideological pacifier—the people's sovereignty—that after 1789 (or, to be historically more exact, after 1792) he could conceive of himself as the true successor and heir to Louis XIV's *grandeur*. The state, in its turn, discovered in those puny details of the household an unsuspected and welcome source of political power, while being fairly sure that this power was now protected by a truly impregnable fortress—since each attack on it by the citizen would force the citizen into a self-destructive fight with his own material interests.

Thus the *dialogue des sourds* that Western democracies embarked upon two centuries ago really made sense to all parties concerned. This may explain why we have been so little inclined to abandon this seemingly fruitless discussion. We will now also be in a position to understand why aesthetic political philosophy is so much better equipped to elucidate our attachment to this strange discussion between state and civil society. To put it briefly, this *dialogue des sourds* perfectly exemplifies the strategy of avoidance adopted by both state and civil society in their interaction, a strategy that was in the interest of both and that had the conditions of its possibility in the notion of representation. As we observed in the first chapter, political representation, by its very nature, entails a division of labor between state and civil society. And such a division of labor, in its turn, entails a readiness to let the other mind his own business and thus, in essence, the adoption of this strategy of avoidance by both state and civil society. The example of Soviet Russia may demonstrate what will happen when the state abandons this prudent strategy of mutual avoidance, and Italy shows us the hardly less disastrous consequences of a too aggressive civil society. We should never forget, therefore, that the protection of our liberties and all the social advantages that we take for granted in Western democracies does not have its origins and guarantees in pedantic and ethically inspired political philosophies, in constitutions, or in fundamental laws—for one can do without all these nice things as long as both state and society stick to this strategy of avoidance (this is why life was better in eighteenth-century England than in Stalin's Russia in spite of the latter's excellent constitution). So what really counts, and what marks the difference between freedom and despotism, must be situated in the adoption of this strategy of mutual avoidance by an ambitious state and a powerful civil society—and emphatically not in any attempt to fatally weaken the one in its relationship to the other, as is required by the die-hards of the left and the right (since ill-considered interventions like these would deprive us of the means necessary for holding on to the *juste milieu* between Russia and Italy). The stronger both the state and civil society are, providing they succeed in avoiding each other, the better this is for all concerned (and I hasten to add that there is an inverse relationship between the state's strength and its size). Freedom and welfare are the results of a strong state and a strong civil society.

Lastly, it is one of the advantages of an aesthetic political philosophy over a Stoic one that it may explain why the coexistence of a strong state and a strong civil society is not in the least a paradox, and why, under certain circumstances, state and civil society may even mutually reinforce each other. Stoic political philosophy will, by its nature, tend to see the relationship between state and civil society as a zero-sum game: for the Stoic theorist the political domain is an unbroken, continuous, and unitary totality, so that the political power gained by either state or civil society is only possible if accompanied by a loss of power by the other. Moreover, seeing the relationship between state and civil society in terms of such a Stoic zero-sum game can even be shown to be a standing invitation to either a complete exaltation or a complete enervation of government power. The Stoic assumption is that the larger the state's power, the less will be that of civil society, but this will automatically weaken the state's power again, since its power now is the power that it possesses over a weak and degenerate civil society. In order to retain the amount of power present in the body politic, an increase of the state's power will occur, and, obviously, this mechanism will ultimately result in despotism. If, however, civil society is the stronger partner of the two, the state may well congratulate itself with being the political director of such a healthy and strong entity, but it will be unable to turn this to its advantage, since what is left of its weak powers will continue to leak away to civil society. And in this case anarchy will be the result. To conclude, the Stoic's zero-sum game in the power relationship between state and civil society will provoke a competition for the available amount of power, and as soon as this competition has begun, and as soon as either of the two parties has won its first victory in this struggle, nothing will stand in the way of a complete degeneration into either despotism or anarchy. Stoic political philosophy thus is fundamentally incompatible with the notion of a *juste milieu* between the state's and civil society's power, since each imbalance between the two will inevitably be the first step toward an even greater imbalance, and so on.

But if (in agreement with aestheticist assumptions) the unitary political domain of the Stoic political theorist is broken into the two domains of the represented and its representation, no room will be left for the Stoic's zero-sum game and its unpleasant implications. As we have seen in Chapter 1, legitimate political power cannot be attributed to either the represented (the people) or the state (its representation), since it originates in the aesthetic gap between the two, in which the (Machiavellian) "brokenness" of the political order in a representative democracy announces itself. And then the question of what state power or the power of civil society will entail for each other does not permit of any clear-cut or a priori answer.

Everything is now possible and can, in theory, be arranged according to our wishes. For example, the increased strength of one can now be used for adding to the strength of the other rather than for diminishing it.

Consider the following argument of the aesthetic political theorist. (Aesthetic) political representation is required since each (civil) society needs an image of itself in order to function properly; without such a mirror image of itself it will stumble around erratically and aimlessly like a blind man. Apart from its better-known and more obvious functions, the state, as the representation of civil society, is such an image to society of itself.[20] And it follows that the clearer and the more vigorous the contours of the state are, the better it may be expected to fulfill its function of being a representation or an image of civil society. On the contrary, the weaker the state is, the more its contours have become lost in what surrounds the state and in what is either below or above it, the less it can function as a mirror in which civil society can see its nature, its legitimate fears and its desires. Thus, the combination of a strong civil society and a weak state would result in a mindless civil society; whereas the combination of a strong state and a weak civil society would give us despotism. On the assumptions of an aesthetic political philosophy, the best political world is therefore the one in which a strong state[21] and a strong civil society coexist in a fruitful symbiosis; whereas we saw just now that political Stoicism, if consistently elaborated, only leaves us with the unpalatable choice between anarchy and despotism. This comparison of the Stoic and the aesthetic political theorists' positions with regard to the balance of power between state and civil society has been entirely an a priori one, but since the Stoic options of either despotism or anarchy are in agreement neither with historical facts about representative democracy, nor with political desirability, we may conclude that both fact and value fit the aesthetic theorist's view better than that of a Stoic opponent. And because both fact and norm have been derived here from a strictly a priori aesthetic argument, this proves, once again, that an aesthetic political philosophy truly is beyond both fact and value.

If contemporary society is far more open and relaxed than any of the political systems preceding representative democracy, this is not (as we all like to believe because of the democratic illusion of popular sovereignty that the state has taught us to cherish) because the state has been made to listen to society and to graciously comply with all its wishes, but rather because the state and civil society have learned, in harmony with the notion of representation lying at the basis of representative democracy, how best to avoid each other: how to mind their own business without being much troubled by each other. This is not a cynical denunciation of our contemporary democracies but may, on the contrary, help us explain and appreciate the unparalleled efficacy of the finely tuned political instrument that representative democracy really is. In many ways it is as if we are living in a beautiful political palace that has been constructed by our ancestors without our being aware of its beauties for even a moment, or as if we always persisted in looking for these beauties in places where they cannot be found. It took one and a half centuries of civil strife, revolutions, and painful experience to build this palace, before the subtle balance between the state and civil society was discovered. It is an achievement of the greatest political wisdom and sophistication that it proved to be possible to have two such immensely powerful and ambitious social entities as the modern state and modern civil society within one body politic, without the two being tempted to enter into an internecine war. On the contrary, they are permanently prepared to make substantial concessions to each other and always intent on discovering the right equilibrium between the two of them. And these concessions and this equilibrium are the unmistakable sign of the good state and society.

We always complain about the immixture of the state in society—and who would deny that this immixture is a reality, or has even been carried further than is in the interest of either or both entities? Nevertheless, what should truly surprise us is that these two huge and potentially aggressive social entities (think of their past behavior toward each other!) have succeeded in living together so peacefully. Indeed, we need only look at history, and to consider the wars that were so frequently and bitterly fought by an immeasurably weaker state and society in order to recognize the true proportions of this unprecedented feat of modern representative democracy. Paradoxically, democracy functions so well and has so much to recommend itself (because of this "living apart together" of state and society) for the same reasons that would invite most people to distrust it and to prefer the unrestricted domination of the one over the other.

The immense mutual benefits resulting from this strategy of avoidance practiced by both state and society, and from the abrasion of potentially sharp edges of conflict by the anonymity of elections once every four years, is mainly exemplified by the modern welfare state and by the blessings that it made accessible to most of the citizenry. Indeed, the modern welfare state can be seen as the paradigmatic result of this strategy of mutual avoidance. For this strategy and for the benefits to be expected from it, civil society was prepared to surrender its claims to control of the state that had been the major stimulus of the political revolutions of the nineteenth century. It was now content to see its freedoms reduced to mere civil or negative freedom. Democratic citizens, however, persisted in the common belief in the self-evident superiority of direct democracy to representative democracy — a curious atavism reflecting down to the present day the illusions fostered first by the iniquities of the relationship of state and social forces preceding this recent tacit deal between the two powers and, second, of the democratic ideals that had once inspired the revolutions of different segments of civil society against the absolute state and its immediate successors. The state's respect for this strongly reinforced civil liberty was institutionalized in the form of the welfare state, which guaranteed to the citizen social, economic, and political security at a level unprecedented in the history of mankind. The state, in its turn, gained by the deal its freedom of maneuver by silently appropriating and absorbing the citizen's political freedom and by discovering in elections a useful detector of nasty institutional illnesses that it might unwittingly have acquired in the course of time. The democratic state (such as Italy) that no longer responds to the diagnosis of elections is like a patient suffering so many ills at once that no sensible diagnosis is possible.

The state had to pay for these advantages by being obliged to care for the welfare state; it knew that abandoning or reducing the welfare state to basics might upset the social contract that had been made with civil society. It was acutely aware that it would be well-nigh impossible to predict what the consequences of its eventual unilateral withdrawal from this social contract might be. If the state's appropriation of the details of the household has been its most significant victory over the citizen, the welfare state has been the citizen's most strategic victory over the state. Only rarely have the state's hands been tied to such an extent as by the post–World War II welfare state.

We have, therefore, every reason to disagree with Habermas's paranoid fears about the "colonization of the life-world" by the state (paranoia being, by the way, the most important and subtle legacy of the neo-Marxism of the seventies to contemporary political theory). Having ransacked the armory of traditional liberalism, Habermas now argues that this "colonization of the life-world" would be the inevitable and reprehensible result of the immixture by the state in the individual's life that is occasioned by the implementation of the welfare state. But in opposition to Habermas we should recognize that the welfare state is by no means an imperialist attack or invasion by the state of civil society, but instead an important concession of the state to civil society entailing considerable risks and dangers for the state itself. Indeed, the maintenance of the welfare state has increasingly absorbed the state's attention and considerably sapped its strength (thereby strongly reducing its capacity to adequately cope with the new kinds of problems that have arisen and that may, as we have seen, threaten our collective future). We need only recall the pre-revolutionary absolute state so easily taking for granted its right to prescribe to the citizen his religion, what he was permitted and not permitted to read, the kind of jobs that he might never obtain because of his social background and so on, in order to realize how fundamentally benign our modern Leviathans actually are.

To complain with Habermas about this "colonization of the life-world" is to behave like Hans Andersen's princess who could not sleep because a pea was hidden under her bed. Perhaps the pea is actually there, but this will be of infinitely little interest to those who are in desperate need of the state's assistance. Furthermore, one wonders how one could possibly satisfy Habermas's self-contradictory wishes: How could the state effectively assist the needy citizen in the way Habermas will be the first to require it to do, without getting the necessary information about whom it should help and in what way this could best be done? Habermas wants to have his cake—the state's assistance of the citizen—and eat it—the state should avoid meddling with the citizen's business. So it may seem that, in the end, civil society has had the better part of the social contract lying at the basis of the modern welfare state. This contract has weakened the state a great deal more than civil society. And I suppose that we will all agree that this state of affairs clearly is insufficient reason for the cultivation of paranoid Habermasian fears about the modern state (which, of course, does not imply that we may not have other and better reasons for worrying about the modern welfare state).

6. Avoidance and Its Dangers for Democracy

But though we may thus applaud the political reality that came into being with the modern welfare state, this does not imply that the strategy of avoidance adopted by state and civil society, from which the welfare state originated, is without its dangers and problems. In the first place, the strategy of avoidance created between the state and civil society a kind of social vacuum that was to be filled by social groups that neither state nor civil society had much reason to fear or to be interested in. If we recall the mechanisms of (political) representation, and the aesthetic gap representation inevitably effects between the represented and its representation, we will see that it will be hard to avoid the coming into being of such a social and political vacuum in a representative democracy. The aesthetic gap will always invite the coming into being of such a vacuum — much in the way that in a family a drifting apart of the parents will tend to leave the children uncared for. For similar reasons the problems posed by this political vacuum may never completely be solved within the matrix of representative democracy. One must also be very careful in choosing one's instruments for solving this problem. To mention one example, every instrument possessing the features of (Stoic) bureaucracy may be expected to dismally fail here — if not to make matters even worse. For the political vacuum is a weakness not of Stoicism but of the representationalism inherent in all representative democracy. It can therefore only be successfully fought by reinvigorating the mechanisms of representation. But since nothing in this world, including representative democracy, can or will ever be perfect, this is, then, how a modern proletariat of dropouts, of asocial groups of unemployed, drug addicts, and criminals living in ghettos increasingly isolated from the rest of society, inevitably originated, and why they will always be the shadow accompanying representative democracy. Even a well-functioning democracy will always generate such a proletariat; and such a proletariat could only be properly reintegrated into civil society after the abolition of representative democracy in favor of something else — for example, a Soviet-style economy (and it has been one of the very few redeeming features of that absurd economic system to successfully avoid the production of such marginalized groups; surely, therefore, one can only feel sympathy for the nostalgia of the elderly people, of the disabled and the jobless in contemporary Russia, for the days of Brezhnev).

This truly is a *modern* proletariat since it is no longer, as mostly was the case in the history of mankind, a proletariat secreted by civil society, but one constructed by the inevitable perversities of the interactions (or rather the avoidance strategy) of the state and society: especially if one considers the West-European welfare states, one cannot fail to be struck by the extent to which state and civil arrangements creating the welfare state have also been responsible for the production and preservation of this modern proletariat. Though for moral (and aesthetic) reasons we have every reason to be disgusted by this particular avatar of the welfare state and, even more so, by

the relative ease with which the welfare state has accepted this new sociological datum, it is not likely that it will, in itself, present a serious threat
to the social contract between state and civil society which is the basis of
contemporary democracies. These groups are typically without power and
influence and are therefore not dangerous as a group, though individual
representatives may sometimes be so. A social danger would only arise if
the equilibrium still existing between social integration and disintegration
would systematically be destabilized and ever larger numbers of individuals would be eaten away from civil society by this modern proletariat, in
the way that Marx had predicted so many years ago. And since the requirements for a proper and moderately successful participation in contemporary civil society tend to become ever higher and more demanding,
it certainly is not entirely improbable that such a systematic destabilization
would actually occur somewhere in the not too distant future. To the extent
that this destabilization would take place and the number of people who
become marginalized by it would increase, a reinvigoration of representative democracy will truly become a matter of life and death for the future
of democracy.

But there are two more direct threats to the social contract between the
state and civil society. In the first place we should observe that the welfare state required the institution of large and complex bureaucracies. We
must recall, next, the argument expounded in the first and second chapters of this study: that bureaucracy always presupposes the acceptance of
an essentially Stoic relationship between the state and civil society; hence,
bureaucracy follows a logic that is fundamentally at odds with the one lying
at the basis of the social contract between state and civil society (note that
I am not saying that this logic would necessarily be at odds with that of
civil society itself). For bureaucracy's logic is "mimetic" and the social contract's logic "aesthetic" (to use the terminology that was proposed in these
chapters). To the extent, then, that the welfare state, and the bureaucracies
necessary for its proper functioning, will claim an ever larger part of the
public sphere, the conflict between these two logics may be expected to become more painfully obvious and will increasingly be felt by all concerned.
This may impinge on the efficacy of the welfare state, and undermine the
confidence that both parties have in the social contract between state and
society and their willingness to tacitly renew it.

But there is an even more alarming danger facing contemporary Western democracies. Their real test will only come when, for whatever reason,

an opposition between state and civil society would come into being. If such a situation would by mischance actually arise, democracy will be in serious trouble, since there is in representative democracy *no* institution that might arbitrate in *this* (type of) conflict. For we have seen in Chapter 3 that the democratic state was created during the Restoration in order to reconcile the immense conflicts existing in society, such as the conflict between the principle of the ancien régime and that of the Revolution or, in a later phase, the conflict between capital and labor. The democratic state that was developed during and after the Restoration was the politically neutralized arena where these fierce political conflicts could be fought out in a generally peaceful and politically creative way; and it has been the state's readiness to offer itself as such an arena in which it found its decisive advantage over the absolutist states of the ancien régime preceding it.

7. Representative Democracy's Fatal Flaw and the Dangers Resulting Therefrom

Under the present circumstances there are, however, two scenarios that might occasion such a disastrous and, in the two centuries' history of representative democracy, unprecedented conflict. The first scenario originates in problems that might arise within the state itself and the other in the increase of financial burdens occasioned by the maintenance of the welfare state.

Let me begin with the first scenario. Though the state developed an impressive autonomy of its own in the course of the historical process described above, it remained in both its own eyes and in those of the public the institution for arbitrating conflicts arising within civil society itself, and not for conflicts between the state and civil society or within the state itself. And this is what the state's proper role is in a representative democracy. The state never functioned (and was not allowed to function) as a party in its own right in its dealings with the public. To the extent that it actually did so, it always took the interests of certain social groups in civil society as its pretext, instead of openly arguing for its own interests (as being potentially opposed to that of civil society). Note, for example, that the state itself, in spite of being such an eminently prominent political agent, is not itself represented in the state. Moreover, it would involve a logical paradox if one were to try to remedy this; it would be like requiring a painting to represent, apart from what it represents, itself as well. As a consequence

the state is supposed to have no specific interests of its own that would permit such a representation.

This confronts us with the fundamental and irreparable flaw within the
concept of representative democracy. In representative democracy the state
itself is, so to speak, held in a representational quarantine. To be more precise, of course the state is not outside democratic control in a representative
democracy—to obtain this democratic control of the state is, in the end,
what representative democracy has always been about; it was created in
order to correct the evident shortcomings of absolutism. But we should not
forget that this control is always restricted to the "outside" of the state; that
is, to the way in which the state presents itself to the electorate, and to how
the electorate may perceive the state from *its* point of view. But this democratic control has no direct constitutional access to "the state from within,"
that is, to the state as an organization. The state as an immensely complex bureaucratic structure, with its own inner rifts, divisions, oppositions,
and inevitable limitations, as these are determined by the kind of unwieldy
and intractable institution that it is, cannot itself be thematized within the
parameters of representative democracy and must remain invisible in such
a democracy. The logic of the relationship between the represented and its
representation, which is so much the pivot of all representative democracy,
is absent from the state, though the institution of the state itself may well
be seen as the heart of representative democracy. And all the refined ways
of dealing with conflict and opposition that representative democracy has
made available to us are therefore curiously inaccessible to the state itself,
though it continuously has to apply these ways of dealing to conflicts that
divide civil society. This one might deem the supreme irony of representative democracy.

We may find here an instructive difference between representative democracy and the regime preceding it, absolute monarchy. The latter had
in this matter the advantage over the former, though there are many excellent reasons to consider absolute monarchy to be far inferior to representative democracy. The theoretically decisive point of view in a representative
democracy is, self-evidently, that of the citizen, however much practice
may sometimes be different; whereas, no less self-evidently, it is the king's
in absolute monarchy. Now, the king, being the center of the state, will not
experience these difficulties noted just now with seeing the state from "the
inside"; in contrast to the point of view of the citizen, his is such that, in a
way, he can see the state *only* from its inside. That may explain, first, why

the state did not generate under absolute monarchy the theoretical problems that it inevitably gives rise to in a representative democracy. The state is, essentially, the king's servant and his household, and if for whatever reason the absolute ruler wanted to make some changes in his household, he was perfectly free to do as he pleased and nobody would have the right to interfere with his measures. The state's organization, size, and criteria of efficiency were the king's sole responsibility and he was, in principle, in the right position for pronouncing on these aspects of the state's activities, for taking the relevant measures and seeing them enacted. To put it briefly, whereas in a representative democracy the apparatus of the state is (temporarily) put *at the disposal* of the administration that has been elected, the absolute king could really be said to *own* the state. More specifically, it would be seriously misleading to say that in a representative democracy the people "own" the state: first, as we have seen in Chapter 1, the thesis of popular sovereignty, according to which the people are the owner of the state, can be found to be at odds with the logic of representative democracy; but, second, insofar as in a representative democracy the people could, from a practical perspective, perhaps be said to "own" the state, this "ownership" is restricted to "the outside of the state," to how the state manifests itself to the public or to those parts of the state that can present themselves to the public with a certain "style"—as we discussed this notion at the end of Chapter 2. "The inside of the state" necessarily remains invisible to the electorate and thus outside the electorate's control.

Both points have their common explanation in the fact that the transition from absolute monarchy to representative democracy entailed a shift of the predominant point of view in the body politic from that of the monarch to that of the citizen. It also follows that an important qualification must be added to the familiar Tocquevillian thesis according to which the modern voter is the heir of the absolute monarch—for what the modern voter could properly be said to have inherited was only the state's "outside," the state as far as the citizen can perceive it from his point of view. In a way this shift in the dominant political perspective actually gave birth to the state as an independent entity (that is, its "inside") in the body politic. Therefore, the beheading of Louis XVI also meant the elimination of the point of view from which the state's inside could still effectively be controlled. One might therefore argue that the state has been the main beneficiary of Louis XVI's sad fate: January 21, 1793, can for good reasons be considered to have been the birthdate of the democratic state. The only one who could still exercise an adequate control of the state as a whole—inside plus outside—had now disappeared from the political scene. And it need not surprise us that the unchecked growth of the state began immediately after the collapse of absolute monarchy. Behind the interface between civil society and itself the state was now no less free to organize itself as it thought best as the absolute monarch had been before 1789.

Undoubtedly there is much truth in the assertion that the French Revolution resulted in the emancipation of the citizen, but there is even more truth in the claim that the Revolution gave us the emancipation of the state. For the emancipation of the citizen was only partial, since he had now given himself with the democratic state a no less severe and omnipresent, though surely more just and more predictable, master than the absolute king had been. So if the French Revolution accomplished anyone's emancipation, it has been the state's rather than the citizen's. It was Stoic ideology that blinded us down to the present day to the state's newly acquired freedom. This may also help explain why so many contemporary theorists who, like Guéhenno, concentrate on this "interface" between state and civil society, and who (correctly) observe that this "interface" is becoming ever more complex and difficult to define, have been able to come to the surprising conclusion that the state has no future, or even no longer exists, and has ceased demanding the political scientist's or the political theorist's attention.[22] It is as if one were to argue that dogs no longer can be said to exist, now that we know that is impossible to tell exactly where the dog's back ends and his tail begins. Surely this has been one of the most resounding recent victories of the democratic state in its continuous effort to make itself invisible.

There is another aspect to this shift of point of view that requires our attention. From the point of view of the king—located at the very center of the state—the distinction between state and civil society was a fairly academic matter: from his point of view he would first perceive the state that he had created around himself and then, slowly and gradually, the state would shade off, from his perspective, into what was to all practical purposes outside his control and therefore belonged to the domain of civil society. The limits of the absolute king's authority were ill-defined and, in practice, determined by tradition, historical precedent, and, even more important, by all the restrictions on the king's power that had been inherited from feudalism (where the brokenness of political reality, as discussed in Chapter 2, manifested itself to the absolute monarch).

Two conclusions follow from this. In the first place, since there are for the absolute monarch, and from his point of view, no well-defined and fundamental limits to be crossed on the trajectory from his own elevated position down to that of the humblest of his subjects, the idea of the *Rechtsstaat* made no sense under absolute monarchy. History, practice, precedent, the mosaic of privileges of citizens and of social classes, accidental contingencies such as the king's personality or that of his main servants, determined the extent of the king's factual power; the ideal of clear and well-defined juridical delimitations as embodied by the *Rechtsstaat* would for absolute monarchy have been as nonsensical as the hopeless effort to tell the upper side of a football from its underside. However, the inapplicability of the notion of the *Rechtsstaat* to ancien régime society does not mean that all was arbitrary in absolute monarchy—on the contrary, the restrictions on the king's power inherited from feudalism often proved to be a nearly as effective though far more erratic protection of the citizen than the modern *Rechtsstaat*. From a practical point of view it did mean, nevertheless, that the king's and the state's authority were subject to a continuous flux that is incompatible with the notion of the *Rechtsstaat*. To maintain this flux was the condition for the absolute monarch's attempts to enlarge his influence over civil society, and the absolute monarch therefore had every reason to firmly resist the introduction of the *Rechtsstaat*, and of the kind of relationship between state and civil society entailed by it—which is why for absolute monarchy the strategy of avoidance adopted by state and civil society in representative democracy was no option to be seriously considered.

And this brings me to my next conclusion. Of course the absolute monarch was well aware of this state of affairs, and he correctly inferred from this that his authority was something to be cherished, to be carefully protected and cultivated by all means at his disposal. This is why the absolute monarch insisted on the sacrosanctity of his person and of his authority (and, therewith, that of the state); he realized that only in this way might he succeed in claiming for himself as large a part of that indefinite no-man's-land between state and civil society as possible. In particular, this explains why the absolute monarch cultivated the inherently feudal notion of crime as lese-majesty, of crime as an attack on the king's person rather than as an infringement on public order. The democratic state could afford to entertain a far more relaxed attitude toward crime (which is, as one might argue, one of the less attractive implications of the notion of the *Rechtsstaat*): in contrast to the absolute monarch, democracy has no reason whatsoever to see in crime an attack on itself. It may allow itself to dispassionately see in crime a mere transgression of the rules that everybody has agreed upon; it has no reason for worrying more about crime than the average citizen (or, rather, even less so, because of its unequaled power to take its revenge on crime committed against the state itself—hence the democratic state's tendency to take crime less seriously than do other political systems, especially absolute monarchy). It is therefore all the more surprising that the democratic state has wished to monopolize to such an extent the retribution for crime, to the almost total exclusion of the victim of crime (obviously, it is penal law that I mainly have in mind here). Though, in contrast to the absolute monarch, the democratic state has far fewer reasons for considering itself a party in the transactions between the (convicted) criminal and his victim, it is illustrative that fines are not paid to the victim but to the state; and especially in the countries of continental Europe the victim of crime is reduced to the status of a forgotten and irrelevant occasion for criminal behavior.

In these countries the police and the judicature are legally entitled to withhold from the victim of crime the identity of its perpetrator, so that the victim in such cases does not even have the means to start a civil suit against the person or party who injured him. The motivation of this scandalous iniquity is that it may help to prevent a victim from taking revenge on the criminal. But in this way the interests of the victim (to obtain indemnification) have been ruthlessly and arrogantly subordinated to those of the state (to assure public order). And the result is an asymmetry absurdly favoring the criminal over his victim. For, to all practical purposes, the criminal has been able to perform his crime, whereas his victim (having so much better reasons for hurting the criminal than the criminal had for hurting his victim) is not only prevented from doing so, but even from obtaining the redress to which he is entitled by the law itself. Of course, one may well warn the victim of a crime of the consequences of taking the law into his own hands, but to withhold from him the name of the criminal is to deal with the victim as if he were a brute and mindless animal. A more striking illustration of the degradation of the citizen by the democratic state will be hard to find.

A possible, though admittedly speculative, explanation of this strange anomaly might run as follows. The coming into being of democracy gave a strong impetus to political Stoicism, since the commensurability of all things political (which is the main aim of political Stoicism) has an obvious elective affinity with the (popular) view of democratic society as a society of equals. Political equality is a doctrine central to political Stoicism (which does not imply that non-Stoic arguments for political equality cannot be given—for example the argument that, first, we need democracy and, second, that democracy requires political equality). Points of view now detached themselves from the individuals or classes of individuals to whom they tended to be fastened in the traditionalist class society of the ancien régime; they could now freely circulate in the body politic. Points of view were now potentially anybody's point of view, and this liberation of the point of view by democracy has greatly contributed to the capacity of the citizens to comprehend each other: successful communication requires the interchangeability of points of view. However, points of view could now strangely coagulate into something like the Hegelian God's-eye point of view (a possibility that proved to be not without its dangers) or even give way to the absence of any point of view (the objectivist ideal of the social sciences). One might plausibly argue, then, that under representative democracy points of view will tend to behave much like small interstellar bodies that may get caught in orbits around the larger political masses—such as the state. In this way the state, to which jurisdiction was already entrusted under the ancien régime, could now appropriate the point of view of the victim—by no means a small prize, since absorbing this point of view within itself would expectedly strongly increase the respect that the law-abiding citizen had for the democratic state. For, unaware of the state's utter lack of interest in his potential role as victim of crime, the citizen now saw in the state a far more effective revenger of injustice than the absolutist state had ever been.

The citizen's naivety with regard to the state's real attitude toward crime is paradigmatic of the citizen's lack of comprehension of what might truly motivate the democratic state's actions, and especially of this dimension of the state's "inside," where these motivations originate. Because this "inside" remains hidden from the citizen, the problems and conflicts that might arise there tend to be excluded from the mechanisms of conflict solving that representative democracy has developed. Admittedly, Parliament or Congress may, at times, discuss problems and conflicts that have arisen within the state itself, but in that case we could not properly speak of democratic control of that "inside" of the state. For at such occasions the people's representatives will find themselves in a strange position: they still are the people's representatives when discussing problems that have arisen within the state, but these concern problems and conflicts in a political realm that they could not possibly be said to represent. They represent the electorate and not the state (and certainly not those specific parts of the state that might have come into conflict with each other). Nevertheless, one might argue that during such discussions in Parliament or Congress about problems within the state, it will be the executive that functions as the state's representative. And when continuing this line of argument, we may observe what constitutional contradictions this type of public problem will necessarily give rise to. For either these conflicts and oppositions are clearly and openly reflected by the executive or they are not. In the former case the executive will have to abandon the unity and indivisibility that it is always supposed to demonstrate in its presentation to Parliament or Congress. The executive will then become divided in itself, with the inevitable consequence (if the issue is serious enough) of the abdication of the administration (and hence the problems that occasioned the fall of the cabinet will be allowed to persist).

This will, obviously, also be the result as long as the executive persists in its unity and indivisibility in its dealings with Parliament or Congress, which would be the other option. But by opting for this strategy the executive would, more or less officially, announce its failure to adequately appreciate the conflict. Of course, unofficially several functionaries and politicians may nevertheless recognize the problem and try to find a solution for it behind the scenes of parliamentary and public discussion. And when the conflicts at stake are relatively unimportant it will obviously be best to deal with them in such a silent and inconspicuous way. In case, however, these conflicts and problems really are quite serious and have truly political proportions, in the sense of having their implications for (parts of) civil society, these problems and conflicts can and should not be kept hidden from the eyes of the public in this way. So in most cases, when problems and conflicts arise within the state itself the result to be expected is that everybody will try to ignore them as well as one can, so that the problems and conflicts in question continue to exist indefinitely. These considerations may explain why the size, the functioning, the internal contradictions, and the inefficiencies of the state are so extremely difficult to get on the political agenda of the representative democracy, and why this flaw really is a serious liability of that otherwise subtle and well-balanced political system. In sum, in the complex machinery of representative democracy the state itself (when seen from the inside) remains a kind of vacuum outside the procedures of representative democracy. Thus in a way the state (from the inside) could be seen as an immensely powerful and resourceful stranger come from abroad, who is now content to live with us and to assist us with a number of essential public services that we (as the electorate) are unable to perform ourselves satisfactorily.

If, then, this giant stranger with whom we have been living in a perfect symbiosis for two centuries begins to get entangled in his own problems, problems for which representative democracy has no proper constitutional solutions, it may start behaving in a way that might be detrimental to the interest of civil society. The state will tend to become absorbed by its own problems and this will stimulate it to develop a clearly articulated notion of its own interests, which need not run parallel to those of civil society. To put it metaphorically, the state will then begin to develop a personality of its own, and will start conceiving of civil society as its natural rival in the public sphere. The natural harmony of interest of state and civil society that has been the solid basis for two hundred years of representative democracy may then be undermined, and a guerrilla war between state and civil society will be the fatal result.

8. Second Scenario

That brings me to the second scenario, according to which, for either economic or ecological reasons, the welfare state will have to be reduced to basics. And if one takes into account the huge budget deficits of several Western welfare states, their economic inflexibilities, and the disquietingly high percentage of jobless people in these democracies, it need not surprise us that many economists and politicians forcefully insist on the necessity of such a reduction of the welfare state. Now, democracy in a growing economy is easy; there will then always be sufficient money for financing the social reconciliation that democracy always had as its main and natural aim since its coming into being during the Restoration. But we can only speculate how democracy will function when national impoverishment really would set in, and when it has to parcel out not the sweet but the bitter fruits of our collective action.

The main problem will then not be that an atmosphere of understandable irritation and frustration will begin to pervade public debate and take away much of the willingness of the parties involved to achieve social reconciliation. The problem is, rather, that the shortage of financial means, occasioned by the increased difficulty in financing the welfare state, will then place the state and civil society in an outright opposition to each other that might easily provoke a relentless struggle between the two for the financial means available. The state will insist upon using these available means for financing the welfare state, whereas civil society would prefer to use these funds for strengthening the economic basis of the welfare state (and the sad irony will then be that this new war between state and civil society will not have been occasioned by a difference of opinions about goals — since both state and civil society have learned to love the welfare state as the child of their fruitful cooperation — but about what the most suitable means are for achieving these goals). As long as the state's own interests can properly be seen as subservient to those of civil society, as long as there exists a certain transparency and convergence of these two sets of interests, this flaw of representative democracy need not have debilitating consequences for the actual functioning of democracies.

Obviously, things would become worse when the two scenarios sketched above would become reality at the same time. And, unfortunately, this is far from being merely hypothetical. For one might well argue that it will be precisely the problems caused by the maintenance of the welfare state (second scenario) that can easily result in conflicts and opposition within the state itself (first scenario). In the first place one could think here of the administrative complexity of the welfare state, which has already, in many countries, involved the state in a number of unpleasant contradictions which are difficult to escape, especially since every attempt to do so might irritate substantial segments of the electorate who have benefited or who hope to benefit from these administrative inconsistencies. But it will be even worse when issues of economic and financial policy will oppose, within the state itself, departments having greater affinity with those parts of civil society that finance the welfare state to departments that spend money on the people who have become dependent on the welfare state.

If such a situation should arise, it is most likely that the state will follow the natural inclination of each institution and wish to begin with an effort to minimize the problematic contradictions in itself. This will invite the state to confront civil society with the contradictions that the politics of the welfare state had created within itself. The state will then try to unload on civil society its own problems instead of attempting to solve those of civil society. It will no longer act as the shock absorber for the problems in civil society that the state has traditionally been, but rather like a screen throwing these problems back on society again (while the state will be tempted to add to these rejected problems of civil society a few more of its own).

Moreover, this will in all likelihood be the silent and underground manner in which that guerrilla conflict between state and society will be fought: we should not believe that this war would take such a primitive form as we remember from the past or from the behavior of Soviet-style communist states. Both state and civil society have become too civilized—and too much aware of the nature of their interests—to fight their wars in such a barbaric, irrational, and utterly uneconomic way. The state will realize that fighting the war in this open and straightforward manner would be counterproductive, and would immediately mobilize the whole powerful potential of civil society's resistance against it. And this would put the state, especially at the initial phase of the struggle, in a most disadvantageous position, since all the traditions, the whole *ethos* of the well-functioning democratic state that has been inherited from the past, as well as all the resources of civil society, could then be put in the field against it. The state would have not the slightest chance of success under such circumstances. Anarchy would be the result, and anarchy is what states fear as much as individual human beings fear their own death. So if the war between state and civil society would actually break out, we should not expect anything so clear and decisive as an open declaration of war of the one on the other. In fact, victories in this war will to a large extent depend on one's success in making one's opponent forget that a war is actually going on. We may therefore expect that each act of aggression in this war will be accompanied by prolix and technical explanations attempting to demonstrate that this act is in the best interests of the opponent. And the real problem (for the citizen) will be to distinguish cases in which this is really true from those in which it is not. The difficulty of properly doing so and the possibilities that this will open to the state for playing off one segment of civil society against another, will be the state's most formidable weapon in its war with civil society.

The only clear and reliable sign of the outbreak of the war would be that gradually and almost imperceptibly a certain shift in the state's behavior toward civil society might be noted, a shift that would have to be observed in a large and variegated set of examples. These would all have in common an increased awareness by the state of its own interests as potentially opposed to those of civil society; it would then begin to privilege these interests over those of civil society. An interesting question would be, of course, whether the first signs of this war can be discerned already. My own intuition would be that, in fact, at least on the European continent the first skirmishes of that war have already taken place some five to ten years ago. And it is not unlikely that the European Union, this trade union of states which, as Milward has recently shown, is so much a construction for the preservation of the nation-state, actually functions as an alliance of the European nation-states against their civil societies; not so much against the economic segments of civil society, since these still are far too powerful to be openly attacked and too much the condition of the economic survival of the state itself, but against the individual citizen. Especially in those countries where the welfare state was most strongly developed, the state has since then confronted the individual citizen with claims and restrictions on his behavior and on the fruits of his labor that this citizen would have every reason to consider as the declaration of war outlined above. And, perhaps, a book like this one could be seen as one of the first responses by the citizenry against our present belligerent Leviathans.

Each institution, even the state, puts its own survival above everything else. The interest of state and civil society will then no longer converge. So if, because of the decline of the welfare state, the state starts to think of itself as having its own interests, different and probably even opposed to those of civil society, that it should at all costs defend against civil society; if then a conflict between the state and civil society would actually break out, this subtle fabric of relationships developed in the course of one century and a half which structures the interactions between state and society will be torn up and destroyed. The state will then attempt to regain the kind of preponderant position that it had had under the ancien régime; while the citizen, in his turn, will lose his confidence in democracy. For he sees that he now has to fight the institution that always was instrumental in solving his problems, and he will realize that the democratic state has turned from a fair and reliable arbiter into his most dangerous enemy.

Moreover, if these insoluble economic and social problems that could incite conflict between state and civil society actually present themselves, these same problems will probably have fatally undermined the citizen's confidence in the democratic state. For democracy has always had a natural affinity with the citizen's trust that all social and political problems, at least in principle, are amenable to a democratic solution. If democracy is the political system that requires the political participation of every citizen—and since it may seem a plausible assumption (though it is not) that there are no problems that could not be solved if every citizen wants a constructive solution—how could democracy then be incapable of solving our collective problems, and, more specifically, that of national impoverishment? If, then, because of such a general impoverishment, democracy failed to satisfy this (apparently) reasonable expectation (but, as explained in the Introduction, only apparently reasonable), democracy will begin to look like "a God that failed." And many citizens will then be tempted to consider alternative, less democratic and more autocratic systems of government. Self-evidently, the state will have no reason whatsoever to discourage or counteract this nascent political mentality; we need only recall the first half of our disastrous and deeply tragic century to know what dangers will then be facing us.

So, once again, the challenge for the political philosopher is to find how to reconcile the stronger state that we may expect for the near future, with democracy, freedom, and those restrictions on government action that experience has taught us will be the minimum prerequisite for a life worthy of a human being both in contemporary and future society. How to create a stronger state within the parameters of democracy is the question upon which our future hinges.

I add one final comment on how the foregoing could be interpreted from the perspective of the argument in Chapter 2. We observed there how "the political object" in the course of time dissolved into the two ultimate tertia of money and language. It was argued, next, that aesthetic rifts at the level of these two tertia might give us back the political object. To these theoretical suggestions a more concrete form can now be given. With the gradual lessening of tensions and conflicts within civil society thanks to the beneficial intervention of the democratic state, civil society became ever more depoliticized (though the state will try to hide this fact as well as it can, since the recognition of it is obviously not in its interest), with the gradual evanescence of the political object as its natural result. Representative democracy now entered a phase of a more or less peaceful coexistence of state and civil society and of all the different segments of civil society; a period of political stasis without very urgent and clearly visible political problems ensued. It now even seemed that all our essential political problems had been solved forever and that therefore, in a sense, we had come to "the end of history." Politics now changed into a busy industry of inventing all kinds of unexpected and pleasant surprises for the citizen, and was no longer that strenuous effort at reconciling real and serious social conflicts that had demanded the attention of the democratic state for the greater part of its life.

But beneath this politically reassuring calm surface a new conflict slowly began to emerge—this time not a conflict having its source and locus in civil society but one between the state and civil society. Whether representative democracy will actually be able to reconcile this new type of conflict by making use of its traditional instruments of conflict-solving can, at present, be only a matter of speculation (though we have every reason to hope that it will). In any case, under the present circumstances the task of political theorists will be twofold. In the first place they must eradicate from their minds the last remnants of Marxist conceptions of the state, according to which the state is the mere agent of the economically predominant segments of civil society; they must now learn to see the state as a very powerful and potentially dangerous institution in our complex societies. It is an institution with a set of interests of its own that need not always converge with the interests of civil society. Next, political theorists must recall that the most appropriate locus for identifying these now diverging interests can best be identified in terms of the two Stoic tertia that have brought us where we now are: money and language. So political theorists must now ask economists to develop economic models that might show us where this divergence of interests between the state and civil society is most likely to be expected. And they may enjoin on the economists that with the construction of such models they will render both ourselves and our children a much greater service than do the models with which so many contemporary economists hope to please mathematicians and that now unfortunately absorb most of their intellectual energy. Next, political theorists will turn to colleagues in the departments of literary criticism and ask them how best to analyze the rhetoric of the monologues that state and civil society address to each other. For in this rhetoric we may find the equivalent on the level of that war of idioms, as discussed above, to that of the war of interests that is being fought over economic issues. An analysis of the rhetoric in use by both parties might show political theorists where their real sensitivities and interests lie, on which the future dialogue between state and civil society could best be grafted.

In this way the future conflicts between state and civil society could be divested of their potential for danger and, perhaps, even be channeled into a direction that might be to the benefit of all concerned. The "political object" demanding our attention most in the future will presumably be this conflict of interests between state and civil society. It is a potentially dangerous type of conflict, since representative democracy has no

time-honored strategies for dealing with it. But if the dangers of the conflict were to become widely recognized, this would already be an important
step toward a solution. Moreover, a society with conflicts is always a better
society than one without them — so even from that point of view there is no
reason for utter despair about those recent developments in our representative democracies that were expounded in this and the previous section.

9. The Ironies of Liberal Reason

As we observed above when discussing Guicciardini, the only already existing idiom capable of dealing with the aesthetic rifts in the political order,
its brokenness, and hence with the transaction between the state and the
citizen, is that of the historian. These aesthetic rifts manifest themselves in
the discrepancies between the politician's intentions and the actual effects
of his actions — it was historians like Machiavelli and Guicciardini who discovered these aesthetic rifts and who were the first to see the unintended
consequences of human action as the true domain of meaningful historical
investigation. At the same time, their insights were meant for the politician — that he should avoid or prevent unintended consequences as much as
possible when making and carrying out his decisions. The good politician is
the politician who gives the historian nothing to write about. But defining
the relationship between politics and history in this way already demonstrates in what impasse the politician is placed by such considerations. For
there is something strangely self-defeating about the task of avoiding unintended consequences: if one succeeds in this task, one has not avoided
any unintended consequences (one cannot avoid what does not exist); if
one fails in the task one has again not avoided unintended consequences.
It seems to be part of the logic of the notion of unintended consequences
that they cannot be avoided (though, of course, politicians may be successful at avoiding the counterproductive consequences of a possible course of
action that are foreseen by them — but these consequences *sui generis* are
not part of the class of unintended consequences). So, whatever the politicians might do, they will supply historians with the material for writing
the account of their failures. This is what is so sad and disappointing about
the historical discipline from the politician's perspective: in history we can
only trace the steps of the Goddess Fortune after she has already passed
by. The irony about all politics is therefore that it should make use of (or,
rather, absorb in itself) the idiom of the historian, hence of an idiom that

exclusively speaks about the past and from which nothing useful is to be
expected for present and future political action.

But perhaps we have been moving too fast here: surely there must be
some truth in the widely shared intuition that history can be useful to the
politician. Let us listen, then, to how that modest and supremely sensible
historian, Leopold von Ranke, defined the relationship between history and
politics in his inaugural address of 1836. He argued that it is

> the task of the historian to demonstrate what is the essence of the state on the
> basis of the events of the past and to further an adequate understanding of these
> events; it is, next, the task of the politician to develop and to complete the histo-
> rian's insights after they have been understood and appropriated by the mind.[23]

Here history is the appropriate propaedeutics for meaningful political
action — not because we can learn lessons from the past, as was suggested
by the Machiavellian topos of "historia magistra vitae," but by a historically
informed awareness of what historical ironies have brought us to where we
are, and by a further extrapolation from that development. As Ranke had
argued in his essays "Die grossen Mächte" and "Das politisches Gespräch,"
politicians should be aware of the ironies of the past as revealed by historians and recognize that here lies the only reliable and necessary (though
insufficient) condition for their successful political aims and strategies.

We should recognize, however, that this is a relatively modern conception of the relationship between politics and (the ironies of) history, one
that could only come into being after speculation about this relationship
has passed the stage that we might identify with Hegel. Before Hegel *historia* was, primarily,[24] "probable" knowledge — not in the sense of "probable" that we associate with probabilism and statistics, but in the sense of
being based on the *doxai* of common sense, therefore ineradicably uncertain and, hence, the opposite of the certain knowledge one expected from
philosophy.[25] With Hegel we see that the paths of philosophy and *historia*
momentarily coincide, since for Hegel dialectical, philosophical truth can
only articulate itself in history. With Ranke (and, speaking generally, the
nineteenth-century intellectual climate) the relationship between history
and philosophy is completely reversed. For it is since then that only history
can give us "certain" knowledge, while the philosophical speculations of
the Hegels and the Marxes about history are now contemptuously rejected
as the delusions of a philosophical reason that has forgotten its inherent
limitations. Hence, if we return to the pre-Hegelian regime of certainties

and to the subordination of history to politics characteristic of it, we will see that in this period history is not yet in the (post-Hegelian) position to ironize politics. Politics still had predominance over history, expressing the fact that it was politics (that is, the notion of *virtù*) that gave us access to the *civitas terrena* and that there is a profound truth in the fact that Guicciardini (the historian) came after Machiavelli (the political theorist) and not the other way around.

A good illustration of this regime of history and politics is the absolute monarch. The political actions of the absolute monarch are no expressions or extrapolations from history but the expression of a quite personal power and majesty, and therefore an emanation of the monarch rather than of a (historical) order existing outside him- or herself. Essential to the actions of the absolute monarch is the legitimacy of those actions, not so much their actual purpose or intent — and with that all that is important has been said. Consequently there is neither need nor room for an ironic objectification of the monarch's actions, as always is effected by *Weltironie*. What the monarch did was done well, for no other reason than that it was the monarch who had done it. An ironization of those actions would have been completely absurd.

The Enlightenment and Romanticism (in this respect, too, so much more the radicalization than the antithesis of the Enlightenment) broke with the "seriousness" of the monarch's political action: *what* was done was now separated from *who* did it, and the idea that there would be some quality specific to the king's actions simply because they are the king's actions now lost all plausibility. Persons are persons and actions are actions and they can be coupled together in any conceivable way. Political action was now "democratized" in the sense that in principle anybody can do anything. In this way (political) action gained an autonomy and independence with regard to the agent, just as a century earlier thinking had already liberated itself from the person who thinks or experiences by means of Descartes's victory over Aristotelianism. Furthermore, the dissolution of action and agent naturally shifted the emphasis from the former (the absolute monarch) to the latter (the state's intervention in society) and all that counted henceforward was the latter's success.

The person of the absolute monarch was thus the last obstacle on the way to the anonymization of all action and thought, which now could begin to lead a life independent of agents and thinkers; the decapitation of Louis XVI was therefore not only the end of a period in political history but also marked the end of traditionalist epistemology and philosophy

of action. Now that actions had become independent entities, the interplay of actions could obtain its own autonomy with regard to the actors. It
was only thanks to this autonomy that it become possible to become aware
of *Weltironie*, and to discern in history a process or development in which
we, as agents, seem to be only indirectly involved. Actions have their own
peculiar logic. They live a life of their own, have their own sympathies and
aversions, and seem to care little about the agents in which they originate.

Thus politics is not intrinsically ironic; it is predominantly history, or,
rather, historical perspective, that ironizes political action. That is true not
only for political action itself but equally for the political philosopher reflecting on political action. Even political philosophy ironizes itself when it
absorbs history. An example of this is given in Spragens's book *The Irony
of Liberal Reason*, a title that can not fail to attract our attention in the
context of the present discussion. Spragens defines irony as follows: "The
ironic situation is distinguished from a pathetic one by the fact that the
person involved in it bears some responsibility for it. It is differentiated
from tragedy by the fact that the responsibility is related to an unconscious
weakness rather than a conscious resolution." [26]

This definition is of course completely in agreement with what was defined above as *Weltironie*. With regard to this so-called irony of liberal
reason Spragens argues as follows: The (proto-) liberalism that came into
being in the course of the seventeenth and eighteenth centuries was the
translation *in politicis* of an absolute confidence in Reason and in the pre-
sumed ability of Reason to solve intellectual, political, and social conflicts
in a satisfactory way. Think, for example, of Grotius's statement in the
"Prolegomena" of his *De iure belli ac pacis*: "It has been my first care to
relate all the matters having to do with natural law to notions that are so
absolutely certain that nobody could deny them unless he were prepared to
violate his own consciousness. The principles of natural law are, if correctly
perceived, self-evident and obvious, in the way this can be said of sensory
perception." [27] We have here a paradigmatic formulation of the rationalism
and logicism of the Stoic tradition, as this tradition is understood throughout this book.

We must see, however, that Reason is in a most unfortunate position. It
is an intellectual faculty with little feeling for balance and equilibrium. As
Reason becomes ever more refined, as has undoubtedly been the case in
the past two and a half centuries, and as Reason became ever more successful at catching ever more people and ever more ideas in unreasonableness,

to that extent the claim that Reason is or could really be our compass in our actions has to be toned down. To the extent that there is ever more for Reason to criticize, Reason inevitably will present itself as little more than a helpless shallop in a sea of unreasonableness. The purer and more "rational" Reason becomes, the more Reason marginalizes itself.

This essentially *historical* process, within which this unfortunate dialectic of Enlightened Reason reveals itself, can best be demonstrated if we consider the problem of the derivation of political norms. It was exactly that relentlessly sharp, hypercritical Reason that taught us that norms can and should not be derived from facts, as was still unproblematically done in the euphoric early years of Enlightened Reason. The most ironic consequence of the discovery of this dichotomy of the "is" and the "ought," of "Sein" versus "Sollen," achieved by critical reason, was that the entire domain of political norms now had to be handed over to irrationality. Paradoxically, it had to be Reason that taught us that habit, arbitrariness, decisionism, or even cruel violence, but certainly not Reason itself, are normally the decisive factors here: "In short, skeptical rationalism, by its renunciation of the very idea of normative knowledge, leaves itself incapable of affirming on rational grounds any constructive political ideals whatsoever." [28] This self-destructive irony of liberal reason is in agreement with the "dialectics of the Enlightenment" that Adorno and Horkheimer had already observed in 1947 and that they described in the following words:

> We hope to contribute with these fragments to an understanding of the fact that the cause of the backsliding of the Enlightenment into mythology is not so much due to the nationalistic, pagan, and other modern mythologies invented especially for the cause of furthering this backsliding, but to the Enlightenment *itself* because it had paralyzed itself by its fear of the truth.[29]

In both cases we may observe that Reason may undergo a historical evolution that causes it to enter into an ironic relationship with its former self: "Reason, the Liberator, becomes Caesar the King," [30] as Spragens succinctly summarizes the process. It is interesting, in the present context, that according to Spragens the political sphere is preeminently the stage on which this unmasking, this ironic suicide of Reason, is enacted. Apparently, more than any other area of human endeavor, politics can be considered the watershed separating Reason itself from its ironical caricatures. On less sensitive territories, areas safely removed from this watershed, the history of the refinement of Reason may still be considered a success story. For what is marginalized by the refinement of scientific Reason need not always be considered an irreparable loss to society that could not possibly be outweighed by its triumphs and successes. Nevertheless, the chaos, disorder, and loss of prestige that befell the humanities after scientific Reason declared itself unable to make any sense of them is one of the more regrettable consequences of this self-purification of scientific Reason since the days of Descartes.

Another conclusion can be derived from this argument concerning the ironic nature of Reason, liberal or not. We are inclined to imagine Reason as a victorious army that, in the course of history, has gradually occupied the territory of the irrational. Once again scientific Reason, as exemplified by the exact sciences, is the best support for such a view. Yet with Adorno, Horkheimer, and Spragens we should realize what is so misleading about this admittedly attractive and reassuring metaphor. In accordance with their suggestions it would be better to say that reason constantly occupies certain points (we hope strategic ones), but this need not mean much for the areas lying between these points, and it is most certainly not the case that these areas are automatically interconnected. Another metaphor of the exploits of Reason would therefore be more appropriate. Let us compare Reason to a microscope or a pair of binoculars. This kind of optical instrument may greatly reinforce our *grip* (the formulation is deliberately Nietzschean) on an extremely well-defined part of reality, but this is always (and here we find the crux of the comparison) at the expense of a loss of clarity and resolution elsewhere. The medical researcher studying bacteria under a microscope cannot at the same time observe the chairs and tables in the laboratory. And so it is with Reason. Reason is no doubt the most powerful intellectual instrument at our disposal for obtaining a grip on our world, but for each individual case it must, just like the microscope, be adjusted to its task. Ironically, this involves a slackening elsewhere of the grip of Reason. In other words, the result of this continuous refinement of Reason will be that a relatively firm but not always satisfactory grasp of large areas of reality is exchanged for an admittedly more satisfactory and more secure grasp of the detail. We pay for our increased insight into the details by a loss of understanding of their interconnection. It is one of the defining characteristics of Reason in the more refined stages of its development that it will be better at details than at coherence. And that is, of course, more or less the diagnosis of our time proposed by postmodernists like Lyotard. What we should learn from these considerations is that Reason is an instrument that we can never do without; it certainly is our only refuge in our dealings with the world and ourselves; but we should never forget that Reason has its own intrinsic shortcomings. More specifically, this means that we would be well advised to recognize that the use of Reason requires a certain *strategy*, just as the choice of a certain magnification of the microscope is always dependent on the kind of objects to be studied. To put it provocatively, Reason should be used in a political way, or rather, our use of Reason must always be guided by the classical virtue of *prudentia*, it must be used prudently: since un-Reason as Reason's permanent shadow can never be completely banished and will always accompany Reason as its alter ego, the only thing one can do is to strive for the narrow optimum between Reason and un-Reason.

This must not be misunderstood. When speaking of a *political* use of Reason, I certainly do not mean by this that science and all other disciplines appealing to Reason should be subject to what we nowadays call "politics." I am not advocating a politicization of Reason. I mean to say, rather, that the decision on what will be the focus of Reason in individual cases will have the *form* or *nature* of a political decision, without it thereby coming to belong to the *domain* of politics. Nor is this an attempt to discredit Enlightened Reason in a subtle and underhand manner—on the contrary. My argument is only a warning against an un-Enlightened and un-Reasonable confidence in the cumulative powers of Reason. So, in fact, I am arguing for a perfection, rather than for a criticism of (the use of) Reason, or, to paraphrase Pascal, for a recognition of the fact that Reason has its reasons that Reason does not know of. More specifically, we must continuously be aware that Reason, always so vulnerable to self-ironization, unfortunately does not score permanent victories. We should realize that the "Enlightenment" brought by Reason is always local and temporary, and always attended by a new darkness occurring where a certain illumination previously seemed to exist. Reason only functions in a chiaroscuro, never in an all-enlightening brightness, as was believed in the happy and boisterous days of the Enlightenment (it was at that time certainly less of an unreasonable conviction than now, considering Enlightenment reason's less perfect and less purified nature compared to contemporary reason). By its very nature, Reason can never give us such an all-enlightening brightness. Indeed, only if we are prepared to recognize this will a relaxed relation with Reason really become possible.

But let me return to the relationship between history and politics from the point of view of irony. If, then, it is only via a history of politics that the ironies of politics will reveal themselves, we may ask whether it is possible to subsume history into politics. This question is far from being merely academic. Hegel's well-known dictum "die Weltgeschichte ist das Weltgericht"—that it is only history that will show us what statesman, politician, or nation is finally put in the right by the ironies of history—implies that such a subsumption of history in politics must necessarily be the statesman's supreme goal. In any case, to the extent that such a subsumption has been achieved by the politician one is surely justified in saying that *then* irony (in the guise of *Weltironie*) has become as much a feature of politics as it always is of history. In the tradition of Romantic German political philosophy suggestions in this direction were often made; moreover, what nowadays is called "practical philosophy" could without much difficulty be seen as a specification of such suggestions.[31] However, the complexities of this two-thousand-year-old Aristotelian tradition of "practical philosophy" are such that an exposition of them adequate in the context of the present discussion would only obscure this possibility of the subsumption of history in politics.

Moreover, on the basis of a suggestion made by Alasdair MacIntyre, we can address the problem more directly than by fighting a way through the recalcitrant intellectual thicket of "practical philosophy." In an influential article MacIntyre dealt with the much-discussed problem of how to decide in the case of a conflict between two Kuhnian paradigms. The answer that MacIntyre proposed for this problem is, roughly, that the best paradigm (out of a set of two or more competing paradigms) is always the paradigm from the perspective of which the *history* of the scientific debate concerned can best be written.[32] Not Cardinal Bellarmin, but Galilei was right—for no other reason than that Galilei would have been capable of writing the best and most convincing story of the relevant intellectual history antedating their difference of opinion. The intuition behind MacIntyre's proposal is that the paradigm enabling one to write the most convincing history, the historical account of the scientific disagreement in question possessing the widest scope and therefore having the greatest explanatory force, will be the paradigm to be preferred.[33] Thus even in exact sciences, in the most decisive phases of their development, we have eventually to rely on narrative criteria (the importance of which for the study of history no one will want to question).

It is obvious what this suggestion implies for politics and for the possibility of a subsumption of politics in history. It implies that politicians must always act in such a way that the point of view from which they consider the political realities of their time and that inspires and justifies their actions will prove to be identical with the point of view from which, perhaps centuries later, historians will prefer to elucidate the course of events in question. Politicians must be able, so to speak, to identify themselves with their later historians, and to transcend or anticipate the differences between themselves and the historians who will, in the future, describe their actions. It is a kind of inversion of Collingwood's reenactment doctrine. Naturally the main idea of the suggestion is that in this way politicians will succeed in diminishing the force of unintended consequences. For it is exactly these (ironic) unintended consequences that will (later) drive historians to choose a point of view outside or opposite that of the politician or historical agent. On the other hand, it will always remain true that the historical perspective can only come into being by virtue of the unintended results. One might thus conclude that there is something oddly self-defeating in the whole proposal: either politicians succeed in subsuming, as it were, the unintended consequences of their actions in these actions themselves — but then we are without a list of unintended consequences that would enable us to assess politicians' political wisdom from a truly historical perspective — or unintended consequences have not been avoided — but in that case our (historical) assessment can only be negative. It seems, therefore, that using the "history criterion" will leave us no other choice than that between a *non liquet* and a negative judgment. This is, arguably, one of the more unfortunate aspects of politicians' predicament: their mistakes will always be much more obvious than their more praiseworthy decisions and will always attract the outsider's attention so much more. The subsumption of unintended consequences within a historical process that the outsider (or later historian) will always accept more or less as a matter of course will blind the outsider to the real merits of politicians' insight and to what have been their most successful actions. This may explain why often politicians who are least noticed during their political careers may, with hindsight, be considered to have been more efficient and effective than politicians with less instinct for the unintended consequences of their actions.

Two other inferences from the foregoing should be noticed here. In the first place, since ethics most often gives us prescriptions regardless of their unintended consequences (one may think here, for example, of Kant's profoundly counter-intuitive "fiat iustitia, pereat mundus"), we should be aware of the dangers of an ethically inspired political practice. Ethics, by its very nature, is not interested in unintended consequences (with the ex-

ception of consequentialism and its variants) and is therefore a powerful
generator of unintended consequences if applied in politics. And indeed,
the modern welfare state is a real *Fundgrube* of examples of how ethically
inspired political decisions may go awry in practice. The best of intentions
often fathers the worst results. One decides that one ought to help a specific category of individuals only to discover that one is subsidizing another
category. And the opposite ethical intuition that, in order to avoid this, one
should *never* help *any* category at all, is, again, doing injustice to the initial category. Hence, both justice and the right-wing justice of injustice are
politically just as counterproductive. Justice and ethics are, here, like the
desire to possess a microscope that will give us a clear view of *all* the sections of the microscopic specimen at one time. The fact of this apparent
asymmetry between politicians' good and bad actions adds further support
to the anti-Stoic arguments developed in Chapter 2: political action is like
a pair of scissors cutting through the seamless texture of the Stoic political
order. There is a real incommensurability between the good and the bad
actions of statesmen: the commensurability that still exists in their delib-
erations about how to act is not mirrored by a similar commensurability as
far as the results of their actions are concerned. In this way the actions of
statesmen always create an essentially "new" world, in the same way that
this can be said of artists' actions. This is what one might properly call
"making history" in the sense that history always is the history of the dis-
turbances of a Stoic order. History is where Stoicism is not.

These considerations may seem fairly academic, and an example is called
for that could clarify the matter. Suitable examples can most easily be
found in the paradoxes of military strategy: what is often difficult to recognize in politics announces itself most clearly in the decisions of military
leaders and their consequences. More than does politics, warfare aims at the
quickest and clearest articulation of the (unintended) consequences of the
actions of its principal agents. More than in politics and diplomacy (where
transactions are often lengthy and not very transparent, and where all kind
of contingencies may frustrate even the soundest decisions), it is necessary
for military strategists to subsume, as much as possible, the future of unintended consequences in their decisions. The world of military strategy
is, perhaps more than any other aspect of human existence and decision-
making, governed by a paradoxical logic in which all the ironies of our
decision-making most clearly present themselves. The old wisdom of "si
vis pacem, para bellum" may well be seen as the model for the interrela-

tion between history, politics, and irony that is the subject of the present discussion. As was suggested by Michael Howard,

> This can be illustrated from elementary tactics. The direct approach to an objective, as Liddell Hart pointed out, will probably be the least productive, since it is likely to be the most strongly defended. The best approach may be the indirect one. But once it is clear that that *is* the best approach it will cease to be so, because the enemy will react appropriately: the direct approach, because it is so evidently the worst, then may become the best. In strategy, therefore, as Luttwak puts it in a phrase worthy of Clausewitz, "a course of action . . . will tend to evolve into its opposite.". . . The great virtue in military operations is therefore flexibility: the capacity to confront the adversary with the unexpected.[34]

We see admirably illustrated here the perplexities caused by the need to subsume the ironies of history in politics, or military strategy.

This wish to subsume unintended consequences as much as possible under political or military action can even lead to a total standstill of history. One can think of nuclear armament, where overlooking unintended consequences has more serious consequences than anywhere else. Overlooking one unintended consequence could easily lead here to the physical destruction of a large part of humanity. In practice this led to a kind of internalizing of the future of political and strategic decisions in the present; it was as if a potential future was rolled back into the present (of decision-making) and was absorbed in it. In this way a potential history (of actual nuclear warfare) was eliminated from the range of possible futures (for good, we may hope). It is as if the act of inventing the nuclear weapon and a political appreciation of the consequences of using this weapon absorbed all potential future acts into itself; it is as if history condensed itself into that one moment of invention. This permits us to establish the following contrast between Thomas Mann's "radical" and the "conservative" politician mentioned in the introduction to this chapter. Precisely by ignoring history (in the sense of the disregard for unintended consequences typical of the radical politician), the radical historian is the creator of history par excellence, whereas the conservative historian attempts to kill history because of his or her respect for it.

All this seems to be an amazing supplement to how Nietzsche in his second untimely meditation characterized the relationship between life and action. Nietzsche argued that all meaningful action, action actually serving the cause of life, will require a certain amount of forgetting. "Just as according to Goethe the person who acts will be unscrupulous [*gewissenlos*]," according to Nietzsche, "so he is also always, to a certain extent, thoughtless [*wissenlos*]. For he must forget all other things to do just this one thing; he is therefore unjust towards what is behind him in the past and he recognizes only one right: the right of what now has to come into being." [35] The coming into being of action, of history, therefore requires a forgetting of history: history originates in those actions that seem to deny its (effective) existence.

This is the counterpart of the argument with regard to the avoidance of nuclear warfare. For there, too, a certain amount of forgetting (of unintended future consequences) is the condition of the coming into being of a specific (disastrous) future history. So both Nietzsche's argument and our own suggest that the subsumption of history into politics (either by the incapacity to forget or by a certain nonchalance with regard to the future) that is discussed here will lead to a standstill in history. The past only comes into being by forgetting, and by a certain nonchalance with regard to the future, since these two things are the prerequisites of action. If we could foresee all the unintended consequences of our actions (a possibility that is, of course, ruled out because such foreknowledge is in contradiction with the notion of *un*-intended consequences) there would be no history—and that suggests, once again, the most intimate relationship between history and the notion of unintended consequences. Without the one we cannot have the other.

This may already make clear what problems will present themselves in relation to MacIntyre's suggestion to subsume history into politics. The extent to which this suggestion appears to be feasible *in politicis*, the extent to which the politician succeeds in acting according to the supreme political maxim, "always act in such a way that your later historian will account for your actions by looking at them from the same point of view as the one from your actions originated," the extent to which this seems possible, will always go hand in hand with the disappearance of history. The criterion for deciding whether the politician has succeeded in overcoming the ironies of history is similar. If politicians do not succeed in overcoming *Weltironie*, then there is indeed history, but it is necessarily the history of the politicians' shortcomings. And it follows that the notion of the subsumption of history in politics is strangely self-defeating. We have to conclude, therefore, that politics is essentially unironical—at least when irony is understood as *Weltironie*.

I want to conclude this section by emphasizing, once again, that the issues that have been discussed here are far from being of a merely academic significance. *Weltironie*, the reign of unintended consequences, can be seen to be so much a determining feature of the contemporary world that one would not be surprised if future historians decided to characterize the end of the second millennium, our age, as the Age of Unintended Consequences. Where Hegel in post-Napoleonic Europe could still optimistically discern in the workings of unintended consequences "the cunning of Reason" we have now learned to see there rather "the betrayal of Reason" or, better, "the self-ironization of Reason." Indeed, no age has been a more powerful generator of unintended consequences than our age of technology and democracy; and, in contrast to the success stories of Hegelian or Marxist dialectics, we unfortunately have had to recognize that the nature of *our* unintended consequences is almost invariably unpleasant.

Certainly in the case of science and technology the range of unintended consequences often exceeds by far that of the intended, desired, and expected consequences. Thus medical science has succeeded miraculously in curing many of the illnesses that killed our ancestors, but it has at the same time effected an aging population in the Western world that will test its resources, financial and otherwise, to the limit, and even worse, a population explosion in the Third World that will only be slowed down in the dismal way predicted by Robert Malthus two centuries ago. Physics created the atom bomb that ended World War II but that may well end human history in World War III, even though, after the disintegration of the Soviet Union, such a world war is, for the time being, less likely than it used to be in the preceding four to five decades.

Technicians developed the combustion engine that mobilized the global population, but that also enveloped the globe in a shell of noise, stench, and pollution. One need not be a pessimist to fear the political conflicts that will arise if, within some 30 to 35 years (according to the most recent predictions), global oil reserves will begin to run out and no substitute has been discovered for this lifeblood of our complex and vulnerable economies. Agriculture has dramatically multiplied its output per acre, but this further increases our demands and destroys an ecological system that is the precarious and vulnerable equilibrium achieved in a process of billions of years. Associated climatological changes may turn large parts of the earth's surface into uninhabitable deserts. The combined effort of scientists, technologists, and the democratic state created a welfare state guaranteeing to most of the population of Western countries a material well-being that previous generations could not even dream of, but at the same time this welfare state, by a logic still far from being understood, let alone counteracted, effected the phenomena of "jobless growth" and of a "fraying" of the middle classes that have always been the backbone of Western society and Western democracy and that are, arguably, the sociological condition for its survival.

These developments of the last few decades are all the more ominous since the kind of unintended consequences that were enumerated just now all have in common the unfortunate feature of being problems that affect us all in a more or less similar way and that therefore, as we observed in Chapter 3, do not fit well in the democratic machinery that was developed in the first half of the nineteenth century and that still is our only political resource for solving our problems. It is as if the relatively well-defined problems that more or less spontaneously announced themselves in the social and political conflicts of the last two hundred years, and that democracy knew to solve so remarkably well, have now been transformed into a set of strangely faceless problems that we must first learn to look for and to recognize. This is what we may expect to be the nature of unintended consequences.

Put differently, the social and political problems of the nineteenth and twentieth centuries were the kind of problems that one was born with and that to a large extent even defined one's life. One really lived the life of the bourgeois or of the proletarian, and one lived the political conflicts resulting from this coinciding of life and social role. It was the very obviousness of the social and political conflicts resulting from such oppositions that was, in fact, a large part of the nature of the social and political conflict in question. Our present main political problems often (though not always, if one thinks, for example, of the ghettos in American cities) have a dimension of chaos that is only vaguely perceived at the edges of our existence and is even denied by those who still believe that political problems can only arise from conflict. Yet this chaos, the unintended consequence of our rational decisions and actions, is a chaos that we have effected in the *Umwelt* and that is the condition for the possibility of all human existence.

So, in a way, we seem to have returned to the medieval world ruled by the Goddess of Fortune. "Reason, the Liberator, became Fortune the Goddess of Chaos": this is how we might paraphrase the statement by Spragens that was cited above, in order to harmonize it more with our present political predicament. It is, perhaps, the supreme irony of Reason that it has brought us, after a bright and marvelous day in the sun of Reason (a very short day, moreover, since it did not last much longer than the third quarter of this century), back into the darkness of the medieval "Fortuna Imperatrix mundi."

10. Romantic Irony

Japp assures us "that history only knows *versions* of irony."[36] Following Japp's suggestion we may agree that *Weltironie* does not provide us with the interesting interaction of irony with politics that we are looking for, but we may nevertheless hold that this need not be the end of our quest. Perhaps there are other versions of irony that will put a different complexion on the issue. So let us enlarge our notion of irony. Since Aristotle and Quintilianus irony has been seen above all as a rhetorical figure of speech, with the speaker meaning the opposite of what he or she is literally saying.[37] Now, it applies to all figures of speech that in a figurative, tropological sense they express something other than what is literally said. It can be argued that metaphor is the most fundamental figure of speech, insofar as it is metaphor rather than any of the others that provides us with the link between literal and figurative uses of language and, hence, elucidates how figurative utterances arise out of literal language—other figures of speech can be demonstrated to be mere further specifications of the semantic inversion effected by the metaphor. The argument in question would show how, under certain circumstances, a set of purely literal statements may coalesce into a metaphor, thus presenting metaphor as a kind of "missing link" between the literal statement and figurative speech.[38] If, then, irony is a further specification of the metaphor (like synecdoche and metonymy), then it seems worthwhile to begin by making a closer comparison between metaphor and irony.[39]

Metaphor and irony behave differently in similar contexts, and studying these differences will deepen our understanding of irony. Let us focus our attention on what happens when we negate figurative utterances.[40] First I will note a general characteristic of negation. Suppose we have the figurative statement "A is B" (for example, the metaphor "John is a pig"); then the negation can have the character of either "it is not true that A is B" or "A is not B." When I speak of a negation of figurative utterances I will especially have the second interpretation in mind. The reason for this is that nearly everything important in figurative utterances takes place between what is to be found in the places of A and of B—and the first interpretation obviously has a position outside the field of interaction between A and B. The first interpretation merely negates whatever the result of the interaction may be, whether or not it constitutes a correct or useful characteristic of (a part of) reality.

Bearing this in mind, let us have a look at what happens when we negate the metaphor "A is B" ("John is a pig"). In accordance with the second interpretation this results in "John is *not* a pig." Let us ignore the fact that this negation, first of all, expresses an uninteresting literal truth (since John is a human being, he cannot be a pig), though it certainly is an interesting fact about metaphor that from the point of view of negation there is an asymmetry between the original (figurative) ironic utterance and its literal, negated counterpart. Leaving aside, then, this transformation of metaphor into literalness by negation, we will observe that the negation of metaphor ordinarily is intended to reject the point of view that was proposed by the original metaphor. If one says, for example, "John is not a pig" one ordinarily will be wishing to express one's disagreement with the suggestion that John eats in an ill-mannered way, behaves rudely, and so on. That is to say — and this is my main point here — the negation tends to move to a semantic area *outside* the "interaction" (to use Black's metaphor of metaphor) of "John" and "pig"; that is, one is saying here that "it is not true that John is a pig, eats without manners," and so on. In other words, negation in the sense of the second interpretation tends to transform into negation in the sense of the first interpretation. This is because the negation apparently does not manage to penetrate into the field of interaction between A and B.

In the case of irony this is different. Suppose we deny the ironic utterance "Ann is a beauty" (in fact Ann is the opposite of a beauty) by saying: "Ann is no beauty." Then it must strike us that the meaning of the ironic utterance "Ann is a beauty" and its negation ("Ann is no beauty") is exactly the same. If we deny a metaphor, the negation is driven outside the metaphoric interaction of the concepts presented in metaphor, as a result of which the metaphoric nature of the utterance can effectively be retained in the negation as well. Denial of irony, however, immediately destroys the figurative nature of the utterance, because the negation can maintain itself in the field of the interaction between A and B and consequently can destroy the figurative nature of the utterance. Judging from its relatively weak resistance to negation, it seems reasonable to conclude that the figurative nature of irony is clearly weaker than that of metaphor.

The differences between irony and metaphor can be illustrated on the basis of the example "John is a greyhound," which has the advantage, from the point of view of the present discussion, that it can be interpreted both ironically and metaphorically. When looking for an example like this it is interesting that metaphoric interpretations are always so much more obvious than ironic ones. The dots in "A is . . ." can be filled with almost anything without making it impossible to think of a plausible metaphoric interpretation of the statement. One only succeeds at an ironic interpretation when the opposite of what we associate with B in the statement "A is B" can be associated with A. In comparison with metaphor this imposes an important limitation on what B can stand for in the ironic interpretation. Moreover, it seems to be the case that in irony much more knowledge of context and of A is required than in the case of metaphor. If one is unacquainted with Ann one will even not recognize the irony of "Ann is a beauty" and see here merely a literal statement (which would be most exceptional in the case of metaphor). Hence, irony is the figure of speech for insiders; because metaphor only focuses attention on itself (namely, on the strong interaction between A and B), metaphor, in contrast to irony, has the power to *unite* outsiders. Metaphor precedes or creates sociability, irony presupposes sociability and feeds on it. In any case, the prevalence of the metaphoric interpretations of "A is B" over ironic interpretations once again proves the relative weakness of irony if compared to metaphor.

Let us now take a closer look at this ambiguous utterance "John is a greyhound" and wonder what will happen in the case of negation. Now, no reasonable language user will interpret the statement "John is *no* greyhound" any differently from "John is slow." If apparently "John is slow" is the opposite of "John is a greyhound," then the favorite interpretation of "John is a greyhound" must of course be "John is fast" (or some other equivalent). Once again we can see the prevalence of metaphor over irony and the weakness of the interaction between A and B in irony's case. Only when one wishes to detect a so-called understatement in "John is no greyhound"—another figure of speech, or simply another variant of irony?—will the irony be retained in the negation.

On the basis of the differences between the metaphor and irony observed just now we can sum up the main characteristics of irony in the following five points:

1. Irony is a specification of metaphor: metaphor is the paradigmatic trope (hence the fact that nearly all the abundant contemporary literature on tropology deals almost exclusively with metaphor), while irony with

its operator of the negation further determines (and thereby weakens) the nature of the metaphoric interaction.

2. Although the semantic range of irony is narrower and more limited than that of metaphor, the meaning of irony still remains vaguer and more open than that of the metaphor. Johnson's ironic statement on Bolingbroke—"He was a holy man"[41]—leaves open a larger variety of semantic options than, for instance, "John is a pig." Irony is directed at divergence, metaphor at convergence. Insofar as figures of speech create an atmosphere of semantic freedom, irony can be associated with negative freedom and the metaphor with positive freedom (to use a political metaphor).

3. Metaphorical meanings of utterances like "A is B" are nearly always possible, while an ironic meaning can only be realized under certain conditions. It is hard to interpret "John is a pig" ironically (and when we nevertheless would wish to force an ironic interpretation, the ironic meaning will only come into being via the more obvious metaphoric interpretation). Probably the negative aspect of this characteristic of John's elicits here the negation of irony so much that the ironic meaning simply does not get enough space to articulate itself at all. On the basis of similar cases one could perhaps derive a general rule concerning the limitations to which irony apparently is subject: unlike positive qualifications (as, for example, "that's a pretty business!" or "fine doings these!") negative qualifications (like "that is sad") can hardly be made into ironic statements. Negative qualifications will remain inexorably literal, however much we may try to interpret them ironically.

4. Metaphor is introverted in the sense that everything comes to focus on what happens between A and B in the figure of speech "A is B." Because the functioning of irony is so much more dependent on what A and B stand for, and on how what they stand for is conceptualized in the figure of speech, than is the case with metaphor, one may conclude that irony is clearly more context-dependent and context-determined than metaphor. Even more so, it is predominantly context that will determine whether a figure of speech will be able to function as irony at all. Phrased differently, where metaphor commits itself to and locks itself within the level of language (where the meanings of A and B are situated), irony mobilizes a nonlinguistic context, a "dehors texte." As we shall see in the last section of Chapter 6, this is even more true of paradox. The difference between irony and paradox is, however, that irony is content merely to appeal to and make use of knowledge of a nonlinguistic context, whereas paradox really forces

us to turn to reality itself, and to acquire a knowledge of the extralinguistic context that we did not possess before. Paradox expresses an even greater respect than the literal statement has for what reality actually is like. But to return to the differences between irony and metaphor: the latter has an affinity with closure (although to a far lesser extent than the literal use of language); irony is open and suggests an intellectual abstinence. Metaphor aims at a closing or a rounding off, at summary and conclusion; irony looks for semantic freedom and dispersion.

5. Distance is manipulated differently by metaphor and irony. Metaphor always starts with shocking us by the initial distance between (or "semantic deviance" of) A and B in the figurative statement, but in order to comprehend metaphor that (semantic) distance must be removed and a certain fusion of A and B effected. However, it is metaphor's purpose to transform this undoing of *semantic* distance into the creation of distance between *language* and *reality*. Horizontal distance on the level of language is exchanged for a vertical distance between the world and the metaphorical point of view from which the metaphor invites us to see reality. In metaphor language is placed at such a distance from reality that we can get the best survey of what goes on in it. And all the intellectual energy mobilized by metaphor is invested in creating this distance rather than in checking the truth of what is seen from the perspective that is proposed by metaphor. Irony, on the other hand, starts with an utterance that may seem to be an unexciting literal statement devoid of semantic deviance (like "Ann is a beauty"), but which on closer examination, by means of our knowledge of or even our direct confrontation with its subject, appears to possess a hidden meaning. Unlike metaphor, irony thus diminishes the distance between language and reality; or it only comes into being in a context when this distance is diminished. But then the reverse of what takes place in metaphor happens: now a wide variety of meanings are left open. "Ann is a beauty" or Johnson's "He was a holy man" suggests rather what we should *not* think than what we *should* think. In sum, metaphor begins with a reduction of (semantic) distance, then creates a distance between language and the world; irony begins with reducing the distance between language and the world and then effects a more or less unchecked dispersion of meaning. To put it metaphorically, irony draws language close to reality and then produces a relatively free dissemination, dispersion, or proliferation of meaning.

Judging from what was said above about irony (in comparison with metaphor), a discussion of so-called romantic irony now recommends itself.

For, out of all forms of irony, romantic irony most closely corresponds to the above five findings. Naturally, the correctness of this observation could only be shown on the basis of an encyclopedic discussion of all forms of irony that have been developed since Socrates. Fortunately, such a procedure would be as unnecessary as it would be tedious. If we suppose that there would indeed be a form of irony harmonizing even better with the above than romantic irony, then this would only result in an even stronger argument in favor of my claims in the rest of this section.

Romantic irony is a creation of Adam Müller, Karl Solger, and especially Friedrich Schlegel. Schlegel does not limit irony to separate sentences. For him a whole literary work can be just as ironic as the individual ironic utterance: "There are old and modern poems, breathing continuously, everywhere and throughout, the divine spirit of irony."[42] Schlegel extols irony to such an extent that it becomes the cornerstone of an all-encompassing aesthetic theory. Schlegel is of the opinion that in the creative process the artist must again and again ironize him- or herself, while continuously ironizing, at the same time, the relationship between the work of art on the one hand and idea and reality on the other. Here irony no longer is a figure of speech that we can prefer to use or not to use, but a dimension that is constitutive of each work of art, and which is the heart of everything we should take seriously in it from an aesthetic point of view.

What is the rationale behind this immoderate expansion of the concept of irony? It is to be found in Schlegel's philosophical psychology of the artist. The recurrent basic idea underlying this philosophical psychology—and this will be central to my argument—is that in Schlegel's view the artist manages to place him- or herself in a relationship to that self. The artist places him- or herself in some relation to that self, at an ironic distance from that self, and only within the area of tension thus arising can the artist create the work of art. Solger's aesthetics may contribute to a better understanding of the idea. To Solger the work of art is the place where idea and reality meet each other; for the work is the *material* object within which an *idea* is given shape. Therefore the work of art is to Solger essentially ironic, because from this intermediate position it effects an ironization of both reality and idea.[43] This clarification is in agreement with what has been said above about irony's effort to move closer to reality, while, during and because of this movement, it will unfold itself in a dissemination or dispersion of contradictory meanings. Meaning is here like a meteor that is torn apart by the gravitational forces of the sun or planet that the meteor encountered during its journey through the solar system. It is as if, in the destruction of the self-referential and deluding structures of language by reality's gravitational forces, an ironic and aesthetic meaning comes into being that brings us closest to reality. And the same is true, according to Schlegel, for the artist. For just as for Solger the work of art is situated between the spheres of what is ideal and what is real, so to Schlegel the work of art is born within the distance that arises when the artist places him- or herself in some ironical relationship to that self—here, too, ironically denying both poles of the relationship thus created. For both Solger and Schlegel the origin of romantic irony is to be situated in—I am now citing Schlegel—"that which refers to the connection or separation of the ideal and the real."[44] Aesthetic truth is not, as in metaphor, a construction of meaning out of already existing "bricks," but a breaking apart of these bricks of meaning that is effected by the pull of reality. Metaphor removes us from reality, irony brings us ever closer to it—and the coherence of meaning is the victim of the movement (as meaning comes into being by our responding to metaphor's call to move away from reality).

It has pleased Schlegel to make use of the word "transcendental" to characterize this effort of the artist to place him- or herself in an ironic relationship to that self; this concept thus has a meaning for Schlegel that is quite different from Kant's and Fichte's use of the word, although the *Wissenschaftslehre* was supposedly an important source of inspiration for Schlegel's aesthetics.[45] For Schlegel the concept "transcendental" does not refer to the conditions for the possibility of knowledge, but to "a relationship of the human being and of the artist to himself that is determined in freedom and, hence, bound in itself."[46] In this transcendental relation to himself the artist can transcend himself in self-irony: hence Schlegel's *dictum* "irony is a permanent 'parekbasis.' "[47] In this self-transcending, self-ironizing *parekbasis* the artist risks himself in the artistic creative process, in which nothing is given to him except for the vertigo of a frightening freedom: aesthetic irony "is the freest of all licenses [*die freyeste aller Licenzen*], since it is through aesthetic irony that one transcends oneself; and yet, at the same time, strictly bound by law, since it is absolutely necessary."[48] In this self-transcendence in freedom, the self is merely the starting point, while the movement of transcendence is itself indefinite and undetermined: irony "contains and evokes a feeling of the insoluble struggle between what is and what is not undetermined."[49] But that does not in the least imply, as one might have expected, that this aesthetic, ironic freedom should be arbitrary; Schlegel always emphasizes (and that is the decisive step in Schlegel's rather uncertain march through this brushwood of oppositions) the need to find a balance in the polarities deliberately created by the artist within himself. The ironic dispersion or distance created by the artist within himself must be such that it will result in a balance between extremes; a balance or equilibrium that Novalis indicated by the two words "reflection" (*Besonnenheit*) and "self-discovery" (*Sichselbstfindung*).[50] Romantic irony is a self-unfolding in a set of ever further proliferating oppositions, but such that these proliferating oppositions achieve a balance that does justice both to the poet and to reality. Romantic irony is therefore essentially a matter of balance, of a "floating" between or above extremes, to put it in the metaphor favored by Romantics themselves that would, as we saw in Chapter 3, so profoundly irritate Carl Schmitt a century later.[51] This, then, is how in Schlegel's aesthetic theory the concepts of irony, of dispersion and distance, of what he understood by the "transcendental" and, above all, by the artist's being in some relationship to himself, were interwoven in his concept of Romantic irony.

Romantic irony was looked upon by Hegel with utter contempt; his dissatisfaction with Romantic irony will further clarify it, and therefore we should devote a few comments to it. One would expect, if one thinks of his speculations on how Spirit moves from negation to negation, that Hegel would be well disposed toward Romantic irony. Yet the very opposite is true. Hegel accused Romantic irony and its theorists, with an uncompromising fierceness anticipating Schmitt, of a complete lack of involvement with the seriousness of life and of history:

> This is the real meaning of this brilliant and divine irony, conceived as a concentration of the self on itself, and for which all restrictions have been eliminated and that is content to live exclusively in the happiness of self-satisfaction. This is the irony that Herr Friedrich von Schlegel has concocted, and many others have already parroted him or parrot him again now.[52]

So where, then, is the essential distinction between Romantic irony and Hegel's own dialectics? What Hegel found so utterly repulsive in Romantic irony is that it seemed to freeze the historical movement of dialectical negation at a certain point instead of developing towards a new negation. To use Hegel's own terminology, Romantic irony got stuck in positivity (*Positivität*) instead of recognizing the development of history that is guaranteed by negation (*Negativität*). It is a kind of halfway dialectics, and therefore in Hegel's eyes a ridiculous parody of his own effort. To put it differently, negation is for Hegel the motor of the dialectical unfolding of the Spirit, but *as such* only instrumental. What really counts are the different contents the Spirit acquires and loses during its dialectical march through history. Hence for Hegel negation and irony are mere shadows in comparison to the majesty of the self-unfolding of the Spirit in history, shadows that are the illusory side-effects of the majestic march of Reason. Negation and irony are merely a graceful dance around the fixed, "serious" line of the gradual self-realization of the Spirit.

That is where we should situate the difference between Hegel's dialectics and Schlegel's Romantic irony: where Hegel sees the seriousness of a continuing historical process within which negation is only of instrumental importance, Schlegel's frivolous Romantic irony feels no urge at all to systematize the results of ironic negation within some speculative philosophy of history. To phrase it pregnantly: confronted with the alternative of "victrix causa Diis placuit, sed victa Catoni," Hegel would have wished to identify himself with the Gods while Schlegel would have been content to be a mere Cato of the lost causes. Put differently, Hegel accuses Schlegel of an unwillingness to move in the same direction as world history: for the semantic dispersion and proliferation of his Romantic irony takes place in a direction *at a right angle* to that of history. And the result is — as Hegel observes with disgust — "an arrogant and complacent attitude, so that one does not really care about the issue itself and thinks oneself to be much superior to it; indeed one does not care about it and believes oneself to be beyond it, indeed one has assumed a position completely alien to the issue itself." [53]

11. *Politics and Romantic Irony*

For all his idealism, Hegel criticized Romantic irony in the name of realism, reasonableness, and meaningful action; his criticism will therefore convince most of us, who will immediately be ready to share Hegel's "nononsense" mentality. Schlegel's ironic freedom, this "freest of all licenses," is, in fact, the empty and irresponsible freedom of not committing oneself to anything, the attitude of someone who is ready to withdraw from everything, from all practical business. It is the intellectual legitimation of a universal nonparticipation in anything that might matter to our world. [54] This famous "floating," which was thought particularly attractive by Schlegel and Adam Müller, permitted them to adopt a position supposedly superior to and so beyond all the issues that were at stake in the historical and political reality of their times. As Hegel sensed, they were actually trying to marginalize their time, but by attempting to do so they succeeded only in marginalizing themselves. A case in point is Müller's ironic suggestion to the Prussian government to have two magazines appear simultaneously under his name: one magazine fervently supporting the government, and another one equally fervently opposing the government. What was to be expected from such a comedy? How could history, or any real interest, be served by not committing oneself to any party, or to commit oneself, as Müller tried, to mutually opposed parties?

However much sympathy we feel for Hegel's no-nonsense attitude toward Romantic irony, it can be argued that the latter was less a cult of irrelevance than may seem to be the case. Let us first of all remember that the possibility of being in a Schlegelian "transcendental relationship" to oneself was, as Hegel had argued elsewhere, perhaps the most important discovery in the whole history of humanity. For in this most moving passage in the whole of his philosophical oeuvre, in his exposition of the tragic conflict between Socrates and the Athenian state, Hegel described how Socrates had been the first, with his unpractical Socratic doubt, to take the same kind of ironic attitude toward himself and toward the "Sittlichkeit" of his age as had been recommended by Schlegel to the artist. And Hegel had impressively shown how all this marked a new phase in world history, since with his irony Socrates had been the first to teach human individuals to think about themselves and to look at themselves from a certain ironic distance.[55] Within the whole argument of Hegel's *Reason in History*, his account of the fate of Socrates is the real and decisive hinge in human history, and thus the strongest historical and philosophical corroboration of Schlegel's speculations on irony that one could possibly imagine. Hegel's exposition of the significance of Socrates' career for human history is certainly not to be regarded as some anomaly in his system, contradicted by its major aims. On the contrary. As Hegel often liked to point out, and actually did on many occasions, civilization and culture presuppose the willingness and ability to objectify oneself, to place oneself in some relation to oneself and thereby also to risk oneself. It is this that distinguishes us from animals, which are typically incapable of placing Reason between themselves and their instinctive urges. Yet in this willingness to objectify and to risk oneself, we may also discern a crucial difference between Romantic irony and Hegel's dialectical irony: unlike Hegel, Schlegel did not offer the dialectical certainty, grandeur, and majesty of the historical unfolding of the Spirit as a reassuring counterweight against self-ironization. The self-ironization of Romantic irony is really and uncompromisingly bottomless; that is where its weakness can be discerned (as Hegel correctly saw), but that is also where it confronts us with a challenge going far beyond Hegel's dialectical irony.

Hegel had characterized the mental revolution effected by Socrates as follows:

> It thus happened that from now on individuals could satisfy themselves in a world of ideas, without chaining themselves to the state. Precisely the greatest people delivered themselves to this world of ideas and thus became unpractical. In this way "rhathymia" [the psychological state of self-dispersion that one may associate with Romantic irony] set in, and from the principle that it is the mind which determines what is right, the questions arose whether there are Gods and what they are, what justice is, what is right and virtuous, etc.[56]

It was Socrates who first gave shape to this *rhathymia*, to this impractical dispersion or dissemination of the self, to this discovery that one may enter into a relationship to oneself. It was thus Socrates who was, in Hegel's view, the creator of all civilization and culture. This Hegelian suggestion to link (the origins of) civilization to the human individual's capacity to be in an ironic relationship to him- or herself finds additional support in Freud's *Civilization and Its Discontents* (whose Hegelian propensities have often been pointed out).[57] Freud argues here that civilization neuroticizes us by forcing us into a continuous frustration of our deepest and most basic urges: "Civilization, therefore, obtains mastery over the individual's dangerous desire for aggression by weakening and disarming it and by setting up an agency within him to watch over it, like a garrison in a conquered city."[58] And in this way, as was suggested by Hegel and in Schlegel's Romantic irony, an opposition is created within ourselves between the "conquered city" and its "garrison"; the strained relationship between the two is the Freudian, psychoanalytic matrix for understanding the ironies of our psyche. And, just like Hegel and Schlegel's psychology of the artist, it is precisely this unhappy opposition in ourselves that not only explains our "discontent" with civilization, but also why this opposition is often most clearly felt by the greatest minds. As Rorty put it, with a Machiavellianism that we will rarely observe when he writes about what goes on *between* human beings, instead of *inside* them: "When Freud told us that we had sexual repression to thank for the hang-ups of the neurotics who created European culture, he meant exactly what he said."[59]

Moreover, Freud's quasi-Hegelian notion of the relationship between the self and civilization (and of how this relationship ironically divides the self against itself) is only one illustration of the ironical nature of psychoanalysis, to which others can be added. To begin with, one may forthrightly state that psychoanalysis is irony systematized into self-knowledge—to enter into an self-ironizing relationship with oneself is, ultimately, what psychoanalysis is all about. Or, to take a more specific example, one could think of the Freudian failure (*Fehlleistung*), where the speaker is determined not to admit a painful or improper thought "to speech, and then one makes a slip of the tongue, i.e. against one's own will the repressed thought or idea is then converted into a statement, by slightly changing the expression of permitted intentions, by mixing itself with the latter, or even completely taking their place."[60] The entering into a relationship to oneself is demonstrated *ad oculos* by the Freudian *Fehlleistung*.

Another powerful confirmation of the Romantic irony that structures our minds can be found in the role played by negation in the practice of psychoanalysis, which manifests itself most clearly in the fact that an emphatic and explicit negation may be expected to hide a confirmation—irony can indeed be considered to be the favorite figure of speech of the language of the soul. But, most of all, within the psychoanalytical matrix mental disorders are conceived of as the victory of one part of the self over others; for example, if the "garrison" of Freud's metaphor becomes a too severe ruler of the "conquered city" and interaction between the two tends to cease, neurosis will be the result. We might, therefore, contrast the "seriousness" of the neurotic with the "Romantic irony" of the healthy self that is able to stand in relationship with itself. Freud would disagree with Schlegel about the psychology of the artist, however, because it is for Freud, unlike Schlegel, the "seriousness" of the neurotic, and not the Romantic irony characteristic of the healthy individual, that created civilization.

Let us now return to our own time and ask ourselves what model is best suited for understanding it: the dialectics of Hegel or Schlegel's Romantic irony? So, Hegel or Schlegel (that is, Fukuyama or the postmodernists)? The answer cannot be difficult: we no longer believe in the Hegelian linearity of the historical process. We now like to smile at the naivety of the great meta-narratives that nineteenth-century liberal bourgeois citizens and twentieth-century proletarians liked to tell each other with so much enthusiasm. Our modern Western European societies are no longer inspired by the desire to fulfill some kind of historical, emancipatory assignment, and will therefore feel little affinity with Hegel's world-historical seriousness. The emancipated society is the ironic society. And of even more importance is this: if we can indeed be said to live in "the Age of Unintended Consequences," in an age where the ironic discrepancy between our intentions and the results of our actions so often and so disagreeably surprises us, and if we thus see ourselves forced to subsume, as much as possible, the consequences of our actions in these actions themselves, the picture emerging from all this is a kind of "freezing" of Hegelian dialectics and a proliferation of actions and self-ironization in a present in which we attempt to slow down historical time as much as possible.

This history of the emancipation of Reason, the bourgeoisie, and the proletariat has been exchanged for the need to suppress history because of our present obligation to confront challenges that do not permit of a dialectical, historical solution. The great struggles of humanity in the past required a Hegelian unfolding in time; our present struggles, in contrast, require us to fold up possible futures in the present—or at least to act as if this were possible. Schlegel, and not Hegel, therefore presents us with the best model for understanding our own time. Hegel celebrates historical time, Schlegel and we attempt to nullify it.

This finally leads us to ask what conclusions regarding the present relationship between irony and politics must follow from our preference, as argued just now, for Schlegel to Hegel. This question can be answered best if we rephrase it in terms of what conceptions of reality we would be justified in attributing to Hegel and Schlegel. I am well aware that, especially with regard to Hegel, this is no small topic. The following comments do not therefore try to be a kind of canned history of philosophy. What I shall be doing is, rather, to contrast two positions with regard to reality and our relation to it, in the confidence that each of these two positions still shows enough of a family resemblance to Hegel's and Schlegel's arguments to justify an identification of these positions with the names of these gentlemen.

For Hegel, then, reality essentially is a dialectical process, and we can only be in a meaningful relationship to this reality if we investigate it from the point of view of dialectical logic. This is the methodological point Hegel wishes to make when, in the beginning of *Reason in History*, we are told that Reason governs the world and that history is a rational process. This is, of course, Hegel's historicized brand of Stoicism. And that means that we can get access to reality only by following, imitating, repeating, reenacting, and so on its ironical and dialectical unfolding. Or, to put it metaphorically, we must *identify* with reality, creep into it and investigate it "from the inside," as it were.

This is different from Schlegel. Schlegel's Romantic irony operates at right angles to Hegel's intellectual route. Schlegel's reality is not historicized—at most one could say that of the poet or the artist. Romantic irony is, therefore, not a feature of reality (as we could describe Hegelian dialectics), but should instead be attributed to the poet or the artist. Romantic irony and the kind of dialectics we might associate with it do not therefore operate in reality (as is the case in Hegel's work), but rather on the line connecting, so to speak, the poet or artist and reality. For Hegel reality must be explored from the inside and by repeating the same moves made by reality itself through the centuries. For Schlegel we can only move toward and away from reality on an imaginary line; it is, for him, Romantic irony that brings us closest to it, though this process of coming ever nearer to reality will always be accompanied by a disintegration, a dispersion into opposite directions, of meaning. In the case of Hegel, closeness to reality will achieve precisely the fullness of meaning.

We can argue, then, that politics seems to have occupied that line on which Schlegel's Romantic irony likes to move forward and backward. To put it differently, Schlegel's irony connects what is close by and far from us. Where the Hegelian conception of reality requires us to preserve or to imitate this regime of the near and far, Schlegel's irony is constructed to destabilize that regime, to permit freedom of movement on the imaginary line connecting the near and the far. Romantic irony ironizes and destabilizes the difference between the near and the far. And this ironic disintegration of the near and far may indeed contribute to a better understanding of contemporary politics. Present-day politics differs most strikingly from "Hegelian" politics in that all the traditional hierarchies of the near and the far—and everything associated with that—tend to turn into their former opposites. This ironic negation or destabilization of the traditional hierarchy of the relation between far and near we find at even the most direct, quasi-physical level. Politicians, royals, scholars, or whoever else is prominent have all become uncannily near in the sense that they now daily enter everyone's living room via television, which reveals everything from their personalities and intellectual abilities down to the peculiarities of their physical appearance; if, as we saw above, the eighteenth-century

Enlightened philosophers tried to pull down politics to the level of the drawing-room, now politics has been so accommodating as to reduce itself to that scale.

On the other hand the administrative lines separating us from those prominent figures have been extended endlessly. An immense bureaucracy has come into being in the domain between the ruler and the ruled, separating them in a way that would have been simply inconceivable in the ancien régime. In short, what used to be close by is now far off and what was far off is now close by. The notion of popular sovereignty has contributed to this confusion of the near and the far: if we now all believe in the peculiar fiction that the people rule (while in fact they obey) and the government obeys (while in fact it rules) then this fact alone must already create a background against which every perspective of far and near becomes possible. Here we see how the Stoic regime of the *tertia* has affected the relationship between the ruler and the ruled. The result is that we no longer have a scale on which to localize power and authority: they may be anywhere on the line connecting ourselves (or perhaps only some *part* of ourselves) to the political elite. A similar observation can be made from the point of view of the state. The state has also become aware that, in its dealings with the citizen, it has, to use the same metaphor as a moment ago, to take into account "lines" extending from itself into unfathomable societal depths, rather than with "points." Both the state and the citizen lack, so to speak, a "point of application" on that imaginary line from which they can have a firm grasp of and on each other. The fixities, certainties, and identifiable points of a Hegelian regime of politics have now become ironized by the smoothness of the line, and a sliding scale has emerged in the relationship between the state and the citizen. On this scale none of the parties concerned can any longer determine its exact position.

This ironical negation or destabilization of distances can even be observed on a global scale, as is argued by Hassan: "Our earth seems caught in the process of planetization, transhumanization, even as it breaks up into sects, tribes, factions of every kind."[61] Elsewhere he writes that "in a sense we have all learned to become minimalists—of that time and space we call our own—though the globe may have become our village."[62] The unknown and alien has become known and close by; the whole world has acquired a nearness sparing nothing and nobody; while what used to be close and within our grasp—a job, a future for our children, and, generally speaking, a certain relationship between what we do (or fail to do) and its consequences—seems to be determined by developments on a global scale completely outside our influence and even outside that of the national state to which we belong. Not being used to this (post-)modern ironization of distance, we still have an embarrassing myopia with regard to the near and presbyopia for the far (produced by a previous regime of the near and the far) blinding us to much that goes on in our contemporary world.

Turning, then, from the global scale to its opposite, that of the individual, a similar story can be told for the norms and values that used to structure our life. Some ten years ago MacIntyre eloquently argued and expressed the general feeling that there has been in contemporary society a loss of norms and values.[63] His argument was that the present "moral vocabulary" is the inconsistent hodgepodge of different and incommensurable moral vocabularies that we have inherited from the past and that linger on in the present. Multiculturalism, which seems to be the fate of our Western democracies, will further reinforce this integration of moral vocabularies. MacIntyre saw here the explanation of this much-lamented loss of moral and intellectual integrity that so many have observed in our societies. For what consistent set of norms can be derived from this moral chaos? I must say that I tend to be skeptical of this alleged loss of norms and values: even a superficial acquaintance with our past will make us realize that what has always been seen as such a loss of values is, ordinarily, little more than an exchange of old values for new ones that the *laudatores temporis acti* simply do not like, and are therefore unwilling or unable to recognize as norms at all. However, the essential anthropological datum is that man is, and has always been, a norm-loving animal. It will be hard to find examples of human societies that were content to live in a normative vacuum. In response to the rejoinder that Nazi Germany and its anti-Semitism provides us with such an obvious example, I would like to point out that many who lived in Nazi Germany were just as prepared to sacrifice their own lives for Nazi ideology as they were ready to sacrifice the lives of the Jews or of those who had the good sense to fight the Third Reich. And this can only be explained by a reference to the norms that these people accepted. Norms do not cease to be norms even if we have every reason to reject them. We should never forget the banal but indisputable truth that bad people may act in conformity with norms that they sincerely believe in, just as do good people.

But though I do not share MacIntyre's fears about a loss of norms and values, there is something more in MacIntyre's argument that deserves our attention. When MacIntyre paints his gloomy picture of contemporary morality as a desert littered by the ruins of the normative strongholds that used to be inhabited by previous generations, he certainly makes us aware of a serious problem. Let me put it this way. Unlike what we think (and would hope), norms and values function less as guidelines for what is and is not allowed in actual human action, than as an instrument to keep incommensurable or even contradictory needs at a reasonable distance from each other. The main function of norms and values is not that they tell us what we ought to do and ought not to do, thus paving the way for a better society. One has to be an incorrigible optimist to believe that norms and values could ever achieve these lofty goals. For as much as human beings are norm-loving animals, they do not hesitate to sin against the norms they accept. Indeed, this is not what norms and values primarily are for.

What makes norms and values indispensable is that they function as a kind of map on which we can quasi-geographically localize ourselves, our needs and desires, our relations with others, and so on, and establish how all these things are connected and what might be the consequences if we chose a certain course of action. In other words, without norms and values we will not so much be disposed to immoral action (the commonsensical opinion) as unable to act *at all*. Norms and values are not rules for how to behave (at least this is not their primary function); rather, they constitute an internalized map on which we can "simulate" our actions and their consequences. In this way they render our actions meaningful, coherent, and, to a certain extent, predictable. That does not mean that our commonsense intuitions with regard to norms and values would be entirely beside the point. It certainly is not my wish to suggest that we are not allowed to express a moral judgment of, let us say, the "moral map" of Nazi Germany and of how that map compares to the one in use in a decent parliamentary democracy. I was only making a statement of how these "maps" function for us as individuals—and then noting that what we customarily associate with norms and values is of a merely secondary practical significance.

For us as individuals moral discussions about why we should do A rather than B are just as pointless as discussions (to pursue the metaphor of the map) about why Paris is closer to London than to New York. What reasonable answer could one give to such a question and why should anyone want to know it? Moral and ethical debate only has a practical impact if whole "moral maps" are compared and contrasted; but if the history of our century has taught us one lesson, it is that we now know what unparalleled disasters may arise from such discussions (if applied outside the drawing-room). Similarly, moral discussions about principles of distributive justice would make sense only after it has been shown how they are located on our "moral map." As long as this issue is avoided the "schöne Seelen" who participate in this kind of discussion are like cartographers who do not trouble to have a look at the coastlines, rivers, cities, and so on that they are mapping.

And that brings me back to MacIntyre's desert littered with the moral ruins left by previous centuries. What is worrying about his characterization of our present predicament is that it suggests the difficulty, or even the impossibility, of making good moral maps anymore. Each moral ruin has, so to speak, its own rules for cartographic projection, its own conventions for what is listed on the legend, and so on, and not only do we miss a map in terms of which all the existing maps can be compared, we are not always capable of telling these different maps apart. An example is how the world of crime is gradually invading that of the state and sometimes even of the police. And one may think of what has recently become known about Italian politicians, their ties with the Mafia, and so on. It would be too easy to see here merely corruption and a loss of political responsibility—though that is undoubtedly true as well. However, it would be shortsighted and unintelligent to see here primarily a sign of political immorality. We should recognize, rather, that this is the inevitable result of different moral maps becoming entangled.[64] And due to that Romantic irony, so all-pervasive in our society, that also produced the blessings of our contemporary democracies (as we observed in Chapter 3), the distance that used to exist between these moral maps can be reduced and stretched arbitrarily—and many politicians and police officers will have observed how easy it is to introduce parts of one moral map into another. All the more so, since what actually transformed the moral maps that we inherited into MacIntyre's ruins has been their loss of exclusiveness. We have become tolerant, we respect each other and each other's moral maps, accept the merely local significance of all moral maps including our own; it is then sufficient to get in touch with people living in a world structured by different moral maps to begin to accept these other maps. And, once again, however much we may regret this confusion of maps, we must realize that we cannot have a democracy as we now have it without this taking place. Romantic irony with its destabilization of distance will inevitably produce this confusion of moral maps.

These unpleasant social phenomena will only go away if we opt for a different kind of democracy.

12. Conclusion: The Irony of Irony

But there is an even more important consideration. From a purely political
point of view the most dangerous consequence of the confusion of maps is
a loss of orientation and an increasing uncertainty in the domain of politics. For without a reliable moral map we will become uncertain about our
reasonable goals, about how others will react to us, about the whole fabric
of society (needless to add, this is not the kind of disorientation that could
be remedied by the social sciences—they would present us just another,
extra map, thereby adding to our perplexity). Hence, what one may expect
in a democracy that increasingly fits the model of Schlegelian Romantic
irony and the ironical disintegration of the regime of the near and the far is
a growing conviction of politicians that their professional life is like walking in a dark room, and that the best they can therefore do is to try to avoid
the nearest unsuspected obstacle while caring little about what part of the
room they are in the meantime moving to. Obviously, the dangers that are
always inherent in democracy's preference for the strategy of avoidance
will be further reinforced by the absence of moral maps, and will stimulate
in the politician a propensity to evade his or her responsibilities by resusci-
tating forms of direct democracy, by closing as much as possible the "aesthetic gap" between him- or herself and the citizen, and by focusing on the
short term rather than on the long term. In short, democracy will develop
all the features of a political regime whose disadvantages are now, perhaps
more than elsewhere in the Western world, visible in California, which is,
in many respects, for the Western world as a whole what America was for
Tocqueville's conceptions of democracy a century and a half ago.

Last, this disruption of the relationship between the near and the far
has an important consequence for the relation between state and society.
With regard to that relation we should begin with the following observation. Each definition of what is close by and far off necessarily presupposes
a background (like a Stoic tertium) against which distance and nearness
can be observed. Ordinarily this background was available in the form of
society itself. To put it differently, politics requires a *substratum* on which to
work—without that politics is as unthinkable as movement without some-

thing that moves—and that substratum is society. The oppositions that divided society against itself presented the politician with this background against which actions and decisions "made a difference": these oppositions provided the politician with the "logical space" within which he or she could locate and orient his or her actions. Politics needs something outside itself—that is, society—to define itself. A self-definition of politics in the absence of such an "outside" would make no sense, or would be a dangerous absurdity. From a logical point of view society is therefore primary to politics.

However, insofar as the above observation concerning the disruption of the relation between the near and the far is correct, we may infer that this will bring about a destabilization of the traditional relationship between politics and society. The state (or the representative) will no longer dare to be the intelligent and responsible solicitor of the represented; it will be judged according to how it (or the representative) serves the latter's interests simply because there are no longer more or less objective or identifiable criteria for coming to a conclusion about his or her freedom of movement with regard to the voter and the representative's (in)dependence of that voter. For the regime of the near and the far is precisely the regime that determines to what extent the politician can afford a certain independence with regard to the represented or not, to what extent it is safe to ignore public opinion in favor of some long-term goal, instead of being merely the mailbox of the voters. Speaking more generally, it determines whether the representative's political actions will be discernible and a possible object of judgment and appreciation at all. The ironization of the distance between the politician and the citizen will therefore result in the elimination of the meaningful contact between the voter and the politician that is the basis of a well-functioning democracy.

With regard to the situation arising as a consequence of this development, we feel initially inclined to distinguish between two alternative possibilities. The first possibility would be that politicians will prefer to return to variants of direct democracy in order to avoid (in the way that democracy always invites its principal agents to a strategy of avoidance) taking responsibilities without there being any sufficient guarantee that they may win rather than lose by assuming these responsibilities. The other alternative would be that politics and the politician will retreat into a sphere of autonomy with regard to the citizen that will safeguard them from conflicts with society. In one word, the Schlegelian ironization of the distance between state (representative) and the citizen (the represented) will force politicians to opt for either an identification with the represented or a movement toward a position altogether outside citizens' horizon. (The latter option can be achieved by becoming technical, by hiding in the bureaucracy or behind the political prescriptions by social scientists, and so on.) Any option between these two extremes can only weaken politicians' position in their contacts both with fellow politicians and with the electorate, and they will therefore avoid it. But we should realize that these two alternatives will, in the end, have the same results. For what both alternatives have in common is an attempt to hide politics from inspection by the citizen as much as possible. Within the former strategy this aim is achieved by suggesting a complete identification of politics with citizens; within the second politics is presented as a science in which only politicians can be expert.

To put it in the aesthetic terms used throughout this book, one could say that in the first alternative the state and the representative are modeled on the *objet trouvé*, where reality and its representation attempt to become indistinguishable, and, at the opposite end of the spectrum, on abstract art that can only be properly appreciated by the connoisseur. In both cases the requirements of representation (that should be formulated in terms of what the citizen, and *not* the state, would recognize as representation) have been circumvented. Romantic irony is, therefore, both the genesis of democracy and its nemesis: it defined the nature and purpose of political representation, but, in the end, it undermines representation in a way similar to how representation gradually became an irrelevancy in contemporary art. Romantic irony is both the lifeblood of democracy and the poison (or Derridean *pharmakon*) that kills it.

Excursus on the Apologetic Character of Political Debate in a Constitutional Democracy

A. INTRODUCTION

In 1661, the year before his death, Pascal wrote a short letter of less than four pages[65] that has been celebrated by Auerbach as "one of the major texts in Christian ethics."[66] As we shall see, this letter is of considerable interest in the context of the discussion in this and the previous chapter. But before turning to that, and to the letter itself, I must comment on the historical circumstances under which the letter was written.

After his conversion to Jansenism, Pascal became involved in the struggle between the Jesuits and the Jansenists that would ultimately result in the papal decree of 1657 requiring the Jansenists to sign a formulary in which they were to abjure their deviant theological convictions. This placed the Jansenists in a dilemma all too familiar in this age of religious struggle: one could submit to the legitimate authorities—in this case both the Pope and the king of France, since Louis XIV supported the Jesuits—or one could remain faithful to what one saw as the only true belief, to one's obligations as a Christian to God. Though the letter does not explicitly say what the Jansenists ought to do in this dilemma, this clearly is what made Pascal write the letter. And it is against this background that it should be read.

B. PASCAL'S LETTER

Pascal did not opt for the usual strategy in the dilemma by invoking his duty toward God as his highest obligation as a Christian. He was aware that this strategy would inevitably "privatize" discussion and eliminate one's chances of convincing others. Instead, with his uncanny (and to the Christian sometimes embarrassing)[67] talent for doing so, Pascal attempted—and succeeded—in reducing the issue from the level of theological speculation to that of a rational debate free from such "private" presuppositions.

Consequently, though Pascal was undoubtedly convinced of the truth of his Jansenist beliefs and of the falsity of those of his Jesuit adversaries, he carefully refrained from relying upon that kind of certainty in his argument. Instead, he preferred to give to it the form of how to deal rationally within a situation of theological conflict without thereby making use of any truth-claims for one's own position. In this way Pascal politicized the theological issue: not theological truth itself, nor what God expects us to do in the case of religious conflict or persecution, but what is rational to do under such circumstances now became the question that Pascal put on the agenda.[68] The "outside" of religion, which is subject to rational and public discussion, is politics in its purest form, as the history of the West has so amply made clear. This is not difficult to comprehend. For this trajectory from inner religious conviction to outward behavior repeats this exchange of the "vertical" relationship to God for "horizontal" social relationships in the Renaissance that was discussed at the beginning of this chapter and from which both modern politics and modern historical consciousness originated. Moreover, the significance of Pascal's letter can be explained by the fact that it focuses on precisely this trajectory.

The first step in Pascal's argument is the idea that for the Christian the same Providence that produces the good, permits what is evil and, once again, that the same Providence that enlightens some of us, may refuse intellectual illumination to others. Hence the same providential power that has allowed us to be in the right, may grant to others both the arguments and the physical violence enabling them to (attempt to) enforce their mistaken views on us. Since the same power (that is, God) works both in us and in our adversaries, we must acquiesce in the presence of the obstacles, as embodied in our adversaries, to our sincere efforts to vindicate the theological truth.

It follows from this that our outward behavior (that is, whether we can or cannot manage to bring ourselves to this resignation) is a more certain sign of our being in the right than our inner motives. For resignation is a better proof of our recognition of theological truth (that is, the fact that both truth and falsity may come from God) than any other (never completely reliable) argument that we might conceive in order to prove our rightness. Resignation embraces, so to speak, both the possibility that we are right and the possibility that we are wrong; it thus is more effective in protecting us against the possibility (which we can never completely exclude) of believing in a mistaken argument. Inner conviction is only sufficient in the case that we are right, whereas resignation covers both truth and falsity.

In a certain sense Pascal follows here a route that is diametrically opposed to the more famous one that was adopted by Descartes in his uncompromising search for the foundations of indubitable truth. Descartes left (publicly accessible) reality in favor of the privacy of inner conviction in order to discover truth there, whereas Pascal turned from that private domain to that of publicly observable behavior in order to be in the right.[69] Hence, when reading Pascal's letter, it is as if the Descartes of the *Meditations* had seen in some aspect or variant of publicly observable behavior the foundation of all truth, instead of finding this in the certainty of his cogito. Pascal's argument here therefore is one of those exceptionally rare examples in the history of Western thought in which, explicitly, the *forum externum* and our outward behavior are given a higher claim to truth than is customarily accorded to the *forum internum*, to conviction and rational argument.[70]

Pascal concludes his argument with a perceptive psychological explanation of why, in opposition to his own proposal, we naturally though mistakenly tend to privilege, with Descartes, the *forum internum*. This is, he writes, because we believe that we have the mission of vindicating the truth, whereas, in fact, our mission is merely to fight for the truth. Or, it is our desire for victory that makes us confuse these two quite different things, since we tend to infer, from our satisfaction about having achieved a victory, the objective proof of our being in the right. But this is a non sequitur.

C. THE POLITICAL SIGNIFICANCE OF THE LETTER

This astounding piece of apologetics can be transposed to political debate in a constitutional democracy. In order to see this we must begin by observing that Pascal's Providence or God puts us (or rather the Jansenist, to retain the context of Pascal's own argument) in much the same situation as the statesman in his dealings with the Goddess of Fortune (whose workings were discussed at length at the beginning of this chapter).

For in both cases truth and (inner) certainties are insufficient guides for meaningful action. In Pascal's case our firm and confident conviction of the right (and our choice to behave accordingly) may well prove to be precisely an indication of our being wrong (as was, according to him, the case with the Jesuits and with the Pope himself). And the Machiavellian statesman knows that neither factual nor moral truths will ever be sufficient for imposing his will on the Goddess of Fortune. But in neither of the two cases does it follow that truth would be irrelevant. How could the good Christian be indifferent to the truth about God and to the endeavor to gain it? The Machiavellian statesman, in his turn, will use all his knowledge and wisdom in order to avoid as much as possible those unpleasant unintended consequences in which the Goddess of Fortune customarily manifests herself. And, again, in both cases it is outward and publicly observable behavior that now takes precedence over inner convictions. If we patiently suffer the obstacles that Providence has put in our way, this is a surer sign of our agreement with Providence than we could ever get by closely and intensely scrutinizing our *forum internum* (as is recommended to us by Descartes and his numerous disciples down to the present day), even if we were to discover absolutely nothing evil or mistaken in it. Similarly, for Machiavelli it is publicly observable behavior, and neither intentions nor convictions, that makes one into a good or a bad statesman. The best of intentions may lead to the worst of results and vice versa.

So Machiavelli and that most Christian Jansenist author of the *Pensées* have more in common than we would have imagined at first sight. To both of them it is our outward behavior that is ultimately decisive, whereas our beliefs and convictions are reduced to mere shadows devoid of practical interest.

D. IMPLICATIONS FOR DEMOCRACY

This shift from our intentions, our convictions, and *forum internum* to our publicly observable behavior or the *forum externum* entails a powerful argument in favor of toleration.

In order to see this, we should begin with the observation that the objects of tolerance and intolerance are always opinions, and not the people that may or may not have these opinions; whereas the two correlated notions of indifference and concern describe how we may feel about people subscribing to opinions that we do not share. For example, we could not possibly "tolerate" the opinion that two plus two equals fifteen, because mistaken opinions about such issues do not permit of "toleration." To "tolerate" the opinion that two plus two equals fifteen would mean the end of the reliability of all our own arithmetic; we could no longer trust anything that we might need to do with numbers. On the other hand, the opinion that the death penalty is a good (or a bad) thing, is an opinion that we can "tolerate," since the opinion is open to reasonable debate and a public discussion of the issue may even be expected to improve the kind of social and political reality we presently live in. However, nothing so serious as "toleration" (or "intolerance") is any longer at stake when we are confronted with people with a different arithmetic than our own, or with other conceptions about the death penalty than we think preferable: for what is then at stake is whether we can permit "indifference" with regard to the existence of such people, or whether we ought to cherish deep-seated reasons to be "concerned" about the presence of such people in the sociopolitical world that we are living in. Generalization is what separates the case of people from that of opinions: opinions require, in principle, their being generally accepted (and then we cannot afford indifference), whereas what one person believes does not allow us to infer what others believe (and then indifference need not be a great risk). We may even observe a certain asymmetry here: for it may well be that opinions that we would not "tolerate" are held by people to whose existence we nevertheless are "indifferent" (think, for example, of people who believe that the earth is flat); on the other hand, we may be very much "concerned," and not in the least "indifferent," about the existence of people adhering to opinions that we nevertheless "tolerate" (as will typically be the case in political debate). The regime of "toleration" versus "intolerance" obeys a logic different from that of the regime of "indifference" versus "concern."

These considerations are in perfect agreement with the argument in Pascal's letter. For there can be no doubt that Pascal would under no circumstances be prepared to "tolerate" the opinions of his Jesuit adversaries, and he certainly would not expect the Jesuits to be prepared to "tolerate" Jansenist opinions. Pascal tended to discuss theological issues with the same uncompromising logic and rationality as his mathematics; and that unequivocally placed these issues outside the realm of what is mistaken, but can be "tolerated." But, as Pascal makes admirably clear, "toleration" simply is not the issue: we must avoid confusing the issue of truth and falsity (and of "toleration" and "intolerance") with the quite different issue of public and outward behavior (and of "indifference" and "concern"), and realize that behavior may have a claim to indubitability that discussions about the truth and falsity of (theological) opinions can never give us. For by behaving *as if* we could never exclude the possibility that we might be wrong (as paradigmatically expressed by our recognition of the truth that even "concern" could never result in "intolerance"), our behavior possesses a greater claim to truth than if we would decide otherwise, since it now embraces both the situation in which we are right *and* the one in which we would prove to be wrong. In a way the strategy is much the same as in Pascal's famous wager: betting on the existence of God is our best option when faced with the choice of whether or not He exists; and the bet invites us to a meta-level in relationship to the object-level of the truth and falsity of the statement that God exists. In both cases Pascal recommends, with good reasons, that we take a meta-position that will enable us to enjoy the best of both worlds (of truth and of falsity).

The following is crucial. All this *also* is an argument that, in its quality of being an argument, could be wrong. Maybe it is; but even its falsity would now no longer be of any importance, if we take into account the following. We should not rely on the (truth of the) argument itself and make the strength of our position dependent on *its* truth or falsity; but we should say, instead, "*if* the argument is correct, it would follow that our being either right or wrong will depend on our outward behavior (that is, whether our behavior expresses the recognition that we might be right or wrong, or not)." This is both sufficient and true. It is sufficient since anyone recognizing it can no longer doubt the superiority of the claims to truth of outward behavior to those of rational argument. Next, it is a truth since nobody could possibly doubt it—for saying that if a statement is correct, it is correct, is a (meta-)truth independent of the truth of the statement in question. So what Pascal essentially did was to bracket issues of truth and falsity by moving on to the (meta-)level of outward behavior—more specifically, to the kind of behavior expressive of a bracketing of issues of truth and falsity—and by showing, next, that this kind of behavior will always have a stronger claim to truth than any opinion one could possibly have, for whatever good reason one might have in favor of that opinion. Hence, Pascal's utterly un-Cartesian insight is that we may discern in our outward behavior a greater potential of truth and wisdom than in whatever rational argument may make us believe.

The sun of truth shines upon our behavior, and our (true and false) opinions are the mere shadows of our behavior as cast by this sun of truth.

In this way Pascal's argument is a remarkably consistent and liberal position with regard to the question of what attitude we must take toward people with other convictions and beliefs than we have. Our lack of "toleration" of opinions that we reject must incite in us an intense urge to demonstrate their falsity (whereas we need feel no such urge with regard to mistaken opinions that we "tolerate"), but this urge can never be a license for not "tolerating" the people who adhere to these "intolerable" opinions. *People* must always "tolerate" each other, since it is only *opinions* that we may, under certain circumstances, decide not to "tolerate." As Pascal put it in his letter, it is our duty to struggle for true opinions, but never to triumph over people.[71]

The advantage of Pascal's analysis in comparison to more customary discussion of toleration is that it succeeds in combining a firm and uncompromising commitment to the truth[72] with an acceptance of the existence of people adhering to convictions that we could not possibly share.

Obviously, this offers the solution to the main problem of French Restoration politics that we discussed in the previous chapter (and, hence, where we may discern the legacy of Christianity to representative democracy). We will recall that this problem required the politicians of the Restoration to reconcile the apparently irreconcilable, that is, to reconcile the ideologies of the ancien régime and of the Revolution. This was the self-contradictory aim that Restoration politics had set itself (an aim that would, in the history of the continental democracies, have to be achieved again and again). And when we speak here about how to reconcile the irreconcilable or about self-contradictory aims, this is because in these cases truly incompatible claims to political "truth" stood in outright and lethal opposition to each other (as was also the case in Pascal's presentation of the conflict between the Jesuits and the Jansenists). For how could one reconcile the ancien régime with the Revolution or, at a later phase of the nineteenth century, capital and labor, without betraying the essence of the political standpoints in question?

However, what Pascal's argument makes clear is that, without abandoning our love of and adherence to the truth and without becoming unprincipled opportunists, there is a solution to the problem of Restoration politics. And this solution exists in this shift of emphasis from our inner ideological conviction to outward behavior. Cutting through these ties between conviction and behavior, and, above all, privileging the latter over the former, enabled the adherents of the ideology of the Revolution to live together peaceably with the adherents of the ideology of the ancien régime, and vice versa.

E. CONSTITUTIONALISM

This dissociation of public behavior and inner conviction came to be reflected in the distinction between the nation's constitution and political ideology.

This distinction is not analogous to the distinction between form and content — as if the constitution should give us the form for how to reach agreement about issues of actual political content. Pascal's dissociation of public behavior and inner conviction effects an analogous dissociation of constitution and form on the one hand, and truth and political conviction on the other. Truth and conviction have no role to play in the realm of public behavior; their domain is that of inner political conviction — though there they are absolutely crucial.

Political debate is quite unlike scientific debate, where we cannot afford to "tolerate" deviant or mistaken opinions; such "toleration" is the point of departure and the presupposition of all politics. Unlike scientific debate, political debate does not aim at *consensus* but at *compromise*. In political debate we typically do not try to convince each other of our being right and our opponent of being wrong (though, admittedly, when dealing with minor and subsidiary issues political debate may sometimes assume this form); rather, on the basis of an acceptance of what the different political parties and their politicians respectively stand for, one tries to elaborate a *juste milieu* that may seem a reasonable compromise to all parties involved. And when exchanging consensus for compromise we don't do so, as is often argued, because there is no final truth to be found in political issues—and that this is, so the argument continues, why we should liberally and tolerantly acquiesce in the existence of a variety of conflicting opinions. In opposition to this degenerate and perverse agnosticism we must realize that nothing is more dangerous to politics than to suggest that rational argument is helpless in deciding the plausibility of political opinions. We should be liberal and tolerant, however, because in political debate we avoid seeing political opinions under the aspect of truth (and Pascal has taught us how to avoid doing so).

In agreement with this, a nation's constitution, when understood as a set of rules[73] to be applied in order to achieve political decisions, is not an instrument for discovering the truth or plausibility of political opinions; for that is the exclusive domain of political ideology or of political philosophy. The constitution is not a *tertium comparationis* (in the sense meant in this work so far) enabling us to identify what opposing political principles may, nevertheless, have in common and what shared background would enable them to be compared. In fact, it is precisely the reverse: the set of constitutional rules that is shared by all the participants in political debate will be used by them for moving away as far as possible from what the participants can still recognize as (their) political truth—until the basis for further compromise finally breaks apart. If we momentarily allow ourselves to use the illegitimate phrase "political truth" for referring to what is shared by all, constitutional political debate is not a movement *toward* the truth, but, on the contrary, a movement *away* from truth. The constitutional rules for publicly observable behavior enable politicians to achieve politically creative compromise even if there is next to nothing that they may agree about without discrediting the notion of (political) truth.

This is how Pascal's apologetics may teach a constitutional democracy to be ready to compromise, and how to avoid both the dangers of a despotic intolerance of people (in the case of an unwillingness to compromise) and those twin dangers of a hypocritical lip service to political truth and conviction and a shallow indifference to them (in the case of a willingness to compromise).

5. Politics and Metaphor

1. Introduction

Perhaps no field is richer in metaphor than political theory. Plato, who is often seen as the first political philosopher in history, incorporated numerous metaphors into his *Republic* and his *Laws*. No less metaphorical are the books written during the Golden Age of Western political philosophy. Hobbes, Locke, Rousseau, and many others all founded the political order on an original contract or covenant entered into by its members. Often they admitted that this contract was a mere historical fiction; but that was of no consequence as long as the idea of the original contract could function as a metaphor in terms of which the legality of the existing political order could be analyzed. Especially in the political writings of that fierce opponent of metaphor, Thomas Hobbes,[1] metaphors abound. For what is the notion of "the body politic" other than an organicist metaphor exploited as such throughout Hobbes's work? Is the commonwealth, the State, or that "artificiall Man" (another metaphor) that forms the subject of Hobbes's book really the monster which Job and the Psalmist refer to by the name of Leviathan? Coming to our own age, we are struck by the force of Foucault's metaphor of "the capillaries of power" and by the Rawlsian metaphor of "the veil of ignorance" behind which our conception of the just society is formed. Most important of all, in these cases even a superficial awareness of the function of these political metaphors forces us to recognize that they do not merely touch the surface but form the essence of the political theories in which they are proposed. Metaphor is no mere ornament or didactic device: the conviction carried by the argument itself depends upon an open or tacit acceptance of the metaphor in question. If metaphor is eliminated the argument of the political philosopher degenerates into a meaningless chaos.[2] Metaphor is the heart that pumps the lifeblood of political philosophy.

Yet political philosophers have only rarely, and only recently, been prepared to recognize the metaphorical nature of their enterprise. In fact, one of the main goals of this essay will be to clarify why and how the perspective of metaphor has run counter to the universalist presumptions of nearly all political theory. But in all fairness I must begin by enumerating a few exceptions to the general and traditional condemnation of metaphor by political philosophers. When William Connolly uses Gallie's notion of the so-called essentially contested concepts for his analysis of political concepts like "democracy" or "the State"—and when he points out that such concepts aim at "describing a situation from the vantage point of certain interests, purposes or standards,"[3] Connolly is already quite close to recognizing the central role played by political metaphor. For it is only a small step from Gallie's "essentially contested concepts" to metaphor. The "essentially contested concept" has in common with metaphor a shift from description or reference to a "seeing as."

Even more explicit was Terence Ball in his book on political discourse.[4] In contrast to Connolly, Ball does not hesitate to emphasize the metaphorical character of Gallie's "essentially contested concepts" if used in a political context. Moreover, with the help of some felicitous examples, Ball explains why metaphor really is an indispensable instrument for the political philosopher. Political philosophers are required to deal with new situations that have arisen in political reality, and it is the semantic newness so often claimed for metaphors that enables them to do so. The newness of the political problem has its linguistic counterpart in the newness characteristic of metaphor. Hence the predominant place which Ball awards to the notion of "conceptual-cum-political" change. An example may be helpful. Ball demonstrates the metaphorical use made by seventeenth-century political philosophers like Hobbes of the Galilean notion of mechanical force: political power as well as its consequences were modeled on the Galilean axiom of inertia.[5] And, to mention a more concrete example, when in the course of the eighteenth century political parties began to form in different European countries, those who applauded the development sought a theoretical justification for this new kind of political association. One of their most successful strategies was to replace the old word "faction" by the word "party." Originally the word "party" was exclusively linked to the juridical sphere. In other words, the unfavorable connotations of the terms "faction" and "factionalism" were neutralized by an implied metaphorical comparison of the political association with the party as it was already known from the perfectly respectable and accepted juridical world.[6] In this way metaphor enabled political philosophers to account for an important new political phenomenon.

Connolly, then, suggests rather than accepts the metaphorical dimension of political theory, while Terence Ball uses the recognition of this dimension for a better understanding of political discourse and its metamorphoses through the centuries. A third step has been taken by James Boyd White. For White the recognition of political theory's metaphorical dimension gives us more than a better understanding of politics. According to him this recognition must also have its implications for actual political practice itself. White, a lawyer, illustrates his thesis with the example of lawgiving. Statutes, orders, and laws are not (at least not primarily) rules for how the citizen should behave; rather, they "establish a set of topics or paradigms or metaphors for how to conceive of social action."[7] That is, a law or statute is a paradigm or metaphor in terms of which we try to see the interaction(s) between citizen and citizen or between the citizen and the state. It follows that lawgiving must not aim at "implementing some a priori principles of (distributive) justice but take into account what room it makes for the officer and the citizen each to say what reasonably can be said from his or her point of view about the transaction . . . that they share."[8]

Here metaphor truly becomes a normative option for lawgiving. Acceptance of this option would have far-reaching consequences for the aims and nature of lawgiving. It would require the lawgiver to guarantee that anything litigants might systematically wish to incorporate into the stories they tell about their case will be reflected in the formulation of the law or statute. And, conversely, what they systematically exclude from their metaphorical points of view must also be kept out of the law and its application. I suppose that this would result in a kind of "democratization" of the law, and would produce a legal system that has more in common with arbitrage than with existing legal procedures. More specifically, it would mean the end of the predominant role of the state as an independent agent in legal procedure: for the state, in most cases, embodies a point of view that is completely alien to that of the litigants. Or so it may seem.

Considering these views of Connolly, Ball, and White, we may conclude that some political philosophers now seem inclined to accept the metaphorical dimension of political theory, but that no consensus yet exists about what the role of metaphor is or ought to be. And opinions differ even more widely about the location of metaphor in political theory. In this kind of situation, where so little seems certain or accepted, a fresh start appears advisable.

2. *Plato's Ship of State*

To begin with the beginning is not a bad strategy if one wishes to make a fresh start. So let us go back to Plato's political writings and find out what metaphors he uses and what their function is in his work. Like most of his work, Plato's political philosophy is particularly rich in metaphors (Plato, the sworn enemy of rhetoric, is Hobbes's most serious rival in combining a prolific use of metaphors with an utter condemnation of them). Especially when Plato embarks on a discussion of the ideal state, of how the ideal state can be realized, and of the role of the statesman, his reliance upon metaphor begins to determine even the substance of his argument. Tendencies in his political thought, tendencies that Plato may not even have been fully aware of himself, stand out if we concentrate on the metaphors he uses. When Plato discusses the statesman and his duties vis à vis the state, the message of his political philosophy is most clearly expressed by the metaphors he uses and the common element that unites them. The metaphors in question are those of the statesman as a painter (who has to start with a clean surface), builder, craftsman, cobbler, physician, or shipwright. What all these metaphors have in common is their suggestion that the statesman must be in the possession of technocratic knowledge (*technē*) which most other people do not have.[9] This obviously accords with all the elitist tendencies of Plato's political philosophy. That tendency is most pronounced in Plato's metaphor of the state as a ship steered by a captain-statesman. This metaphor is even more suggestive of the necessity of technocratic knowledge than the ones I mentioned a moment ago, since, unlike the painter, the cobbler, and the others, the captain of a ship really controls the destiny of fellow human beings whose life and security depend on his seamanship.

Since this metaphor of the state as a ship seems to be the most felicitous
and suggestive one from Plato's perspective, I shall focus my attention on
it not only in this section but in the whole of this essay.

Plato's metaphor has irritated many of his modern commentators. Thus
Michael Walzer resents the technocratic undertone of the metaphor and
the implied disregard for all interaction between the rulers and the ruled:
in Plato's metaphor the captain does not bother about the wishes, if they
have any, of his crew or passengers.[10] In a similar vein Bambrough complained that normally the passengers or the owner of the ship determine its
destination, whereas Plato seems to assign this crucial task to the captain
as well. The captain's technological knowledge apparently also gives him
the right to choose the ship's destination, and it is characteristic of Plato
that he so easily makes the transition from *technē* to goal.[11]

Surely the technocratic implications of Plato's metaphor are damaging
to some extent, and it is quite true that these are at odds with our modern,
democratic notion of the state and of its relation with the citizen. There is,
however, another and more important dimension to Plato's metaphor that
still harmonizes with how even nowadays we customarily conceive of the
state and with the very essence of how the state has always been perceived in
the Western political tradition. I have in mind here the simple but decisive
fact that the metaphor invites us to see the state as an entity with a certain
unity that can and ought to be steered in the right direction by a competent
and responsible statesman.[12] I do not think that critics of Plato like Walzer
or Bambrough would wish to disagree with *this* element of the metaphor.
As we shall see, an intuition like this has been behind the greater part of
the Western political tradition. If this intuition is abandoned, large parts of
that tradition lose much of their meaning and practical significance.

We must be grateful to W. J. Witteveen for drawing our attention to this
fact. In his introductory essay to a volume that takes Plato's metaphor as
its leitmotiv, Witteveen has given us a competent and convincing account
of how the complexities of modern government and bureaucracy and the
(in)effectiveness of government policy can be fruitfully analyzed from the
point of view defined by Plato's metaphor of the state as a ship.[13] Witteveen
is clearly implying that precisely because Plato's metaphor has always been
a tacit assumption behind most of Western political theory, practice, and
science, it provides us with the ideal background for gaining a better perception of the problems addressed in these areas. For as soon as we say that

the state has the obligation to solve social and political problems and to strive for a better and more just society, regardless of how we define social progress, we are unavoidably presupposing that the state is like a ship that can be set on a certain course. We can already draw an important conclusion at this early stage of our argument. If we nowadays encounter strange and unnerving obstacles on our route to a better and more just society, this need not mean that our technocratic knowledge is insufficient, or that we should now heed the highly impractical treatises of German philosophers on so-called practical philosophy, or that government agencies have become too unwieldy for effective action. It may mean, rather, that there is something wrong with the metaphorical background against which politics has commonly been defined in the Western tradition.

With a view to what I wish to do in the remainder of this chapter, it will be necessary to dissect Plato's metaphor. The metaphor is complex, as we have seen, and can only be fruitfully dealt with if its constituent elements are scrutinized separately. This procedure is not without risk, since metaphors often lose by being taken apart. But I believe that if the following three elements are discerned in Plato's metaphor no serious injustice will be done to it. The metaphor's first suggestion is that the ship of state ought to follow a certain *course* toward a certain goal—obviously here Plato's ideal state. Whether the ideal state is in fact an attainable goal, or whether it depends on some sudden epiphany of political truth, or whether, as was suggested by Julia Annas, the Platonic ideal state functions rather as a compass for existing states, is a matter of no consequence in this connection.[14] Second, the metaphor, by separating the helmsman from both the ship itself and from its crew, implies a *distance* between the center of decision-making and the people for whom and on behalf of whom these decisions are made. In Plato's ideal state this distance found its expression in the way the *phylakes* were separated from the other classes in the state, but usually the notion of distance is not emphasized by such radical social divisions. All I wish to maintain is that there must be some location, place, or perspective separate from either the ship or the state itself which allows the captain or the statesman to make his decisions about the course that the ship will follow. Without this notion of distance, or some variant of it, the whole metaphor collapses into absurdity. Third, like the ship the state must have a certain *coherence* and *unity*: one cannot navigate with a chaotic farrago of boards, ropes, and sails. Plato himself used to be quite explicit about the unity of the state. He considered the unity of the polis to be its paramount property,[15] and even compared his ideal state with the human individual, which certainly implies a very high degree of integration.[16]

I can now outline what I intend to do in this chapter. First I hope to demonstrate the plausibility of Plato's metaphor insofar as the metaphor entails the three ideas of goal, distance, and unity I mentioned a moment ago. My argument will be, roughly, that political action is metaphorical and, next, that as such political action involves an acceptance of these three notions. Hence my argument will be somewhat indirect. Instead of starting with Plato's metaphor in order to show its appropriateness, I shall begin with political action and try to deduce Plato's metaphor by showing that the universe of political action is defined by the three dimensions of goal, distance, and unity. I hope to explain next why the metaphorical nature of political theory and practice has been so often and so consistently ignored. Having reached this stage, my argument will move into a different, apparently even opposite, direction: I will discuss the considerations that seem to militate against Plato's metaphor. Such considerations find their justification in the changing boundaries of the political in the modern political order. These changing boundaries seriously diminish the room left for the three notions of goal, distance, and unity that we have associated with Plato's metaphor. This makes us wonder what it might be like to have a politics without metaphor and a state that can no longer be compared to a ship. As we shall see at the end of this chapter, Japanese politics suggests an answer to this question.

I am well aware that I am attacking no small problem. But I think it is wrong to avoid big problems, as so many contemporary philosophers are apt to do. I suppose that if there is such a thing as a philosophical truth that makes the efforts of the philosopher worthwhile, truth must, metaphorically speaking, be a fairly sizable thing that is best found by investigating big problems. However, both the procedures and the topology of much modern philosophy appear to be fed by the opposite intuition: that truth is rather a particularly elusive thing that prefers to hide in the most secret and unlikely places. It is as if one were looking for elephants under a microscope. In my opinion political philosophy, of all philosophical disciplines, is least likely to survive this minimalist approach. I hope that this chapter will be, among other things, an argument in support of that conviction.

3. The Deduction of Plato's Metaphor

"For we all of us," George Eliot wrote in *Middlemarch*, "get our thoughts entangled in metaphors and act fatally on the strength of them."[17] If we wish to understand the metaphorical basis of action, especially of political action, it is best to start with Donald Schön's so-called generative metaphor. In political action we must distinguish, Schön writes, between problem setting and problem solving, and Schön emphasizes the priority of problem setting. After all, we do not act in a void but always on the basis of a more or less clear idea of the situation we wish to improve; problem solving is thus logically dependent on problem setting. According to Schön, then, problem setting is mainly a matter of finding the appropriate metaphor. "My point here," he writes, "is not that we *ought* to think metaphorically about social policy problems but that we already *do* think about them in terms of certain pervasive generative metaphors."[18] Schön proposes the term "generative metaphor," since the kind of metaphor in question "generates new perceptions and inventions."[19]

Two proposals for the renewal of a slum area may illustrate Schön's view of generative metaphor. According to the first proposal the slum area is metaphorically seen as a diseased body, or as a cancer within the larger city, and it is not hard to imagine what policy and solution for the slum area follow from this way of setting the problem. On the other hand, if the slum area is metaphorically seen as a natural community, whose natural growth has been stifled, a different policy is called for. All this sounds fairly convincing and I should like to add the following comment. Metaphor, as conceived by Schön, is the missing link between the "is" and the "ought." As Schön's examples make clear, metaphors in this context will logically have the character of proposals: they invite us to see part of (social) reality from a certain point of view that automatically leads to a certain kind of action. In other words, apart from their capacity to characterize an existing social situation, metaphors predispose us in favor of a specific line of action, and it is because metaphors embody proposals that they produce this effect. Thus, the goal-directedness we defined as the first of three elements in Plato's metaphor is more or less thrown in our lap by Schön's analysis. Finally, one can point out that the generative metaphor is neither description nor action itself, so that it truly can be said to be the missing link between the "is" and the "ought," and not identified with either.

Now I come to the heart of Schön's analysis. Schön says that the two metaphors used for the problem setting of the slum area owe their origin to a *story* or *history* that is or can be told of the slum area. Generative metaphors are condensed histories.[20] The first metaphor condenses a story of blight and renewal and the other a story of the natural community and its deterioration.[21] Different stories, different metaphors, and vice versa. Governments characteristically act when they recognize that something has gone wrong (or is perceived to be wrong) and such recognition necessarily requires a quasi-historical assessment of the problem involved. On a far larger scale than Schön has in mind, this fact is most strikingly illustrated by all nineteenth- and twentieth-century ideologies, which until recently were the most powerful sources of political action. The social and political problems these ideologies attempted to solve were always defined in terms of a historical interpretation of Western history. There has always been considerable overlap between what one might somewhat pompously call "the logic of politics" and "the logic of the writing of history."

Schön's thesis of the similarities between metaphor and narrative as expounded above is quite useful and will enable us to increase our understanding of both metaphor and narrative and also, in passing, of the nature of rhetoric. I shall begin with the question of how metaphor can be used for a better grasp of narrative. If we have the metaphor "X is A" there must be a *prima facie* incompatibility between X and A—without this incompatibility we would not have a metaphor. I shall naively assume that we are right in attributing to metaphor the capacity to offer a more or less precise description of part of reality. I shall call this the descriptive meaning of metaphor and in the case of the metaphor "X is A" the descriptive meaning is expressed by the literal statement "X is B." Most discussions of the semantics of metaphor concern this difficult and complex translation problem and I therefore do not want to commit myself to anything more than the rather trivial and uncontroversial claim I made just now. In the present context it is sufficient to notice that the metaphor "X is A" and its descriptive meaning "X is B" are not equivalent. This is made clear by negating the metaphorical statement. The metaphorical statement then turns into a literal statement and will be perfectly compatible with the original metaphor's descriptive meaning "X is B." Now, no two statements can have an identical meaning if the negation of the former is compatible with the latter, and that implies that the meaning of the metaphor and its descriptive meaning cannot be identical. If we inquire next where and why the metaphor and its descriptive meaning are not equivalent, we will naturally turn to the capacity of the metaphor to individuate a point of view. It is this capacity that is lost when we make the transition from the metaphorical statement to its descriptive meaning and where the two are *not* equivalent.

Because of the logical similarity between metaphor and narrative established by Schön, we can make a similar claim for (historical) narrative. Narrative consists of statements; when taken separately these statements describe sociohistorical reality and embody the descriptive meaning of the narrative in question. When taken together, these statements individuate the metaphorical point of view from which the historian or politician invites us to see part of sociohistorical reality.[22] It should be observed that the narrative's point of view arises out of the descriptive meaning of the narrative's statements—apparently the metaphorical character of narrative lies closer to descriptive meaning than that of metaphor itself. If metaphor is the missing link between the "is" and the "ought," narrative is the missing link between descriptive meaning—in other words, the "is"—and metaphor.

Next, and more importantly, we may ask what the logical similarity between narrative and metaphor can add to our understanding of the latter. Aristotle defined metaphor as follows: "Metaphor consists in giving the thing a name that belongs to something else,"[23] and this is not in conflict with most modern definitions of metaphor.[24] The customary idea is that the metaphorical statement "X is A" requires us to look at X from the point of view of A. And this only makes sense if both A and X are more or less familiar to speaker and hearer prior to the formulation of the metaphor. This is the case in Schön's generative metaphor. The slum area is compared either to a cancer or to a living thing whose growth has been stifled. An even more striking example is Schön's account of how difficulties with a new type of paintbrush were successfully solved by seeing the paintbrush as a kind of pump. Now, this state of affairs is not wholly unknown in (historical) narrative. The historian may see part of the past as a renaissance or as an Indian summer. But most often in historiographical metaphor, the A in "seeing X as A" is *not* previously given, and the metaphorical image has to be created ad hoc for the purpose. In historiography, metaphor is to be identified with the point of view from which the historian proposes to see the past, and this point of view owes both its origin and its identity to the set of statements used by the historian for writing the historical narrative. Obviously, in the majority of cases in historiography metaphor at the same time *presupposes* and *develops* the point of view from which the past is seen. And because problem setting precedes meaningful political action, the same can be said for political action.

But if we give credence to Derrida this already has its precedent in the writings of Aristotle himself. Commenting on Aristotle's so-called helio-trope, the metaphor par excellence,[25] Derrida quotes Aristotle as follows: "Thus to cast forth corns is called 'sowing' (speirein); but to cast forth its flames, as said of the sun [and here we have the heliotrope] has no special name." Derrida adds the following rhetorical question: "When has it ever been *seen* that there is the same relation between the sun and its rays as be-tween sowing and seeds?"[26] Just as in the case of narrative metaphor we do not have here two more or less well-known entities that are seen metaphori-cally in light of each other. For prior to the heliotrope the sun's sowing its flames was still a "nameless act," to use the words of Derrida.

We observe here an essential difference between the heliotrope and nar-rative metaphor on the one hand and models on the other. The heliotrope does not urge us to see, for instance, the pump as a model for the paint-brush or, generally speaking, a less familiar system in terms of a better known system. Here the metaphor creates its own subject. Much is there-fore to be said for Derrida's contention that we should bestow on the helio-trope—and therefore also on narrative metaphor—the honor of being the metaphor of metaphors.[27] For the "newness" of the relation between the metaphor's tenor and vehicle, to use Richards's terminology,[28] is here not restricted to that relation only, but pervades the domains of both tenor and vehicle themselves. We do not merely have here—as with the model—a new view of an "old" thing: in the heliotrope and in narrative metaphor we have a new word for a new thing. But if all this is true, we may ask, what still differentiates the heliotrope from literal language? For if the heliotrope introduces new words for new things, we shall look in vain for the semantic tension that is characteristic of all metaphor. Derrida considers this objec-tion, insofar as he deals with metaphor and the heliotrope throughout his essay, from the perspective of *usure*.

As Alan Bass has pointed out, the French word *usure* is ambiguous, and refers to use and to a deterioration through use.[29] The suggestion is, clearly, that the heliotrope is the use of metaphor that tends to obscure its metaphorical character—a tendency that is, of course, even more clearly visible in narrative metaphor than in Aristotle's heliotrope itself. What, then, is right and what is wrong in the objection I mentioned a moment ago becomes clear if we contrast the heliotrope and its *usure*, as explained just now, with catachresis. With regard to the tension between metaphoricity and literality we can say that the pseudo-literality of catachresis arises from our tendency to forget about its (original) metaphoricity, whereas in the case of the heliotrope we have not yet come to recognize its metaphoricity (once again, narrative metaphor is an even better illustration than the heliotrope). In sum, the heliotrope, this metaphor of metaphors, is, paradoxically, the metaphor that most wishes to make us forget about its metaphoricity (think of the objectivist *eros* that has always inspired both historians and philosophers of history). And the heliotrope tries to achieve this goal of self-occultation by bathing everything in a clear and even light that makes us forget that the light must have a source. The heliotrope is therefore all too easily taken as guaranteeing a literal and realist presentation of the world. As we shall see in the next section, this is why metaphor in political theory has always presented itself in the guise of the heliotrope.

I shall now add a comment on rhetoric and its relation to narrative metaphor. Since rhetoric plays such a prominent part in politics, this excursion seems pardonable. To begin with, we can distinguish between two traditional conceptions of rhetoric. Both conceptions are hinted at in the opening sentences of McCloskey's and Megill's pathbreaking volume on what they call the rhetoric of inquiry. Their introduction begins as follows: "Scholarship uses argument and argument uses rhetoric. The 'rhetoric' is not mere ornament or manipulation or trickery. It is rhetoric in the ancient sense of persuasive discourse." [30] According to one conception, rejected by Megill and McCloskey, rhetoric is mere adornment and adds nothing substantial to the argument itself. According to the other conception, adopted by both authors, rhetoric is a deep structure underlying argument itself; a deep structure that has hitherto been underplayed, ignored, or repressed in the Freudian sense of the word. It should be observed that although the conceptions may differ, both agree that rhetoric is distinct from argument.

Our analysis of metaphor, however, permits us to see a third conception of rhetoric that does not dissociate rhetoric from argument. All that is needed is a readiness to cast rhetoric in the mold of metaphor. No one doubts that metaphor is prominent in rhetoric, so in the absence of this readiness I am happy to restrict my argument to rhetoric only insofar as it makes use of metaphors. Because of the affinity of rhetoric and metaphor the following can also be seen as a statement about metaphorical argument. We saw a moment ago that the narrative metaphor proposed by the historian or the politician is defined or individuated by the statements that have been used for writing the narrative. It follows that statements about what statements a narrative metaphor does or does not contain are all analytically true or false: it is part of the notion of a narrative metaphor that it contains certain statements and that these statements can be analytically derived from this notion.[31] Thus the construction or deconstruction of narrative metaphors has all the characteristics of an argument—even of analytical argument. On the other hand, narrative argument, the individuation of narrative proposals, shares with rhetoric the desire to convince by persuasion: not by having recourse to fact but by making use of a linguistic construct. Persuasion here is aesthetic rather than factual, though not necessarily in conflict with fact.

In short, from the perspective of narrative metaphor, rhetoric is neither mere embellishment of language nor its hidden deep structure: rhetoric is argument itself and vice versa. The positivist tradition has conditioned us to associate truth and argument primarily with factual truth and deductive argument; this has made us insensitive to the kind of constructive argument one finds in rhetoric or metaphor and in disciplines like history or politics, which make use of constructive, aesthetic argument. Nevertheless, as this statement suggests, recognition of the possibility of rhetorical argument does not rule out the possibility of distinguishing between rhetorical and rational argument. Rhetorical argument is always related to metaphorical or narrative constructs and these constructs only appear, and only support rhetorical argument, against the background of a specific culture containing these constructs. Rational argument may convince a god or a Neanderthal man if only these beings are rational. Rhetoric and rhetorical argument, on the other hand, if they are to be effective, presuppose a knowledge of the metaphors that are in the mind of whoever one wishes to convince. In contrast to rational argument, rhetorical argument presupposes both self-knowledge and empathy with others.

Finally, we have to consider in this section the three elements of Plato's metaphor—goal-directedness, unity, and distance—and try to derive them from the nature of metaphor. Having dealt with goal-directedness in the beginning of this section, I now turn to the notion of unity. That metaphor provides unity and coherence is fairly undisputed.[32] The main idea is that metaphor is not knowledge but rather the organization of knowledge, while unity and coherence are due to the organizational patterns, or gestalts, proposed by metaphor. From the point of view of political action an interesting complication can be observed here. The unity of the gestalt stands out against a diffuse background lacking this unity. Where, then, should we situate political reality? If we grant reality the connotation of "externality" ordinarily associated with it, the background must be reality from a *cognitive* view and the gestalt must be reality from the view of political *action*. The background embodies externality when political metaphors are to be constructed; such metaphors, however, embody externality when one wishes to act on reality. It seems natural that political action will tend to avoid this realist dilemma as much as possible, and this can be achieved by concentrating on the borderline between the world of the gestalts and that of the background rather than on either of these two worlds themselves. Hence politics will not feel at home in spheres that are either completely narrativized and metaphorized or not narrativized at all. Both the lifeworld (according to philosophers like Ricoeur or Carr the richest source of narrativity) and nature therefore tend to fall outside the scope of politics. This means that it will be particularly difficult for politics to deal effectively with ecological problems, since these problems are far removed from the borderland where politics is most at ease and since they have their center both in the lifeworld and in nature.

That leaves us, finally, with the notion of distance. We must recognize with Danto the self-referential character of metaphor.[33] The metaphorical meaning of the statements of a historical or political narrative lies not in what these statements express about sociohistorical reality but in what they contribute to the proposed metaphor itself. Reference to or correspondence with reality obstructs metaphor's striving for self-reference and thereby weakens metaphor. The greater the distance between the metaphor or its point of view and the world metaphorized by it, the more successful metaphor is. In its most perfect form metaphor becomes part of a substitute reality in the way Gombrich's hobby-horse is a substitute for a real horse. Insofar as political action is inspired by metaphor it will demonstrate a similar affinity with distance. It is surely no coincidence that in the West the paradigm for effective action is the action of God, who is farthest removed from our world and who looks at us, so to speak, from the perspective of the sun. We find a secularized version in Louis XIV, "le roi soleil," who wished to emphasize the majesty of his absolutist kingship by moving from Paris to Versailles. "This was absolutism in its most perfect form," writes Kossmann,

> it had cut its roots. It did not associate itself with any particular class or group of the French population. It withdrew from society and from institutions which

had been created by the French monarchy. . . . But to be alone and superior the king must also withdraw from the centre of the country and build, at Versailles, not just a new palace but the very symbol of absolutism.[34]

If one has achieved, like God or Louis XIV, this maximal distance, one's actions seem no longer inspired by questionable metaphors but by the nature of political reality itself. Here the absolutism of Louis XIV and natural law philosophy mutually reinforce one another. This, then, is another sense we may give to the heliotrope.

Having found that the three notions of goal-directedness, unity, and distance that embody the essence of Plato's metaphor are also essential characteristics of political metaphor in general, we may conclude that Plato's metaphor is a metaphor of political metaphor. Small wonder that political practice and political theory have always been inspired by the idea that the state can be seen as a ship, nor should we be surprised by the fact that so few political philosophers have seen this: presuppositions can only function as such so long as we are not aware of them.

4. Why Metaphor Has Been Ignored by Political Philosophers

Let us listen to how Rawls defines his notion of the "veil of ignorance" behind which we decide on matters of distributive justice:

> In justice as fairness the original position of equality corresponds to the state of nature in the traditional theory of the social contract. The original position is not, of course, thought of as an actual historical state of affairs, much less as a primitive condition of culture. It is understood as a purely hypothetical situation characterized so as to lead to a conception of justice. Among the essential features of this situation is that no one knows his place in society, his class or social status, nor does anyone know his fortune or the distribution of natural assets and abilities, his intelligence, strength and the like. I shall even assume that the parties do not know their conceptions of the good or their special psychological propensities. The principles of justice are chosen behind a veil of ignorance.[35]

The metaphorical character of the Rawlsian notion of the veil of ignorance will be obvious to anyone. It can even be argued that we have to do here with a complex interweaving of two metaphors: the metaphor of the veil of ignorance and the time-honored metaphor of natural society that is presented here under the guise of the "original position."

With its mixing of the metaphor of the original position and the meta-phor of the veil of ignorance, Rawls's political philosophy is the most illus-trative example of how Western political philosophy has always attempted to obscure and neutralize its metaphorical nature. Unlike his predecessors, the natural law philosophers of the seventeenth and eighteenth centuries, Rawls is not content to see contemporary society metaphorically in terms of a state of nature. Rawls also attempts to free the state of nature or the original position of all perspectivism necessarily present in the use of meta-phor. Rawls's two metaphors are juxtaposed in such a way as to cancel out each other's metaphoricity. It is as if Rawls wants to tell us, "Look here, I know that the original position is not historical but a metaphorical fiction. But with my veil of ignorance I am able to show that the original position is a metaphor acceptable to each rational person, and therefore, in practice no different from reality itself or from deductive argument. So you may be sure that nothing has been constructed or 'invented' here." There is a universal-ism in Rawls's argument that one will not find even in Hobbes or Rousseau, where it is always softened by the quasi-metaphorical specificity of some psychological or sociological assumptions. Rawls wants to do without any such assumptions, and it is this wish which necessitated the introduction of some notion like the veil of ignorance. The less a political philosophy has empirical content, the more it is inclined to eliminate political action from its scope (and Rawls's book is completely devoid of political action), the more it will be forced to deny explicitly its metaphorical character. In sum, Rawls's veil of ignorance, this metaphor that has no other purpose than to wipe out metaphoricity, is a perfect instance of the political heliotrope as we defined it in the previous section, following on from Derrida.

To explain this fascination with the political heliotrope we must turn to the transcendentalism of Western epistemology. Kress and Gunnell already noticed the affinity of transcendentalism with what we have called here the political heliotrope: the quest for a solid foundation of the political order as we find it in the writings of Rawls, Dworkin, or Ackerman is the politi-cal counterpart of that quest for absolute foundations of knowledge that is characteristic of the Western transcendentalist tradition since Descartes.[36] And it has always been the transcendental self in which such absolute foun-dations were located.

In a crucial passage Kant characterized the transcendental self as an entity that accompanies each of our thoughts but of which we can have no knowledge as such. Kant argues that our thoughts can be said to be the predicates of this transcendental self, but since we have access only to these thoughts themselves or what they are about, the transcendental self itself remains an unknown X, an indefinite peg on which to hang our thoughts.[37] Hence right at the heart of the knowing subject lies a transcendental self that must necessarily remain completely unspecific, since specificity is to be associated exclusively with the manifold of experience and thought, and since the transcendental self is *ex hypothesi* never tainted by this specificity. Thus the (metaphorical) point of view we would naively associate with the transcendental self can never function as such, since the latter is devoid of all specificity and is rather anybody's point of view. An even more striking example can be found in Wittgenstein's *Tractatus*:

> Where in the world can a metaphysical subject be discerned? You say it is here as with the eye and the field of vision. But the eye you really don't see. And there is nothing in the field of vision suggesting that it is seen by an eye.[38]

This is truly the exact analogue of Rawls's veil of ignorance. Of course we have to do here with a metaphor—the metaphor is even a metaphor of the point of view, which is a most convenient circumstance in this context. But the very purpose of the metaphor is to eliminate metaphor, since the whole drift of Wittgenstein's transcendentalist argument here is to rob the metaphorical point of view of its capacity to function as a point of view in the proper sense of the word. For we can only see what is within our scope, and that excludes the eye—the point of view—itself. Just as in Rawls's veil of ignorance, the point of view is only introduced so as to be eliminated again. The contrast with narrative metaphor could not be greater. For where the Kantian transcendental self remains a bare peg on which to hang thoughts, narrative metaphor and its point of view completely identify themselves with the narrative statements that individuate them. Narrative metaphor is as specific as the unique set of perhaps thousands and thousands of statements that make up a specific historical narrative. Here (narrative) metaphor is truly radically opposed to the transcendentalist or political heliotrope.

The Rawlsian citizen who has retired from the historical world behind a veil of ignorance is thus the political analogue of the Kantian transcendental self. Given Rawls's explicit approval of Kant's demand that ethics should be completely free from empirical considerations, the affinity between Kantian transcendentalism and Rawls's veil of ignorance need not astonish us. Yet this is only part of the story. For the transcendental seduc-

tion has also given us the modern notion of the sovereign state. Perhaps no
political philosopher since Bodin has contributed more to the development
of this notion than Hobbes, so let us consider *Leviathan* for a moment. One
should resist a proto-totalitarian reading of *Leviathan*, though the well-
known frontispiece of the book seems to invite us to do so. For what is
united in and by Leviathan, the modern sovereign state, are not individual
citizens but their points of view. The difference is far from academic, since
it marks the distinction between collectivism and the possibility of pluralism *within* an acceptance of the modern state. This is not hard to see: to
pursue exclusively one's own egoistic, antisocial interests is not at all necessarily incompatible with the acceptance of a united point of view in the
form of the modern sovereign state. On the contrary, it may well be that
we can best serve our own egoistic interests and organize our self-directed
actions most successfully if we are prepared to look at ourselves from that
elevated point of view. In fact, this is precisely the essence of Hobbes's
argument: the mere introduction of this unified point of view, while leaving
everything else, our egoism or aggression and so on, unchanged, will transform initial social chaos into a well-ordered body politic. It must be emphasized that the political heliotrope certainly does not exclude pluralism.
If one should wish to attack the political heliotrope, the accusation of collectivism decidedly is beside the point. The state is, in fact, nothing but
the institutionalization of our readiness to look at ourselves from the top
down, from the perspective of the state, and it is immaterial whether we
do so for egoistic or altruistic purposes. In the course of time, however, we
have become so accustomed to looking at ourselves and our interests from
the top down that we find it very difficult to conceive that things might be
otherwise. But as we shall see, there actually are societies where the top
is "blown off," so to speak, and that are nevertheless no less successful in
dealing with the challenges of the modern world than our own.

Thus, the Hobbesian state in which we have lived until at least quite
recently is an indivisible point of sovereignty that is created through a unification of individual points of view. (Once again, this does not at all imply
that what is seen from this unified point of view will in all cases be exactly
identical, so that no room is left for pluralism.) This unification is only
possible by denying the citizen's point of view its specificity, which we cannot even begin to do as long as we are aware that a nonspecific point of
view is a *contradictio in terminis*. A political variant of transcendentalism,
however, which had elsewhere already succeeded in planting a completely

unspecific entity right in the heart of the individual, permitted this crass denial of the metaphorical point of view's specificity. The modern state is our shared political, transcendental self, not only mine, but also yours and anybody's. This is why metaphoricity has always been both present and absent in Western political philosophy and why the heliotrope could guide the development of the latter.

The affinities between transcendentalism and the political heliotrope invite a last comment that will only be developed in outline here. Several philosophers, most notably the Wittgenstein of the *Tractatus*, have noted the propensity of transcendentalism for solipsism. The idea goes roughly as follows. If we "go transcendental" there is no obvious stop demarcating the self from the nonself on the route from the empirical self to the transcendental self. The borderline between the self and the nonself becomes an arbitrary choice, and the same will obviously be true for each proposal to distinguish between outward reality and the self. Solipsism and pure realism tend to coincide: "Here one will observe that solipsism, if consistently applied, coincides with pure realism. The 'I' of solipsism shrinks into an extensionless point, while remaining the reality absorbed within it." [39] That political transcendentalism has this same tendency will be obvious if one recalls, as we saw a moment ago, that the state is anybody's political transcendental self. Here the distinction between the state and what is not the state is as arbitrary as in the case of solipsism. Now, solipsism, despite its spectacular appearance, is in fact a most harmless and innocuous philosophical doctrine. Probably no philosophical doctrine has fewer consequences, whether one subscribes to it or not. It is like changing from summertime to wintertime: there are new denominations for everything but for the rest everything remains as it was. As far as I can see the same applies to the solipsism of political transcendentalism.

There is, nevertheless, one consequence that deserves our attention from the perspective of intellectual history. Political solipsism tends to paralyze our instincts and intuitions about demarcations—in this case, about demarcations between the state and what is not the state, between the state and the citizen, and so on. In other words, political transcendentalism has the tendency to create a discourse in which one can move around with surprising ease. The really amazing amount of political positions that have been developed in the Western world since the seventeenth century, and the fact that individual people have sometimes moved from the extreme left to the extreme right without blinking an eyelid, can perhaps be explained with an appeal to the solipsism of political transcendentalism. Similarly, if the anti-transcendentalism that has recently become fashionable will also affect political thinking, the broad spectrum of political opinions that we used to have may be expected to become much narrower. Surely, this anti-transcendentalism or anti-foundationalism is bound to cause some intellectual heavy weather for Plato's ship of state.

5. The Disintegration of Plato's Metaphor: The Anatomy of Independence

Nevertheless, we ought to be realists and recognize that if Plato's ship is threatened it will be by social or political storms rather than by philosophical ones. That will be the topic of this section. First of all, the political heliotrope has never been in complete harmony with the realities of politics. The indivisible point of view of the heliotrope was never realized. Sovereign political power was always divided constitutionally and in actual political practice. Moreover, it is hard to reconcile political representation with the aims and requirements of the heliotrope, though this may not be impossible. An argument can be devised that turns representation into an ally rather than an enemy of the heliotrope.[40]

But, more important, a number of political developments in most Western societies over the last few decades all suggest the gradual disintegration of Plato's ship. Postmodernist distrust of the grand metanarratives that always gave the ship of state its direction undermines the notion of goal-directedness. State and civil society are anything but a unity and tend to dissolve into a number of more or less independent islands; little distance seems left between the state and civil society nowadays. In the remainder of this section I shall concentrate on the third development—the dissolution of the state in civil society—since it is not difficult to extrapolate from this development to the other two.

If there is one fact contemporary political philosophers and political scientists agree about, it is that the traditional boundaries between state and civil society are disappearing. "The distinction between the state and civil society seems to have largely collapsed," writes Maier in his volume on the changing boundaries of the political.[41] Keane even speaks of "a 'magma' of overlapping hybrid institutions no longer discernible as either 'political' or 'social' entities."[42] Though this may be an exaggeration, it cannot be gainsaid that the state is no longer the unitary agent it used to be in the nineteenth century; it has lost much of its freedom of movement to transnational organizations on the one hand and to a multiplicity of sub-governments with their own systems of decision-making on the other.[43]

And Claus Offe, Habermas's discussion partner in so many social and political debates, has brilliantly shown in a recent analysis that the increasing entanglement of state and civil society and the increasing impact of the state on the citizen has spawned an entirely new political culture. This "new paradigm" for politics as characterized by Offe has materialized in the counterpolitics of the "green parties," with their emphasis on ecology, their insistence that we must undo what Habermas called "the colonization of the lifeworld." Two things must be noticed about this new political paradigm. It truly is a new paradigm, because both in form and in content the alternative politics of the "greens" and their like cuts across the whole spectrum of traditional political ideologies and parties. On the other hand, as Offe emphasizes, the new paradigm does aim at a reinvigoration or even restoration of politics and its former preeminence. According to Offe, the new paradigm is decidedly modern in its "evident belief that the course of history and society can be changed and created by people and social forces determined to do so."[44]

Insofar as the complexities of contemporary political life are both the expression and the result of the increased entanglement of state and civil society, these complexities have been widely discussed by numerous political scientists. I shall refrain from reviewing their discussions here. I am no expert in this field, and there is a more fundamental reason to be reticent. When political scientists discuss these problems they do so from the outside, as it were: from a safe distance they discern two previously given entities, the state and civil society, and then they try to analyze how and why these two entities became ensnared in one another. No less than do the greens or the neoconservatives, therefore, political scientists look at the problem from the point of view of the heliotrope. The political scientist's approach is thus handicapped by presupposing what is really part of the problem. I therefore prefer to approach the problem from the inside—that is to say, by taking the notions of the state and of civil society *themselves* as my point of departure, and not what is denoted by them. I shall inquire next what dialectics governs the relation between the two. This approach compels us to follow the path of political philosophy rather than that of political science, and if we follow this path the first political philosopher likely to be of help is Benjamin Constant, whom we discussed in the previous chapter. He gave us the first and the clearest definition of the concepts of the state and civil society. Moreover, as we shall see, his writings contain a surprising analysis of the very dialectics that we are looking for. No political philosopher has surpassed Constant's analysis of the relation between state and civil society in depth and subtlety. The fact that in both his personal and public life Constant had an almost neurotic obsession with all the problems this relation may give rise to—especially where freedom and independence are concerned—may explain the penetration of his insight and why he still is considered to be one of the best thinkers on the subject.

The concepts that do most of the work for Constant are those of freedom and independence. The latter is perhaps the more important, since it gives the right flavor to the notion of freedom and since we can also apply it to institutional spheres like the state and civil society, to which the concept of freedom does not apply. The central role of freedom and independence (or freedom *as* independence) in Constant's political philosophy is already exemplified by his definition of the state and civil society in those terms. In contrast to Constant, modern writers do not make the notions of state and civil society conceptually dependent on other notions; this may partly explain their helplessness.

This conceptual relation is defined in Constant's treatise on the contrast between ancient and modern liberty, in which all the threads of his political philosophy are adroitly woven together into one powerful intellectual web. He pointed out that ancient liberty, or what we now call "political liberty," consisted in the citizen's right to participate in the process of policymaking. Modern or "civil liberty," on the other hand, is the freedom of the citizen from immixture of the state in his or her affairs, and is thus primarily an *independence* from the state. Ancient or political liberty is best suited to the small state of the classical polis, whereas modern or civil liberty is required for the large states of modern Europe. "It becomes clear from my exposition that we can no longer practice the liberty of the ancients, consisting in active and constant participation in political decisionmaking. Our liberty must consist in the peaceful enjoyment of private independence."[45] The following qualification must be added: Constant does not wish the citizen of the modern European state to renounce political freedom: on the contrary, political liberty as exercised within a system of representative government is a necessary condition for safeguarding civil liberty.

We can therefore say that Constant's distinction between ancient and modern liberty is analogous to the distinction between direct democracy

and representative government—a distinction that was the point of departure for most political debates in his day. But if we consider how the two
forms of liberty were defined by Constant we shall see that the association
of political liberty with the state and of liberty as independence with civil
society must follow as a matter of course. Independence is the crucial concept here: both spheres are defined in terms of their being independent of
each other, and civil society can even be seen as the incarnation of independence. Last, although Constant never explicitly says so himself, the notion
of civil freedom as used throughout his work often has the connotation of
"security": the citizen is "secure" when and insofar as he is independent
from the state. This is interesting because one can say that the modern
welfare state considers its main task to lie in organizing the security of the
citizen within a complex system of welfare facilities. What used to belong
to the domain of civil society—security—has now become the very raison
d'être of the state. So here we meet for the first time the conceptual dialectics between state and civil society that will demand our attention for the
rest of this section.

In a most remarkable way Constant dramatizes the mutual independence of the state and civil society by also assigning to each a different
regime of truth. Constant's surprising thesis is that deceit, dissimulation,
pretext—in short, hypocrisy—may in many cases prove to be an unquali-
fied good in the public sphere of the state,[46] a thesis that earned the young
Constant the honor of a debate with Kant. In the words of Holmes, Constant's most recent biographer, "dissimulation and fraud are an integral
part of modern freedom." [47] Constant's thesis is all the more surprising because, as Hannah Arendt has shown, late eighteenth-century intellectuals
unanimously agreed that hypocrisy was the supreme vice in politics. Their
argument was that hypocrisy teaches us not only to play a role toward
others but toward ourselves as well; thus the last court of appeal for the
cause of truth and justice would be corrupted. The authenticity and sincerity that form the ultimate basis for the state and good government would
be undermined by hypocrisy.[48] When Constant permitted the state to yield,
under certain circumstances,[49] to the seductions of hypocrisy, he gave the
following argument. What is at first only hypocritically feigned by the state
may, in the end, become a true part of its character. Hypocrisy may therefore be instrumental in the education, or edification, of the state. If the
state improves its character, so to speak, this does not happen overnight
but only after an intermediate phase during which the state merely feigns

that it has bettered its ways. Because of his insistence on the educational value of hypocrisy, Constant's defense of state deceit should decidedly not be put on a par with Plato's "noble lie" or with Machiavelli's eulogies of pretext and lying.

From the perspective of the entanglement of state and civil society—the sphere of the individual citizen—it is interesting that Constant translated his proposition about the hypocritical state to the individual citizen. And, as we might expect from that perspective, his argument is that politics even intrudes upon the privacy of the citizen's inner sanctuary. The hypocrisy of the state has its counterpart in our hypocrisy toward ourselves.

In the mental struggles of the characters in his two novels Constant is out to demonstrate the impossibility of discovering or laying bare our truest or innermost feelings. Constant's own experience was the source of this insight into the insincerity of sincerity. For example, Constant observed that when writing his diary, even if he did his utmost to be sincere about himself, he felt an irresistible urge "to speak for the gallery."[50] There is in Constant an almost Derridian resistance to "a metaphysics of presence": even if we wish to get to the truth about ourselves, we have no privileged access to ourselves that might guarantee such a metaphysics of presence. Each attempt to penetrate into the recesses of our mind chases away something else, and so disturbs the psychological mechanism we wish to grasp. Constant is here far superior to the psychological utopia of Rousseau's *Confessions* (although Rousseau's urge "to speak for the gallery" was undoubtedly even stronger than that of Constant). Thus the dialectics of the insincerity of sincerity makes us aware that even in our most private inner world, which we always believed to be the foundation and incarnation of our independence, this independence is successfully challenged by the political and the social in the form of an absent "gallery." In Constant's rejection of the possibility of being sincere to oneself we encounter for the first time his recognition of the intrinsic weakness of independence.

But it is only in his novel *Adolphe* that Constant gave a full account of this weakness and showed why the desire for independence is self-defeating. This bleak and bitter story of the love between Adolphe and Ellénore has been interpreted in many different ways over the last century and a half. To the dismay of both Mme de Staël and of Constant, contemporaries saw the novel above all as an autobiographical account of their love affair—and this is certainly part of the truth. In a more recent interpretation Todorov proposed to read *Adolphe* as proof of the immense performative power of words and speech.[51] That already brings us closer to our goal. For I shall discuss the novel for what it most manifestly is: a thesis about the anatomy of independence and of power and freedom. In doing so I follow Holmes's approach when he says that the novel must be seen "as a commentary on the emptiness of negative freedom"[52]—that is, of freedom as independence. It cannot be doubted that independence is the book's guiding theme; the word makes its appearance at every crucial phase of the story. *Adolphe* is a highly political text, no less political than Rousseau's novels or Dostoyevski's *Demons*.

The tone of the novel is set by the manner in which Adolphe loses his independence. Bored by the social life at the tiny German court of D—— and intrigued by the ecstatic stories of a friend's love affair, Adolphe decides that starting a love affair himself might dispel his ennui. He talks himself into a passion for Ellénore and (typically Constantesque!) is so successful that he soon believes that his whole life, future, and happiness depend on the favors of Ellénore. The message is, clearly, that our independence is something we seldom have very precise ideas about, and if we have them it is usually after we have already lost it. Independence is an active factor in our lives in its absence, more than when we possess it. Knowledge about our independence is characteristically a wisdom after the event.

Almost as soon as Adolphe succeeds in winning Ellénore's heart their relationship becomes strained and unsatisfactory to Adolphe. The mistress of Count P——, Ellénore was barely respectable before she began her affair with Adolphe. But after this relationship has started she becomes a social outcast, and she is now wholly dependent on Adolphe. Paradoxically, this only further restricts Adolphe's freedom and room for maneuver: from now on it is he who is entirely responsible for Ellénore. Thus Ellénore's dependence on Adolphe generates Adolphe's dependence on Ellénore. There is apparently no law of the conservation of energy in human relations: all the independence there was in the beginning may turn into mutual dependence. And in the case of Adolphe and Ellénore the result is an impasse that lasts for the greater part of the novel and ends only with the tragic death of Ellénore, after she has read the letters sent to her by Baron de T—— about Adolphe's decision to leave her.

The clue to the novel can be found in that chilly but lucid letter Adolphe's father writes him after his departure for Poland together with Ellénore: "I can only pity you because you always do what you don't want to do in spite of your desire for independence."[53] This is the paradox in the story of Adolphe's life as related by Constant: his passion for independence merely results in dependence and in situations where he has to do what he never wanted to do. But is it really a paradox? The main lesson of Constant's novel is that it is *not* a paradox; on the contrary, we are mistaken if we suppose that Adolphe's (or anybody's) desire for independence should result in his freedom to do what he wants to.

If we ask how Constant's novel teaches us this counter-intuitive lesson, we must note that all action in the novel originates in Adolphe's strained relationship with Ellénore. There is *no* action outside this relationship and its history. Adolphe's life before he came to know Ellénore was an irrelevancy, and after Ellénore's death Adolphe failed to become the successful man his father and Baron de T—— had expected and hoped. Instead, he became that shadow of a man encountered somewhere in the south of Italy by the supposed source of the novel's text.

Adolphe's regained independence did not turn out to be the necessary condition for new independent action on his part. And this is not because Adolphe was a weak man, though that is true as well. It is rather the reverse: it was because he was a weak man that Adolphe became so passionately interested in his independence. Adolphe says so himself at the beginning of the novel: he explains there how his weakness and inherited timidity kindled in him "un désir ardent d'indépendance."[54] So we must conclude that the kind of action (or, rather, inaction) arising from and associated with the desire for independence can only be found *in* Adolphe's relationship with Ellénore and not *outside* or *beyond* it. This implies in turn that independence only plays its role within a context of dependence. Independence is like a fish swimming in a fishbowl of dependency. Independence is not an autonomous factor but rather something to be regretted or to be restored; in both cases independence presupposes the presence of dependence. Quite revealing here is what Adolphe says much later about his state of mind immediately after the death of Ellénore: "How heavily it weighed upon me, this liberty that I had regretted so much. How much did I miss this dependence that used to revolt me so often."[55] Adolphe always regretted his independence, but as he has now come to realize, what really lay behind this regret was his desire for dependence. Independence and dependence are not each other's opposites at an equal level; independence is rather a feeling about or a reaction to the wish for dependency, and thereby presupposes the latter.

It is not hard to spell out what this implies for the relationship between the state and civil society—another very untidy love affair. When in the field of force between dependence and independence the latter systematically proves to be the weaker of the two, the mutual independence of the state and civil society cannot last for long. All the more so since one of the two, civil society, is the political embodiment of independence, and is therefore by its nature destined to undermine their initial relationship. That it has nevertheless been possible to make the distinction between the state and civil society, and that the distinction was reasonably clear for a century and a half, partly finds its explanation in the absolutism that preceded the political world we have lived in since the beginning of the last century.

Absolutism, as defined by "droit divin" theorists like King James I, Robert Filmer, or Bossuet, only recognized the rulers and the ruled. It had no use for a system of dependence and independence (that is where it differs both from the modern world and from feudalism). The terms "dependence" and "independence" are not part of the vocabulary of absolutism. Admittedly, there is *some* conceptual overlap between the dichotomy of rulers versus ruled and that of dependence versus independence, but this overlap covers only part of their respective meanings. Being ruled differs from dependence. My life may depend on the airplane pilot, but I am not ruled by him; Voltaire was ruled by Louis XV but it would be odd to say that Voltaire was dependent on this monarch. And think of independence: Are we not at first inclined to say that the ruler is independent because he is independent of those he rules? Yet throughout this section we have learned to associate independence with civil society, the sphere of those who are ruled. If we wish to capture the difference between the two dichotomies, we might point out that the distance between ruler and ruled far exceeds that between dependence and independence—not least because of the dialectics between the notions of dependence and independence expounded above. (When I use the word "distance" here, I take it to refer to the metaphorical distance we encountered in our analysis of Plato's metaphor, the distance that proved to be a condition for the maneuverability of the ship of state.)

From the nineteenth century on, however, the system of dependence and independence was grafted onto that of the rulers and the ruled. The inconsistencies between the two systems were concealed by that most obscure concept of all political philosophy, the concept of popular sovereignty. This concept conveniently confounded the two systems in such a way that the politicians and political philosophers who used it could at all times produce the outcome required by the circumstances. For example, because in representative government the rulers are to some extent dependent on the electorate, the sophistry arose that not those who effectively ruled but those who are ruled are the real rulers. The major shortcoming of political thought since the nineteenth century is that it has always failed to distinguish between the system of rulers and ruled and the system of dependence and independence. As we shall see in a moment, that has obscured from view a specific form of political power.

In any case, the absolutist system of rulers and ruled had accumulated over time what we might call a large "capital of (metaphorical) distance." For a century and a half Western politics has lived comfortably on this capital of distance; it is this capital that long made the distinction between the state and civil society both acceptable and realistic. The capital of distance was, however, gradually consumed by the system of dependence and independence. And when the capital of distance was exhausted by the dialectics between dependence and independence, that dialectics had to gain the upper hand, since the system of rulers and ruled now could no longer slow it down. This meant both the dissolution of the boundaries between the state and civil society and a rudderless ship of state.[56]

If we want a closer look at the results of the dialectics of dependence and independence, the story of Adolphe is once again an instructive guide. We should not forget that a great deal happens in the novel: there are outbursts of emotion, there is a passionate love affair, an ensuing concatenation of miseries, and, finally, the death of Ellénore and Adolphe's dwindling into a mere shadow of his former self. Yet all these things happen without anybody seeming to be in charge. A great deal of power is implied in the drama acted out by Ellénore and Adolphe, yet this power does not seem to find its origin in either Ellénore or Adolphe. Their relationship is in many respects similar to that depicted by Hegel in the famous chapter of the *Phenomenology* on the master-slave relationship (in which Hegel also made use of the terminology of dependence and independence). In both cases power relations that originally seem clear and unambiguous are subverted and changed beyond recognition. Thus one could plausibly argue that Adolphe holds all the winning cards whereas Ellénore is condemned to a passive role. But just as strong a case could be made for the opposite view: that Ellénore is in the stronger position. Is not the story of the novel impressive proof of the power she exerts over Adolphe? Yet both views would be incorrect, and they would both fail to do justice to that peculiar dialectics of dependence and independence that governs the relationship between Adolphe and Ellénore. It is perhaps the supreme achievement of Constant's novel that it successfully demonstrates how even in the tiny microcosm of a relationship between two

individuals power can already become anonymous. Power—and as I said a
moment ago, power has been immensely effective in the novel—has been
swept from its foundations in the will, the desires, or the goals of the actors
involved. Power freely circulates here between Adolphe and Ellénore, and
although it occasionally absorbs in its course some external influences like
that of Adolphe's father or of Baron de T——, it largely remains a self-
propelling and self-perpetuating factor that is in nobody's control.

We might therefore discover in *Adolphe* a third paradigm of power; one
that we can only begin to perceive owing to the dialectics of dependence
and independence. The first paradigm of power is that of the heliotrope,
the power of the *roi soleil* to rule his country. Right at the opposite end of
the power spectrum we find Foucault's "capillaries of power," that insidi-
ous kind of power that conceals itself in disciplinary discourse. Foucault's
power is a subtle kind of power, felt or even noticed only by a few, but
nevertheless quite real. It was undoubtedly Foucault's insistence that we
still "have to cut off the King's head" that made him proceed to this other
extreme in the power spectrum without considering any intermediate form
of power. Between the power of the heliotrope and disciplinary power we
can, however, situate a third paradigm of power. This is an anonymous
and unpredictable kind of power, without traceable origins or foundations,
freely circulating around, much like those immense and elusive clouds of
money moving around the financial world in a way that worries so many
contemporary economists; a power whose existence was first suggested by
Constant with his anatomy of independence. This form of power is no less
real, but a great deal more visible, than Foucault's disciplinary power. In
fact, we have already been aware of this kind of power for a long time, albeit
only as an absence, as power*less*ness. But the powerlessness of the modern
state I have in mind here, its inability to steer the ship of state, should
not be seen as mere powerlessness, as an absence of power, as degree zero
on the power scale. Rather, there is another, anonymous kind of power at
work whose operations are still largely a secret to us. In the next section I
shall try to lift a corner of the veil that has covered the mechanism of this
anonymous power that seems to lack foundations.

6. The Empty Versus the Sovereign Center

The gradual dissolution of the boundaries of the state, the increasing entanglement of state and civil society, and the resulting loss of state ma-

neuverability are considered by both politicians and political philosophers to be perhaps the most alarming evolution within contemporary political practice. The intuition underlying their alarm is obviously that these and related developments are unnatural in the sense of being at odds with how we traditionally conceive the nature of the state and of politics itself. The major problem for a correct grasp of this dissolution of the boundaries of the state is that we find it difficult to imagine a political order in which the natural is what we consider unnatural and a degeneration of all political clarity and rationality — and, surely, as long as we accept the heliotrope we cannot do otherwise. Yet such an "unnatural" political order already exists. In many ways this political order and the society supporting it are remarkably successful and effective, perhaps even more so than our own. We all know this society. It is what has been called "the Japanese system."[57] To put it succinctly, the absence of a political center, of a sovereign center — the absence, in short, of the heliotrope — is not accidental to the Japanese political system, but its very essence. Over against our metaphor of the sovereign center, from which the ship of state is steered, Japan places its metaphor of the empty center.

Before entering into a discussion of the Japanese empty center I should comment on some differences between Western and Japanese value systems insofar as these differences are relevant to our subject. Within the Western theological and philosophical tradition some kind of payoff has always been expected from the discussion and identification of universal values. However skeptical, antitheoretical, or antifoundationalist we may have become, we still believe that such universal values are necessary for determining large-scale political action, since they function, so to speak, as the compass for the ship of state. Japan, on the contrary, has little or no use for universal values. A most striking example is given by Edward Seidensticker when he reports that a Japanese student, asked what values she accepted, came up with the following list: "Marxism, non-Marxist socialism, liberalism, humanism, pragmatism, anarchism, nihilism, existentialism, nationalism, hedonism, ideology-free," and, last but not least, "others."[58] The example is extreme, but other inquiries confirm the impression that even educated Japanese simply have no instinct for universal values. And we should not take *that* to be their universal value — the Japanese are no nihilists. The explanation is, rather, that they do not wish to play our game of seeing the political and social order in terms of such universal values. They do not see political reality from the point of view of such values, nor can they believe that these values create political reality. In his magisterial book on Japanese political practice Van Wolferen situates the crucial factor in the exercise of political power in Japan in this "near absence of any idea that there can be truths, rules, principles or morals that always apply, no matter what the circumstances. Most Westerners as well as most Asians who have stayed for any length of time in Japan will be struck by this absence; and some Japanese thinkers also have seen it as the ultimate determinant of Japanese public behavior."[59] The Japanese are not motivated by universal values but by values that are radically particularist, that is, values that are directly related to the wish to realize some specific goal.[60] This leads to a preference for "performance," or to achieving success in individual cases, over "maintenance," or what are the conditions of the achievement of success, since maintenance is a background for discerning particularist goals rather than being such a particularist goal or value itself.[61] This preference may partly explain the dynamism of Japanese society and the surprising ease with which it adapts to new and changing circumstances.

Yet to a certain extent this picture is misleading, for Japan is not completely without universalist values. In his book on the history of Japanese political thought Najita describes this thought as a continuous search for the balance between bureaucracy (*kanryoshugi*) on the one hand and universalist idealism (*ningensi* or *kokoro*) on the other.[62] Right from the beginning of the Tokugawa period, for two to three hundred years longer than the West, the Japanese have been discussing the phenomenon of bureaucracy and the values from which it should draw inspiration. However (and there's the rub), Japanese universal values are, in comparison with those of the West, peculiarly empty and devoid of positive content. Such values are, for example, filial piety, devotion to the Emperor, a striving for *wa*, that is, harmony and consensus, or for striking the right balance between *giri* and *ninjo* or between *on* and *hoon*. These last terms refer to the extreme sense of obligation Japanese are apt to feel toward anybody who has done them a service, however small. This sense of obligation sometimes takes on the features of a kind of social original sin.[63] All in all, such Japanese universal values as there are have the character of loyalties rather than of commitment to what society ought to be like from the point of view of certain ethical or political goals. The emptiness of Japanese values is notably illustrated by an often cited anecdote about a samurai who found himself in the difficult position of having to choose between two such conflicting loyalties. Because of the very emptiness of the two loyalties there was no way for him to decide between them. He had no choice but to commit suicide. The story reminds one of the breakdown of a computer that has been asked to solve some logical contradiction.[64]

But perhaps the emptiness of Japanese universal values is best illustrated by Shinto, Japan's more or less official religion. Shinto is a religion without dogmas, holy books, ethical prescriptions, and so on; it is what we would nowadays call a typically "anti-foundationalist" religion. Now, what one does find in a Shinto shrine, in its holiest of holies, is not an image of the deity, a relic, or some sacred text, but, of all things, a mirror—a mirror, moreover, that neither priest nor worshipper is permitted to look at or in. The mirror has this honored function because, as Ono explains,

> it symbolizes the stainless mind of the kami [the spirit that inheres in all things]. . . . Everything good and bad, right and wrong, is reflected without fail. The mirror is the source of honesty because it has the virtue of responding according to the shape of objects. It points out the fairness and the impartiality of the divine will.[65]

It is precisely the emptiness of the mirror that permits it to reflect what is, without adding anything of itself. The mirror gives us a doubling of reality—one is reminded of the *dédoublement* that Roland Barthes believed to be so characteristic of the Japanese use of the sign[66]—rather than that it gives us a *perspective* on what is. The mirror is "literalist" and "anti-metaphorical."

Most writers on Japan agree that Japanese culture, religion, and politics are very closely related; so much is already suggested by the fact that the word used for referring to politics, *matsurigoto*, originally meant a religious observance.[67] Yet politics is the sphere where the notions and practices of culture and religion are, in a way, recapitulated.[68] Politics is all-pervasive in Japan. We may therefore expect that Japanese politics has an analogue to the empty center in ethics and religion. This is in fact the case, according to the main thesis of Van Wolferen's book on how power functions in the Japanese system. In Japan, writes Van Wolferen, there is

> a hierarchy, or rather a complex of overlapping hierarchies. But it has no peak: it is a truncated pyramid. There is no supreme institution with ultimate policy-making jurisdiction. Hence there is no place where, as Harry Truman would have said, the buck stops. In Japan, the buck keeps circulating.[69]

The irony about Japan is that it impresses outsiders with the idea that it is an economic giant deliberately and singlemindedly bent on the economic conquest of the world. But there is no master plan behind it all for the very simple reason that Japan lacks the political center for developing such a master plan.[70] Nor should it be thought that this political center has abolished itself and delegated its right to and its capacity for policy-making to other institutions. For exactly the same pattern emerges when we look closely at the bureaucracy and the world of trade and industry. Whether we have to do with the relations between the state, the bureaucracy, and the world of trade and industry, or whether we have to deal with each of these spheres individually, decision-making and policy-making in Japan differ from what we are accustomed to in the West in that it always seems intent on blurring the lines of responsibility and accountability; it is as if hierarchy only exists in order to conceal and to raise an impenetrable mist around what really goes on (or *should* be going on according to Western premises).[71] Thus, it has been found that the process of coming to a conclusion or decision is in Japan effectively rounded off by deliberately creating a "final ambiguity with respect to authority and responsibility for the proposal." [72] If the hierarchy's function is to hide what really goes on—and as such it is a vital necessity!—it follows that Japan has no use whatsoever for strong charismatic leaders. A Napoleon would be utterly inconceivable in Japan,[73] and there can be no greater mistake than to believe that the Japanese leaders during the Second World War had anything in common with Hitler or Mussolini.

The prime example of all this is the Japanese emperor and his function in the Japanese political universe. One is inclined to put the Japanese emperor on a level with Europe's remaining constitutional monarchs, since there is in both cases a discrepancy between hierarchical status and the possession of real power. But the apparent similarity is misleading. Generally speaking, the outward appearances of Japanese parliamentary democracy must not be misinterpreted as evidencing the existence of a real parliamentary democracy. For one thing, whereas the ancestors of the European constitutional monarchs once possessed real power, this has never been the case with the emperor in Japanese history. There never has been a Japanese *roi soleil* (even if the emperor is believed to be a descendant of the sun, or of Amiterasu, the goddess of the sun). The powerlessness of the Japanese emperor already amazed Chinese chroniclers in the third century A.D.[74] The powerlessness of the emperor is not an ingenious solution for a constitutional problem—in the way that Benjamin Constant came to circumscribe the role of the constitutional monarch as "un pouvoir neutre" with the task of arbitrating between Montesquieu's three powers[75]—but is paradigmatic for how the Japanese wish to screen the origins and exercise of effective power. That the powerlessness of the emperor is paradigmatic of the anonymity of Japanese political power rather than the result of a constitutional arrangement is also clear from the fact that exactly the same phenomenon is repeated at lower levels: official dignitaries below the emperor often functioned as no less visible but in fact powerless screens behind which real power was exercised.[76] And yet the institution of imperial rule was never abolished; such an abolition was never contemplated in the whole of recorded Japanese history. We are thus left with the conclusion that the institution of the emperor served a hidden but vital purpose: namely, the creation of an empty political center and of an anonymous power without foundations, since these foundations so obviously could not be where they *seemed* to be.

The full sovereign political center typical of the West, however this center may be defined, exists because we are prepared to look at ourselves in a political context from the top down. As we found when discussing the Western political heliotrope and the Hobbesian concept of the state, we in the West are required to identify with the point of view of the sovereign center, and are inclined to even if we have only our own selfish interests at heart. In Japan the movement is exactly opposite. It is a movement that the Japanese refer to by the word *rengo-sei*, that is, "super-subordination":[77] the superior moves downwards, so to speak, to the subordinate and by doing so sanctions the latter's actions. The superior is required to identify with the point of view of the subordinate rather than the other way round. Thus the emperor has been described by Najita as "a constant spiritual presence accessible to and, indeed, coincidental with everyone."[78] It will be clear—and this is the key to the secret—that this coincidence of the emperor with everyone is only possible to the extent that the emperor remains a completely empty presence: only thanks to this emptiness is such a "dissemination" of his presence conceivable. Any concreteness of imperial will would upset the movement of *rengo-sei* and put an end to the anonymity of political power.

In the West the sovereign is situated, as it were, "ahead of us": the citizen and the civil servant follow the sovereign by identifying themselves with his heliotropic point of view (that they may contribute to its material definition does not alter this). In Japan the sovereign is, rather, "behind" the citizen or civil servant, for the sovereign is prevented by his emptiness from giving actual guidance. This does not mean that the Japanese equivalent of the Western sovereign legitimates *ex post facto* the actions of the civil servant. For the notion of legitimacy has its origin in the heliotrope, which does not apply to Japan. Even more beside the point would be the suggestion that the Japanese exercise of power is more democratic than that of the West, owing to the absence of a sovereign will in the empty center. It is not illuminating to see the differences between the West and Japan in terms of democracy; these differences rather concern the notion of sovereignty itself, and that is an issue prior to questions of democracy. It would be no exaggeration to say, instead, that the Japanese metaphor of the empty center is, from the Western point of view, a formal denial of the notion of sovereignty. For Japanese politics only needs a supposedly sovereign center so that it can deny this center the quality of being the source, origin, or foundation of power—though as such the center is absolutely vital. It is like Magritte's painting of a pipe with the caption underneath saying that this is not a pipe—and, indeed, the painting *is* not a pipe. Surely, all this is mindboggling for us, who are accustomed to Western patterns of power; but a grasp of the Japanese system can also help us understand the new kind of political power that is slowly emerging from the familiar constitutional constraints of our own Western politics.

The exercise of political power does not take place in a vacuum. The psychology of a people and its sociological characteristics are not only a reflection but a part of power. A political philosophy neglecting psychological and sociological determinants must necessarily remain, as was stressed some years ago by Maurice Sandel in his debate with Rawls,[79] a purely academic game only of interest to a few professional philosophers. I therefore turn now to the psychological explanation of the Japanese empty center given by Takeo Doi in his *Anatomy of Dependence*.[80] Central to Doi's argument is the concept of *amae* and the related verb *amaeru*. The word *amae* is the center of a complicated web of other words whose meanings lack exact analogues in Western languages and, even more surprisingly, suggest different translations that actually contradict one another.[81] The Japanese mind really seems to be incommensurable here with that of the West. The *Daigenkai*, the Japanese dictionary, translates the word *amae* as "to lean on a person's good will";[82] *amaeru* means to behave self-indulgently in the safe and reassuring confidence that the other will love you all the more for it.[83] *Amae* has its origin in the nursery and is closely related to the process during which the child separates itself from its mother and begins to give itself an identity of its own. Doi clarifies *amae* by contrasting positive and negative love and by associating *amae* with the latter. Positive love is a reaching for the loved object; negative love is creating, by showing *amae* behavior, a kind of emotional void or suction that will attract the loved object and make it reach for *you*. With its *amae* behavior the child displays a specific kind of dependence aimed at making the mother identify with the child. In negative love and in *amae* we encounter once again the wish to make the outside world identify with the subject, a wish we discussed a moment ago in the form of *rengo-sei*. In both cases there is a psychological or emotional inversion.

It is Doi's conviction that the concept of *amae* is essential for a proper understanding of the nature of Japanese politics. He backs his claim by presenting the emperor as the embodiment of the nation's desire to *amaeru*. What *amae*, taken politically, aims at is establishing a relation of dependence—hence the title of his book. But it is a peculiar kind of dependence which is in some respects different from the notion of dependence we talked about in connection with Constant's *Adolphe*. This kind of dependence has nothing to do with, for example, the relation between a medieval knight and his feudal lord. It is, writes Doi, the kind of dependence we must ascribe to the Japanese emperor. The emperor depends entirely on his subordinates, who shoulder all actual responsibilities and fulfill all the actual tasks of government: "The emperor is in a position to expect that those about him will attend to all matters great and small, including, of course, the government of the country. In one sense he is entirely dependent on those about him, yet status-wise it is those about him who are subordinate to the emperor. When his degree of dependence is considered, he is no different from a babe in arms, yet his rank is the highest in the land, a fact which is surely proof of the respect accorded to infantile dependence in Japan."[84] The emperor is the embodiment of the Japanese desire for *amae*: that is, for combining complete dependence with being the center of everything. And that is why we find at the center of Japanese politics an emptiness that is occupied by a person as helpless and dependent as a newborn; indeed, it is precisely this utter helplessness and dependence that qualifies him for this position. How far are we removed here from the *roi soleil* and his modern successors in the West!

Political power in the West owes its legitimacy, its visibility, and its origin to the fact that it is reducible to a well-defined center, be it God; God's lieutenant on earth, the absolute monarch; the people; or, in constitutional practice, that point where parliament and government meet. Through this reducibility political power in the West is always its own double: it always has—or at least ought to have—its shadow or counterpart in its origins or foundations. Power in the West has a fondness for the cloak of representation: Western power always prefers to represent something else, God, a social order, the people, history or the structure of the human being or of society. This is where Western power differs from that of Japan. Japanese power has no double, is not reducible to certain origins or foundations: it is what it is. Yet Japanese power is no less well-organized, no less subtle than that of the West. It would be a grave mistake to interpret this kind of anonymous power, as we find it on a large scale in Japan, with chaos or mere arbitrariness. So it may appear if we forget to abrogate our Western, heliotropic presuppositions. But anonymous power is very well able to organize a complex social and political world.

No one has expressed this better than Roland Barthes, who used the map of Tokyo as metaphor for the Japanese empty center. Tokyo is a highly complex city without a clear and well-defined plan; strangers have the greatest difficulty in finding their way about. Road signs are often lacking and only elaborate maps drawn for the purpose by inhabitants show strangers how to get from one place to another. The only obvious landmark in the city is the center. But it is a secret and forbidden center, since it is the palace of the emperor. "Tokyo does have a center, but this center is empty. The whole city circulates around a place both forbidden and indifferent." [85] And yet this ill-ordered city, turning around an empty center that has nothing to hide, this urban metaphor of the Japanese "system of power," has now become the economic capital of the modern world.

7. *Conclusion*

My point of departure in this chapter has been the controllability of the state by the statesman—or of civil society by the state, if, unlike Plato, we decide to distinguish between the state and civil society. We have seen that political metaphor is instrumental in securing this control. More specifically, metaphor creates the distance between the political helmsman and social and political reality required for all meaningful political action. Distance stabilizes political reality. Thus metaphor assumes the form of the heliotrope, as it often has in the history of Western political thought; an initially diffuse political reality will harden into an objective, external reality like the physical reality investigated by the scientist. Political metaphor—

or rather the heliotrope—and political reality are each other's counterparts and presuppose one another. Hence the permanent tendency of Western political thought to develop political systems pretending to be accurate reflections of the actual nature of political reality, and its no less permanent ambition to claim for these political systems the capacity to put an end to all politics. For if a political system correctly reflects the nature of political reality it can show us the way to a situation in which future political action will no longer be needed. This is obviously true for Plato's ideal state, for the natural law philosophies of the early modern period, and for their subsequent nineteenth-century historicizations as found in Hegel or Marx; only Machiavellianism and *raison d'état* doctrines are the exceptions to this rule.

Thanks to this metaphorical distance most Western political philosophies imply and emphasize referentiality: they always are theories about a supposedly theory-independent political reality, and from this metaphorical distance they tell us how best to deal with it. Here I would like to recall the tendency of Western political philosophy to see political power as representative of something outside itself (whether it be God, the nature of the body politic, or the people). In other words, the distance between political language and a heliotropically defined political reality is in the Western tradition not merely a fine epistemological point about the relation between words and things: this distance is the birthplace of the kind of political power we know in the West. Political action and political power only become possible after the two have been separated in this way.[86] By seeing words and things as mutually independent in the sphere of politics, Western political theorists implicitly defined the kind of political power that would rule our world. Political power in the West is the power of the heliotropical word that presents itself as independent of a heliotropically defined political reality. Political power is the power of language—a thesis, of course, that has been elaborated *ad nauseam* by countless theorists of political ideology and by Foucault's followers.

In contrast to this *power of language*, we find in the Japanese system the *language of power*. As the Japanese counterpart to the political metaphor of the West we may think of the haiku. These unpretentious, homely, and often rather trivial three-line poems seem very far removed from the sphere of politics. But if our analysis of political metaphor has taught us anything it is that we must put aside our naivety with regard to the political significance of linguistic phenomena. Moreover, if the haiku seems irrelevant to us from a political point of view, that may well be because the haiku prevents us from recognizing its political import by being the very opposite of political metaphor.

Indeed, I propose to consider the haiku here for no other reason than that its contrast with political metaphor is so striking. I follow here Roland Barthes. In a few brilliant pages Barthes argued that the haiku effects "une exemption du sens,"[87] an abstention from giving meaning to reality; or, at least, the haiku suggests "un sens obstrué."[88] Where political metaphor gives meaning to reality or even defines it, the haiku seems to have no other purpose than to take meaning back again. For the haiku possesses no clear, developed, rhetorical meaning as does poetic language in the West; the haiku does not aim at expressing something deep or universal about either the world or ourselves. Whereas language in the West wants to erase itself by being transparent with regard to an underlying reality to which it refers and that is represented by it, the haiku is merely suggestive of an interplay of language with itself. As Barthes put it, language in the West has the aspiration "de suspendre le language, non de le provoquer"—whereas the aim of the haiku is this provocation of language.[89] And the haiku achieves this provocation of language by its having no pronounced sense or meaning itself. Barthes here compares the haiku to a self-effacing host who invites his guests to make themselves as comfortable as possible.[90] Precisely because the haiku is a kind of semantic void, a semantic emptiness, it can provoke a circulation of language and meaning. Because of its high degree of readability, its almost platitudinous openness, the haiku allows any number of associations or interpretations. The haiku is like an exchangeable coin going from hand to hand, which all can use for their own purposes. According to Barthes this emptiness of the haiku's semantic center is even typical of the Japanese use of the sign in general. Is Japan then, Barthes asks, "l'empire des signes?" and he answers: "Oui, si l'on entend que ces signes sont vides et que le rituel est sans dieu [Yes, if one agrees that these signs are empty and that the ritual is without a god]."[91]

So it is with political power. Power does not represent in Japan; it is not the substitute for or the double of another reality behind which it tries to hide itself. Power is just what it is. Power goes from one hand to the other like money or the haiku and its movements do not reflect a deeper structure of social or political reality. Thus, in the transition from the political metaphor of the West to the Japanese haiku we witness the transition from a Foucauldian *power of language* to the *language of power*, to a power with no double. This power, which is rather a *speaking* than a *speaking about*, we may expect to find in societies without deep social cleavages and where even the scars of earlier social strife and conflict tend to disappear. For social cleavages and conflicts were always the paramount producers of political metaphor. It is an uncertain kind of power in that it no longer urges us to follow the path of history as defined within some grand historical meta-narrative. But in spite of its uncertainty it is quite capable of, and even ideally suited to, structuring the postindustrial societies of the present and of the near future. No less than language itself, the language of power is a subtle and refined structure that permits us to tell any number of stories without *presupposing* any one of them.

6. Metaphor and Paradox in Tocqueville's Political Writings

> All this can be taken as evidence of the recognition that narrative, far from being merely a form of discourse that can be filled with different contents, real or imaginary as the case may be, already possesses a content prior to any given actualization of it in speech or in writing.
>
> —H. White, *The Content of the Form*

1. Introduction

No theorist of democracy has received more praise than Tocqueville. From Tocqueville's contemporary John Stuart Mill down to present-day authors like D. Riesman, D. A. Dahl, or F. Furet, political theorists, sociologists, and historians have found in Tocqueville's oeuvre their major inspiration for an analysis of democracy and its historical origins.[1] But although Tocqueville's views have been so very influential, it is surprisingly difficult to summarize his theory of democracy. This is all the more surprising since the major textbooks appear to have little difficulty in identifying convincingly a few central theses in Tocqueville's political philosophy. One can think here of Tocqueville's insight into the strained relation between freedom and equality, his thesis about the continuity between the ancien régime and the Revolution or about democracy's inclination to develop into a "tutelary despotism." Indeed, no one will contest the presence of these views in Tocqueville's oeuvre, nor that he doubted their truth and significance, nor that Tocqueville's wish to make his contemporaries aware of these insights into the nature and the origins of democracy was the chief aim of his writing. Yet the more detailed one's analysis of Tocqueville's work becomes, the less happy one will be with these and similar summaries. Of course we lose something in summarizing, but in most cases we are prepared to accept the loss, since we get a grasp of the whole in return. But the peculiar thing about Tocqueville's oeuvre is that we seem to lose precisely the essence or a grasp of the whole by attempting to reduce it to its essence. Summarizing Tocqueville seems inevitably to result in some stale and relatively uninteresting truths; it reduces the intellectual depth of his thought to the level of trivial conversation. It is as if the essence of his oeuvre is that it does *not* have an essence; as if we could not better summarize his work than by saying that it cannot be summarized.

Two reasons can be given for this peculiar resistance to summary. First, such major theses as we can find in Tocqueville's work are in many cases contradicted by other passages in it; the truth is that Western political thought knows few texts so conspicuous for lack of consistency as those of Tocqueville. Second, close reading of the text suggests that Tocqueville's major insights can only be found at what one might call the micro-level. There is much truth in Elster's remark that in Tocqueville's work "the details are more interesting than the whole, the arguments more forceful than the conclusions, the individual mechanisms more robust than its general theories."[2] There seems to be no "macro-theory" present in his writings. One might infer from this that, despite appearances, Tocqueville has no "theory of democracy" in the proper sense of the word to offer to his readers; it may seem that his work is not an attempt to lay bare the hitherto hidden essence or nature of democracy. Or, to put the same idea in a more positive, possibly truer, and certainly more interesting way, it might be that we ought to interpret Tocqueville as saying that, in fact, no theory of democracy is possible and that precisely our effort to theorize about democracy will prevent us from seeing what is really new and interesting about it.[3]

It will be my main purpose in this chapter to demonstrate the plausibility of such an antitheoretical interpretation of Tocqueville's texts; I hope to make it clear that both the form and the content of Tocqueville's work are a protest against the attempt to objectify democracy, to look at it from a certain distance in order to develop a theory of it. If one tries to take a stand outside democracy itself in order to get a clear view of it, democracy will lose its contours and our analysis will be automatically transformed into some latter-day variant of aristocracy, that is, into a theory of despotism (and this is what actually happens in certain parts of Tocqueville's oeuvre itself). To the extent that we allow ourselves to be convinced, or even only intrigued, by Tocqueville's analysis, Tocqueville's texts are an implicit suggestion about which manner or style we ought to adopt if we wish to say anything useful about democracy. In a curiously oblique way Tocqueville's texts show that its antitheoretical, antimetaphorical, and paradoxical style is the only key to the secrets of democracy. In contrast to relatively crude political systems like feudalism, aristocracy, or absolutism, the philosophical web of democracy is so subtle and intricate that we will tear it apart if we approach it with an unsuitable stylistic apparatus. Before starting to think or to write about democracy, we will have to make up our mind about the style to adopt for doing so; reversing that order will inevitably make us blind to its most interesting features. Never is an acute awareness of White's thesis of the content of the form more necessary than when we start talking about democracy.

2. Social Meaning

"Aristocracy had made a chain of all the members of the community, from the peasant to the king; democracy breaks that chain and severs every link of it" (*Dem. II*, 105). Aristocracy knew a sociological or social "great chain of being," expressive of the harmony existing in the social order; each social rank, from the highest station to the lowest, was necessary and indispensable. The social system was truly a chain because all ranks were closely tied together, so much so that all members of society could satisfy themselves by defining their rank or position in terms of the other ranks that were closest to their own. For what one could say about the members of the aristocracy — namely, that each of them "was a vassal as well as a lord" (*Dem. II*, 245) — was metaphysically true of *all* the members of aristocratic society. Precisely because all members of the social hierarchy could sufficiently define themselves or their social rank in terms of their social neighbors, the social chain could take on an aspect of objectivity: nobody needed to appeal to the great chain as a whole. As a whole it could remain an entity in its own right lying beyond the grasp (intellectual or political) of all the members of society. Thus it became an objective reality like the natural order.

Here lies the explanation of the fact noted by Tocqueville that patriotism is inconceivable in feudal, aristocratic society (*Dem. II*, 246). Because the social chain of being was experienced as an objective, external reality, nobody, not even the king, could identify himself with it. Not even the king could be a patriot. For like the sea, a mountain, or a tree, the social chain can never truly be a part of ourselves. Patriotism or nationalism presupposes not so much an awareness of the national character as the end of the objective existence of the social chain of being; it therefore is a prelude to the death of aristocracy. It subjectifies an objective reality, makes us part of it and thus brings us democracy.

Thanks to this hierarchization of aristocratic society, social meaning can become unexpectedly clear and precise. For precision is an aristocratic virtue. Object and meaning, action or language, and what is expressed by action and language are tied together by very precise referential laws in aristocracy. Tocqueville explains the mechanism producing fixed social meaning in his discussion of honor in aristocratic and democratic societies. Since honor is given such a different content in different (ranks of) societies and is often the supreme code of behavior, honor is perhaps paradigmatic of all social meaning and for the same reasons is probably the best locus for investigating it.

The precision of social meaning in aristocracy is explained by Tocqueville as follows:

> It is surprising, at first sight, that when the sense of honor is most predominant, its injunctions are usually most strange; so that the further it is removed from common reason, the better it is obeyed; whence it has sometimes been inferred that the laws of honor were strengthened by their own extravagance. The two things, indeed, originate from the same source, but the one is not derived from the other. Honor becomes fantastic in proportion to the peculiarity of the wants that it denotes and the paucity of them by whom those wants are felt; and it is because it denotes wants of this kind that its influence is great. Thus the notion of honor is not the stronger for being fantastic, but it is fantastic and strong from the selfsame cause. (*Dem. II*, 253)

Hence it is this "paucity" of the number of people accepting a certain code of honor—or, put differently, the fact that moral codes or codes of honor are class-specific—which explains *both* the power that these codes exercise *and* the fact that these codes come to be very well articulated. It seems self-evident that the tendency of these codes to become "fantastic" is a derivative of the urge for articulation of the codes: the more fantastic they are, the more successful they will be in distinguishing themselves from other codes (and the classes adopting these other codes). In other words, social meaning requires for its clarity and articulation the background of a social hierarchy to which it can be related and to which it can be better related the more this hierarchy is experienced as an objective reality. In aristocratic society it was not the character of the action itself but its relation to the social hierarchy that determined its meaning and thus guaranteed that meaning was precise: in the feudal world actions were not praised or blamed with reference to their intrinsic worth but rather "appreciated exclusively with reference to the person who was the actor or the object of them" (*Dem. II*, 243).

Tocqueville does not wish to deny that in democracy (that is, in America) some reminiscences of the notion of aristocratic honor survived, like a religion that has still a few temples left standing (*Dem. II*, 247), but, generally speaking, he believes the notion of honor has lost both its content and its former precision in democracy. This is not because more and more people in democratic society pretended to accept the same social code so that no room was left anymore for the category of the fantastic that gave aristocratic social meaning its precision and articulation (although this undoubtedly is also part of the truth). What is more important is that social meaning lost its referential anchors in an objective outside of a fixed social hierarchy. Or, as Tocqueville puts it himself: "Thus, to comprise all my meaning in a single proposition, the dissimilarities and inequalities of men gave rise to the notion of honor; that notion is weakened in proportion as these differences are obliterated, and with them it would disappear" (*Dem. II*, 255). In aristocracy social meaning has an outside (that is, the social chain), to which it refers or which it reflects, that is absent in democracy. Social meaning in democracy therefore lacks the clarity, precision, and articulation it used to have in aristocracy.

This pattern of the gradual disintegration of social meaning with the advent of democracy is repeated within the sphere of linguistic meaning. Tocqueville observes that in aristocracy different segments of society, although all sharing a common origin, may nevertheless become complete strangers to each other (*Dem. II*, 71). This process may go so far that these different segments experience each other as if they were different races (*Dem. II*, 16). As an example Tocqueville cites a letter of Mme de Sévigné written in 1675 to her daughter; the letter demonstrates her complete inability to identify with, or to feel even the slightest compassion for, the sufferings of the lower classes. Yet, Tocqueville adds, we would be mistaken to believe Mme de Sévigné to be a selfish or cruel person (*Dem. II*, 174, 175). According to Tocqueville, this segregation of society, as exemplified by Mme de Sévigné, goes together with a corresponding segregation of the languages spoken by the nobleman, the citizen, or the peasant. But, contrary to what one might expect, this social and linguistic differentiation does not lead to confusion, but to an unparalleled precision in the way language is or was used and spoken (*Dem. II*, 71, 72). For when asked by Nassau Senior what he considered to be the Golden Age of French literature, Tocqueville pronounced in favor of aristocratic seventeenth century authors like Pascal and Bossuet, followed at a short distance by "les Quatre" of the no less aristocratic eighteenth century: Voltaire, Montesquieu, Rousseau, and Buffon.[4]

What attracted him so much in these authors and what, in his eyes, set them so much apart from contemporary Romantic writers like Lamartine, was the clarity, simplicity, and directness of their style. Lamartine, like most "democratic" authors, is typically incapable of such clarity, since he wishes to bridge the gap between private and public in his attempt to make his readers his "accomplices."[5] Social uncertainty or confusion leads in the democratic use of language to uncertainty in meaning. The literary men of the seventeenth and eighteenth centuries did not attempt, like Lamartine, to make common cause with their readers. They were therefore not seduced to achieve a (con)fusion of viewpoints: "Style was then the mere vehicle of thought. First of all to be perspicuous, and then being perspicuous, to be concise was all they aimed at."[6] This was enough—and it was feasible.

Democracy fuses the different segments of society into one undifferentiated mass, and by doing so transposes confusion from the social sphere to that of meaning and language. The main feature of the latter process is a loosening of the ties between words and their referents. The motor behind this estrangement between language and the world in democracy is, according to Tocqueville, democracy's passion for abstraction. He considers this to be one of the most dangerous and most objectionable propensities of democracy; "nothing," he declares, "is more unproductive to the mind than an abstract idea" (*Dem. II*, 243). As soon as abstraction becomes popular, meaning no longer originates in a relation to the world, but in the interplay between abstractions; an interplay intensified by democracy through an exaggerated use of figures of speech and the attempt to tie together metaphorically what is different in reality (*Dem. II*, 70). "Abstraction" thus repeats in the domain of language and meaning democracy's rejection of an objective social great chain of being. It is therefore only in a democracy that we can come across highly abstract locutions like "la force des choses veut que les capacités gouvernent [the force of things requires that the capacities govern]" (*Dem. II*, 73). And Tocqueville ruefully concedes that his own use of the term "equality" shows how much he himself has fallen victim to democracy's fatal love of abstractions.[7] No writer of the age of Louis XIV would ever have used the word "equality" in the way he does; in aristocratic society one would have used the word exclusively when applied to a particular thing (*Dem. II*, 73). Apparently, as soon as "democratic" language comes into being, it is impossible *not* to use it. The unclarity of democratic social meaning serves a vital purpose after the advent of democracy.

Tocqueville's thesis about the clarity and referentiality of social (and linguistic) meaning under aristocracy—and the subsequent loss of this clarity and referentiality in democratic society—seems to be contradicted by his conviction expressed elsewhere that democracy, in contrast with aristocracy, adores realism and is in love with "hard facts." Americans, writes Tocqueville, are only interested in facts and not in opinions (*Dem. II*, 195). This seems to tie language and meaning to reality in a way we would rather have expected in aristocracy, as presented by him. Democracy's love of realism is already manifest, Tocqueville argues, in what one might call democratic art. In democratic art (he mentions David as an example), reality is followed with the utmost fidelity, nothing of the mind is added and no idealist correction of reality (as found in the aristocratic art of Rafael) is permitted. In short, democracy puts the real in the place of the ideal (*Dem. II*, 54). And we might add still another reason for democracy's realist preoccupations. If social meaning can no longer be tied referentially to the social great chain of being of aristocracy, if such a differentiation of the social hierarchy no longer guarantees the articulation of meaning, what is more natural under such circumstances than to anchor meaning in objective, real facts functioning as a surrogate for that great chain of being? If we have no longer a *social* basis for meaning, objective *reality* is what we should resort to; we can recognize ourselves and each other in its terms. An objective (social) *order* is thus replaced by an objective (natural) *mirror*. And, surely, all this seems hard to reconcile with the idea that aristocracy surpasses democracy in the attempt to create clear and intersubjective meaning.

If we ask Tocqueville how we must explain and account for this apparent contradiction, his answer runs as follows. The crucial datum is that, in contrast to people in an aristocracy, democratic people are always a prey to doubt. In aristocracies life is relatively stable, whereas in democracies one's situation is forever uncertain and changing. It is this extreme mobility of their fortunes that prevents people in democracy from holding on to any of their opinions and to the linguistic means used for expressing it. People in democracies, writes Tocqueville, will therefore require "loose expressions" in order to convey and represent their uncertainties and unstable convictions (*Dem. II*, 74).

What emerges from this is the following picture. In a certain sense it is true that the urge for realism is stronger in democracy than in an aristocracy. But the interesting fact is, rather, that aristocracies and democracy each entertain different notions of what realism is and what we can expect from it. Aristocracy's realism consists mainly of being true to the facts, whereas democracy requires a kind of realism that will allow it to come to terms with its permanent instability and uncertainty. For aristocracy reality is something that is unproblematically given; for democracy realism is, to put it paradoxically, a sublime and almost unattainable ideal. Aristocratic reality has a firm and solid support in the social great chain of being; in a democracy reality is something we must rather strive for, it is what we passionately wish to identify with for fear of losing it forever. Reality here is not a given but a goal.

The contrasts between aristocratic and democratic drama exemplify this difference. Aristocratic drama, with its display of classical heroes and its interest in the (mis)fortunes of kings, did not, at least according to Tocqueville, call for an identification of the public with the events on the stage. Instead, in the days of Louis XIV, the audience focused on the probability of the plot, the consistency of the characters, and the plausibility of their actions (*Dem. II*, 87). In democracy, on the other hand, the public above all wishes to be able to identify with what takes place on the stage; the democratic spectators wish "to see on the stage that medley of conditions, feelings and opinions that occurs before their eyes" (*Dem. II*, 81). In aristocracy, reality is what can be *correctly represented*, and the emphasis is on truth and plausibility; in democracy reality is what we can and will *identify* with, and the hidden emphasis is on illusion, or on the "reality effect" in the sense meant by Barthes.

And now we can solve the contradiction between democracy's love of realism on the one hand and its abandonment of aristocratic clarity and precision on the other. First, democracy's perpetual fight for reality (realism, the facts) is a far more dramatic and desperate one than in aristocracy. The easy assurance of aristocracy's attitude toward reality having been lost, democracy hopes to bridge the gap between reality and itself by an energetic effort to identify with, or to become part of, reality. Second, the "public" means for achieving such an identification—language, art, and drama being the domains singled out by Tocqueville—are continuously put into question by the instability and uncertainty of the fortunes of people in democracy. If the politician, the dramatist, or the novelist wants, like Lamartine, to make the public an "accomplice" in giving it the (doubtful) suggestion of a shared reality, a certain amount of unclarity and abstraction (hiding differences), which corresponds to the instability of the fortunes of democratic people and the differences among them, is not only inevitable but even desirable. And this is why realism and imprecision or unclarity must go together in democracy. For it is precisely democracy's realism that requires it to create a kind of semantic void or no man's land at the heart of everything that is said and done. It is this semantic void that enables democratic social meaning to satisfy these two requirements: permitting an illusion of reality; and being adapted to the changeability of democratic social conditions.

The same pattern is repeated if we take a look at democratic poetry or rhetorics and at the public monuments erected by democracy—those bearers of social meaning par excellence. Democratic poetry is no longer interested in the gods and classical heroes that abound in aristocratic poetry. And since the democratic poet feels only occasionally challenged by inanimate nature, he or she will naturally focus on humankind itself. This interest in humanness provokes once again that peculiar or even paradoxical dualism we noted above. For if the poet focuses on individual people "he will be engaged in the contemplation of a very puny object, himself. But if he raises his looks higher, he perceives only the immense face of society or the still more imposing aspect of mankind" (*Dem. II*, 82). Democratic poetry and rhetorics will therefore always hesitate between being absorbed by the smallest details on the one hand and a proclivity to "exaggerated descriptions," "strange creations," and "fantastic beings" on the other (*Dem. II*, 83). Poetry, like the ideas and interests of democratic people themselves, will be "either extremely minute and clear or extremely vague and general; what lies between is a void" (*Dem. II*, 82).

The same is true for public monuments. During his journey through the United States Tocqueville noted that Americans raise many insignificant monuments and a few of the largest scale, "but between the two extremes there is a blank" (*Dem. II*, 56). Social meaning as exemplified by public monuments is polarized in democracy between the petty detail and the large, pathetic gesture and moves around the empty center that comes into being thanks to this polarization.

Let us summarize now Tocqueville's insights into social and linguistic meaning. Meaning in democracy is realist. But democracy lacks aristocracy's capacity to generate an objective (social) reality as embodied by the social great chain of being. Democracy's love of realism is therefore predominantly a wish to repossess what has been lost; it surely does not originate from the confident choice of a solid referential basis for all social meaning. Next, Tocqueville's sociology of knowledge demonstrates how social meaning is pulled in two mutually opposed directions by this intense effort to regain access to reality. As a result social meaning gets polarized between the concrete detail and empty abstraction. Between these two opposites a void or blank comes into being around which social meaning continuously oscillates.

3. Opinion

In the previous section we saw that meaning in democracy, both social and linguistic, is systematically out of focus. Tocqueville makes clear that the same is true for opinion in democracy. Since social meaning and opinion are not far apart from one another, this need not surprise us.

"It was remarked by a man of genius," writes Tocqueville, "that ignorance lies at the two ends of knowledge," and he adds the following clarification: "perhaps it would have been more correct to say that strong convictions are found only at the ends and that doubt lives in the middle" (*Dem. II*, 196). Individuals start with having very firm, though often incorrect, opinions. Next the activity of the press, so effective in democracy, exposes them to a wealth of different opinions—and individuals begin to doubt. Those who persevere in their quest for truth may ultimately find knowledge after having crossed this sea of doubt and skepticism lying between the two states of firm conviction. As a critic of democracy Tocqueville is quick to point out the dangers of this regime of knowledge and opinion in democracy: he fears that belief will prefer the domain of opinion to that of knowledge and that people gradually will lose the habit of exposing opinion to what opinion is about. This regime of knowledge and opinion cannot fail to dull the mind. On the other hand, Tocqueville graciously grants the indispensability of the domain of opinion. If we would have to convince ourselves of the validity of all our beliefs, life would become impossible. The intellect of the individual who nevertheless decides to take up this heroic stance would be "at once independent and powerless" (*Dem. II*, 10)—which seems to justify the amazing paradox that the potential exercise of power presupposes dependence. So to a certain extent our subjection to public opinion can best be seen as a "salutary servitude" (*Dem. II*, 10).

Opinion in democracy, therefore, is governed by a remarkable mixture of skepticism and credulity. The set of publicly held beliefs that are born from this mixture is what we call "public opinion." Since this mixture of skepticism and credulity is inconceivable for knowledge and science (many contemporary philosophers of science would probably disagree with Tocqueville here) this is how we can distinguish between knowledge or science and public opinion. But apart from this fairly natural distinction there is a more interesting feature of public opinion that we ought to take into account. The term "public opinion" is suggestive of something solid, unitary, and well defined. It is true that this suggestion is sometimes in agreement with Tocqueville's manifest intentions — for example, when he discusses (in many places) the "tyranny" of public opinion or when he personifies public opinion (in a manner reminiscent of Jacques Offenbach, that other deconstructivist *avant la lettre*, in his best-known opera) as "more than ever the mistress of the world" (*Dem. II*, 11).

But in other places where Tocqueville is more careful, it becomes clear that the suggestion is mistaken. Once more, the contrast between aristocracy and democracy is the best point of departure. In aristocracy opinion originates with "a superior person" or "a superior class of persons" (*Dem. II*, 11). In democracy, on the other hand, public opinion is the result of a complex interplay of the opinions held by the persons constituting the multitude. As a result, (public) opinion in aristocracy will have the well-defined and precise character of an assent to dogma. In democracy, on the other hand, public opinion is a fragmentary cloud of private opinions subject to a constant metamorphosis that nobody can predict or command. One could express Tocqueville's intentions by saying that democracy demonstrates the "privatization" of a domain that was still public or a public property in aristocracy (consequently, the term "public opinion" is an oxymoron). Opinion has become something that one may change, exchange, destroy, or cultivate, as one can do with one's own private possessions (whereas opinion in aristocracy is inviolable for the individual; there it truly is a public possession). And public opinion is the (largely unintended) result of what the public, "the multitude" in Tocqueville's terminology, decides to do with its collective intellectual property. But this constitutes no more of a self-contained unity than the gross national product. Indeed, Tocqueville himself emphasizes this equivalence of property and opinion when he writes that "in democracy men are no longer bound by ideas, but by interests; and it would seem as if human opinions were reduced to a sort of intellectual dust, scattered on every side, unable to collect, unable to cohere" (*Dem. II*, 7). In democracy public opinion truly is an "intellectual dust," an indefinite and ever-changing list of commonly held beliefs, rather than a dogma or a fixed Weltanschauung as was the case under aristocracy.

Let us now cast a quick look at religion, which might, of course, be seen as the paradigm of public opinion throughout the history of Western civilization. Tocqueville considers religion when discussing the chances of Catholicism and Protestantism under the condition of democracy. It is his view that Catholicism has the best chances since it is, more than Protestantism, in agreement with the nature of democracy. This view is slightly surprising, most of all because it was customary in Tocqueville's time to see a connection between Protestantism, revolution, and democracy. This was, for example, the view expounded by Guizot in his lectures on the history of Western civilization that were so assiduously attended by Tocqueville and his friend Gustave de Beaumont.[8] Tocqueville's deviance from the accepted view can perhaps be explained by his own robust Catholicism and his unwillingness to face the idea of a future that is both Protestant and democratic (democracy being bad enough already). With religion we apparently reach the limits of Tocqueville's tolerance and of his readiness to provide his readers with a cool and disinterested picture of the future. Yet it remains all the more remarkable that he was prepared to argue for an elective affinity between Catholicism and a democracy that he distrusted so much.

Tocqueville discusses the issue twice, once in the first volume and once in the second volume of *Democracy*. The arguments he gives for Catholicism's supremacy at these two occasions are (as so often in Tocqueville) diametrically opposed. The opposition is all the more interesting here since it is an exact replica of the major conflict present throughout the work: the conflict between the center and what the center is the center of. In the first volume Tocqueville argues that Catholicism effects an equality of the faithful before the priest (the center) that is structurally similar to what we find in the democratic, centralized state. Moreover, Protestantism breeds an attitude of independence, a term that is part of Tocqueville's conceptual inventory when he wishes to praise aristocracy (*Dem. I*, 311). But in the second volume it is not *equality* of the faithful but the existence of a *central authority* itself that explains Catholicism's affinity with democracy (the shift is, of course, characteristic of the more pessimistic mood of the second volume) (*Dem. II*, 30). What is so peculiar, however, is that Tocqueville immediately goes on to deconstruct this Catholic model of religious unity and its preference for a well-defined center. For when discussing religious content a moment later, Tocqueville says that he is convinced (like many of his contemporaries, for example, Michelet)[9] that democracy will feel a natural affinity with pantheism:

> The idea of unity so possesses man and is sought by him so generally that if he thinks he has found it, he readily yields himself to repose in that belief. Not content with the discovery that there is nothing in the world but a creation and a Creator, he is still embarrassed by this primary division of things and seeks to expand and simplify by including God and the universe in one great whole. (*Dem. II*, 32)

Hence, we move here from a paroxysm of unity to a dispersion of that unity over the whole cosmos, with the result that no center is left. As in the Leibnizian universe, everything is both center (from which the whole universe is perceived) and an insignificant part of that universe. Religious unification ultimately yields to dispersion.

Tocqueville's sociology of religious belief offers a similar picture. Tocqueville intelligently observes the peculiar paradox that people will change their religious beliefs in times of great religious fervor rather than in times of religious skepticism. The explanation is that skepticism breeds religious indifference and indifferent people do not bother to change their religious convictions (*Dem. II*, 197). Democracy stimulates skepticism, and Tocqueville acidly comments that if Luther had lived in an age of democracy, his attempt to reform people's religious convictions would not have met with the slightest success (*Dem. II*, 273). So in a democracy the natural unit or cell of religious belief is not the *center* from which dogma or the dispensation of grace proceeds but is rather *individuals* themselves. Their skepticism makes them impervious to religious change or exhortations to that effect. In sum, religion in democracy has its natural focus not in the center but in the *weak* (but paradoxically *immutable*) persuasions of the separate individual.

The pathetic picture of Luther vainly trying to change the religious consciousness of complacent, democratic, nineteenth-century citizens is true, Tocqueville argues, for all bold and ambitious innovators in democracy. Unlike Luther, however, the innovator will not be opposed outright or attacked; on the contrary, he or she may even be applauded. Nevertheless, in most cases the innovator will be slowed by the indifference, inertia, and lack of interest of the majority. The innovator wishing to impose ideas on society and to change public opinion thereby may "strain himself to rouse the indifferent and distracted multitude, and find at last that he is reduced to impotence, not because he is conquered, but because he is alone" (*Dem. II,* 269). And the same is true for forceful new ideas themselves: they will soon lose their impetus in a soft mixture of skepticism and lack of interest. It is as if one would try to force a metal bullet through a viscid liquid.

There are two reasons for this frustration of deliberate attempts to effect intellectual change or influence public opinion. First, insofar as there is change in public opinion in democracy—and despite his thesis about the ineffectivity of the bold innovator, Tocqueville is impressed by the amount of change we will find in democracy—this is rarely the result of public debate or of an open and declared intellectual fight between the new and the old. "Time, events, or the unaided individual action of the mind will sometimes undermine or destroy an opinion," Tocqueville writes,

> without an outward sign of the change. It has not openly been assailed, no conspiracy has been formed to make war on it, but its followers one by one noiselessly secede; day by day a few of them will abandon it, until at last it is only professed by a minority. (*Dem. II,* 276)

Hence progression or change in public opinion is the result of avoidance rather than of conflict (obviously, this is the most antidialectical model of intellectual change one could imagine). Put differently, the innovator or a new idea lack a point of application from which they can purposefully affect public opinion. Knowledge and opinion (like power) are "infinitely subdivided" (*Dem. II,* 61),[10] and therefore necessarily outside the reach of the innovator and the new idea. Second, it is true that democracy is always intent upon something new, but because of its essentially practical and pragmatic character, newness is only valued insofar as it can be grafted upon the old and thus made useful within an already existing context (see *Dem. II,* chaps. 1, 2, 4). Democracy does not make old things new; rather, it "ages" the new.

An analysis of the interaction between the two principles mentioned in the previous section may deepen our insight into the strange ways of democracy. This becomes clear if we consider Tocqueville's question whether democracy will necessarily end in anarchy, as many of his contemporaries believed (*Dem. II,* 304). Surely, the centrifugal mechanism of avoidance seems to point toward anarchy. The fact that there is no universally respected source of truth or of social and intellectual change reinforces this movement in the direction of anarchy. Yet Tocqueville believed that such fears are unfounded. But this is not a historical thesis, saying that if we take a few steps backwards and consider historically the process of intellectual change in democracy we will be able to discover a method in the madness. Although Tocqueville is deeply aware of the power of the unintended consequences of intentional human action, he never invokes the Hegelian point of view in order to clarify the functioning of democracy. His approach is always synchronic rather than diachronic. What makes democracy avoid anarchy, according to Tocqueville, is its capacity to develop an orderly disorder (or disorderly order). What effectively curbs anarchy and the anarchist tendencies of the first mechanism can be found in democracy's tendency to reduce the new to the dimensions of the old, which we observed in the previous section. For the latter principle guarantees that change and newness are not random but always an adaptation of the existing system (of public beliefs). The secret of the movement of democratic public opinion, Tocqueville discovers, lies in "infinitely varying the consequences of known principles and in seeking for new consequences rather for new principles. Its motion is one of rapid circumvolution rather than of straightforward impulse by rapid or direct effort" (*Dem. II*, 272). In democracy it sometimes happens "that the human mind would willingly change its position, but as nothing urges or guides it forward, it oscillates to and fro without progressive motion" (*Dem. II*, 274).[11] The key words in these two quotes are the terms "circumvolution" and "oscillation," and we will be able to find Tocqueville's intentions when we unpack these two spatial metaphors.

What Tocqueville wishes to convey with these metaphors is that there is only a center and a foundation of general principles insofar as they enable democracy and democratic public opinion to circle around the center without ever coinciding exactly with that center itself. There is, therefore, truly a center in democracy that keeps democracy together and that prevents anarchy and complete disintegration, but this center can only perform its function properly as long as it remains inactive itself, or remains, so to speak, an "empty" center, in the sense used in Chapter 5. Thus, in a way reminiscent of what we found at the end of the previous section, we also see here, in the midst of the busy movement of public opinion and change in democracy, a blank or void, an emptiness where nothing happens but which is nevertheless crucial in the sense that it is the motionless stimulator of motion and change. As with the variations that a composer might write on a certain theme, all that counts is how and when these variations differ from the original theme. The theme itself is present precisely because of its absence. And in a striking passage Tocqueville himself offers us the following metaphor: "Imitation diamonds are now made which may be easily mistaken for real ones; as soon as the art of fabricating false diamonds becomes so perfect that they cannot be distinguished from the real ones, it is probable that both will be abandoned and become mere pebbles again" (*Dem. II*, 53). From here, obviously, it is only a small step to Walter Benjamin's "work of art in the age of mechanical reproduction" and to Baudrillard's simulacra. Center, theme, and original yield to variation, imitation, and simulacrum while nevertheless remaining present in and by their absence.

4. The Roots of Ambivalence

In what is perhaps the most moving passage in his whole oeuvre, Tocqueville describes how just before the elections of April 1848 he spent a few days at the castle of Tocqueville where he grew up. His old home, tucked away in the fields near the sea in Normandy, had been uninhabited for some time. Clocks had run out and dust was on the furniture.

> But through the desolation of the present I could see, as if looking out from the bottom of a tomb, the tenderest and gayest memories of my life. It is wonderful how much brighter and more vivid than reality are the colors of man's imagination. I had just seen the monarchy fall; since then I have witnessed the most terrible scenes of bloodshed. All the same I declare that neither at the time nor now in recollection do I feel such deep and poignant emotion about any of those disasters as I felt that day at the sight of the ancient home of my ancestors and at the memory of the quiet, happy days I passed there without realizing how precious they were. Believe me, it was then and there that I most fully understood the utter bitterness of revolutions [*toute l'amertume des révolutions*]. (*Rec.* 94, 95)

The cause of Tocqueville's extreme sadness was not that the events of faraway Paris had destroyed the memories of his happy childhood, nor that he felt unable to revive those memories. On the contrary, these memories presented themselves to him with clarity and great intensity. What happened, however, was that he realized that his continuous awareness of the events in Paris had wiped away the original colors of his memories and now cloaked them in a different hue; and that something similar happened to his far more recent memories of the fall of the monarchy.

To be more precise, at this moment Tocqueville experienced the mutual infection, so to speak, of the private and the public. Remembering his happy childhood from the perspective of the political realities of April

1848 made him see it as from "the bottom of a tomb," and his imagination proved only too eager an accomplice in this estrangement from his memories. On the other hand, seeing the existing political realities from the point of view of his childhood years, Tocqueville feels strangely and disquietingly remote from them. It is only then that his mood becomes full of this "bitterness of revolutions." Tocqueville underwent a progressive estrangement from *both* realms of experience precisely because of their becoming intermingled or interrelated. Both realities, both realms—that of his childhood and that of the revolution of 1848—stand before his eyes with utmost clarity at this rare moment of private reflection. It is exactly because of that clarity that Tocqueville can become aware of what each has lost to the other. More specifically, the confusion of the private and the public domains did not make him a citizen of both: it was "the bitterness of revolutions" that now *excluded* him from both. And this is not only effected by revolutions: elsewhere Tocqueville indicates how democracy itself, no less than a revolution, turns the public domain into another part, aspect, or continuous presence in our private daily life, and makes it even dominate our dreams (*Dem. II*, 308). No less than revolution does democracy produce a confusion of the private and the public, while eviscerating both.

It may very well be that democratic theory or practice has been the inventor of the distinction between the private and the public. But, as Tocqueville apparently realizes at this moment, this is the artificial reformulation of a distinction that was still natural before the advent of democracy and that will only remain natural as long as it remains unacknowledged and therefore unknown. It is a distinction we can only "live." The introduction of the distinction into political theory and practice inevitably means its death; this makes the citizen the inhabitant of a third realm that shares the misfortunes of the private and the public while not giving us any of its certainties in return—hence Tocqueville's immense distress. Here we find what is perhaps Tocqueville's deepest insight into the nature of life under the condition of democracy, an insight that far surpasses those more mechanistic and dualist notions of modern theorists, like Habermas, who have written about the relation between the private and the public in contemporary democratic society.[12]

Although he devoted a large part of his work to an analysis of the influence of democracy on the psychology of the democratic citizen, it is the other movement, the invasion of the public by the private, that clearly interests Tocqueville most. He is here the political theorist rather than the sociologist or the psychologist. One of the most striking effects of democracy is its success in abasing traditional aristocratic politics. Politics in the grand style, politics as a clear manifestation of the public, politics striving for a "grandeur" worthy of the nation, had had to give way to the politics of the household. I agree here with Shiner when he argues that this transition, so much regretted by Tocqueville, is a major theme in the *Recollections*.[13] This death of the public domain and of traditional public grandeur already announced itself in the July monarchy, that French tryout of democratic government. For when, after 1830, the bourgeoisie became the directors of French society, "a marked lull ensued in every political passion, a sort of universal shrinkage [*rapetissement*] and at the same time a rapid growth in public wealth" (*Rec.*, 5).

The result was a kind of politics Tocqueville felt utterly unable to comprehend; it did not offer to him a metaphorical center from which he could grasp it; it was to him nothing but an accumulation of small and petty incidents without coherence, goal, or principle, and was even lacking a history in the proper sense of the word. Politics seemed to oscillate, to persist in a movement of permanent "circumvolution" while avoiding the center that might have organized the movement and given it a (historical) meaning. It is natural, therefore, that the aristocrat Tocqueville, in spite of his distaste for the revolution of 1848, experienced a feeling of immense relief at its outbreak (*Rec.*, 81): the world had again become comprehensible and meaningful to him. Politically, however strange it may seem, revolutions exemplify the same mentality as aristocracy. They both differ from democracy—hence Tocqueville's surprising thesis that a revolution will be inconceivable in a well-developed democracy (*Dem. II*, chap. 21). For a short moment, as Tocqueville saw it, an end had come to the embarrassing uncertainties of a proto-democracy that was continually out of focus; for a short period strong convictions about what is good and what is wrong, about truth and falsehood, returned to the center of the political scene (*Rec.*, 84). But of course this could not last long.

It could not last long since democracy—and in the long run democracy would be the inevitable outcome of the political struggle dominating the contemporary world—is irresistibly drawn from an interest in grand and central questions to an interest in the small detail. The revolution could only temporally undo this "universal shrinkage" effected by the triumph of democracy. A strange alliance of the respective strengths and weaknesses of the democratic state and citizen may, at least partly, explain this paradoxical inversion of the traditional regime of the important and the unimportant. In representative democracy, Tocqueville argues, it will be the central and major political issues that can still attract the attention of the public. But precisely for that reason central and major political issues will disappear from public political debate.

Because of the avoidance mechanism we discussed in the previous section, and more elaborately in Chapter 4, the democratic state instinctively tends to leave such matters to the free will of the public. To compensate for this, the state develops a true love and devotion for the small (administrative) detail; in other words, the state will try to satisfy its natural hunger for power by choosing the line of least resistance. This line will necessarily lead to an exploitation of the power vacuum that the state discovers in the small and apparently insignificant detail. Since in representative government the state attempts at all costs to avoid a conflict with the public, it will naturally focus on matters of mere administrative detail, and attempt to create a political reality that enables it to "transfigure" mere detail into matters of real importance to itself (*Dem. II*, 338, 339). We will always find the state at those places where it has the best chance for making itself, if not invisible, at least as inconspicuous as possible. That is why the state (the "public") tries to "hide" itself in the sphere of the private. An inversion of the traditional regime of the important and the unimportant — or, rather, a mutual exploitation of what the state and the citizen consider to be important — is the result. It should not be seen as the outcome of a battle for power, and it is not experienced by the two parties in that way. Once again, the democratic state will do anything to avoid a clear-cut conflict with the public that is suggestive of such a battle for power. The very real influence that the state and civil society exercise over each other is, paradoxically, the result of the wish on the part of both the state and civil society to *avoid* each other. If the amount of power circulating in democratic society exceeds by far that of the aristocratic state, the main reason is that this power is born from avoidance and not from confrontation; it is a kind of "negative" power, which is all the more subtle and penetrating for that. What is unique to democracy is its discovery of this almost unlimited potential of negative power: it is thanks to this discovery that democracy differs from all the regimes that have preceded it. Nonetheless, one can only be amazed by the paradox of the ease with which the state abandons great and important issues (which were its natural domain) to civil society, while civil society is completely sanguine about the invasion of the sphere of the household (its proper domain) by the state. It is as if the deconstruction of the important has blinded both state and civil society to what ought to be of importance to them.

As one might have expected, what is historically important undergoes, with the advent of democracy, a transition parallel to that which occurs in politics. The intentions and actions of kings or great statesmen are no longer of central importance in the eyes of democratic historians, in contrast to those of their aristocratic predecessors. What is of historical importance or significance is looked for in the patterns historians may discover in a labyrinthine myriad of seemingly irrelevant facts. Just as the state attempts to assert its position vis à vis the citizen by organizing the world of detail, so democratic historians are looking for the "general facts" that are hidden in the irrelevancies the past has left us. "General facts serve to explain more things in democratic than in aristocratic ages," writes Tocqueville, "and fewer things are then assignable to individual influences. During periods of aristocracy the reverse takes place: special influences are stronger, general causes weaker" (*Dem. II*, 91). And because of the parallelism between democratic historians' interest and that of the democratic state, one must conclude that democratic historians play the game of the state rather than that of the public and the citizen (*Dem. II*, 93). Here democratic historians do *not* distance themselves from their aristocratic predecessors.

In a passage worthy of Foucault, Tocqueville expresses his awareness of the dangers of democracy's inversion of the important and the unimportant for civil freedom. Discussing the division of power and the relation of the important and the unimportant in democracy, Tocqueville writes,

> I admit that, by this means, room is left for the intervention of individuals in the more important affairs; but it is not the less suppressed in the smaller and more private ones. It must not be forgotten that it is especially dangerous to enslave men in the minor details of life. For my own part, I should be inclined to think freedom less necessary in great things than in little ones, if it were possible to be secure of the one without possessing the other. (*Dem. II*, 338)

The spirit of independence in the individual is broken by the *semper cadendo* of the state's domination in the sphere of administrative detail; on the other hand, obedience incidentally enforced by the state in issues of importance will always be recognized by the individual as a manifestation of the state's power and will therefore foster the spirit of independence rather than weaken it. The despotism we are to fear, says Tocqueville, does not descend from above, but slowly and insidiously works its way up from below. Despotism characteristic of democracy is "not to be fierce or cruel, but minute and meddling" (*Dem. II*, 148). Thus the unimportant becomes doubly important for Tocqueville, not only because of the factual truth that the unimportant is the preferred sphere of action for the democratic state but also for the moral reason that a permanent attention to the smallest details in the relation between state and public is our only guarantee against despotism (*Dem. II*, 344, 345).

Notions about what is politically and historically important are always closely related to our conceptions about what we should see as the foundations of the social and political order. Obviously, any such foundations will have to be looked for in what politically or historically is of paramount importance. After Tocqueville's deconstruction of the important and the unimportant, we may for good reasons doubt his willingness to identify (the nature of) the foundations of the democratic state. Indeed, as we shall see, that is ultimately his position. But before we can see our conjectures confirmed, we must first consider two possible candidates for the foundational task: enlightened self-interest and freedom. Enlightened self-interest is a plausible candidate since Tocqueville makes many remarks to the effect that "private interest is the only immutable point in the human heart" (*Dem. I*, 255). Behind all the vicissitudes of democratic government we will expect to find the old truth that men always act in conformity with what they see as their enlightened self-interest; and it may seem that this truth shows us where to find the foundations of democratic government.

Yet two reasons can be adduced for why Tocqueville would resist such a utilitarian or economist foundation of democratic political theory. These two reasons are incompatible, but the fact that Tocqueville cites two such different arguments against self-interest as the foundation of political theory only suggests more strongly his profound distaste for any attempt to reduce politics to enlightened self-interest. First, Tocqueville notes that in a democracy like America one is always focused "on some point in which private and public interest meet and amalgamate" (*Dem. II*, 129). It will be clear that democratic practice here apparently voices its agreement with the kind of arguments we discussed in this section a moment ago. For when public and private interests meet, the traditional relation of the private and the public is deconstructed insofar as that relation ordinarily presupposes, if not an opposition, at least a difference between the two domains. It will be obvious that after such a deconstruction it is not possible to discover any foundation of what is essentially and exclusively political. Foundations require differences: a practice can only be founded in what it is *not*.

But this is not the mainstream of Tocqueville's argument. On many occasions he relates self-interest to a desire for physical well-being or with love of physical gratifications (*bien-être*). This love of well-being is surely one of the major themes in the whole of Tocqueville's oeuvre, to the point of becoming a kind of obsession with him. And wherever the theme is dealt with, Tocqueville's distaste and contempt for the love of well-being is always quite pronounced. The continually recurring suggestion is that the love of well-being can never be the foundation of a sound political order, not even of democracy, since it is inherently antipolitical. Hence we should not interpret Tocqueville's condemnation of the love of well-being as a critique of democracy's tolerance of well-being (although this is undoubtedly true as well). His criticism of the love of well-being reaches further than that: he wants to make it clear that the growth of the love of well-being will inevitably mean the disintegration of *each* political order into its smallest components: the household or even only the selfish individual—and that would mean the death of all politics, however conceived.

More indicative of Tocqueville's hatred of the love of well-being than any well-considered argument could be is his tendency to associate the love of well-being with the female. Well-being belongs to the sphere of the household, which is the realm of the housewife and therefore intrinsically antipolitical. Quite characteristic are the harsh words used by Tocqueville to condemn his sister-in-law's exclusive interest in the well-being of the members of her family during the stormy days of the revolution of 1848:

> What made me most impatient was that my sister-in-law had no thought for the country's fate in the lamentations she poured out concerning her dear ones. There was neither depth of feeling nor breadth of sympathy in her demonstrative sensibility. She was, after all, very kind and even intelligent, but her mind had contracted and her heart frozen as both were restricted within the narrow limits of a pious egotism, so that both mind and heart were solely concerned with the good God, her husband, her children and especially her health, with no interest left over for other people. She was the most respectable woman and the worst citizen one could find. (*Rec.*, 39, 40).

But despite his contempt for women like his sister-in-law, this is nevertheless how women ought to behave, according to Tocqueville's etiquette for the sexes. For he admits that he had no less antipathy for women like

Georges Sand, who did write and, worse still, liked to speak out on political matters (so that when he once met her and talked to her, she could only exceed his expectations) (*Rec.* 134, 135). Generally speaking, he regarded the influence of women on politics as "mischievous" and, in his view, one of the very few redeeming features of the revolution of 1848 in comparison to that of 1789 was that women were so much less conspicuously present in the former.[14] The idea behind these and similar pronouncements by Tocqueville is that the female and the love of well-being belong together and that both are intrinsically antipolitical in that they require by their very nature a seclusion from society and from the domain of politics. Well-being, therefore, could never be the foundation of politics since it is diametrically opposed to all politics.

What we see here is, in fact, a dramatic reversal of natural law philosophy. For without doubting the significance and social power of natural principles like the love of well-being or the desire of physical gratification, or, better, precisely because he is so very well aware of the hold these principles may exercise over human behavior, Tocqueville rejects them unconditionally as possible foundations of the political order. Where the natural law philosopher saw the origin and legitimation of the political order, Tocqueville only finds its ultimate dissolution. A political world in which private interest and the domain of the private determine the orientation of the citizen would for Tocqueville be nothing less than a return to the state of nature. For Tocqueville (a return to) the state of nature is not, as it was for the natural law philosophers, a theoretical construct used for *founding* the political order, but a very real and concrete historical possibility that had to be avoided at all costs because it would entail the *dissolution* of that order. And this is all the more true for democracy, since it has (perhaps partly because of its indebtedness to the prerevolutionary natural law philosophers) a natural propensity to develop into this state of nature. Other than, for example, Hobbes's *Leviathan*, democracy is not a political system for putting an end to the *bellum omnium contra omnes*, but for creating the circumstances so that this war can be fought in a decent way. In a perverse way natural law philosophy is the glorification of the private over the public, and by a strange reversal democracy comes closest to a realization of the tendencies implicit in natural law philosophy.

But what about freedom, if self-interest cannot function as the foundation of the political order? A superficial acquaintance with Tocqueville's political writings is already sufficient for the recognition that freedom is the highest god in Tocqueville's conceptual pantheon. Characteristic is his assertion "the man who asks of freedom anything other than itself is born to be a slave" (OR, 169). The idea, clearly, is that freedom is the highest political and moral desideratum, since it is no longer a mere instrument to achieve a still more elevated goal. It might therefore seem that in Tocqueville's view, the love of freedom ought to be the foundation of the political order, or the principle from which everything else can be derived. But here we encounter the following difficulty. Neither in *Democracy* nor in *The Old Regime* is it Tocqueville's intention to develop a political theory outlining the good and just political society. Tocqueville's goal was more modest: he wanted to investigate the origins and nature of one specific political model—democracy. So it might be plausibly argued that foundations are not his business: he accepts democracy for what it is and makes no attempt to justify it philosophically. Moreover, if only because of his all too apparent distrust of democracy, we could hardly expect Tocqueville to be interested in a search for its theoretical foundations. But this obviously is only part of the truth. For Tocqueville's analysis of democracy is intended to make us aware of the strengths, weaknesses, and dangers of democracy. Surely an assessment of democracy's positive and negative aspects is only possible if it is measured according to a quasi-objective standard embodying the foundation of the good political order. Undoubtedly this standard for Tocqueville is freedom. Next, if the standard is to be applied it must be given a content that is appropriate for the purpose. As we shall see in the remainder of this section, it was the concept of independence in terms of which Tocqueville attempted to expound the fortunes and misfortunes of freedom under the condition of democracy.

Independence is one of the most important notions in Tocqueville's intellectual inventory. The concept becomes more and more prominent as Tocqueville's argument progresses, and is most frequently used in the short fourth book of the second volume where the final judgment on democracy is passed. Generally the concept has a favorable connotation (which seems to suggest the compatibility of freedom and democracy), as when Tocqueville equates independence with "self-reliance and pride" (*Dem. II*, 311). Tocqueville praises democracy's Cartesian independence of mind and its religious independence (*Dem. II*, 23); public associations (Tocqueville's main remedy against the ills of democracy) and independence mutually presuppose each other (*Dem. II*, 115, 341); centralized government, on the other hand, stifles the "independent will [*volonté indépendent*]" (*AR*, 121) of both individuals and institutions. In these and similar cases we see how freedom manifests itself in democracy in the guise of independence.

But the term is also used in contexts where Tocqueville discusses the gravest dangers facing the citizen under the conditions of democracy. In such cases Tocqueville often associates independence with isolation and weakness: "When on the contrary, all the citizens are independent of one another, and each is individually weak, no one is seen to exert a great and still less a lasting power over the community" (*Dem. II*, 90). Independence accustoms the citizen to live apart from other people and reinforces both the animosities between the social classes caused by the inequalities aristocracy has left to democracy and the small jealousies stimulated by democracy itself. Thus "the habit of inattention" that Tocqueville sees as the "greatest defect of democratic character" (*Dem. II*, 235) will in the end take possession of the democratic citizen — a criticism of democratic society that would be echoed a century and a half later in Richard Rorty's writings on ethics.[15] The great chain of mutual dependence that we discussed in the first section of this essay is apparently a better guarantee for independence than democratic independence itself. In democracy independence will always be a vulnerable "product of art" (*Dem. II*, 313): it will always tend to destroy itself and to change into either dependence or into a condition of isolated existence that is a sad caricature of what independence initially was.

One can summarize Tocqueville's views as follows. Independence is the notion in terms of which we can analyze the paradox of freedom under the condition of democracy. On the one hand independence in democracy is the heir of aristocratic freedom, of the spirit of freedom that gave both the aristocracy itself and the municipalities of the feudal period the courage to resist central authority (*AR*, 49). On the other hand, independence in democracy fosters weakness and isolation and thus makes the citizen dependent on others, most specifically on central authority (*Dem. II*, 185). The state is not only tolerated but even invited by the citizen to invade the sphere that had hitherto been reserved for private independence (*Dem. II*, 323). Thus the profound paradox arises that in democracy the individual wants both to be free or independent and to be led (*Dem. II*, 337). In this way, democracy fosters both freedom and despotism (*Dem. I*, 340; *Dem. II*, 342). But even this is not yet all. Independence is not only the *cause* of its own destruction; paradoxically it is also the only *remedy* against the despotism resulting from this self-destruction: "this complete independence" which democratic citizens enjoy "tends to make them look upon all authority with a jealous eye and speedily suggests to them the notion and the love of political freedom. . . . The instinctive inclination for political independence . . . thus prepares the remedy for the ills which it engenders. It is precisely for this reason that I cling to it" (*Dem. II*, 304, 305, see also *AR*, 52). Hence all essential (and often contradictory) movements of democracy have their origin in independence.

Here, then, we confront the paradox of independence lying at the heart of Tocqueville's analysis of democracy.[16] When we look for the foundations of democracy we are looking for the point where the language we use for speaking about reality and the reality of democratic practice come closest to one another. Having arrived at this point, Tocqueville presents us with the concept of independence. That we find a concept at that foundational level is only natural, for it is neither in the statement, nor in theory, but in interpretive concepts (like independence) that language and reality come closest to each other. Normal discourse as we find it in the statement or as systematized by theory is the result of a process of abstraction and, consequently, of an estrangement between reality and language that is still absent at the level of the interpretive concept.[17]

It is more surprising, however, that the concept of independence that we encounter at this foundational level is the personal union of two *opposite* movements. In a paradoxical way the concept of independence ties together a movement toward freedom and a contrary one toward despotism. Thus at the heart of democracy we find an ambivalence beyond which we cannot go, which does not permit reduction to a deeper level where the paradox is eliminated (it is interesting that the paradox only announces itself as such when the notion of independence is projected onto the opposition of two more general concepts, those of freedom and despotism). Hence it is in the notion of independence that we discover the roots of the ambivalence of democratic government. It is a foundation that in a curious way at the same time discredits itself as a foundation because of its paradoxical nature.

Paradox and the centrifugality of paradox form the ambiguous basis of democracy. The movement of social meaning and of opinion we discussed in the previous sections, a movement of "oscillation" and of "circumvolution" around a center that does not commit itself and therefore remains a mere "void" or "blank," to use Tocqueville's own spatial metaphors, ultimately has its origin in the paradox we discover at the heart of democracy.

Paradox destroys the fixity that might stop the movement. It is the paradox of independence that gives us a political system—democracy—which has a center that is no center and a foundation that is no foundation.

5. Metaphor and Paradox

Metaphor is the trope that comes naturally to both historiography and political theory.

Historical discourse presents us with a text that—when taken as a whole—does not refer to or correspond to reality like the constative statement. One cannot compare a historical representation of the past as given in the text as a whole to a historical reality, as we can with the statement. Instead, we should conceive of the historical text as a substitute, present for us here and now, for an absent past. Instead of an objective and publicly accessible and perceivable historical reality that is given to historians when they speak about and discuss the past, we have the historical representations historians have proposed as its substitutes. This may explain the essentially metaphorical character of historical representation. For just as the historical representation is used for speaking about the absent historical reality that is represented, so metaphor proposes the metaphorically used expression (and the semantic field that is commonly associated with it) for speaking about the subject of the metaphorical utterance. And there is an additional reason for the historian's reliance on metaphor. What makes metaphor especially valuable in historical discourse is its capacity to organize knowledge. A simple metaphor like "the earth is a spaceship" effects an organization and hierarchization of hitherto insufficiently integrated knowledge we have about the earth, the pollution of the ecosystem, about the biosphere being a closed system, and so on. A good metaphor may be so successful at organizing knowledge that it even suggests a certain course of action—the metaphor given just now is a good example (I will return to that in a moment). Metaphor achieves such an organization of knowledge because it proposes a point of view or perspective on (historical or political) reality. As is suggested by the notion of perspective or point of view, metaphor effects a distancing from the reality metaphorized. Thanks to the distance thus created, a hierarchization of knowledge, of what is important or unimportant, can take place. Similarly, because of its metaphorical character, the historical text will show its reader what is of central significance and what is merely peripheral for understanding the nature of a particular part of the past. Depth, distance, relief, a textual *clair obscur*, a contrast between foreground and background, hierarchization of the important and the unimportant, a differentiation between center and periphery, are all achieved if historians make use of the resources of metaphor.[18] At the same time we discover here the political uses of metaphor. For all political action requires a point of application, so to speak, from which social or political reality is changed or influenced. And metaphor offers both the political theorist and the politician such a point of application. Obviously, the point of view proposed by the historical text or a political analysis is closely related to, if not identical to, the point at which political thought and action are applied to reality. As expounded already in Chapter 5, D. A. Schön has given us a few striking examples of how metaphors adopted by city planners ("this part of the city is a cancer" versus "this part of the city is stifled in its natural growth") give rise to different programs for urban renewal (here: demolishing and rebuilding versus an improvement of the infrastructure).[19] Metaphor enables us to "comprehend" political reality, to get a grip on it so that it cannot be changed except in the way suggested by the metaphors used. The close relation between history and political action is undoubtedly an old cliché, and was already expressed in Ranke's inaugural lecture of 1836, as quoted in Chapter 4. But it is less of a cliché to say that it is metaphor that provides us with the *trait d'union* between history and politics: only thanks to metaphor could history assume the Faustian task of transforming the social and political face of the Western world and be so successful in executing it.

If contemporary historians do sometimes experiment with nonmetaphorical organizations of the past, nineteenth-century historians, Michelet perhaps being the outstanding example,[20] almost universally opted for metaphor.[21] The explanation for this infatuation with metaphor (apart from the Faustian intellectual climate I referred to a moment ago) lies in the historism that was almost universally accepted by nineteenth-century historians. Historism, with its insistence that sociohistorical reality — even as it is here and now — can only be understood if conceived as the result of historical evolution, could not possibly exist without historical metaphor. For metaphor (with a movement identical to that of the transcendental self of Kantian and post-Kantian epistemology) placed the historian at a transhistorical distance from the flow of historical time itself, so that this flow could be objectified. Only then did it become possible to write a survey of the historical evolution in question. Thus, historism, metaphor, and a preference for narrative representation of both the past and the present naturally went together in nineteenth- and most of twentieth-century historiography.

Against this background we would not be astonished by the metaphoricity of Tocqueville's analysis of democracy and of its historical origins. And we do find metaphors in his work. Every reader of the *Recollections* will surely remember Tocqueville's amusing caricature description of Louis Blanc, when the latter used all the force in his small frame to resist the attempt to get him on the rostrum on that eventful May 15, as "a snake having its tail pinched" (*Rec.*, 121) or his contemptuous metaphor of the members of the Chambre after Guizot's announcement of his resignation as "a pack of hounds whose prey has been snatched from their half-full mouths" (*Rec.*, 32). Yet such metaphors, however effective, remain mere adornments of language (quite rare, incidentally, in *Democracy* and in *The Old Regime*). More interesting is Tocqueville's (metaphorical) characterization of the period after the Restoration as one of an "industrial revolution," though even he was not the first to use the term (*Rec.*, 62).[22]

We certainly cannot afford to ignore the spatial metaphors referred to in the previous sections: the movement of "circumvolution" and of "oscillation" so typical of the vicissitudes of social meaning and opinion in democracy. What is particularly interesting about these two metaphors is that they seem to have no other purpose than to obviate the narrativism so natural to (historist) historical metaphor. These metaphors are used by Tocqueville to freeze the flow of time rather than to attempt to step outside it (their use is immanent rather than transcendent). "Oscillation" and "circumvolution," in the context in which Tocqueville used the terms, refer to a movement "to and fro without progression" (*Dem. II*, 274); the suggestion is that democracy has absorbed in itself the flow of time and the historian can no longer hope to assume a neutral point of view from which evolution could be charted. The historian is also borne along on the flow of democratic historical time and is therefore unable to perceive fundamental social or political change: in democratic society "men and things are always changing but it is monotonous because all these changes are alike" (*Dem. II*, 239). To the historian of democratic times, democracy offers the spectacle of an endless and busy variation of a fixed number of virtually immutable principles, and it therefore lacks the marks of true historical change.

Democracy, Tocqueville seems to imply, is essentially antihistorical: all the pages of history written by democracy are "soon wafted away forever, like the leaves of the Sibyl, by the smallest breeze" (*Dem. I*, 219). Hence,

Tocqueville's use of these two spatial metaphors is antimetaphorical in the sense that it has no other purpose than to rob metaphor of its (traditional) capacity for organizing our knowledge of historical change within a narrative frame. Because of his effort to pit metaphor against itself in this way, we might characterize Tocqueville's use of metaphor in the examples offered here as "paradoxical."

The same paradox, and consequently the same transcendence of metaphor, are found when we consider Tocqueville's book as a whole. Nowhere is metaphor more freely embraced by Tocqueville than at the end of the first volume. He offers there a characterization of his enterprise with the following words:

> I am approaching the close of my inquiry; hitherto in speaking of the future destiny of the United States, I have endeavored to divide my subject into distinct portions in order to study each of them with more attention. My present object is to embrace the whole from one point of view; the remarks I shall make will be less detailed, but they will be more sure. I shall perceive each object less distinctly, but I shall describe the principal facts with more certainty. A traveller who has just left a vast city climbs the neighboring hill; as he goes farther off, he loses sight of the men whom he has just quitted; their dwellings are confused in a dense mass; he can no longer distinguish the public squares and can scarcely trace out the great thoroughfares; but his eye has less difficulty in following the boundaries of the city, and for the first time he sees the shape of the whole. Such is the future of the British race in North America to my eye; the details of the immense picture are lost in the shade, but I conceive a clear idea of the entire subject. (*Dem. I,* 447)

Such seems to be the nature and the purpose of his analysis of democracy: to gain access to the point of view from which past, present and even the future of the American democracy can be perceived. It is in assertions like these that we see reflected in Tocqueville's enterprise the program of the whole of nineteenth-century (metaphorical) historiography. A similar seemingly unconditional acceptance of metaphorical historical narrative is found in Tocqueville's other great book, *The Old Regime,* when he writes that at the time the work was written, humanity found itself at that precise point ("que nous soyons placés aujourd'hui à ce point précis," *AR,* 61) from which one can best perceive and pass judgment on the French Revolution.[23] At that (short) moment the great revolution stands out clearest against the encompassing background of French and European history. But in spite of statements like these, both *Democracy* and *The Old Regime* do not put metaphor to its natural use, placing us outside a historical evolution so that we can enjoy a historical survey of it; rather, it seems to be Tocqueville's purpose to circumvent historical change and evolution and to opt for immanence instead of historical transcendence. As we shall see, Tocqueville, in a paradoxical way, likes to play off metaphor against itself.

An indication of Tocqueville's paradoxical use of metaphor, of his apparent wish to deny metaphor what it always aims at—that is, the identification of a point of view at which historical synthesis, unity, and political practice coincide—is already found in his proud assertion at the beginning of *Democracy*: "I conclude by pointing out myself what many readers will consider the principal defect of the work. The book is written to favor no particular view, and in composing it I have entertained no design of serving or attacking any party" (*Dem. I*, 17). The foreword to *The Old Regime* gives us additional information about Tocqueville's program for avoiding the metaphorical point of view: his book is a "study"; it is analytical and not a (narrative) history (*AR*, 43). A letter written to his friend Kergorlay may further clarify his antinarrativism and his avoidance of historiographical metaphor: "Besides, the principal merit of the historian is to give a good account of the tissue of facts, and I am not sure whether my talents lie there. What, up until now, I have been most successful at, is to assess facts, rather than recounting them" (*AR*, 13). But instead of considering these declarations of intent, we had better turn our attention to Tocqueville's works themselves.

If narrative always requires a space between two different historical episodes or phenomena so that they can be narratively tied up again, then we cannot fail to be struck by the antinarrativism of *The Old Regime*. In a brilliant analysis of the book Linda Orr has argued that the ancien régime and the Revolution are so intimately tied together in it, and that they can be so little dissociated either chronologically or as an absence with regard to one another, that the ancien régime rather seems a duplication of the Revolution and vice versa.[24] It was the notion of centralization that enabled Tocqueville to pull the ancien régime and the Revolution so close together that any distinction becomes a merely historical and misleading pedantry. It is misleading because it might invite us to see differences where it is essential that we do not see them. Causes and effects, beginnings and endings, symbols and what symbols stand for are ruthlessly taken together by Tocqueville, with the result, as Orr has pointed out, that the book could have been more properly entitled *L'Ancien Régime est la Révolution* instead of *L'Ancien Régime et la Révolution*.[25] Tocqueville effected this elimination of narrative contrast by focusing on the love of centralization, a love shared by the ancien régime and the Revolution, so that each attempt at temporal and narrative differentiation of the two became impossible.

It might be objected now, however, that the narrative, metaphorical point of view, by placing itself outside the flow of time (in order to describe it), also strives for such a position of neutrality with regard to time. Is not *The Old Regime* and the Revolution, then, the very consummation of narrative, metaphorical historiography? Might one not argue that the concept of centralization fulfills the same role in Tocqueville's book as, say, "the people" in Michelet's *Histoire de France*? One can think of the anecdote of Michelet's visit to Reims cathedral just after he had finished the part of his book devoted to the Middle Ages. Seeing in the vault, above the spot where traditionally the kings of France down to Charles X were crowned, the sad and singularly moving images of poor and mutilated people, Michelet suddenly realized that "the people" were the immutable subject of French history. Thanks to his insight into this immutability of the people Michelet saw that he could provisionally pass over the history of the ancien régime—a most welcome insight, since he shrank from the task of writing that part of French history—and proceed with that of the great Revolution: there would be no danger of a change of subject and the requirements of narrative continuity would be upheld.[26] Would it not seem therefore that Tocqueville's notion of centralization plays exactly the same role in his *Old Regime* as that of "the people" in that most metaphorical of all historiographies, Michelet's *Histoire de France*?

Yet seeing these similarities will at the same time make us aware of the differences. For Michelet "the people" were the guarantee of the continuity of French history that he could now properly *narrate*, thanks to his discovery of this source of continuity. Centralization, on the other hand, enables Tocqueville to *confuse* narrative. For it is only thanks to the notion of centralization that Tocqueville can write a book purportedly about the causes of the French Revolution that does not end but starts (in the first book) with a meditation about the essence of the Revolution, then proceeds with a (masterly) characterization of the ancien régime, ends with the enumeration of a few accidental causes of the Revolution, and succeeds in doing all this without ever dealing with the Revolution itself as an autonomous phase in French history. To use another spatial metaphor: Michelet places "the people" at a point outside the line described by French history through time; Tocqueville places himself in an extension of that line so that all narrative episodes of history seem to coincide. As this image may suggest, Tocqueville's use of narrative metaphor is again truly paradoxical: his metaphorical point of view is both outside and inside the flow of time in French political history, and neither position is destroyed by the other (that would give us irony). Both are maintained at the same time.

Nor is this all. When considering the requirements the subject he was going to write about ought to satisfy, Tocqueville told Gustave de Beaumont: "Il me le fallait *contemporain* [my italics] et qui me fournît le moyen de mêler les faits avec mes idées, la philosophie de l'histoire à l'histoire même [It had to be part of *our own time* and enable me to mix facts with my ideas, philosophy of history with history itself]" (*AR*, 9). Hence, narrative time should be broken not only in the direction of the past but also in that of the future (that is, with regard to what is later than the Revolution). Once again it is centralization that unites the Revolution's future with itself. When in 1856 Tocqueville can say about the Revolution that "it is still operative" (*OR*, 20), it is centralization in terms of which the present can be tied to the past. Hence, centralization is not the metaphorical point of view that enables Tocqueville (as "the people" enabled Michelet) to *narrate* French history; on the contrary, it allows him to transcend and to annul narrative. Centralization, the political idea shared by the ancien régime, the Revolution, and contemporary France, renders French history untellable and transforms it into a number of variations on the same principle — in a way reminiscent of democracy's fondness for variations. And just as democracy questions the possibility, or rather the very meaningfulness, of narratable history, so Tocqueville uses metaphor (centralization) in a paradoxical gesture to destroy metaphorical historiography.

Democracy in America presents us with a roughly similar picture. At the beginning of his book it looks as if Tocqueville intends to write a narrative history of how democracy developed in America. In a pronouncedly historist vein Tocqueville declares at the outset that America and American democracy can only be understood if seen as the result of a complex historical evolution, and he assures his readers that he is going to tell them that history. Nations will always bear "the marks of their origin" (*Dem. I*, 28) and we will have to retrace those origins if we wish to grasp the nature of American democracy. Furthermore, an exposition of the history of America will contain "the germ of all that is to follow and the key to almost the whole work" (*Dem. I*, 29). Having said this, Tocqueville immediately abandons the historist program. Apart from a few incidental remarks about the democratic tendencies of Puritanism (*Dem. I*, 33) or about how the tradition of municipal government inherited from the Old World fostered the love of freedom (*Dem. I*, 63), historical references are virtually absent in the two volumes of *Democracy*. Hence, a pseudo-historist opening suggesting that the reader is presented with the beginning of a narrative history merely functions as a Tocquevillian ploy for entering into the nonnarrative analysis developed in the rest of his book. In that sense we might properly say that the book has no beginning: such a beginning as there is initiates a book that Tocqueville never wrote. No more did Tocqueville succeed in providing his book with an acceptable (narrative) end. It is even somewhat comical to see how the book ends several times, only to be taken further. The book ends for a first time with the last section of chapter 17, which, characteristically, is a prolepsis of the second volume. With chapter 28, which is really an appendix to the first volume, the book ends for a second time. Then the book ends for a third time with the anacoluthon of the third book of the second volume. Last, as if he had himself become impatient with his inability to find a suitable ending, the book ends for a fourth time with the resounding kettledrum beat of the short fourth book. But even here the end, like the final chords of a Beethoven symphony, is spread out over the last three chapters, any of which would have been the right place to stop the book. So if we wish we can discern in the book no less than six or seven endings.

Thus, if the book has no beginning in the proper sense of the word, it has also no end. It is as if the Tocquevillian text arises out of a narrativist textual *Umwelt* that is not only alien but even inimical to it. And it is as if this hostility between the text itself and its narrativist context is necessary in order to emphasize the text's own antinarrativism. This rejection of narrative coherence is further confirmed by the text's being divided into some 93 more or less self-sufficient little essays, each of them a variation on a continuously reiterated theme rather than contributors to one thesis running through the text as a whole. If *Democracy in America* is nonnarrativist, it does not have the characteristics of analytical argument either. Analytical argument always entails certain formal requirements for what the argument in question should or should not contain. It is, however, one of the strangest peculiarities of *Democracy in America* that one cannot possibly say that it does or does not contain what it *ought* to contain given the aims and purposes of the investigation. After having read the book one can indicate neither omissions nor superfluities in it. What Tocqueville has had to say seems to be both necessary and accidental. It thus supersedes our notions of narrative or argumentative coherence. As we shall see, this peculiar formal characteristic of Tocqueville's text is an accurate reflection of democracy itself. Just like the text itself, democracy seems to transform the notions of coherence and incoherence into inapplicable terms.

But the haphazard organization of the *Recollections* surpasses by far even the orderly disorder of *Democracy in America*. To begin with, apart from the sarcastic and unfriendly portraits of a number of the protagonists of the events of 1848 scattered throughout the book, and apart from a few quotes from the January speech in which Tocqueville had predicted the revolution, Tocqueville provides his reader with no background information for understanding the origins and nature of the revolution. We are thrust *in medias res*. The end of the book is no less abrupt. After a detailed account of the diplomatic imbroglio concerning a few revolutionaries of 1848 who had fled to Turkey (an affair devoid of any significance), the reader is informed that the cabinet of which Tocqueville was foreign secretary was about to fall. Curious to learn more about this important event, one turns the page and finds oneself confronted with the appendix. If the *Recollections* are, as Shiner somewhat unconvincingly argues, Tocqueville's "sole historical narrative,"[27] it is certainly a most peculiar one. It has a large gap of some eight months in the middle (from September 1848 to May 1849), and it stops before Napoleon III's coup d'état, although this event was in Tocqueville's own view the logical outcome of the events since the outbreak of the revolution. The book seems to have its center neither in Tocqueville's private history (as the title of the book suggests it would have) nor in French political history. It does not attempt to put forward even the semblance of an explanation of the revolution nor to provide any consistency in Tocqueville's own reaction to the events. Finally, on the one hand Tocqueville abhors the revolution, but on the other he appears less shocked than relieved by it. And his attitude toward Napoleon III is the height of ambivalence, if I am permitted this expression.

The resistance to metaphor expressed by this antinarrativism is reinforced by another feature of Tocqueville's texts. It has been correctly observed by Lord Bryce about Tocqueville that "the facts he uses are rather the illustrations than the sources of his conclusions." Even if one is unwilling to follow Lord Bryce in his assertion that Tocqueville consciously evaded facts that might have contradicted his views,[28] the implication that Tocqueville's argument is a priorist rather than empiricist seems correct to me.[29] This a priorism becomes all the more apparent if we realize that

Tocqueville's texts are constructed around a limited number of political or historical notions, such as aristocracy, democracy, freedom, equality, centralization, and independence (to mention the six most important ones). These notions function in his text like the dramatis personae in a play. What these dramatis personae "say" to each other derives from the character that Tocqueville has chosen to give to each of them, and makes up the essence of his texts. They are, however, never reducible by the nature of this procedure to one single (metaphorical) point of view. Tocqueville's exposition both in *Democracy* and in *The Old Regime* is curiously reminiscent of Collingwood's "re-enactment of the past." It is as if a number of agents active in the past itself repeat their actions on the stage of the Tocquevillian text while, because of the procedure followed, the text makes no attempt to gloss over the untidiness of their interaction. The text has a number of centers (each of them to be identified with one of the conceptual dramatis personae) and no effort is made to harmonize or hierarchize these different centers. The texts represent a broken world that is not amenable to a metaphorical reduction; nor does it permit one center to subsume the others. In fact, exactly the opposite is the case. In order to respect the autonomy and the authenticity of each of the centers, a direct and open confrontation between the conceptual dramatis personae they represent is carefully avoided. There is then in Tocqueville's text a strong tendency to move away from the essence to the detail; or, to put it differently, Tocqueville's text shuns a direct and straightforward exposition of what the dramatis personae of the text symbolize, stand for, or represent, and prefers to focus on what they "say" to each other and on how they "interact." Essence is bound up with the detail, and the detail is not derived from the essence in the way metaphor always wants to have it. Once again we see how in Tocqueville's text a movement that is initially metaphorical is ultimately turned in exactly the opposite direction. The metaphorically inspired attempt to understand the details of the past in terms of a central (set of) historical or political notion(s) has to give way to a subordination of these notions to the historical detail.

Few texts in the history of Western political thought have so much personality, are so immediately recognizable, and possess such extraordinary rhetorical vigor as Tocqueville's books on American democracy and on the nature of the French Revolution. So if it is *not* metaphor with its affinity with unity, hierarchical organization, the dominance of the center over the periphery, with its reliance upon narrative and chronology and causal relation, then *what* did Tocqueville choose as his stylistic code? It will be my thesis that Tocqueville's break with the historiographical traditions of his (and our own) time mainly consists in his abandonment of metaphor in favor of paradox. And surely we may expect a penchant for paradox in an author who, like Tocqueville, presents to his readers the French Revolution as being, in fact, no revolution at all or who describes democracy as being, in fact, a despotism of the multitude and as a political system that is essentially conservative (the last paradox undoubtedly being the most amazing of the three to Tocqueville's contemporaries). In each of these three examples it is Tocqueville's strategy to present a historical or political thesis by means of its opposition to an accepted truth; the rhetorical strength of his argument is derived from this opposition, which is carefully upheld in the text.

We find paradoxes on nearly every page of Tocqueville's books; every time he reaches a conclusion that pleases or interests him it is molded in the form of paradox. Since much of my argument in this essay rests on this replacement of metaphor by paradox, I may be expected to be generous with examples. To begin with, Tocqueville, considering himself, notes the paradoxes of the human heart: "I need not traverse earth and sky to discover a wondrous object woven of contrasts; of infinite greatness and littleness, of intense gloom and amazing brightness, capable at once of exciting pity, admiration, terror, contempt. I have only to look at myself" (*Dem. II*, 80). In the years before 1848 notions of right and wrong, good and bad seemed to have become confused in the paradoxical turmoil of his mind. In desperation he cries out: "Where was truth? Where was falsehood? On which side were the evil ones? And on which side the well-intentioned?" (*Rec.*, 84). And here is a paradox with regard to another individual human being: Napoleon III owed his rise to the presidency to his good sense just as well as to a little vein of madness running through his character (*Rec.*, 203). The character of nations and of peoples is no less paradoxical: thus the Americans are "at once constrained and without constraint" (*Dem. II*, 229); America is the country "where the precepts of Descartes are least studied and best applied" (*Dem. II*, 4); and in spite of all their Cartesianism and their confidence in their own resources, Americans are more gullible than any other people (*Dem. II*, 11). Even more paradoxical is the French national character: the French care about property but not about their lives; they are "equally bent on reasoning and on being unreasonable" (*Rec.*, 114). And a two-page list of the paradoxes of the French national character is drawn up as a kind of afterword to *The Old Regime* (*AR*, 320, 321). Humanity in general fares no better: people can do things that are far from honest with a good conscience (*Rec.*, 84); humanity has the paradoxical desire both to be free and to be led (*Dem. II*, 337).

French history adds a few other items to the list of paradoxes. The notables of 1787 became popular because of their obstruction of what popular welfare would have required,[30] the monarchy fell not because of its weakness but because of its strength,[31] and in revolutionary times "popularity may be united with hostility to the rights of the people and the secret slave of tyranny may be the professed lover of freedom" (*Dem. I*, 100). Similarly, during a revolution exceptional laws obtain that "tolerate murder and allow devastation, but theft is strictly forbidden" (*Rec.*, 72). With regard to the great Revolution of 1789 Tocqueville comments that never were events "mieux préparés et moins prévus" (*AR*, 57; in the English translation— "better prepared and less foreseen"—part of the paradox is lost), while "the governments it [the Revolution] set up were less stable [*plus fragiles*] than any of those it overthrew; yet, paradoxically, . . . they were infinitely more powerful [*plus puissants*]" (*OR*, 9) and for that reason the Revolution was for the princes of Europe "à la fois leur fléau et leur institutrice" (*AR*, 67, here the English translation—"at once their plague and their teacher"—is also less pointed than the original).

But what most catches the eye, and contains a good deal of the essence of Tocqueville's argument, are his sociological and political paradoxes. It is true that the prerevolutionary period is not completely free of paradoxes— in aristocracy "some actions have been held to be at the same time virtuous and dishonorable; a refusal to fight a duel is an instance" (*Dem. II*, 242)—but it seems impossible for Tocqueville to describe democracy without an appeal to paradox, and paradoxes multiply in this portion of his work. With the rise of equality, for instance, landowners remain unaware of social leveling because rents tend to rise in this phase of history (*Dem. I*, 198). Equality fosters a kind of "virtuous materialism" (certainly an oxymoron in Tocqueville's eyes) and, what is more important,

> the democratic nations that have introduced freedom into their political constitution at the same time they were augmenting the despotism of their administrative constitution [a condition typical of democracy] have been led into strange paradoxes. To manage those minor affairs in which good sense is all that is wanted, the people are held unequal to the task; but when the government of

the country is at stake, the people are invested with immense powers; they are alternately made the plaything of their rulers, and his masters, more than kings and less than men. (*Dem. II*, 339)

American democracy offers the paradoxical spectacle of freedom of the press "without independence of mind and real freedom of discussion" (*Dem. I*, 273); also, political power will "be more extensive and more mild" in a democracy than in other political systems (*Dem. II*, 335). Nothing is more common in democracy than to "recognize superior wisdom in the person of one's oppressor" (*Dem. II*, 12). In contrast to this paradox Tocqueville elsewhere presents us the paradox that in democracy power increases when authority diminishes and vice versa. But of all the characteristics of democracy that are "most formidable but least foreseen" (*Dem. II*, 348), surely democracy's most surprising feat is to have created a society in which everything changes and yet everything remains the same (*Dem. II*, 239). Tocqueville even succeeds in introducing paradox at the phonetic level when he explains in *The Old Regime* "comment on souleva le peuple en voulant le soulager" ("how one aroused the people by attempting to assuage them" — the title of chap. 5, book III); and nowhere is Tocqueville's genius for paradox more impressive than when he succeeds in the tour de force of grafting paradox on metaphor by means of his description of a few members of the National Guard during the revolution of 1848 as "furious sheep" (*des moutons enragés*) (*Rec.* 162).

If we wish to understand the meaning of Tocqueville's exchange of metaphor for paradox, it will be necessary to devote some attention to the similarities and dissimilarities of the two tropes. In both cases, in metaphor no less than in paradox, we have to do with semantic deviance, with an apparent conflict at the semantic level. Both metaphor and paradox interrupt the easy flow of literal language. But the way in which semantic conflict is solved is different in each case. As we have seen at the beginning of this section, metaphor solves semantic conflict by the identification and fixation of a semantic point where the conflict disappears and significant meaning originates. In the case of historiography this semantic point is the point of view from which we are invited to see the past.[32]

It must be noted, next, that such points of view are outside and independent of historical reality itself, and this is no coincidence. For metaphorical historiography requires of the historian a movement of estrangement from historical reality (a movement often associated by historians with the pursuit of the state of objectivity); it is a movement that results in the opposition of, on the one hand, a now "objective" or even "objectively given" historical reality and, on the other hand, a metaphorical point of view whose preferably maximum distance from that objective reality guarantees that an objective survey or account can be given of it. One must realize, then, that in metaphorical historiography historical truth comes into being only thanks to this movement of withdrawal from what is to *become* historical reality. Historical truth is achieved when the distance between the past and the point of view is infinite (and yet all the details are respected and still clearly visible), so that all perspectivism has thus been eliminated.

As we have seen, Tocqueville himself gave a perfect account of this ideal of metaphorical historiography (*Dem. I,* 447). In the previous chapter I have called this ideal of historical metaphor—historiography's analogue of transcendentalist epistemology—the "heliotrope": the heliotrope is the metaphor that, by its apparent avoidance of perspectivism, succeeds in annulling its own metaphoricity. The supreme (historical) metaphor is the metaphor that we no longer recognize as such, which has become indiscernible from literal truth.[33] It is the heliotrope that succeeds in presenting (metaphorical) representation as mere description.

Paradox favors a movement that is precisely the *opposite* of that of metaphor. Take, for instance, Tocqueville's paradox of the governments that have succeeded that of the great Revolution: "The governments it [the Revolution] set up were less stable [*plus fragiles*] than any of those it overthrew; yet, paradoxically, they were infinitely more powerful [*plus puissants*]" (*OR,* 9). Semantic conflict exists, as in metaphor, in the paradoxical notion of a government that is both more fragile and more powerful than the government that preceded it; language resists this conjunction of concepts. Yet—and this is essential—paradox does not invite us (as metaphor does) to resolve the conflict at a linguistic level, but requires us to look at historical reality itself in order to find that *both* halves of the paradoxical assertion are true. Postrevolutionary governments *are* both more fragile and more powerful than those of the ancien régime; we are misguided by language in presuming a conflict here. What paradox lays bare, therefore, is the betrayal of language (if I may put it in this slightly paranoid way). Paradox teaches us that language erroneously makes us see oppositions or incompatibilities where in reality they do not exist. Metaphor trusts language unconditionally; all the possibilities of linguistic friction, of linguistic double play that language offers, are used confidently for the cognitive purposes of the historian and the politician. Paradox, by contrast, firmly turns away from language and redirects our attention to reality itself. It is deeply aware of the shortcomings of language and of the blind alleys into which language may lead us. As we saw in the previous paragraph, metaphor effects a movement of redoubling in which (metaphorical) language and reality are set opposite to each other, but in such a way that the former determines the nature of the latter; paradox, on the other hand, effects a rehabilitation of reality in its relation to language. Paradox shows us that reality is stranger than language suggests.

At first sight paradox and irony do not seem to lie too far apart. What is known as *Weltironie*, "cosmic irony," or the "irony of events"[34] expresses the insight that there is often a paradoxical relation between what we intend to do and what is actually the result of our actions. Political thinkers such as Mandeville, Adam Smith, Hegel, and, indeed, Tocqueville himself, have pointed out the paradoxical workings of cosmic irony. It is therefore not surprising that Hayden White should see Tocqueville's oeuvre as dominated primarily by the trope of irony.[35] But there are two differences between irony and paradox that we cannot afford to ignore. First, when being ironical we say one thing but mean the contrary of what we say (just as in cosmic irony the effects of our actions are contrary to our intentions). We expect the hearer or reader to see our point and to exchange what we say for what we really intended to express. But here irony differs from paradox. In the case of paradox semantic opposition should *not* be obliterated—as irony expects us to do—but has to be respected. At most one could say that paradox and so-called Romantic irony come quite close to each other. In Chapter 4 we saw that, for theorists of Romantic irony such as Friedrich von Schlegel (Romantic), irony is a precarious and momentary equilibrium between two opposites; the secret of Romantic irony, like that of paradox, lies in the requirement that neither of the two opposites yield to the other.[36] The second and perhaps more important difference between irony and paradox is that an understanding of the former always depends upon additional knowledge (knowledge that is not provided by the ironical assertion itself). One must have at least some acquaintance with Viscount Bolingbroke's most dubious political career in order to appreciate (or even recognize) the irony of Samuel Johnson's remark that "he was a holy man." The irony is, in fact, an interplay of the ironic utterance itself with the associations we already have with the subject of the utterance. Hence, like metaphor, irony tends to stay on the level of language and thought, on the level of associations and knowledge we already have. Paradox, on the other hand, is the trope that inexorably sends us back to reality after the holidays we have spent at the linguistic level in the company of metaphor and irony. It demonstrates the shortcomings of our knowledge and our system of associations. Metaphor and irony are a celebration of language and are given to idealistic patterns of thought; paradox is a celebration of reality. In its insistence on redirecting our attention to reality and its effectiveness in doing so, it is even more persistent than the literal statement.[37]

Tocqueville's rehabilitation of political and historical reality by means of his use of the trope of paradox is reinforced by his recognition of the sublimity of history and of the long historical process that gave us democracy. (Historical) reality is something we can only undergo, and that we shall rarely, and even then only partially, get into our cognitive grasp. Reality will always exceed what we can say and think about it. We find this respect for the sublimity of history clearly announced in Tocqueville's description of the revolutionary days of May and June 1848. What Tocqueville achieves in his account of these days is an amazing dissociation of the seemingly irrelevant actions of puny individuals (including those of the Parisian crowd) and the immense historical groundswell that completely overwhelmed all those individuals. This impression of the unleashing of historical forces that we should not even attempt to understand or catch in language is reinforced by Tocqueville's all too apparent lack of interest in the proper explanation of the revolution itself and of the course that it took.

But, more important, it is perhaps the supreme paradox of all of Tocqueville's paradoxes that he has the courage to posit the sublimity of democracy, of that apparently so homely, so petty, and so utterly lusterless political system. Surely Shiner is right when he writes that for Tocqueville the advent of democracy meant the final triumph of pettiness over "grandeur,"[38] but the exactness of this assertion might make us forget that, according to Tocqueville, precisely democracy's love of well-being, of petty pleasures and of petty details, has unleashed a political force that makes those of aristocracy and the ancien régime dwindle into mere insignificance. More than any other previous political system, democracy is not what it seems. It mobilizes every potential source of political strength and action in society—nothing will be allowed to remain as it was before the advent of democracy. Democracy has given us a "providential, and creative power" (*Dem. II*, 309) of the same sublimity as the raging seas or the distant stars that so deeply impressed Kant.

This is how we ought to interpret Tocqueville's famous characterization of the birth of democracy as "a providential fact" (*Dem. I*, 6), as a historical event that must fill our minds with a kind of "religious awe" (*Dem. I*, 7). Tocqueville could be so sensitive to the sublimity of democracy itself and of the historical process to which it owed its birth because he looked at democracy with the peculiar and paradoxical mixture of feelings that the sublime awakens in us. Consider the confession found among Tocqueville's papers after his death:

> J'ai pour les institutions démocratiques un goût de tête, mais je suis aristocrate par instinct; c'est à dire que je méprise et crains la foule. J'aime avec passion la liberté, la légalité, le respect des droits, mais non la démocratie. Voilà le fond de l'âme.[39]

> Intellectually I can approve of democratic institutions, but I am an aristocrat by instinct. I passionately love liberty, legality, the respect for rights; but not democracy. That is the essence of my personality.

Tocqueville hated, or, better, feared democracy, but at the same time he was prepared to recognize that democracy would realize the equality that "the Creator and Preserver of man has set as man's highest historical goal" (*Dem. II*, 351). When Schiller describes the sublime as "dieses einzige Schreckliche, *was er* [man] *nur musz und nicht will* [this absolutely terrible thing, which man has but does not want to undergo]" (Schiller's emphasis)[40] and which evokes in us the contradictory feeling of both *Wehsein* (pain) and *Frohsein* (joy),[41] this captures exactly Tocqueville's paradoxical attitude to democracy and to its entrance on the scene of world history.

6. Centralization

In Tocqueville's text paradox is not restricted to the description of political realities; in harmony with its nature, paradox in Tocqueville's work even elicits its opposite. This is the ultimate consequence of paradox. For if paradox did not deny itself in the text, the insight into the necessary paradoxical nature of a text dealing with democracy would in the end degenerate into (or give rise again to the antiparadox of) metaphor. This means that we must see democratic society from the (metaphorical) point of view of paradox. By a curious inversion, then, paradox can only maintain itself insofar as it is prepared to cede some latitude to its opposite—metaphor. A complete avoidance of metaphor would finally result in an equally complete surrender to it. Thus, to the extent that we may associate democracy with paradox and the absence of a center, both democracy and paradox can only be upheld by the partial acceptance of what is *not* paradoxical: that which does not question the position of the center but affirms it.

This recognition that paradox itself requires the reappearance of metaphor may shed some new light on Tocqueville's increasing obsession with centralization. He uses metaphors in discussing centralization and its character in a democracy. First we must observe the close affinity of centralization and metaphor. Metaphor defines the point of view from which sociohistorical reality is seen. This point of view is the obvious center for the political action inspired by the metaphor used. The idea that society has to be ruled from a strong, well-defined center will come naturally to anybody whose weltanschauung specifies that the sociohistorical order can be understood in terms of powerful and convincing metaphors. On the other hand, the center will remain politically inactive and ineffective to the degree that people tend to conceive of society with the help of linguistic or analytical means other than metaphor. It is therefore not surprising that metaphor and centralization make their entrance at exactly the same time in Tocqueville's text, and that when they do so they are strongly dependent on one another.

Although Tocqueville's work is aswarm with paradoxes, it contains only one powerful metaphor. But this metaphor is extremely strong; so much so that it has even succeeded in hiding from view the potential for paradox that is present in the text as a whole. It has convinced many of Tocqueville's readers that the text should be seen in terms of it. The metaphor is that of the democratic state as the "guardian" (*tuteur*) of the democratic citizen. Although it was already used by Tocqueville at the end of the first volume (*Dem. I*, 340), the metaphor only makes its real appearance in the fourth book of the second volume. From there, however, it casts its long and sinister shadow over the whole of the text preceding it. The metaphor is introduced by Tocqueville in the following way:

> When I consider the petty passions of our contemporaries, the mildness of their manners, the extent of their education, the gentleness of their morality, their regular and industrious habits, and the restraint which they almost all observe in their vices no less than in their virtues, I have no fear that they will meet with tyranny in their rule(r)s, but rather with guardians. (*Dem. II*, 336)

There are two aspects to this metaphor which require our attention. First, we will note, as was predicted in the previous paragraph, that this metaphor is suggestive of a process of centralization; in fact, it *is* a metaphor of centralization. "If I seek to trace the novel features under which despotism may appear in the world," writes Tocqueville,

> the first thing that strikes the observation is an innumerable multitude of men, all equal and alike, incessantly endeavoring to procure the petty and paltry plea-sures with which they glut their lives. . . . Above this race of men stands an immense and tutelary power, which takes upon itself alone to secure their grati-fications and to watch over their fate. That power is absolute, minute, regular, provident and mild. It would be like the authority of a parent if, like that au-thority, its object was to prepare men for manhood; but it seeks, on the contrary, to keep them in perpetual childhood: it is well content that the people should rejoice, provided that they think of nothing but rejoicing. (*Dem. II*, 336)

Democratic citizens will become more and more isolated from one another in their search for private well-being, and ever less capable of solving either individually or in mutual cooperation what they experience to be the prob-lems of their social and political life. It is the democratic state to which they will therefore unanimously turn. Thus there comes into being a cen-tral authority in which ever more power will be invested. The guardianship of the state will create a powerful center. Yet that power will not be used arbitrarily or despotically; it will bend the wills of the individual citizens rather than break or directly oppose them.

And that brings us to the other feature of the metaphor that we have to take into account. It generally is the task of the guardian to identify with the interests and the point of view of the person(s) entrusted to his guardian-ship. More specifically, the guardian ought not pursue his own interests if these are hostile or detrimental to those of his ward(s). Since the relation-ship between the state and the citizen is constructed by Tocqueville in such a way that a conflict of interests between the state and the public is far from imaginary, this puts the state in a highly ambiguous and even paradoxical position. The benevolence Tocqueville expects from the democratic state in its behavior toward the public reflects this uncertainty of the position of the state. Its benevolence clearly bears the marks of paradox: "benevolent" power is the kind of power that does not want to be what it is (but without being any less ugly or degrading for that). Hence, if we take Tocqueville's metaphor of the state as a "tutelary power" seriously—and the metaphor certainly accords with his relevant intentions—this means that the demo-cratic state will necessarily be divided against itself because it always has to reconcile in its actions two perspectives standing in a paradoxical rela-tion to each other. The conclusion—not actually drawn by Tocqueville—

would seem to be that the state will tend to cultivate the area of potential action that escapes from this paradox; that is, the state will have a natural propensity to develop a domain where it feels capable of free and meaningful action without being entangled in the paradoxes that its relations with the public ordinarily give rise to. That may partly explain why over the last century the democratic state has built large governmental apparatuses that it can afford to rule in a way that would never be possible with civil society.

This paradoxical attitude of the state with regard to the citizen has its counterpart in the paradoxical way the state is perceived by the citizen. On the one hand, citizens in isolation will tend to rely on the state in order to ensure their well-being, and they are willing, therefore, to surrender their independence to the state. On the other hand, it is precisely in this state of isolation that citizens become aware of their quasi-existential independence. Independence incorporates both the misery and the glory of the democratic citizen. In independence lies therefore both the cause of and the remedy for the evils of democracy. For example, Tocqueville is prepared to acquiesce in democracy's love of equality for no other reason than that it "lodges in the very depth of each man's mind and heart that indefinable feeling, the instinctive inclination for political independence and *thus* [my italics] prepares the remedy for the ill which it [democratic equality] engenders" (*Dem. II*, 305). As we have seen at the end of section 3 of this chapter, the willingness to turn to the state that is caused by independence paradoxically always goes together with a tendency to resist the state (or even a proclivity toward anarchy; *Dem. II*, 304), that has the selfsame origin.

The fact that paradox requires a partial acceptance of its opposite, metaphor, may help us to answer one last question occasioned by Tocqueville's account of democracy. If we recall Tocqueville's metaphor of the "oscillation" and "circumvolution" of social meaning and of opinion in democracy, we may wonder what is responsible for this circular movement *around a center* that is so clearly suggested by these two metaphors. What ties that movement to a center without ever coinciding with it? The question becomes all the more urgent if we remember, furthermore, the implication of Tocqueville's argument that democracy has no unambiguous basis nor ultimate foundation, and his fears, expressed at many places throughout his oeuvre, that equality and the love of well-being will effect a disintegration of state and society. If we see only these aspects of democracy, which are all so obviously related to paradox and the destruction of unity and coherence caused by paradox, we will be susceptible only to the centrifugal tendencies of democracy. But it will be clear from the partial acceptance of metaphor *within the rule of paradox itself* that there must also be a movement of centripetality to counteract centrifugality. Thanks to this presence of metaphor the movement of social meaning and opinion in democracy remains enclosed within a magic circle in a way that reminds one of how one day physicists hope to control nuclear fission by preventing the natural expansion of the thermonuclear plasma with the help of very strong magnetic fields. Because of this equilibrium between centrifugality and centripetality democracy can do without foundations.

One final comment must be added. I do not want to suggest that the equilibrium between centrifugality and centripetality, or between paradox and metaphor, as sketched here should be in conformity with Tocqueville's own intentions. When Tocqueville discusses centralization (centripetality) in the later parts of *Democracy*, his obsession with it is rather the result of a shift of emphasis in that work—a shift of emphasis that would be continued in *The Old Regime*—than of a search for equilibrium. That is to say, if we take seriously the Tocqueville of the first volume of *Democracy* and the first three books of the second volume, we will discover in him the painter of a democracy ruled by paradox. On the other hand, the fourth book of *Democracy*—and the relevant parts of *The Old Regime*—give us a picture of a democracy dominated by centralization and metaphor. A balance between the two is not deliberately pursued by Tocqueville and is even difficult to imagine within Tocqueville's pessimistic conception of democracy. It seems likely that Tocqueville was suspicious of *both* the centrifugal and centripetal tendencies of democracy. The idea of a multiplication of evils is therefore probably closer to his mind than the idea of a wholesome balance. I have attempted to show, however, that the Tocquevillian text itself contains sufficient arguments for confidence about the possibility of such balance. Of special relevance here is Tocqueville's proposal to reintroduce paradox into metaphor when he makes use of the metaphor of the state as a guardian, and the insight that paradox, in its turn, must give rise again to metaphor. The implication is that metaphor and paradox—and all that we have learned to associate with these two tropes—are mutually dependent without either of them dominating the other. Democracy is the "oscillation" between these two tropes.

7. Conclusion

As was suggested in the introduction to this chapter, writing a conclusion to an essay on Tocqueville is a task fraught with dangers. Conclusions always present us with a number of general insights that summarize what has been said before and, in a case like this, the main themes in the work of the author investigated. Summaries and conclusions are therefore ineradicably metaphorical in the sense meant in this essay. For that very reason a summary of so paradoxical an oeuvre as Tocqueville's could be nothing but a *contradictio in terminis*. In order to avoid this trap of metaphorizing paradox, I shall not attempt to offer a conclusion in the normal sense of the word; I will instead make a final remark about how Tocqueville should be read and about what this direction for use implies, both for democracy itself and for any future attempts to analyze that sublime political system. And is not *all* interpretation in the end a direction for future use of the interpreted text?

In a penetrating and intelligent commentary, John Elster has written of Tocqueville, "One should be absolutely clear about this: there is no great thinker who so often and so strikingly contradicts himself over such central issues." [42] Confronted with the contradiction and paradoxes in Tocqueville's work, Elster develops a number of "rules for decoding" that will enable him to straighten out these contradictions. It is his expectation that these decoding principles will give us both a Tocqueville more true to his own manifest intentions and a better and more responsible theory of democracy. It would certainly be quixotic to go to war with this interpretive strategy. Elster's own study not only demonstrates that it results in new and interesting sociological insights, but even more that the Tocquevillian text certainly contains a number of inconsistencies it can do without. Yet for all his assiduity, even Elster has to concede that "these salvage operations do not always succeed, and, besides, they are never completely successful." [43] I agree with Elster, but would rather reverse the emphasis in his approach to Tocqueville's writings: what is really interesting in Tocqueville, in my opinion, is not what lends itself to a reduction to consistency, coherence, and logical argument, but rather the paradoxes and inconsistencies that resist such a reduction.

Tocqueville's inconsistencies and paradoxes are not simply a regrettable defect in his argument (if only because Tocqueville, not being quite the most obtuse of political philosophers, would undoubtedly have been capable of avoiding them if he had thought that their presence might interfere with the nature of his enterprise). I therefore propose to see these inconsistencies and paradoxes rather as marks or signs of the brakes provided by the text *itself* to resist any Elsterian attempt to force it willy-nilly into a coherent and consistent "theory" of democracy or social action. Seeing these inconsistencies and paradoxes as the textual signs that discourage the construction of "theory" implies furthermore that it would be mere pedantry to distinguish between contradictions (on the linguistic level); inconsistencies that might arise between two statements against the background of Tocqueville's acceptance of a third statement that is compatible with only one of the two; paradoxes in the proper sense of the word; and so on. The logical nature of these problematic conjunctions is largely irrelevant: what counts is that they all point in one direction—avoidance of "theory" and a recognition of the sublime character of the democratic system. The text does not offer a theory; if one would prefer to put it that way, it is at most a theory saying that no theory of democracy is possible. For as soon as one starts to theorize about democracy, this elusive political system will make us see only the reflection of the theorist, behind which it will carefully hide itself.

The tradition of Western epistemological thought generally upholds the distinction between form and content, between what we say and what we talk about. The idea that language and thought should somehow mimic their content is rejected within this tradition. As undergraduates we have all been taught the naivety of the idea that the description of something round should itself be round. Yet here we are confronted with an example that is in conflict with this common epistemological wisdom. We should not describe democracy, nor develop theories about it, but democracy must be represented or "depicted"; and as the depiction of a tree always ought to share some structural features (for example, of form and color) with the tree itself, so there should be some structural resemblances between democracy and the text about democracy. More specifically, if Tocqueville is correct in saying that democracy has no center, that it has neither essence nor nature of its own, this requires us to adopt a style that bestows on the text exactly the *same* characteristics. If we opt for metaphorical analysis, as almost all contemporary historical, sociological, and political writing does, democracy will remain invisible forever. As the last chapters of *Democracy* prove, metaphor will provide us with a theoretical model that is no longer a model of democracy itself; it will inevitably present to us a political system with a center. Metaphor inevitably generates centers. It is only the trope of paradox that will give us access to the sublimity of democracy, and that will respect the anti-essentialism and centerlessness of democracy.

Already in his own time Tocqueville was rightfully considered to be the greatest thinker on democracy. Now that democracy at the end of the millennium seems to be beginning its triumphal procession over our entire globe, Tocqueville is still our best guide if we wish to understand democracy. Tocqueville has an undeniable right to such praise, since no other political thinker has been more deeply aware of the paradoxes and the sublimity that are forever the glory of democracy.

Democracy in the Age of Unintended Consequences

1. Self-Government

Since the days of Aristotle and Polybius political philosophers like to enumerate the different forms of government, to describe their properties, and to speculate on which of these properties ought to be considered as the indispensable ingredients of the best form of government (most often identified with the *regimen mixtum*, which is generally recognized to be the precursor of contemporary representative democracy).[1] There is, however, one aspect of the differences between monarchy, aristocracy, and democracy that was rarely noticed by them, but that is of great importance in the present context. Monarchy, aristocracy, and their respective degenerate forms all have in common—and in this respect they all differ from democracy—that they define who rules whom, while the ruler and the ruled are not identical. There is always an "outside" to the ruler himself, a more or less passive *substratum* on which he exerts his political power. This is different in democracy: democracy is self-government, government in the style of "the middle voice," as Hayden White might have put it. There is something contradictory about the very notion of self-government—or, at least, the notion only seems to make sense to the extent that a certain doubling takes place in the political entity democratically governing itself.

This process of doubling, this folding over oneself, is not an idea without its antecedents in the history of political thought. It is appealed to with regard to political systems other than democracy. When the notion actually is discussed for other political systems, however, it will not surprise us that it is discussed exclusively within the matrix of *self*-government (which is the essence of democracy) insofar as this matrix can be part of those other political systems. Let us listen to how Montesquieu defines honor, which he saw as the primary virtue in aristocracies and as the moral compass for the gentleman's "self-government." A person's honor, he writes, concerns those virtues which "are always less what he owes to others than what one owes to oneself; they are not what calls to our fellow citizens so much as what distinguishes us from them." [2] The self-government demanded by honor thus functions like a kind of Freudian superego, though this superego emphatically does not have its origin in the internalization of universal social rules and norms, as it does in Freud's description. On the contrary, it is essential to honor to have this origin exclusively in the individual's own conception of his or her (ideal) individual self.

In this way aristocratic doubling essentially differs from democratic doubling, since democratic self-government, in the case of the individual and in that of politics, always involves the immixture of others. Unlike the aristocratic self, the democratic self (both the private individual and the citizen) has disseminated itself over other individuals. In this sense the democratic self is inevitably a less complete and self-sufficient human being than the eighteenth-century nobleman respecting the commandments of honor. The latter should be seen as more of an individual (as being really "ein heiler Mensch," as nineteenth-century Germans would have put it) than our modern, more typically Freudian selves. In a quasi-Nietzschean way the eighteenth-century nobleman was the creator of his own superego. This may suggest what has been our gravest loss in the transition from aristocracy to democratic society: the eighteenth-century "man of honor" can exist in contemporary democracy only in its nasty caricature of the Mafia godfather. In our own democratic age of "men without chests," to use Fukuyama's terminology, we can only regret the eighteenth-century aristocrat (or rather his ideal) whose moral and political independence necessarily is a thing of the past.

However, as Kinneging interestingly suggested, the Romantic notion of the self, more specifically that of the artist, could be seen as a modern variant of this classical, Roman notion of honor that Montesquieu had in mind.[3] Combining these two insights, we may say that Schlegel's Romantic psychology of the artist (discussed in Chapter 4), according to which it is the defining characteristic of the artist that he should be able "to stand in a relationship to himself," is a Romantic version of how classical honor puts the man of honor in a relationship to himself. This is the condition for his being the man of honor that he wants to be—even if this would require him to commit suicide. So at least in theory the Romantic individual, especially the poetic genius, can be seen as the democratic successor to the eighteenth-century gentleman.[4]

2. Self-Government and Aesthetic Political Philosophy

In fact this democratic "honorable doubling" is what this book has been about all along. When I have been arguing in favor of the aesthetic gap that effects a doubling of the represented and the representative (or representation); when I proposed to see in this gap both the origin of all legitimate political power and the only guarantee for the possibility of an effective democratic control of the exercise of legitimate power; when I have so relentlessly been criticizing all that could be associated with (ideals of) direct democracy—in all of these the motivation was, again and again, that democracy puts us in a relationship to ourselves and that we should distrust all efforts, in political theory and in practice, aiming to undo this doubling by seducing us with deceitful visions of unity and harmony. It is only thanks to this being in a relationship to itself that democracy can be an "honorable" political system. Only this relation can ensure that in democracy the tensions, frictions, and oppositions can be created that will illuminate and make visible the kind of political problems that we will have to address. It is only in this way that democracy can succeed in safeguarding its "honor" and in exercising the self-restraint that honor demands.

Direct democracy "dishonors" democracy by extraditing it to the boundless and unlimited desires of a collective political "libido." By ignoring friction and conflict it stimulates the supreme classical political vice of immoderateness. As Machiavelli correctly saw, a body politic without tensions, frictions, and conflicts (or where these tensions are feared) will first set a course of boundless and arbitrary self-gratification before disintegrating into an incoherent mass of self-seeking, egoistic individuals. By its nature representative democracy (insofar as it differs from direct democracy) must retain for itself the restraints that honor placed upon the eighteenth-century aristocrat. Those restraints had taught the aristocrat to recognize and respect the conflicts that the requirements of honor inevitably confronted him with. "Standing in a relationship to oneself" and conflict belong to each other no less than being a human being and being capable of rational thought.

As we have seen in Chapter 3, the grandeur of democracy has always lain in its capacity to recognize conflict and to reconcile it: its strategy of avoidance never seduced it into ignoring conflict, as direct democracy requires us to do. "Dishonorable" direct democracy ignores conflict and naively believes in a kind of preestablished harmony within the political domain; "honorable" aesthetic democracy wants to solve conflict by avoiding it in its peculiar and politically creative way, and can only succeed in this by *not* ignoring it. Self-evidently, one can only be successful in avoiding something if one is aware of this something. As we have seen in Chapter 6, most of the successes of democracy originated in the recognition of conflict and the consequent awareness that its solution requires the creation of a new political reality, the new reality of the *juste milieu*.

But, admittedly, the distinction between these two attitudes toward conflict, between reconciling and sidestepping conflict, will, in actual political practice, be a matter of emphasis rather than of outright opposition. Hence, we may discern in democracy's strategy of avoidance one of the permanent temptations of democracy, which may all too easily succeed in perverting it. Avoidance is democracy's heel of Achilles; it is both its greatest force and its greatest weakness. Avoidance and indifference are the supreme achievements and the greatest threats to democracy.

3. Aesthetic Political Philosophy and Republicanism

Though taking a different route, many contemporary political philosophers came to similar conclusions (or to similar fears) with regard to democracy's future. I am thinking here of the so-called republican tradition—not coincidentally often traced back to Machiavelli.[5] Insofar as these political philosophers are prepared to pronounce on the predicament of contemporary Western democracies, they tend to be worried by citizens' increased lack of willingness to identify with the public interest. In order to remedy this dangerous (in their eyes) degeneration of democracy, and in order to counteract the indifference of citizens to the major political issues that have to be addressed and require political decision-making, they attempt to define the political responsibilities belonging to what they call "the office of citizenship" and to develop a kind of public morality circumscribing the virtues belonging to that "office."[6] In this way the republican hopes to counteract democracy's tendency to disintegrate and to become a helpless political system unable to define and to adequately deal with its greatest challenges.

Obviously the development of such a set of citizenly virtues is a most praiseworthy enterprise; yet as long as the majority of us remains uninformed about or disinclined to effectively internalize these civic virtues, the republican program will sadly remain devoid of all practical significance. What surely is of great value in the republican proposal, however, is its insight into the indispensability of this "standing in a relationship to oneself" for the proper functioning of the political machinery. Indeed, *somewhere* in the political machinery, this dimension has to be realized in order to prevent the kind of danger that republicans so rightly fear. No democracy can survive from which the dimension of "standing in a relationship to oneself" is absent.

Consequently, what is most valuable in republicanism for a better understanding of democracy is its awareness of the central role played by civic virtues (always having to do with this "standing in a relationship to oneself"), or, as we would now say, of the "mentalities" guaranteeing the proper functioning of political systems. Indeed, the modern term "mentality" is, from this perspective, to be preferred to its classical alternative, "virtue," because the former avoids the association with ethics that is invited by the latter. And we need only think of Machiavelli, who was, as Pocock has demonstrated, one of the principal exponents of the republican tradition, in order to realize how mistaken the latter association in many cases would be. It is here that contemporary republicans speculating about the ethical duties implied by "the office of being a citizen" still have to learn quite a lot from Machiavelli, his insight in the brokenness of the political world, and in what that means for the place to be assigned to ethics. More often than not, ethics is a poor guide for adequate political action. Speaking more generally, the greatest advantage of the (Machiavellian) republican tradition when compared to either the liberal or the communitarian tradition is the republican appeal to the aristocratic, classical tradition of political theory. The realism, even cynicism, of this tradition is our very best guarantee for a better understanding of our contemporary political situation. Republicanism is superior in that it permits itself to speak in a quasi-sociological vein *about* virtues and to assess realistically their respective merits, instead of being content to *develop* some lofty civic virtue and to recommend that in the way that the many *schöne Seelen* in the history of political thought have done.

Indeed, now that our familiar ideological "moral maps" have become confused and ethics is more politically helpless than ever before, and now that attempts to develop such civic virtues immediately betray their arbitrary idleness, talking about existing civic virtues makes more sense than trying to devise new ones. Once again we may expect more from the historical perspective than from systems suggesting an illusory ahistorical transparency of the political domain. Democracy has come of age, it has acquired its own history, it has gone through several metamorphoses, and nothing is to be expected from analyses that do not have the rich and variegated historical development of democracy since the Restoration as their natural background. Dispensing with this background is like the attempt to guess the plot of a book on the basis of a single page, instead of recalling to mind all that one has read up to that page. Contemporary democracy can only be adequately understood if its history is taken into account. Aesthetic political philosophy, with its rootedness in the same logic of representation as historical writing, is here quite close to the detached if not cynical attitude characteristic of the classical and aristocratic phases of republicanism. And, indeed, we observed in Chapter 4 how aristocratic republicanism contributed to the emergence of modern historical consciousness. It is history that almost naturally emerges from this contemporary confusion of our "moral maps" and that provides us with the only means of bringing some order in the chaos.

Turning next to the practice of contemporary democracy, we must observe that neither the conflicts between these moral maps nor these maps themselves can any longer generate and guarantee the indispensable tensions and frictions in democratic society. Democracy has become so much satiated with its own history that the attempt to understand and to mend the practice of democracy with the help of such moral maps can only add to the confusion. On the politically relevant level moral maps have lost the capacity to guide us in our actions, and the sphere where they may still be of practical relevance is far removed from the domain of politics. Contemporary politics is not so much amoral or immoral as beyond ethics—and this is, once again, what we share with Machiavelli's outlook. Ethics simply lacks the matrix that we need for understanding the nature and the size of our political problems.

We will, in agreement with this evolution (whether we like it or not), have to abandon the ideological and normative perspective on politics. The politically essential tensions and frictions no longer originate in oppositions within civil society. They rise rather from the relationship between state and civil society, and from differing expectations about the role of the state in addressing social and political problems that face us all in more or less the same way. Not, for example, the old struggle between capital and labor, but the question as to the nature, the future, and the tasks of the state is nowadays our primary political problem. This is the contemporary type of political problem, and it urges us to develop an aesthetic political philosophy.

But this is also where republicanism and aesthetic political philosophy each go their own way. The republican tradition would resist any such concentration on the state. We need only recall in this context the seventeenth- and eighteenth-century struggle — as recorded by Pocock — between the republican "country" tradition and the "court" tradition. Whereas the country tradition concentrates on the citizen and argues (or presupposes) the state's transparency with regard to the citizen, it was precisely the opposing court tradition that recognized the autonomy of the state in the political domain. And this deliberate blindness to the state is, remarkably enough, shared by those predominantly left-wing philosophers who like to call themselves "republicans" and the conservative voters of Reagan's or Gingrich's Republican Party. Most of the remainder of this conclusion will therefore be devoted to the role of the state in political philosophy.

4. The Death of Ideology

This brings us to the heart of the matter. What I want to suggest below is that the opposition between republicanism and aesthetic political philosophy as defined just now is only part of the whole story. More specifically, the disappearance of ideology will be shown to be the major complicating factor in the initially relatively clear and simple relationship between republicanism (versus the autonomy of the state) and aesthetic political philosophy (in favor of the autonomy of the state). My argument will be that the death of ideology forces the contemporary observer into a subsumption of the republican's notion of the divided political self within the matrix of aesthetic political philosophy. We are forced to consider how the divided political self of republicanism and aesthetic political philosophy's traditional focus on the state hang together. In sum, aesthetic political philosophy is not so much republicanism's theoretical adversary as a mutation of republicanism caused by the new social and political *Umwelt* in which democracy attempts to survive.

Let us begin, then, with considering what changes in the political realm have been effected by the death of ideology. First we should observe that there must be an elective affinity between republicanism and ideology. Obviously ideology is the best instrument for achieving this identification of citizens with the collectivity and its interests that republicanism originally was devised for. Weighing their own interests against those of the nation compelled citizens to enter into relationship with themselves (as was discussed above). Taking this into account, the death of ideology seems to have destroyed this biotope of republicanism. Citizens have now lost the possibility of linking their own station of life to the public interest in the meaningful way ideology always used to suggest; citizens now seem to have been reduced to the same situation as Pocock's sixteenth-century Florentine citizen after the link between the individual and the *civitas dei* had been cut through (see Chapter 4). As a consequence, with the death of ideology the relationship between the state and the citizen took on the form best described as "living apart together" (as also described in Chapter 4). From our ideological past we have inherited a large and complex state, but citizens have lost the (ideological) instrument for developing for themselves a meaningful relationship with that state. And as in marriage the phase of living apart together expresses the *fait accompli* that actually living together merely irritates both partners and is the first step toward a divorce, because the partners even lack the stamina to put up a fight. So did the de-ideologization of politics announce a divorce of state and citizen. The state and the citizen withdrew into their own worlds and any contact between the two could now only be perceived as pointless, a time-, energy-, and especially money-consuming nuisance.

This, indeed, is the pattern that we may discern in the increasing mutual animosity between the state and citizens in most contemporary Western democracies: citizens often think that they would be better off without a state and desperately want to be rid of all government interference, while politicians like to complain of the sudden unpredictable, ungrateful,[7] calculating, and selfish behavior of citizens. Between the politician and the citizen this has led to a climate of irritation and frustration about each other's behavior that is quite unlike the matrix of respect, confidence — even fear, sometimes — but in any case, an awareness of mutual dependence, that used to characterize democracy in its ideological phase.

Before proceeding further, I want to return briefly to the distant relationship between state and citizen that came about because of the death of

ideology. This may seem counterintuitive to most readers. Should the disappearance of ideological conflict from our modern democracies not have
effected a *rapprochement* between the state and citizens, instead of an estrangement? For, as we might argue, both politicians and citizens must
surely feel that they are so much closer to each other than ever before, now
that the political universe is no longer defined by the dimensions of different and warring ideologies. Did the death of ideology not imply the disappearance of what used to separate citizens from each other and from the
state (often in the hands of a feared or distrusted ideology)? Did the end of
ideological polarization not show us our fellow citizens for the first time in
history as fundamentally the same individual as ourselves, with more or less
the same outlook, beliefs, private interests and desires? And did this not
imply that the state, as the ship that is carrying us all, cannot be divorced
from our private interests? We will recall that this is how Tocqueville described the political climate under Louis Philippe, when much of the ideological tensions of the previous years had disappeared. In the *rapetissement
général* of that period everybody, citizens and state, recognized the other
in the all-pervasive mentality of the *"enrichissez-vous,"* which was ascribed
to Guizot. There was a unanimous and universal cooperation to get ever
richer and to make life ever more comfortable—for the members of the
politically relevant classes, that is. State and society cooperated in a common enterprise. And is this not, *mutatis mutandis*, what we have also seen
in Western democracies after the death of ideology?

Moreover, is this picture not empirically confirmed by political science
when its practitioners emphasize again and again that, in fact, the state and
society have come so close to each other that traditional distinctions between the two seem to have lost all justification and practical significance?
And is this increased entanglement of state and society not both the result and the measure of the de-ideologization of politics? And was not the
argument in Chapter 3 that democracy always lives and thrives on the reconciliation of political conflict and that our present difficulty is precisely
that we have too little political conflict to feed into the machinery of democratic government? So what else could all this mean but that, inevitably,
the distance between the state and society has been diminished tremendously after the death of ideology?

This objection confronts us, once again, with the kind of paradox that
discussions of social and political reality so often produce. We should not
distrust them, as was demonstrated in our analysis of Tocqueville's politi-

cal writings. We should consider them rather as the royal road to all true political insight. Certainly, we may ask, how could the death of ideology *both* increase *and* diminish the distance between the state and the citizen? The notion of "distance" does not permit of this conjunction. Nevertheless, I think it is of the utmost importance to realize that there is nothing fundamentally wrong with either argument. I believe, therefore, that we should not try to force the issue by proving one view of the consequences of the death of ideology correct, so that we can safely reject the other. Generally speaking, historical changes both in the political domain itself and in our conception of it are the result of how we react to such paradoxes — and in this way each time a fundamentally new political reality is born. So instead of attempting to decide between the two views we should rather heed Tocqueville's wisdom and ask ourselves how both views *could* possibly be correct. Then we need to inquire how we will have to rearrange our unconscious political intuitions in order to account for this *coincidentia oppositorum*. This is how political insight ordinarily comes into being.

5. *The State as the Natural Object of Aesthetic Political Philosophy After the Death of Ideology*

The paradox of distance that is both increased and diminished may suggest, by way of solution, the idea of a systematic *indetermination* and *indefiniteness* in the relationship between state and citizens. From the paradox of a distance that is both increased and diminished we may infer the failure of measuring, and if measuring has to be abandoned, indetermination and indefiniteness are to be expected. Two comments should be made on this result.

First of all, this diagnosis seems to be in agreement with the present political climate. We may think here of the indecision of so many contemporary politicians: they no longer know in what relationship they stand to their electorate; they become ready to respond to all kinds of accidental impulses and abandon all long-term policy to the requirements of short-term policy goals; in short, they begin to demonstrate that kind of brainless and erratic behavior that may, at first sight, be quite endearing in view of the immense power that they actually wield but that is, in fact, just as dangerous as leaving the flight control of a large international airport to a class of schoolchildren. On the one hand they command a political apparatus compared to which Hobbes's *Leviathan* and the majestic states of the absolute monarchs are mere dwarfs, but on the other hand, they lack any clue to the purpose for which this immense and powerful apparatus has to be used. And in the same way that we like to project our own ideas and wishes on uncertain people, so we also like to think that the indecision and uncertainties of the state and the all too apparent readiness of politicians to react immediately to what catches the attention of the public, proves that now the requirements of direct democracy (democracy's old dishonorable alter ego) are finally becoming realized. And our frustration and irritation about politicians' behavior is that they always somehow refuse to make this last natural step toward direct democracy—that is, to listen to the *gesundes Volksempfinden*, to simply do what we ask them to do, and thus realize direct democracy.

This may demonstrate that we may have our doubts about the common lamentation that all our problems originate in an estrangement between politics and citizens. In fact, we have little reason to rejoice in a *rapprochement* between the state and citizens. There has been too much *rapprochement* between state and citizen in the recent past rather than too little. Precisely because politicians felt tempted to nestle as closely as possible to voters they lost the appetite for independent action and became the mere executors of the changing, chaotic, and ill-defined political intuitions of citizens. The justified expectations of both citizens and the state with regard to each other's behavior (originating in an awareness of *difference*) were now systematically disappointed. The final result was that our main political problem became a problem *about* politics as such and *about* how the political machinery should function instead of how we should deal with a number of increasingly serious problems that confront contemporary democratic societies. In an age that can no longer afford the holiday of a revolution, it may be quite dangerous to get stuck in this kind of preliminary problem, occasioned by the dysfunctioning of our political "overhead."

Second, the thesis of the indeterminacy and indefiniteness of the relationship between the citizen and the state is in agreement with the analysis of democracy given in this book. For with the continuous refinement and thereby the continuous erosion of the ideological tertia until, in the end, nothing remained to us but money and language, we also lost the "political object." As we observed in Chapter 2, because of this evolution, the political object gradually evaporated and tended to lose all the contours that previous, coarser tertia were still prepared to leave to it. For the refinement of the tertia, as we saw, did not result in a clearer and better articulation of the political object, as one would have expected, but rather in its ultimate dissolution, in the way that a drop of ink may be seen to dissolve in a glass of water. Hence, indetermination and indefiniteness mark both the death of ideology and the victory of the tertia over what is compared in terms of them. This state of affairs is interesting since one would have expected a parallelism of the fate of ideology and that of the tertia: did not ideology function as a tertium ordering the objects of the political universe? The problem could be solved by saying that the ultimate tertia, money and language, have become the ideologies of the contemporary world. And this would permit the conclusion that the tertia are politically a stronger force than ideology and that these two ultimate tertia have hungrily absorbed ideology, that formerly awe-inspiring political force, within themselves. The tertia are a political and historical power that nobody and nothing—not even ideology—can successfully withstand.

I return to the indeterminacy and indefiniteness of the relationship between the citizen and the state that was mentioned above. This indeterminacy and indefiniteness that has been created by the tertia must now be the major challenge to political philosophy. Politics requires well-considered decisions, and if politics becomes paralyzed—as now seems to be the case in most Western democracies—by the indeterminacy and indefiniteness ruling the political domain so that neither voter nor politician can have any clear conception of in what direction we should move, political philosophy has a double task. First, it should explain how this state of affairs has come into being; second, it should indicate what kind of issues we should focus on in order to regain our grasp of political reality.

The diagnosis given above of our present political predicament will suggest an obvious answer to that second question. For if indeterminacy and indefiniteness now characterize the relationship between the citizen and the state this self-evidently directs the gaze of the political philosopher to that relationship: it is here that more clarity is a first requirement for a shoring up of our present, faltering democracies. Moreover, this indeterminacy and indefiniteness can only be adequately dealt with if we take seriously what we find at *both* ends of this problematic and indeterminate trajectory in our contemporary political landscape. An aesthetic political philosophy, originating in the recognition of the indeterminacy of the aesthetic relationship between the represented and the representation, and asking itself how to properly deal with this, is the best premise for a successful discussion on the future of democracy. And it will be no less obvious that a primary condition for the success of such a discussion will be a recognition of the autonomy of the state (reflecting the autonomy of the representation with regard to the represented that was discussed in Chapter 1) and to see in the state the natural object of contemporary political philosophy.

One more argument can be given for my plea in favor of a political philosophy mainly focusing on the state. The death of ideology has substantially weakened the state's position with regard to citizens. If we wish to comprehend this loss of the state's authority over citizens, we must realize that ideology is always metaphorical. Ideology defines a point of view from which we are invited to see social and political reality. For example, the metaphor "the earth is a spaceship" invites us to model the ecosystem of the earth on the cramped quarters of a spaceship. Metaphor also suggests a certain kind of action or behavior: when hearing the metaphor mentioned just now, we all understand that it means to say that we should stop exploiting our ecosystem. Metaphor really is the missing link between the "is" and the "ought" that philosophers have so long been looking for: it links description to prescription.[8]

But, as we have seen in Chapter 5, the state itself also automatically places itself in a metaphorical relationship to society — and the implication of this conjunction of state and ideology is that the disappearance of ideology from the contemporary political scene is not, as some people argue, a liberation of the state from its previous ideological fetters, but a sign that the state has now lost its strongest ally and traditionally most powerful support. It is true that the state avoids (or ought to avoid) identifying itself with a specific ideology, but without ideological conflict it is like a flower that is no longer watered. Its fate will be no different from that flower. Ideological conflict is the lifeblood of the democratic state.

For this close alliance between the state and ideology two arguments can be given. First, if metaphor defines a certain political "point of view" from which social reality is conceptualized, it is the state onto which this point of view can be projected. The state enables us to translate ideological, metaphorical insight into concrete political action. Without a state, ideology is helpless, without ideology the state has no program for political action. A nonideological state is then a *contradictio in terminis*, and it may seem that one cannot have one without the other. Second, the relationship between the citizen and the state or party representing the citizen is intrinsically metaphorical. For if A represents B, this is an invitation to us to see B in terms of A; the same applies to the metaphorical utterance "A is B." Representation is essentially metaphorical and this is no less true of political representation.[9] If, then, both the state and ideology are intrinsically metaphorical, we should now recall from Chapter 5 that metaphor is the trope of distance: the most successful metaphor places us at such a distance from reality that we can integrate its elements into one coherent "picture." And both the state and ideology mimic this gesture. Taking this into account, it will be clear what the evanescence of ideology will have to mean for the state. In the first place the disappearance of ideology will further contribute to the diminishing of the distance between the citizen and the state that was already discussed above—and we have therefore every reason to agree with those authors who argue that our present political discontent and our irritation about contemporary politics have to do with a reduction rather than with an augmentation of the distance between state and citizen.[10]

This may help us to explain some unpleasant features of contemporary politics. For suppose that we are moving ever closer to a painting and yet we hope to retain the survey of the painting as a whole that was still easily achieved when it was looked at from a proper distance. We shall now have to turn our head in this direction, then in quite another; everything we see must be looked at with much more attention than before; we shall have to be able to memorize all kinds of details; and so on. In short, we shall have to develop the kind of all-encompassing attention to the painting that the state has gradually developed with regard to society. And yet, by such a "bureaucratization" of our attention, we will inevitably lose our grasp of the whole:[11] the more we "perceive," the less we "see." In fact, this argument is a repetition of the argument of Chapter 4, when we observed that with this victory of (Romantic) irony over metaphor and with the reduction of the metaphorical distance between the state and the citizen, we will also lose our capacity to conceptualize social and political problems. And this will result in a loss of the state's political power, which is necessary for putting our solutions into practice. In short, the result of these developments will be an increased brainlessness, bureaucratization, and ineffectiveness of government. The nonideological state is a stupid and ineffective state, and its capacity to learn will decrease accordingly.[12] Needless to say, I am not wishing to contribute here further to that popular and all-too-easy *culte de l'incompétence* of the politician; we have no reason to suppose that contemporary individual politicians are less intelligent or less devoted to the public welfare than those of a few decades ago. I only want to point out that the present relationship between the state and society has become such that the politician is forced almost willy-nilly to behave unintelligently and short-sightedly. About a century ago, mass psychologists like Tarde and Le Bon argued that the democratic mass is always as unintelligent as the stupidest of its members and therefore will require strong and charismatic leaders; now we may observe the reverse: an enigmatic and unfathomable society is ruled by a state and by politicians who (probably much to their own dismay) find themselves placed in institutional circumstances that force them, often against their own will, to yield to their most primitive reflexes.

In sum, if contemporary (aesthetic) political philosophy has one task, a task that is more important than ever before and on which I would not hesitate to say that a large part of our political future hinges, it is to investigate anew, with all the energy and rigor we can bring to it, the democratic state and the mechanisms that keep it moving (that is, if it still moves at all). Put differently, if this book has had one purpose, if I hope that it will have taught the reader one lesson, this lesson is that the state ought, more than anything else, to be once again the primary focus of interest in political philosophy—such was the main aim of the argument in Chapter 4. We should not let ourselves be blinded by the uncertain, bungling, and inefficient behavior of the state; nor by how it so often allows itself to be humiliated by lobbies, pressure groups, corporations, and so on; nor by the stories that political scientists enthusiastically tell us about how much power the state has lost to supranational organizations or to the kind of quasi-feudal institutions that have grown up between the state and the citizen; nor by the contempt and disrepute into which the state has fallen in the eyes of most of the public. All these sad facts about the contemporary democratic state are unfortunately more true than ever, but instead of seeing here an argument for declaring the state an irrelevancy, we should see in these facts rather an indication of the scale of the difficulties threatening democracy's future—and of the difficulties facing the political philosopher in any attempt to understand democracy's predicament. Whether we like it or not, our political future is closely bound up with that of the democratic state. The democratic state may be the ship safely carrying us over the seas of our collective future, but it may also be like the proverbial millstone around our collective neck that may drown us as soon as either it or we make a wrong movement.

Hence, all the recent developments that seem to be so much the unmistakable signs of the erosion of the state, of its sinking away helplessly into the morass of society, should not make us turn away from the state as an object that is no longer worthy of the attention of the political philosopher.

On the contrary, all these obscurities with regard to the state and its loss of contours—which I do not contest—should exhort us to have a better look than ever before at the state. Moreover, we should realize that whatever may be true of a relative loss or gain in the power of the state, this does not prevent the state from remaining the only institution that can address, at least with any hope of success, the social and political problems facing us. The number and size of these problems will increase rather than decrease in the foreseeable future. Those political philosophers who wish to present the state as an irrelevancy in the power relationships in contemporary democracy, and whose worldly-wise sneer that focusing our attention on the state can never be more than an idle attempt to return to an outdated and obsolete form of political philosophy, in fact recommend us to forget about the only institution we now possess for solving our present and future political problems. As this book will have made clear, I am far from being unaware of the weaknesses of the present democratic state, but, for better or for worse, for the time being we have nothing else to rely upon. *If the state does not solve our collective problems, nothing and nobody else will*; so we had better ask ourselves how to reconstruct the democratic state so that we may expect it to be more equal to its present and future tasks than it currently is.

6. The Voter After the Death of Ideology

It was said above that the abandonment of ideology diminished the distance between the state and the citizen (though with results differing from those we would have expected from this evolution). I now want to consider this same evolution from the perspective of voters finding themselves at the other end of that problematic trajectory between citizens and state. The crucial datum here is that the realization of so many of the aims of traditional ideological politics has effected a number of unintended consequences that average citizens hate as much as they have learned to love the fruits of ideological politics. So citizens now find themselves caught up in the hitherto unknown paradox of willing both the realization of certain ideological goals and the avoidance of their inevitable unintended consequences. Contemporary voters, to mention some examples, may want lower taxes but at the same time better and more expensive social security; they may want higher wages but, at the same time, less unemployment; they may want to be able to go on driving their cars but at the same time they require the state to put an end to traffic jams; they hate sitting in traffic

jams but at the same time they cause them; they want more and cheaper
meat and fruit, but at the same time they ask the state to stop the pollution
of the environment caused by intensive agriculture; they want more individualism and less government interference but at the same time they want
the government to be tougher on crime—and so one could go on. Now, nobody can prevent voters from cherishing all these mutually exclusive political goals that, admittedly, all make perfect sense from their point of view.
Since nobody can do so, we may expect voters not to feel in the least inhib-
ited in this respect. Our ideal world is by no means a consistent world, and
consistency certainly is not an ideal of most people. And why should it be
different? The average voter has little in common with the kind of strictly
rational individuals that are discussed in the rational choice theories of the
Chicago sociologists. Voters might well point out that it may actually further their interest to be irrational and to want, for example, both higher
wages and less unemployment. Besides, not *all* sets of causes with their unintended consequences would mutually exclude each other, and to a certain
extent one can effectively realize incompatible goals, albeit at considerable
cost elsewhere. Our social world itself often is no less inconsistent than are
voters (one more lesson from our insight in the aesthetic brokenness of the
social and political world we live in).

But if voters will not feel inclined to properly sort out causes and unintended consequences themselves, and even if they wish to have the best of
the world of ideological goals as well as avoiding their unintended consequences (as most often will be the case), this does not prevent them from
being confronted with the need to make choices. This new situation will
have two results. In the first place citizens will tend to hesitate between
a satisfaction of ideological desires and the counteracting of such satisfaction's unintended results; there is little that will consistently bind citizens
to either of the two options. The smallest of accidents may make them
change their minds from one moment to the next. For example, citizens
may fiercely resist the building of new highways as long as their own freedom of movement is not denied, but they may become just as ardent an
advocate of new highways after having been caught up in traffic jams—
and vice versa. Small and unforeseeable contingencies on either a local or
a national scale (as, for example, an unexpected resurgence or decline of
the economy) may dramatically change the minds of large parts of the electorate because of this subtle balance between social causes and their unintended effects.

Of course, since Schumpeter's famous observation that the average voter spends more time on a game of bridge than on thinking over political choices, the (ir-)rationality of the voter has been a favorite target in political science. The results of Converse's and Campbell's analyses of the American voter are well known. They demonstrated to what surprising extent any voter's political wishes may be inconsistent, with politicians themselves scoring a little better.[13] I want to emphasize, however, that, disappointing as these results may be, they need not in the least imply a serious threat to democracy for as long as voters remain consistent in their inconsistencies. Democracies have functioned excellently in the recent past with Schumpeter's inconsistent and infantile voters. Inconsistencies can even become pillars of a well-functioning democracy, as long as they will determine the decisions of voters in a certain and consistent manner and enable the politicians to sufficiently predict the voter's reactions to their proposals and decisions. But what we may observe for our own age of unintended consequences is more serious—that is, not so much the *inconsistent* but the *unstable* or *floating* voter. Our contemporary nonideological voter will be a systematically unstable voter. And as we will see in a moment, it is here that we must discern a real threat to democracy.

To the extent that citizens become aware of this unpleasant conjunction of ideological desires and the unintended effects of the realization of these desires, to the extent that they become aware of the "catch 22" situation in which they suddenly find themselves, political conflict and opposition will no longer be a matter of opposing one part of the electorate to another (as was the case in the happy and unproblematic days of democracy). Citizens will now become divided against and within themselves. In other words— and this brings me to the essence of my argument—in contemporary post-ideological politics the individual citizen is confronted with the inconsistency of his or her own seemingly legitimate political desires. The citizen him- or herself now becomes a microcosm of traditional ideological politics. The macrocosm—the impact of our collective action on our social and physical *Umwelt*—now has its counterpart in a microcosm—how the voter determines his or her political options. We could describe this remarkable internalization of political conflict in Freudian terms: the citizen now learns to see him- or herself as the place where the conflict is fought out between the "libido" of one's ideological desires and the "superego" of one's new insight into the need to counter the unintended consequences effected by the realization of one's ideological desires.

Or to put it in the terms that were used at the beginning of this con-clusion, not the electorate as a whole, but the *individual* voter now finds him- or herself placed "in a relationship to him- or herself"—though this relationship in which he or she now stands to him- or herself can, for two reasons, be shown to be quite different from the traditional one.

First, whereas traditionally the politicized individual was transposed onto the non- or prepolitical individual, now *both* poles in the opposition are political and suggest the individual's subsumption in politics while that individual's prepolitical self is denied its customary role as a compass for political desires. Consequently, the voter feels disoriented because, as we observed above, this internal political struggle, where his strongest oppo-nent now is part of himself, is unfamiliar. Traditional democracy requires politically undivided individuals and the voter feels that this requirement can no longer be satisfied. It need not surprise us, therefore, that, as was the case in Freud's speculations about the relationship between the indi-vidual and civilization, this also stimulated in the democratic voter a "dis-content" with politics: politics itself now forces the voter into a struggle with him- or herself and presents itself simply as incapable of fulfilling even the most rational and apparently most justified collective desires. All sin-cere attempts to improve society only seem to result in the creation of new problems that will often be worse than those that we already had.

If, then, we take these two facts about the nonideological voter together, we will be able to explain many of the features that politics has acquired over the last five years in most Western democracies. We will now under-stand why contemporary democratic politics is caught up within a matrix determined by an increasingly inconsistent, irritated, and "Freudian" voter who is getting more and more frustrated about the incapacity of the state to do what seems to be such an obvious thing to do (though the next moment the very opposite thing may seem to the voter to be the obvious course of action). We will see why politicians desperately ask themselves why their attempts to come as close as possible to the voter (which is their natural reaction to all this) only reinforces the voter's erratic behavior, and why politicians must observe that their capacity to comprehend what goes on in society and to act accordingly decreases year after year.

Second, this internal struggle of the modern voter with him- or herself may remind us of the picture given in the beginning of this conclusion of the citizen within the republican tradition. For one of the attractive aspects of republicanism is that, just like aesthetic political philosophy, it emphasizes that as a citizen one ought "to stand in a relationship to oneself." But there is one fundamental difference here. Within the republican tradition the issue of the citizen's struggle was always fairly obvious: it always had to do with how to weigh one's *own* interests against the *public* interest. Thus, as a true republican theorist, Machiavelli required the citizen to be ready to risk his own life for the safety of the state. But this clear-cut opposition between private and public interest has now disappeared. For the indecision of the voter with regard to the implementation of ideological desires or the avoidance of the unpleasant unintended consequences of that implementation cannot be decided within the old, trustworthy matrix of private versus public interest. The implemention of these ideological desires, after all, may serve or threaten the voter's private interest—as it may also serve or threaten the public interest. The old comfortable (republican) dilemma of being either selfish or public-spirited has now evaporated.

We should not interpret this new situation as if a systematic indeterminacy has come into being between private and public interest, as if we now live in a world where the republicans (opting for public-spiritedness) and Mandeville (opting for enlightened self-interest) are fighting a neverending war. It is, rather, that the identification of what is our self-interest and what is public interest has become a meaningless issue: all our options can be constructed as public options, just as well as all our options can be seen as private options. This state of affairs should not be confused with the one that Mandeville had in mind: Mandeville argued for a harmony or coincidence of private and public interest and not for their being identical or indiscernible. He did not wish to say that the notions of the "public interest" and of the "private interest" had the same referent: what he wanted to make clear was, rather, that there exists a means-to-ends relationship between the two in the sense that the public interest is best served by citizens who allow themselves to be guided by their enlightened self-interest. The state of affairs that has come into existence in our contemporary democracies should rather be compared to Frege's argument about the names "the morning star" and "the evening star" having the same referent (that is, the planet Venus). And, as in Frege's argument, the identifying descriptions "public interest" and "private interest" may well retain their different meanings, whereas it would be an empirical discovery of some importance that, under the present circumstances, the two identifying descriptions apparently refer to one and the same (still unnamed) thing. Indeed, our present political predicament is comparable to that of the astronomers who were using the names "the morning star" and "the evening star" without being aware that both names have the same referent.

On the one hand it may seem that an awareness of this fact about our present political predicament must provoke in us an intense feeling of profound satisfaction: for had not all politics, since it came into being in the dawn of mankind, the reconciliation of the public and the private interest as its highest and most supreme goal? And has this most desirable reconciliation not been brought about when we can make in the realm of politics that same kind of empirical discovery that Frege was thinking of in the realm of astronomy? Has utopia silently been realized in our complex and highly sophisticated contemporary democracies? Perhaps this is how one could look at the achievements of late twentieth-century democracy; traditional definitions of utopia certainly seem to fit part of how contemporary democracy succeeded in readjusting and redefining the relationship between private and public interest.

On the other hand, one might well argue that the realization of this utopia is at odds with the nature of the human being as well as that of (democratic) politics. We should recall here the republican's insistence on the necessity of this "standing in a relationship" to oneself for a properly functioning political machinery. If we no longer have any vital interests outside the public interest, and if the public interest coincides with the private interest, we will have entered a new political world in which the machinery of republicanism simply lacks a point of application since the distinction between public and private interest has lost its meaning. If all democratic politics, somewhere, somehow, and in whatever way defined or implemented, requires the dimension of representation in which this "standing in a relationship to oneself" can articulate itself—if there is no longer a dimension enabling us to objectify or "represent" ourselves and our interests—democratic politics becomes like a dismounted clock. The voter now lacks the means necessary for his political orientation. No need, then, to be surprised about the instability of the contemporary voter who finds himself, after having lived for generations in the relatively stable and orderly world of ideological conflict, in a new political reality that seems simply to lack the means for articulating his own interests against those of the community. How helpless he must feel in a world in which the opposition between public and private interest gradually became an obsolete and useless construction. He must now feel as if History had surrendered him to the expert as the only person still able to tell him who he actually is and what his true political interests are; not only is the expert the only one still capable of answering his political questions (as was already the case in Daniel Bell's technocratic utopia of half a century ago), the expert now also dictates to him what are the really important questions that he should ask.

Or, even worse, the citizen may now conclude that all his political intuitions and desires have become strangely unrelated to his true interests, since he is now living in a world that he will never understand well enough to serve even his most direct interests, those lying closest to his desires; he may conclude that, therefore, his opinions and actions have become politically irrelevant. Now, this conjunction of desires and interests truly is a minimum condition of democratic politics: nothing could be more effective in excluding, expelling, or alienating the citizen from the realm of democratic politics than cutting through the ties between his desires and interests. To use once again the metaphor of the clock, this conjunction of desires and interests is, in politics, like the pendulum of a pendulum clock: without the pendulum the clock will run down wildly and uncontrollably. A functioning democracy is unthinkable if in the mind of the citizen this conjunction of desire and interest is destroyed, so that his desires, beliefs, interests, and actions seem to him inconsequential from a political point of view. The best way to keep the pendulum of democracy in its place is therefore to take care that the terms "public interest" and "private interest" retain their capacity to refer to different things. And, obviously, a certain rehabilitation of the notions of self-interest and of egoism (so much discredited in contemporary, ethically inspired political systems such as the one developed by Rawls) would, in its turn, be the most appropriate means to that end. For egoism and self-interest have always been the most efficient and reliable means for tying desire and interest together.

I hasten to add three qualifications to my eulogy of egoism—a eulogy that will undoubtedly strike most people as unduly cynical. In the first place, it is certainly true that the conjunction of desire and interest could also be reinforced by a reinvigoration of altruism. Theoretically, altruism is not necessarily less effective than egoism in achieving a redefinition of the relationship between desires and interests. However, altruism would be a less secure and effective instrument to that effect, since egoism and self-interest have always proven to be stronger determinants of social and political action than altruism: egoism pushes, so to speak, in a certain direction whereas altruism merely corresponds to a movement of giving way. This observation brings me to my second qualification: one can only successfully push in a certain direction if there is something else in that direction to yield to the increased pressure. Hence, an increased egoism can only bring about its wholesome effects if it is accompanied by an increased altruism. Put differently, though the emphasis would have to remain on egoism, an increased polarization in the citizen between egoism and altruism would be the best description of what is needed for a reanimation of our contemporary democracies (at least, as far as the citizen is concerned).

When praising the virtues of egoism here, I am not making an ethical statement; from the point of view of ethics my plea for egoism has surely little to recommend itself. My claim is that for a functioning democracy an increase of egoism (and a concomitant increase of altruism) is an important condition: my claim is a claim about democracy and not about ethics. So one will have to chose between being a good democrat or being ethically in the right — and one cannot be both at the same time. This is not because democracy should be inherently unethical or amoral: the explanation is, rather, that the aestheticism of representative democracy places democracy beyond the realms of both fact and value.

My claim can be further substantiated as follows. The disintegration of the traditional opposition between self-interest and public interest and the one between desire and interest will cause havoc in the mind of the voter. He will now be without the strong and infallible guide for his political preferences and actions that he used to have in the age of ideology. Inevitably this will condemn him to indecision, instability, and self-entanglement. And it is of the greatest importance that we realize that this will undermine another essential presupposition underlying all democratic decision-making. When the process of democratic decision-making (whatever the process may look like in actual constitutional detail) no longer has its foundation in a voter who can adhere with at least a minimum degree of consistency over at least a certain minimum of time to some political option, when the voter is ready to change political affiliation because of the smallest accidental event, when voters will support political efforts to reduce traffic as long as they are not themselves prevented from using their cars, but will resist those efforts the very moment they get caught up in a traffic jam, then one of the minimum conditions of democracy is no longer fulfilled. When the voter's political preferences behave in the same unstable, erratic, and unpredictable way as the gas molecules in a chamber, neither a political party nor the state will any longer be able to connect with citizens — and either a total paralysis of politics or a brute autocracy becomes inevitable (two different consequences, by the way, of one and the same cause). And we may expect that this situation will arise if the self of the citizen becomes polarized between ideological "libido" on the one hand and the fears of the unintended consequences of the realization of ideological desires on the level of the "superego" on the other. The modern sophisticated, politically tormented individual citizen, torn between his desires and the fears of the realization of his desires, may in most relevant aspects be a morally more responsible and respectable citizen than his parents were—but he will destroy democracy.

A further complication is that, paradoxically, we will need precisely this morally more responsible voter if we wish even to begin to deal with the kind of problem that will face us in the near future. The uncertain and confused voter, entangled in his desires and the fears of the undesired results of the realization of his desires, the voter that so much thwarts the functioning of democracy, is no less the voter that we will need if we wish even to try to effectively counter the unintended consequences of our ideological political action. The dilemma seems to be that we succumb in a democratic way to the problems that we have created, or we succeed in an undemocratic way in securing the continuation of at least part of the kind of life that we have become accustomed to in the second half of this century.

7. Conclusion

Now, whatever one might wish to say to the detriment of ideological politics, ideologies had at least the advantage that they gave some minimum coherence and consistency to voters' political desires. Party ideologues were aware, though perhaps not always sufficiently, that wanting one thing often would automatically exclude wanting something else as well. Since voters were inclined to accept their expertise in these matters and to agree with their regime of political desiderata, this provided ideological politics with a fairly solid basis—a basis that is absent in contemporary politics. This absence is the cause of the indecision and instability of both the voter and the politician. If, then, this is what we owed to ideological politics, we may discern here another argument in favor of a stronger state and, more specifically, a far more crucial role for political parties. The instability of the voter, which is such a serious threat to democracy, can only be counteracted effectively by limiting the voter's options in a way that may recall the traditional role of ideologies. More specifically, henceforward it will become an additional task of the political party to sort out all the mutually incompatible wishes that the electorate might have, to discern certain configurations in them all, and to see what does and does not belong together.

When saying that this means a stronger state, I hasten to add that this does not imply that the state will thus get a preponderance over the citizen that it did not hitherto possess. For we should remember that, to a certain extent, parties have *always* been doing this: citizens *never* voted for a certain policy, voters vote for parties and not for political ideals or ideologies (though of course political ideals and ideologies may determine the voter's preferences). It is, once again, one of the naive delusions inspired by the notion of popular sovereignty to believe that the political wishes of the electorate are "represented" as such by the state and that parties are a mere intermediary channeling these wishes to the level of the state. The voter may decide about the future of political parties, but parties decide about the future of the state. And this is how it ought to be—or, rather, since Arrow's "impossibility theorem" [14] we know that there is no other workable way for translating the preferences of the voter into actual policy.

But in spite of this continuity, which I am the first to admit, my proposal with regard to the new role of the political party will grant to it additional responsibilities, and will require of politicians an awareness of all the implications of their new preponderance in their relationship to the citizens. If the ideological politician had the now enviable privilege of merely having to deal with political conflicts that had already been trimmed down by ideology into a recognizable and manageable form (of course, I am not in the least belittling the gravity of these conflicts and am referring here merely to their formal characteristics) and if both the voter and the political party were in a position subservient to ideology, this can now no longer be the case. Once again the explanation lies in the unintended consequences of traditional ideological politics and in the paradoxes which, as we saw in chapter 6, democracy gives rise to.

Now, it is a most unfortunate peculiarity of these unintended consequences and of these paradoxes that they persistently refuse to demonstrate the same most convenient consistency and coherence that was characteristic of the (ideological) policies that called them into being; they are rather a kind of echo, so to speak, and may come from all directions (an echo of the finiteness of our *Umwelt*, to put it poetically). And an extra problem, as we observed in Chapter 3, is that these echoes have the unpleasant habit of presenting themselves in a fairly similar way to the electorate as a whole—

and, therefore, possess a form that the democratic political machinery aiming at reconciliation can only digest with the greatest difficulty. Its most natural reaction is to ignore them and to act as if these problems do not exist. Here we face, once again, the second of those two supreme vices of democracy: immoderateness, and the tendency to ignore unpleasant facts.

Nevertheless, as may be inferred from this, if the main task of previous politics was to look for an *Ausgleich* between ideological and social conflict, democracy now has to solve the problems posed by the unintended consequences that were brought about in the age of ideological democratic politics. I will not insist here on the urgency of problems like these: overpopulation, climatological change, pollution, the decay of the welfare state, crime; combined with the social problems caused by the conflation of moral maps that was discussed in Chapter 4, the tremendous political problems arising when oil reserves run out with no suitable alternatives—since this book was not written for those who are unwilling or unable to see their urgency. More specifically, if it has been my argument at several places in this book that all meaningful political philosophy originates in the recognition of some urgent political problem, on the solution of which, according to the political philosopher, the well-being of future society depends, then one may discern here the kind of problem that has stimulated me to write this book. But if we are convinced that these problems are our most serious political challenge, we will recognize that it will be the new and future task of political parties to single out certain configurations of unintended consequences that, in their view, are the most serious threats to the future of humanity, and to explain to the voter with all the arguments and the rhetorical skill they can muster the merits of the choices that they have made. *It is only the political party that effectively and efficiently can end the present political impasse.* The new preponderance of the party with regard to the voter is the new fuel that we shall have to feed into the machinery of the democratic state, which may get it going again.[15] Somewhere a new source of political power has to be created, some rearrangement in the relations of political power has to be effected, and, under the present circumstances and in conformity with the intuitions of aesthetic political philosophy, a strongly increased autonomy of the political party with regard to the voter seems the best and safest way to do this.

If we recall the argument in Chapter 1 that the political party is part of the state rather than an extension of the voter, this will undoubtedly imply a stronger state as well. One suggestion for how to counterbalance this increased power of the state follows, once again, both from the analysis of our contemporary political predicament and from aesthetic political philosophy. We should realize that the ideological tie between the citizen and the state has always been the most powerful remnant of mimetic representation in parliamentary democracy: in terms of ideology the "identity" between citizen and state (as recommended by Gerhard Leibholz) was achieved. And this identity found its constitutional expression in the fact that in most Western democracies the citizen is asked to vote for one party only. Now that aesthetic distance between citizen and the party or the state will have to be increased more than ever before, it will be necessary to abandon this absurd demand that the voter should pronounce on one party only. The pathetic declaration of political love for one party that is expected of the voter during elections, and that is now more at odds than ever with how the voter conceives of politics and the state, has to be exchanged for a system where the voter can express judgment on *all* existing parties. Or to use the most appropriate term: the voter must be asked to present his or her "representation" of political reality by giving a verdict on the behavior of *all* political parties. This will require the political party not to satisfy just one ideologically congenial section of the electorate, but to develop a party program that can be attractive to any voter. Not ideologically defined interests of *sections* of the electorate, but visions of the future of the *whole* of the nation will now be the issue in the struggle of political parties for the voter's favor. Only in this way will constitutional practice be harmonized again with the contemporary political realities of the relationship between the voter, the political party, and the state.

In sum, a stronger and more determined state than we presently possess will be needed if we wish even to begin to grapple with this kind of new problem that history has placed on our political agenda. The state and, more specifically, political parties have to define certain configurations of unintended consequences that they think must be counteracted first; this may guide the mind of the voter. Even more so, when dealing with these problems the state may at times find itself opposed by almost the whole electorate because the type of political problem we may expect for the future will often face society as a whole and not just one part of it—and yet the state should under such circumstances be able to summon the strength and the courage not to yield before the immense pressure to which it will then be exposed. The state now knows that whereas its former role, inherited from the political constellation of the Restoration, was to function as the scene where a reconciliation of opposing ideologies could be enacted, it now may, under certain circumstances, find itself in conflict with *all* political denominations existing in civil society. It is only an aesthetic political philosophy, which does not fear the aesthetic gap between the state and the citizen, that may, under the circumstances in question, provide the state with a theoretical justification of its firm decision to persist in what it sees as the only possible course of political action and yet allow it to be confident that, by doing so, it will nevertheless remain within the framework of a democracy that is dear to us all, and the only guarantee we have for a livable future for all of us and for our children. It is only in this way that the new source of legitimate political power can be tapped that will enable democracy to survive, both physically and politically, the Age of Unintended Consequences.

In a word, the supreme challenge for contemporary political philosophy is to develop a conception of democracy that grants to the state the more extensive powers that can enable it to deal effectively with the immense problems that one may expect for the next century while, at the same time, democratic control of political parties and of the state is defined in such a way as to avoid the dangers of despotism.[16] We must realize that a stronger state is not in the least incompatible with democracy: on the contrary, as Spinoza and Tocqueville correctly saw, no political system generates so much power and is so much dependent for its proper functioning on the presence of political power as democracy: democratic liberty and political power entail rather than exclude each other. And this is, in the end, what aesthetic political philosophy is all about.

Reference Matter

Notes

Preface

1. In order to avoid confusion both here and in the rest of this book, a short terminological clarification of the terms "historism" and "historicism" will be necessary. The latter term gained currency in the Anglo-Saxon world mainly thanks to Popper's influential *The Poverty of Historicism* (1944). In this book Popper fiercely attacked so-called speculative philosophies of history, i.e. the kind of systems developed by Hegel, Marx, Spengler, or Toynbee for finding meaning in human history. Popper convincingly demonstrated (1) that the predictions of the future were often unsound because they were based upon unwarranted applications of the methods of science to the domain of history and (2) that much of the unprecedented political disasters of the first half of this century had their intellectual origins in these "historicist" speculative systems.

The word "historicism," however, may also have a different and, in fact, almost opposite meaning from the one that Popper gave to it. It may also refer to the kind of historical theory that inspired the practice of historical writing as exemplified by the writings of nineteenth-century German historians such as Ranke and to which Humboldt devoted his brilliant and famous theoretical exposition of 1827 entitled *Über die Aufgabe des Historikers*. This variant of "historicism" has been defined by Maurice Mandelbaum as follows: "Historicism is the belief that an adequate understanding of the nature of any phenomenon and an adequate assessment of its value are to be gained through considering it in terms of the place which it occupied and the role which it played within a process of development." See M. Mandelbaum, *History, Man, & Reason. A Study in Nineteenth-century Thought* (Baltimore and London 1974, 41). For an exposition of the other most current definitions of the word "historicism" and for the way that these definitions are interrelated, see my *Denken over Geschiedenis* (Groningen 1986), 185 ff. Both in theory and practice the adherents of the latter definition will reject the kind of speculative systems that the former refers to: we need only recall here that Ranke's historicism was to a large extent inspired by his intense dislike of Hegelianism and of the historical apriorism that he discerned in Fichte.

In order to avoid confusion, I shall use the term "historism" for the Rankean variant and the term "historicism" for the speculative systems or "grand narratives," as one presently likes to call them, of philosophers like Hegel or Marx.

To properly appreciate the Rankean definition, one may think of the following. Suppose that we write a history of Napoleon. In that case we can be sure about the subject of that history: undoubtedly this is the human being of flesh and blood who lived from 1769 to 1821 and became emperor of the French. But suppose, now, that we are writing a history of the labor movement and ask ourselves, again, what is the subject of *that* history. Apparently, this subject is not "labor," which is "moving in one way or another," as suggested by the phrase "labor movement" itself. Rather, if there is such a subject, we shall have to associate it with what went on in the minds of nineteenth- and twentieth-century workers and in that of their political leaders and with the political programs developed by these leaders. Undoubtedly, a certain amount of knowledge of Marx, of resistance to capitalism or expectations about the future social revolution, will be part of that subject. But what about, for instance, the attitude toward the clergy or knowledge of the French Revolution? Are these also part of that subject that a history of the labor movement is about? Here historians will tend to disagree.

And then something of considerable interest can be observed. For this disagreement will be exactly the same disagreement as we shall find in historical discussions about *the history* of the labor movement. Hence, the *subject* of a historical discussion about the labor movement, or what such a discussion *is about*, only becomes clear and can only be articulated in and by a *history* of the labor movement (and this is why we find ourselves here in a situation so much different from that of the Napoleon example). Put differently, in case of a history of the labor movement we cannot distinguish between the subject of the work of history and the history that is presented of it—and this, obviously, has made us repeat the historist definition (à la Ranke and Humboldt), according to which a thing is what its history is.

Obviously the claim should not be confused with the absurdist claim that histories make the past: the past will always remain what it has been regardless of what historians will decide to say about it. Historians do not *create* the past; however, what they decide to say about the past will determine what entities we shall wish to discern in it.

Introduction

1. In the *Times Literary Supplement* of July 3, 1992. Shapiro summarizes the academic criticism that has been elicited by Rawls's *magnum opus* over the years as follows: "There is a great skepticism, first concerning the neo-Kantians' much debated aspiration toward a moral neutralism. . . . Second, there is widespread disaffection with the neo-Kantians' failure to offer a satisfying account of political community. . . . There is disaffection, third, with the neo-Kantians' search for substantive principles of social organization that are deontological in form. . . . People are concerned, last, with the ideological dimensions of the neo-Kantian arguments." See Ian Shapiro, *Political Criticism* (Berkeley 1992), 9 ff.

2. Nevertheless Berlin sometimes comes quite close to the aesthetic political philosophy that is advocated in this book. As will be expounded in Chapter 3, aesthetic political philosophy has one of its major sources in Machiavelli's perspectivism. This perspectivism was already noted and correctly appreciated by Berlin: "What he [Machiavelli] institutes is something that cuts deeper still—a differentiation between two incompatible ideals of life, and therefore of two moralities. One is the morality of the pagan world: its values are courage, vigour, fortitude in adversity, public achievement, order, discipline, happiness, strength, justice, above all assertion of one's proper claims and the knowledge and the power needed to secure their satisfaction. . . . Against this moral universe . . . stands in the first and foremost place, Christian morality." See Isaiah Berlin, "The Originality of Machiavelli," in Berlin, *Against the Current* (Oxford 1983), 45. And it is a matter of "perspective" (p. 40) which morality one will choose; the two moralities share no common background that could help us to choose.

3. Who never tired of pointing out the disastrous unintended consequences of attempts to realize precisely the most lofty political ideals—thus combining their individualism with a keen awareness of the limits of individualism.

4. Quoted in P. Rosanvallon, *Le moment Guizot* (Paris 1985), 302.

5. See Chap. 4, section 2.

6. I must make an exception here for Jon Elster's subtle arguments for how the numerous "prisoner's dilemmas" of our contemporary political world can be solved in a strictly rational way from the perspective of collectivism. See, especially, J. Elster, *Nuts and Bolts for the Social Sciences* (Cambridge, Eng., 1989), chap. 4.

7. Quite characteristic of our contemporary embarrassment at unintended consequences is the chapter devoted to them in Elster, *Nuts and Bolts*. Instead of asking how unintended consequences come into being, Elster focuses on the subsidiary question of whether in the social sciences explanations may be phrased in the language of unintended consequences. In this way the trajectory between intention and unintended consequences is left unexplored. Or, to be more precise, in the discussions of, for example, the so-called hog cycle (systematically frustrating

hog farmers in their intentions and expectation with regard to the price for hogs), unintended consequences are presented in Elster's account as a sociological fact or datum, rather than as the occasion for an investigation into the philosophy of action, or of the question what this datum must imply for meaningful social and political action.

8. A. Kinneging, *Aristocracy, Antiquity, and History: An Essay on Classicism in Political Thought* (The Hague 1994), 187.

9. This is my argument in *History and Tropology* (Berkeley 1994), chap. 3.

10. P. Duvenage, *Die estetiese heling van die instrumentele rede: 'n kritiese interpretasie van Jürgen Habermas se sosiale filosofie* (Port Elizabeth 1993). An English version of this book was published in 1995 by Polity Press.

11. See, for this notion, the last section of Chapter 4. This may also explain why we may expect corruption to be worse in large countries (in case of the loss of an external enemy) than in small countries under the same circumstances.

Chapter 1

1. In *The Aesthetic State: A Quest in Modern German Thought* (Berkeley 1989), Josef Chytry explores the German tradition of aesthetic political philosophy since the eighteenth century. Schiller is the central figure in his account. See the conclusion to this chapter for my objection to the tradition described by Chytry.

2. F. Schiller, "Über die ästhetische Erziehung des Menschen." In *Einer Reihe von Briefen*, in *Schillers sämtliche Werke*, vol. 12 (Stuttgart n.d.), 86.

3. F. Schiller, "Über den moralischen Nutzen ästhetischer Sitten," in *Schillers sämtliche Werke*, vol. 12 (Stuttgart n.d.), 188.

4. F. Guizot, *Histoire des origines du gouvernement représentatif en Europe*, vol. 2 (Paris 1851), 82, 83. See also, for example, A. de Grazia, "Representation: Theory," in D. L. Sills, ed., *International Encyclopedia of the Social Sciences*, vol. 13 (New York 1968), 462.

5. H. B. Mayo, *An Introduction to Democratic Theory* (New York 1960), 103.

6. H. F. Pitkin, *The Concept of Representation* (Berkeley 1967), 2; De Grazia, "Representation: Theory," 463.

7. F. Guizot, *Histoire des origines du gouvernement représentatif en Europe*, vol. 2 (Paris 1851), 94 ff. See also the "sixième leçon" in vol. 1 of Guizot's book.

8. This is the leitmotiv in E. Voegelin, *The New Science of Politics* (Chicago 1952).

9. "Dazu kommt, dass die soziale Repräsentation durchweg Inhalt von Kollektivvorstellungen ist, die nie über sich selbst hinaus bis zu philosophischen Abstraktionen ('Ideen an sich') gelangen können. Das im Repräsentanten verkörpert Gedachte (z.B. die 'Gerechtigkeit') bleibt stets blosser Gegenstand von Vorstellungen, wirdt nicht Gegenstand 'reiner Erkenntnis,' ist notwendig empirisch und kann nicht apriorisch sein oder werden, auch wenn der Inhalt der Vorstellung mit dem einer Erkenntnis vollkommen übereinstimmt. Personell repräsentierbar ist

nur, was personifizierbar ist"; see H. J. Wolff, "Die Repräsentation," in H. Rausch, ed., *Zur Theorie und Geschichte der Repräsentation* (Darmstadt 1968), 154.

10. The term is Burke's. See, for a discussion of it, Pitkin, *Concept of Representation*, 171–80. From a deliberately socialist perspective, Cole too advocated representation of interests; see G. D. H. Cole, *Social Theory* (London 1920), 104. For a discussion of the problems resulting from the representation of interests, see J. Roland Pennock, *Democratic Political Theory* (Princeton 1979), 352 ff.

11. Wolff, "Die Repräsentation," 197. And Köttgen writes: "Für die konstitutionelle Staatstheorie galt ein Adressat als Wesensmerkmal jeder Repräsentation"; see A. Köttgen, "Das Wesen der Repräsentation," in the same collection (Rausch, ed., *Theorie und Geschichte*), 80. See also Pitkin, *Concept of Representation*, 105 ff.

12. G. Sartori, "Representational Systems," in D. L. Sills, ed., *International Encyclopedia of the Social Sciences*, vol. 13 (New York 1968), 467. See also B. J. Diggs, "Practical Representation," in J. Roland Pennock and J. W. Chapman, eds., *Representation* (New York 1968), 36; H. C. Mansfield, Jr., "Modern and Medieval Representation," in the same collection, 78.

13. Sartori, "Representational Systems," 467.

14. J. H. Prins, *Over representatie en identiteit* (Deventer 1978), 5 ff.

15. Quoted in Pitkin, *Concept of Representation*, 60.

16. "Auch bei dem wichtigsten menschlichen Verbande, dem Staate, der gleichfalls nur durch einzelne Menschen denken, wollen und handeln kann, ist ja die Repräsentation nur ein Notbefehl, bleiben also selbstverständlich und unvermeidbar, bleiben geradezu per definitionem Spannungen zwischen dem, was ideal wäre, und dem, was einzelne Menschen als die Repräsentanten wirklich leisten und überhaupt nur leisten können"; see M. Drath, "Die Entwicklung der Volksrepräsentation," in Rausch, ed., *Theorie und Geschichte*, 261.

17. J. J. Rousseau, *Du contrat social* (Paris 1962), 302.

18. See C. Schmitt, *Verfassungslehre* (Leipzig 1928).

19. T. Hobbes, *Leviathan* (London 1970; I am using the Everyman's Library edition), 84.

20. For an analysis of the dubious parallels between Schmitt and Leibholz, see W. Mantl, *Repräsentation und Identität* (Vienna 1975), 149–99.

21. I am referring here to J. Habermas, *Strukturwandel der Öffentlichkeit: Untersuchungen zu einer Kategorie der bürgerlichen Gesellschaft* (Neuwied 1971).

22. The fact that modern, twentieth-century totalitarian concepts do nevertheless have their origins in eighteenth-century political theory was defended, as is well known, by J. L. Talmon in his *Origins of Totalitarian Democracy* (London 1952).

23. See O. von Gierke, *Das deutsche Genossenschaftsrecht*, 4 vols. (Berlin 1868–1913); a source edition on the legacy passed on to the sixteenth century from the Middle Ages concerning representation is G. Griffiths, *Representative Government in Western Europe in the Sixteenth Century* (Oxford 1968).

24. Mansfield, "Modern and Medieval Representation," 80.

25. B. Williams, *Descartes* (Harmondsworth 1978), 65.

26. To refer to this concept, which is so essential to my argument, I had to choose between the term used by E. H. Gombrich—"tertium comparationis" (see Gombrich, "Meditations on a Hobby Horse," in M. Philipson and P. J. Gudel, *Aesthetics Today* [New York 1980], 175) and the term "tertia" used in an exactly similar context by Richard Rorty in his "Pragmatism, Davidson and Truth," a chapter in his *Philosophical Papers: I. Objectivism, Relativism and Truth* (Cambridge, Eng., 1991).

27. G. W. Leibniz, *The Monadology*, section 78, in L. E. Loemker, ed., Gottfried Wilhelm Leibniz, *Philosophical Papers and Letters* (Dordrecht 1976), 651.

28. Quoted in N. Lobkowicz, *Theory and Practice: History of a Concept from Aristotle to Marx* (London 1962), 50.

29. Ibid., 51.

30. I. Kant, *Grundlegung zur Metaphysik der Sitten* (Reklam edn., Stuttgart 1970), 68.

31. This terminology is still used by Guizot: "Il s'agit de découvrir tous les éléments du pouvoir légitime disséminés dans la societé [that is, the memory of the logoi spermatikoi evoked by the term 'disséminés'], et de les organiser en pouvoir de fait. . . . Ce qu'on appelle la représentation n'est autre chose que le *moyen* d'arriver à ce résultat." See F. Guizot, *Histoire des origines du gouvernement représentatif en Europe* (Paris 1851), 95.

32. G. W. F. Hegel, *Vorlesungen über die Philosophie der Weltgeschichte. Band I. Die Vernunft in der Geschichte* (Hamburg 1970), 88.

33. Williams's argument against the Cartesian need of an "absolute concept of reality"—which is his tertium comparationis—is as follows. If we want to form an opinion of the correctness of a particular representation R of the reality W, we will have to form for ourselves a representation R' of that part of the reality W' in which the relation between R and W is objectified. And we can go on in this way. The only way to put a stop to this infinite regression is in fact the postulate of an absolute concept of reality. In that case, however, it is true that "we may have some determinate picture of what the world is like independent of any knowledge or representation in thought; but then that is open to the reflection, once more, that that is only one particular representation of it, our own, and that we have no independent point of leverage for raising this into the absolute representation of reality"; in B. Williams, *Descartes* (Harmondsworth 1978), 65. Rorty offers a similar argument against the tertia, which are said to encompass the representation and what is represented; see R. Rorty, "Pragmatism, Davidson and Truth," in Rorty, *Philosophical Papers. I. Objectivity, Relativism and Truth* (Cambridge, Eng., 1991), 138, 139.

These early modern conceptions persistently keep appearing today in attempts, in particular by Germans, to develop a "practical philosophy." These practical philosophers are once again aiming at a unity between action and thought in which the latter takes on the form of a practical rationality. However, nostalgia is a bad counsellor in philosophy.

34. Elsewhere I have argued that narrative and metaphor provide us with the *trait d'union* between the "is" and the "ought." See my *History and Tropology* (Berkeley 1994), chap. 2.

35. In chaps. 4 and 5 she deals with the representation of thought and opinions and in chaps. 6 and 7 that of action. In connection with this, see also the clarifying debate between Diggs and Pitkin on pictorial representation (thought) versus practical representation (action): B. J. Diggs, "Practical Representation," in Pennock and Chapman, eds., *Representation*, and Pitkin's reaction in the same collection under the title "Commentary: The Paradox of Representation."

36. The argument had already been formulated by Burke; see Pitkin, *Concept of Representation* (Berkeley 1967), 147.

37. For a more detailed exposition of these claims about the nature of representation, see my *History and Tropology*, chap. 3.

38. Quoted in E. Gombrich, *Art and Illusion* (London 1977), 263.

39. See my *Narrative Logic: A Semantic Analysis of the Historian's Language* (The Hague 1983), chap. 4.

40. Pitkin, *Concept of Representation* (Berkeley 1967), 82.

41. J. Roland Pennock, "Political Representation: An Overview," in Pennock and Chapman, *Representation*, 14 ff.; Pennock, *Democratic Political Theory*, 323 ff.; Pitkin, *Concept of Representation*, chap. 7.

42. Pitkin, *Concept of Representation*, 53–59; see also her critical discussion of Hobbes in chap. 2; G. Sartori, "Representational Systems," 464, 467.

43. Pitkin, *Concept of Representation*, 234.

44. H. Eulau and P. D. Karps, "The Puzzle of Representation," in Eulau and J. C. Wahlke, *The Politics of Representation* (London 1978), 60 ff. The authors of the above-mentioned article describe the year in which Pitkin's book appeared as the "watershed year" in the research of representation, see p. 59. This enthusiasm is also to be found in H. Eulau and J. C. Wahlke, "Introduction," in Eulau and Wahlke, *Politics of Representation*, 16.

45. E. H. Gombrich, "Meditations on a Hobby Horse," in M. Philipson and P. J. Gudel, eds., *Aesthetics Today* (New York 1980), 175.

46. Gombrich, "Meditations," 175; Gombrich continues: "The clay horse or servant buried in the tomb of the mighty takes the place of the living. The idol takes the place of the God. The question whether it represents the 'external form' of the particular divinity or, for that matter, of a class of demons does not come in at all. The idol serves as the substitute of the God in worship and ritual."

47. Gombrich elaborated on this line of thought in a number of books from his *Art and Illusion* up to and including his recent *Image and the Eye*. As I attempted to show in my "Historical Representation" in my *History and Tropology*, there is an

intrinsic conflict between the idea that art is a substitute for reality (see previous note) and the idea that art should offer an illusion of reality. The second thought comes more and more to the fore in Gombrich. Gombrich was criticized for this by, among others, Wollheim and Scruton.

48. A. C. Danto, *The Transfiguration of the Commonplace* (Cambridge, Mass., 1983), 15; see, for Danto's variant of the "substitution theory" of art, 18–21.

49. A. C. Danto, "Artworks and Real Things," in Philipson and Gudel, *Aesthetics Today*, 323; see also 335.

50. Danto, *Transfiguration of the Commonplace*, 77. See, furthermore, my "Historical Representation."

51. E. J. Sieyès, "Überblick über die Ausführungsmittel, die den Repräsentanten Frankreichs in 1789 zur Verfügung stehen," in E. Schmitt and R. Reichardt, eds., *Emmanuel Joseph Sieyès: Politische Schriften, 1788–1790* (Darmstadt 1975), 34, 35.

52. Quoted in M. Prélot, *Histoire des idées politiques* (Paris 1970), 452.

53. E. J. Sieyès, "Opinion de Sieyès sur plusieurs articles des titres IV et V du projet de constitution, prononcée à la Convention le 2 thermidor de l'an troisième de la République; imprimée par ordre de la Convention Nationale," in P. Bastid, ed., *Les discours de Sieyès dans les débats constitutionnels de l'an III* (Paris 1939) is the most impressive ode to political representation that he ever wrote: "Tout est représentation dans l'état social. Elle se trouve partout dans l'ordre privé comme dans l'ordre public; elle est la mère de l'industrie productive et commerciale, comme des progrès libéraux et politiques. Je dis plus, elle se confond avec l'essence même de la vie sociale. . . . Je voulais prouver qu'il y a tout à gagner pour le peuple à mettre en représentation toutes les natures de pouvoir dont se compose l'établissement public, en se réservant le seul pouvoir de commettre tous les ans des hommes sensés et immédiatement connus de lui, pour renouveller la portion sortante de ses représentants pétitionnaires, législatifs et communaux. . . . Il est constant que se faire représenter dans le plus des choses possibles, c'est accroître sa liberté, comme c'est la diminuer que d'accumuler des représentations diverses sur les mêmes personnes. Voyez dans l'ordre privé, si celui-là n'est pas le plus libre, qui fait le plus travailler pour soi; comme aussi tout le monde convient qu'un homme se met d'autant plus dans la dépendance d'autrui, qu'il accumule plus de représentation dans la même personne, au point qu'il arriverait jusqu'à une sorte d'aliénation de lui-même, s'il concentrait tous ses pouvoirs dans le même individu" (16–17). See also E. J. Sieyès, *Von dem Zuwachse der Freiheit in dem Gesellschaftsstande und in dem Stellvertretungssystem*, in K. E. Ölsner, *Emmanuel Sieyès, politische Schriften vollständig gesammelt von dem Deutschen Übersetzer nebst zwei Vorreden über Sieyès Lebengeschichte, seine politische Rolle, seinen Charakter, seine Schriften*, 1796.

54. Pitkin, *Concept of Representation*, 191.

55. Chytry, *The Aesthetic State*.

56. Ibid., 85.

57. F. Guizot, *Histoire du gouvernement représentatif en Europe*, vol. 1 (Paris 1852), 88.

58. Quoted in R. A. Steininger, *Soziologische Theorie der politischen Parteien* (Frankfurt 1984), 9.

59. A. Ware, "Political Parties," in D. Held and C. Pollitt, eds., *New Forms of Democracy* (London 1986), 112.

60. B. Barry, *Democracy, Power and Justice* (Oxford 1989).

61. See p. 27.

62. G. Leibholz, *Verfassungsstaat — Verfassungsrecht* (Stuttgart 1973), 90.

63. G. Leibholz, *Strukturprobleme der modernen Demokratie* (Frankfurt am Main 1974), 95.

64. See Chap. 3 for an elaboration of this paradox.

65. Cf. W. Hennis, *Die missverstandene Demokratie* (Freiburg 1973), 63: "Die Theorie vom Identität aufgebauten Parteienstaat provoziert geradezu die Abkehr von und die Verachtung des Parteiwesens, denn an diesem Massstab der Identität gemessen ist das Parteiwesen eine tiefe Unwahrhaftigkeit, die nur durch die noch grössere totalitäre Identifikation überwunden werden kann."

66. K. von Beyme, *Parteien in westlichen Demokratien* (Munich 1982), 22.

67. Quoted in T. Ball, "The Prehistory of Party," in Ball, *Transforming Political Discourse* (Oxford 1988), 29.

68. Ibid., 30.

69. Quoted in J. A. O. Eskes, "Het Nederlandse beeld van politieke partijen tussen 1813 en 1848," in *Jaarboek 1991 DNPP* (Groningen 1992), 62.

70. This is the argument in Ball's essay (referred to in note 6).

71. Beyme, *Parteien in westlichen Demokratien*, 24.

72. J. J. A. Thomassen, "Het functioneren van de representatieve democratie," in Thomassen, ed., *Hedendaagse democratie* (Alphen aan de Rijn 1992), 175. Anglo-Saxon literature on democracy has no analogue to this excellent collection, which is up-to-date, well-informed, well-argued, and informative.

Chapter 2

1. R. Dallmayr, *Polis and Praxis* (Cambridge, Eng., 1984), 42.

2. E. H. Kossmann, "Veertig Jaren," in Kossmann, *Politieke theorie en geschiedenis* (Amsterdam 1987), 475–76.

3. A. de Tocqueville, *Democracy in America: The Henry Reeve Text as Revised by Francis Bowen*, vol. 2 (New York 1945), 243.

4. J. G. Gunnell, "In Search of the Political Object: Beyond Methodology and Transcendentalism," in J. Nelson, ed., *What Should Political Theory Be Now?* (Albany 1983), 42.

5. W. Dilthey, *Gesammelte Schriften*, vol. 2, *Weltanschauung und Analyse des Menschens seit der Renaissance und Reformation* (Leipzig 1914), 93.

6. See M. Spanneut, *Permanence du Stoïcisme: De Zénon à Malraux* (Gembloux

1973). The number of authors who have stressed the importance of the Stoic legacy is relatively small; examples are P. Barth, M. Pohlenz, R. M. Wenley, and the Polish logician J. Lukasiewicz.

7. See, for a more detailed exposition of these Stoic concepts, Spanneut, *Permanence*, especially chaps. 1, 2, and 3; and M. van Straaten, *Kerngedachten van de Stoa* (Roermond 1969).

8. G. Oestreich, *Geist und Gestalt des frühmodernen Staates* (Berlin 1969).

9. For an assessment of Rorty's ultimately unsuccessful attack on epistemology (or Stoicism), see my "Can We Experience the Past" (forthcoming) and my "Van taal naar ervaring," in S. Alexandrescu, ed., *Richard Rorty* (Kampen 1995).

10. Especially in Rorty's brand of pragmatism language functions as a Stoic tertium—as may become clear from Rorty's criticism of Nagel's essay "What Is It Like to Be a Bat?" For an exposition of Rorty's abandonment of the promises of pragmatism for the limitations of "Stoicism," see my "Van taal naar ervaring," in Alexandrescu, ed., *Richard Rorty*, 54–99.

11. A. C. Danto, *The Transfiguration of the Commonplace* (Cambridge, Mass., 1983), 207.

12. See R. G. Collingwood, *The Idea of History* (Oxford 1970), 282. See also W. H. Dray, *Laws and Explanation in History* (Oxford 1970); and G. H. von Wright, *Explanation and Understanding* (London 1971). The amount of "Stoic" literature on intentional explanation is immense.

13. F. R. Ankersmit, *History and Tropology: The Rise and Fall of Metaphor* (Berkeley 1994), chap. 3.

14. As has been pointed out by historians such as D. Kelley, modern historical consciousness came into being with the sixteenth-century revolt against religious universalism (the Stoicism of the Middle Ages, so to speak) only to be extinguished again by the modern Stoicism of Cartesian rationalism. See also Chap. 4, section 2.

15. G. W. F. Hegel, *Vorlesungen über die Philosophie der Weltgeschichte*, vol. 1, *Die Vernunft in der Geschichte* (Hamburg 1955), 28.

16. For the continuity between the natural law tradition and Hegel, see B. Croce, "La naissance de l'historisme," *Revue de métaphysique et de morale* (1937), 606 ff. Remarkably enough, this article is not discussed in D. D. Roberts's excellent and impressive *Benedetto Croce and the Uses of Historicism* (Berkeley 1987). For a forceful attempt to close the gap between speculative systems and historiography, see H. Fain, *Between Philosophy and History* (Princeton 1973). The same tendency is present in H. White, *Metahistory: The Historical Imagination in Nineteenth-Century Europe* (Baltimore 1973) and in P. Munz, *The Shapes of Time* (Middletown 1978).

17. It is only in the so-called narrativist tradition that the aesthetic character of historical writing is best respected. And even there aestheticism sometimes shades off into Stoicism; insofar as White's tropology offers a structure within which all historical writing can find its proper place, we may hear in White's aestheticist narrativism a strong Stoic undertone.

18. See the introduction to Ankersmit, *History*.

19. T. Hobbes, *Leviathan* (London 1970; Everyman's Library), 84, 90.

20. J. J. Rousseau, *Du contrat social* (Paris 1962; Classiques Garnier), 244.

21. J. Schumpeter, *History of Economic Analysis* (London 1951), 141, 142.

22. J. L. Cohen and A. Arato, *Civil Society and Political Theory* (Cambridge, Mass., 1992), 186.

23. P. Self, *Political Theories of Modern Government: Its Role and Reform* (London 1985), 111.

24. The two concepts of the corporatist and the interventionist state are closely related: if the state is an institution that can claim no more than to be a *primus inter pares* if compared with other institutions, the term "intervention" nicely defines the limits of its power. See J. W. de Beus and J. A. A. van Doorn, *De interventiestaat* (Meppel 1984).

25. Self, *Political Theories*, 141.

26. M. Walzer, "The Politics of Michel Foucault," in D. C. Hoy, ed., *Foucault: A Critical Reader* (Oxford 1986), 53.

27. In the next chapter it will be argued that democracy was created in the beginning of the previous century mainly for reconciling political conflict.

28. Hobbes, *Leviathan*, chap. 4, 369; J. W. Danford, *Wittgenstein and Political Philosophy* (Chicago 1978), 16–73.

29. F. M. Barnard, *Herder's Social and Political Thought* (Oxford 1965), chap. 3.

30. According to Oakeshott, moral and political practice "compose a vernacular language of colloquial intercourse" (*On Human Conduct* [Oxford 1975], 63). Just like Herder, Oakeshott endows moral and political language with the capacity both to achieve moral and political communication *and* to constitute ourselves as moral and political beings. The former capacity is called by Oakeshott "self-disclosure" and the latter "self-enactment."

31. See, for example, H. Arendt, *The Human Condition* (Chicago 1958), 4; M. Oakeshott, *On Human Conduct* (Oxford 1975), 63 ff.; J. Derrida, "Préjugés—devant la loi," in *La faculté de juger* (Paris 1985); M. Foucault, *Power/Knowledge* (New York 1980); J. G. A. Pocock, "Verbalizing a Political Act," in M. Shapiro, *Language and Politics* (Oxford 1984); J. G. A. Pocock, "Languages and Their Implications: The Transformation of the Study of Political Thought," in Pocock, *Politics, Language and Time* (New York 1973); Q. Skinner, "Meaning and Understanding in the History of Ideas," *History and Theory* 8 (1969), 3 ff.; Skinner, "Conventions and the Understanding of Speech Acts," in P. King, ed., *The History of Ideas* (London 1983), 259 ff.; H. V. White, *Tropics of Discourse* (Baltimore 1978); White, *The Content of the Form* (Baltimore 1987); M. Edelman, *Constructing the Political Spectacle* (Chicago 1988); and M. J. Schapiro, *Reading the Postmodern Polity: Political Theory as Textual Practice* (Minnesota 1992). Representative of linguistic political philosophy are also the essays in Nelson, ed., *What Should Political Theory Be Now?*. J. Habermas, *Theorie des kommunikativen Handelns*, 2 vols. (Frankfurt am Main 1982) has

inspired a whole Habermasian galaxy of political studies: for example, J. S. Dryzek, *Discursive Democracy: Politics, Policy and Political Science* (Cambridge, Eng., 1990) and the huge and dinosaurian J. L. Cohen and A. Arato, *Civil Society and Political Theory* (Cambridge, Mass., 1992). Other representative works are M. Schapiro, ed., *Language and Politics*, (Oxford 1984); C. C. Lemert, *Sociology and the Twilight of Man* (Carbondale 1979); R. Harvey Brown, *Society as Text: Essays on Rhetoric, Reason and Reality* (Chicago 1987); and F. Dallmayr, *Language and Politics* (Notre Dame 1984). Of course this list is a mere spoonful out of the kettle.

32. D. Lodge, *Nice Work* (London 1989), 153.

33. Of course I am referring here to the speculation against the British pound of the autumn of 1992, which forced Norman Lamont to withdraw the pound from the European Monetary System (EMS).

34. J. Millman, *The Vandal's Crown* (New York 1995), 178.

35. For a more detailed analysis of the Machiavellian opposition of Fortuna and "virtù," see Chap. 4, section 2.

36. L. Wittgenstein, *Philosophical Investigations* (Oxford 1974), section 107.

37. For the notion of "variation" as characteristic of contemporary democracy, see Chap. 3, section 4.

38. In an eloquent argument Frank Lentricchia has indeed accused linguistic political philosophy of political quietism, of what he refers to as "political acedia." See F. Lentricchia, *Criticism and Social Change* (Chicago 1983). Lentricchia's main target was Paul de Man, whose literary criticism clearly entails a political philosophy. In a way that is reminiscent of Nietzsche's argument in his second *Unzeitgemässe Gedanken* an absolute forgetting, an absolute disregard of what is and has been, appears to be for De Man the prerequisite for all true political action. And because of the rejection by linguistic political philosophy of any referential or ontological anchor for language as a political tertium, this is what one might have expected (De Man's embrace of anti-Semitism, which was discovered a few years ago, undoubtedly made forgetting all the more attractive to him). Thus nothing short of a total revolution can be considered meaningful political change. The inevitable result is, according to Lentricchia, "a paralysis of praxis" and the "inculcation of a matrix of despair, resignation, futility, frustration, cynicism and hopelessness" (see Lentricchia, *Criticism*, 42, 51, 49). And, needless to say, the same accusation has often been leveled at that other great proponent of a linguistic political philosophy, Michel Foucault. Thus when Walzer speaks of "the catastrophic weakness" of Foucault's political philosophy, he has in mind Foucault's all too apparent inability to steer a prudent middle course between a conservative acceptance of the powers that be and a total revolution reducing the Stalinist and the Maoist revolutions to mere child's play. See M. Walzer, "The Politics of Foucault," in D. C. Hoy, ed., *Foucault: A Critical Reader* (Oxford 1986), 67.

39. J. Schumpeter, *Capitalism, Socialism and Democracy* (London 1976; 1942),

261, 262; P. E. Converse, "The Nature of Belief Systems in Mass Publics," in D. E. Apter, ed., *Ideology and Discontent* (New York 1964).

40. W. Bagehot, *The English Constitution* (Oxford 1928), 236.

41. C. Lefort, "The Permanence of the Theological-Political," in Lefort, *Democracy and Political Theory* (Oxford 1986), 214 ff.

42. R. Sennett, *The Uses of Disorder* (New York 1970), 198 ff. This also is the main thesis of his *Fall of Public Man* (New York 1977).

43. See especially the next chapter, section 3.

44. See Chap. 6 for an exposition of Tocqueville's political theory and of its relevance to a proper understanding of democracy.

45. A. de Tocqueville, *Democracy in America*, vol. 2 (New York 1945; Vintage Books), 276.

46. Ibid., 338.

47. I am thinking here of the kind of political problems that no longer have their origin in the opposition of one part of society to another (for example, labor versus capital), but that confront all of us in a more or less similar way. For a good albeit tentative discussion of this new kind of political problem, see U. Beck, *Politik in der Risikogesellschaft* (Frankfurt am Main).

48. I am not speaking here about political science, where the state, the political party, the voter, the influence of lobbies, and so on were investigated intensively.

Chapter 3

1. T. Hobbes, *Leviathan* (London 1970; Everyman's Library), 8.

2. Ibid., 89.

3. Ibid.

4. D. Easton, "Political Science," in D. L. Sills, ed., *International Encyclopedia of the Social Sciences*, vol. 12 (London 1968), 282.

5. N. Machiavelli, *The Prince*, (Harmondsworth 1984), 30.

6. What is meant here by "aesthetic" or "practical" political theory cannot, in spite of an obvious affinity, be identified with what is ordinarily considered to be practical philosophy. Traditional practical philosophy is Aristotelian in origin and discusses the application of general political or moral rules to concrete historical circumstances. However, the kind of practical political theory meant here aims at finding out how an agreement can be found between distinct and often conflicting political rules or ideologies. What both ideas of practical political theory have in common is an affinity for moderation and for the *juste milieu*. For an excellent brief explanation of the nature and background of traditional practical political theory, see J. C. Den Hollander, "Conservatisme en historisme," *Bijdragen en mededelingen betreffende de geschiedenis der Nederlanden 102* (1987), 380–402; see particularly 392–95.

7. A. T. van Deursen, *Geschiedenis en toekomstverwachting* (Kampen 1971). Van

Deursen here shows how in the eighteenth-century German tradition of the so-called statistics, *raison d'état* thinking transformed itself into a social science that might be valuable for political practice. See F. Meinecke, *Die Idee der Staatsräson in der neueren Geschichte* (Munich 1957) for how historism developed out of the *raison d'état* tradition.

8. See W. J. Witteveen, *Evenwicht van machten* (Zwolle 1991); Witteveen emphasizes here that Montesquieu was not so much concerned with a separation (as he is usually interpreted), but rather with a balance, with what one might call the *juste milieu* of the three powers.

9. For the potential conflict between these two metaphysical foundations of democracy, see J. J. A. Thomassen, "Democratie, problemen en spanningsvelden," in Thomassen, ed., *Hedendaagse democratie* (Alphen aan de Rijn 1991), especially 1. In later essays in this useful collection this paradox of democracy is further specified.

10. For the good and bad sides of Carl Schmitt, see the dissertation of T. W. A. de Wit, *De onontkoombaarheid van de politiek: De souvereine vijand in de politieke filosofie van Carl Schmitt* (Ubbergen 1992).

11. For the importance of Hobbes to Schmitt, see Günter Maschke's epilogue to C. Schmitt, *Der Leviathan* (Cologne 1982 [1938]).

12. K. R. Popper, *The Open Society and Its Enemies*, 2 parts (London 1968 [1945]); J. L. Talmon, *The Origins of Totalitarian Democracy* (London 1952); B. Lang, *Act and Idea in the Nazi Genocide* (Chicago 1990).

13. C. Schmitt, *Politische Romantik* (Leipzig 1991), 20 ("Alles ist Anfang eines unendlichen Roman"). All the translations from German into English in this chapter are mine.

14. Ibid., 77 ("eine allgemeine Unfähigkeit ein bedeutendes politisches Idee fest zu halten").

15. Ibid., 83.

16. Ibid. ("jede Begründing ist falsch denn mit einer Grund ist auch eine Grenze gegeben"—a statement that seems to anticipate Rorty's antifoundationalism). What is characteristic here is Müller's distinction between what he refers to as an "atomistic" and a "dynamic" definition; he prefers the latter to the former. He describes the latter as follows: "The dynamic definition: definition is the explanation of an entity through another entity that is conceived to be in a contrary movement and in opposition to the former; or definition can be described as that which stands in opposition to an anti-definition," and he ends his discussion on definitions as follows: "In an exhausting definition of things and concepts similarly lies the thing's exhaustion and its death. It is in ideas that life manifests itself! Who tells me, who narrates to me the histories of how the concept developed into an idea?" See A. Müller, "Vom Wesen der Definitionen," in Müller, *Kritische/ästhetische und philosophische Schriften 2* (Neuwied 1967), 255, 256.

17. Schmitt, *Romantik*, 222.

18. Ibid., 105 ("Der Romantiker weicht der Wirklichkeit aus, aber ironisch und mit Gesinnung der Intrige"). It can be argued that democracy has its greatest strength exactly in this strategy of avoidance. See also Chaps. 2, 4, and 6.

19. Schmitt, *Romantik*, 70.

20. For a hard, though not unsympathetic exposition of the absurdly unpractical and utterly unworldly conservative conceptions of the two gentlemen in question, see E. H. Kossmann, "Over Conservatisme: Johan Huizinga-lezing," in Kossmann, *Politieke Theorie: Verspreide Opstellen en Voordrachten* (Amsterdam 1987), 9–26, especially 13 ff.

21. For a more detailed account of Guizot's historical and political theory, see my *De Spiegel van het Verleden: Exploraties*, vol. 1 (Kampen 1996), chap. 4.

22. E. H. Kossmann, "De Doctrinairen tijdens de Restauratie," in Kossmann, *Politieke Theorie en Geschiedenis: Verspreide Opstellen en Voordrachten* (Amsterdam 1987), 277.

23. Kossmann, "Doctrinairen," 258.

24. A similar "universal shrinkage" taking place under similar conditions is recorded by Putnam in his recent and much discussed book, when he describes there the consequences of the democratization of local politics in Italy because of the great reforms of the 1970s: "Councilors came to interpret their role less as being 'responsive to' and more as being 'responsible for,' less as eloquent tribunes for popular causes and more as competent trustees of the public interest. . . . Practical questions of administration, legislation and financing became more salient. Councilors now spoke more of efficient service delivery and of investment in roads and vocational education, and less of 'capitalism' or 'socialism,' 'liberty' or 'exploitation.'" See R. R. Putnam, *Making Democracy Work* (Princeton 1993); 34. In both cases, in Guizot's France and in Putnam's Italy, large and fundamental political questions dissolved into a myriad of small and precise questions concerning the most practical and down-to-earth-issues.

25. A. de Tocqueville, *Recollections: The French Revolution of 1848*, New Brunswick 1987; 5.

26. Thus Lamartine exclaimed in 1848 in the Assemblée: "Je ne vois que de misérables chiffres se heurtant contre des autres misérables chiffres. Je n'entends que des questions de de boire et manger, de spolier, de conserver, d'attaquer, de défendre; des questions purement alimentaires, des questions de produit net, de spoliation par les uns, de retenue avare et cupide par les autres; pas une pensée qui dépasse les limites des compoirs de l'industrie ou des champs! En vérité, il semble que vous pourriez effacer ces trois mots magnifiques que nous nous proposons d'inscrire sur le frontispiece de votre constitution: Liberté, Egalité, Fraternité, et les remplacer par ces deux mots immondes, vendre et acheter." Quoted in F. Méliono, "Les Libéraux Français et leur Histoire," in S. Stuurman ed., *Les Libé-*

ralismes, la Théorie Politique et l'Histoire (Amsterdam 1994), 38–39. The irony is, furthermore, that Guizot himself had the habit of walking out of the cabinet council as soon as financial matters came to be discussed.

27. What Guizot really said was: "enrichissez-vous par le travail et l'épargne" — and this obviously is a far less ignominious exclamation, if it is this at all. Furthermore the context makes abundantly clear that Guizot's words were certainly not intended as the exhortation to the narrow egoism that one customarily reads in it.

28. Quoted in P. Rosanvallon, *Le moment Guizot* (Paris 1985), 27.

29. The statement is by Johan Rudolf Thorbecke, the creator of the political system functioning in the Netherlands down to the present day. See E. H. Kossmann, "Thorbecke en het Historisme" in Kossmann, *Poliieke Theorie en Geschiedenis: Verspreide Opstellen en Voordrachten* (Amsterdam 1987), 335. Both politically and qua personality Thorbecke strikingly resembles Guizot—ironically, however, Thorbecke could only come to power in the Netherlands because of the revolution of February 1848 that marked the end of Guizot's political career.

30. R. Koselleck, *Kritik und Krise* (Frankfurt am Main 1973). Koselleck's view on the genesis of the modern state in the early modern period, as expounded in this profoundly thought-provoking book, is similar to that of Schmitt. It will be hard to find a book in which the origins of our modern political *Umwelt* have been depicted with greater originality and accuracy.

31. B. Constant, *Écrits et discours politiques: Présenté par O. Pozzo di Borgo*, vol. 2 (n.p. 1964), 46. Hegel expresses a similar idea, curiously enough in his aesthetics: "Similarly the monarchs of our days are no longer a concrete culmination of everything, as the heroes of the mythical Middle Ages were, but rather a more or less abstract center inside for regulations already developed and fixed by law and constitution. The monarchs of our days have relinquished the most important acts of governing; they no longer administer justice themselves, finances, civil order and certainty are no longer their own special concern, war and peace are determined by the generally customary political relations." G. W. F. Hegel, *Vorlesungen über die Ästhetik*, vol. 1 (Frankfurt am Main 1986), 253–54.

32. See Chap. 6, section 3.

33. Spinoza argues that there is an optimum between the complete chaos of the state of nature in which each individual follows his own impulses and the quasi-totalitarian power of a state imposing certain religious convictions; if this optimum is effectively realized the citizen's freedom does not weaken the state's power (as seems, on the face of it, inevitable), but rather increases it. The state becomes vulnerable as soon as and insofar as it abandons this optimum in the relationship between state and citizen that can best be realized in democracy. It might be argued that this insight is the beginning of all wisdom in political theory. See B. Spinoza, *Tractatus theologico politicus*, in *Benedict de Spinoza: The Political Works* (Oxford 1958), especially chap. 20. As for Tocqueville, see Chaps. 2 and 6.

34. What Rawls, in his recent work, refers to as "constructivism" leaves no room at all for how we can reach consensus and compromise in politics without thereby forsaking the political principles that are at stake in our dealings with our political opponents. But this is what democracy is all about: in democracy we often reach agreement *without* having been convinced of the validity of the views of our opponents. Whoever ignores this fact has lost sight of one of the most interesting and important features of public argument in democracy; they can even be considered to be (perhaps unwitting) adherents of totalitarian politics. One may recall in this connection the amount of energy totalitarian societies like Mao's China always invested in the attempt to convince their opponents of their supreme political wisdom. Democracy requires us "to do business" with even our most sincere and deeply felt political principles. This is not a weakness; it is the paramount strength of democracy. Rawls does not take sufficiently into account the differences between debate in the academic world (which seems to be the model he is unable to cast aside) and in politics, where the conditions for reaching consensus and compromise have a very different background.

35. G. H. Dodge, *Benjamin Constant's Philosophy of Liberalism: A Study in Politics and Religion* (Chapel Hill 1980), 144.

36. B. Fontana, *Benjamin Constant and the Post-Revolutionary Mind* (New Haven 1991), 106; see also Constant, *Écrits*, vol. 1, 64–65.

37. Schmitt, *Romantik*, 191, 192.

38. Constant, *Écrits*, vol. 2, 10 ff. One of the most alarming aspects of present-day political practice is that the executive and legislative powers tend to coagulate into one undifferentiated mass that is often labeled "government" or "administration." It is because of this that in contemporary democracies the absolute crucial role of the legislative power to control the executive has been eroded and why in this book a renewed emphasis on representation and on the notion of political style is so much recommended.

39. One is reminded of Claude Lefort's speculations about the empty center in democratic politics, and of the position of the Japanese emperor, which will be discussed in the final section of Chap. 5. Nevertheless, the empty center of the European constitutional monarchy has a function different from that in Japan. In Europe the neutral power of the king is a background against which political dissension can *articulate* itself; in Japan it serves the function of *hiding* dissension. See also Chap. 2.

40. J. Culler, *On Deconstruction: Theory and Criticism After Structuralism* (London 1983), 80, 81, 96, 145, 202, 234, 246, 247.

41. A good example is F. Lentricchia, *Criticism and Social Change* (Chicago 1983). Much of Lentricchia's argument has a certain "family resemblance" to Schmitt's impatience with political Romanticism. See also Chap. 2.

42. Something similar can be said for historism, which can well be seen as one

of the most influential expressions of Romanticism. See the last chapter of my *History and Tropology* (Berkeley 1994), where I argue that postmodernism is a radical form of historism.

43. Cited by H. Prang, *Die romantische Ironie* (Darmstadt 1972), 8. See also Chap. 4.

44. A. Müller, "Die Lehre vom Gegensatz," in Müller, *Kritische/ästhetische*, 198.

45. R. Rorty, "Philosophy as a Kind of Writing: An Essay on Derrida," in Rorty, *Consequences of Pragmatism* (Brighton 1982), 90-110.

46. The translation might run as follows:

> I wish I were the Emperor,
> But while Joseph will fulfill
> During his life what also is my will
> And all wise men rejoice in that
> So let him always be the Emperor!

47. De Wit, *Onontkoombaarheid*, 97-103.

48. Orr accordingly suggests that Tocqueville should have given his second major book the title *L'Ancien Régime est la Révolution*, instead of *L'Ancien Régime et la Révolution*. See L. Orr, *Headless History* (Ithaca 1990), 100.

49. F. Schlegel, *Kritische und theoretische Schriften* (Stuttgart 1978), 140.

50. E. Ostermann, "Der Begriff des Fragments als Leitmetapher der ästhetischen Moderne," *Athenäum* 2 (1992), 189-205. See the end of the article for a comparison with deconstructionism.

51. J. F. Lyotard, *Het postmoderne weten* (Kampen 1988 [1979]), 26. This is the Dutch translation of Lyotard's *La condition moderne*.

52. Lyotard, *Weten*, 26.

53. To Hobbes, as to all natural law theorists, the state was the institution in terms of which all individuals become comparable, or to use the most suitable word in this context, commensurable. Lyotard's thesis concerning the postmodern *in*commensurability of individuals reflects from that perspective an attempt to conceive (contemporary) society in terms of the state of nature as conceived by the natural law theorists. As may be clear from my argument in this chapter, what is good in Lyotard's proposal is his emphasis on the irrevocability of political conflict. But what is bad in it is that he does not see that this poses the subsidiary but no less important question whether political conflict will have to be conceptualized in the modernistic Hobbes/Schmitt tradition or be aestheticized as is done in this book.

54. "Ich kann von meinem ganzen Ich kein anderes Echantillon geben, als ein System von Fragmenten, weil ich selbst dergleichen bin." Cited in E. Behler, *Friedrich Schlegel in Selbstzeugnissen und Bilddokumenten* (Reinbek 1966), 72.

55. R. Rorty, "Postmodernist Bourgeois Liberalism," in Rorty, *Objectivism, Relativism and Truth* (Cambridge, Eng., 1991), 197-203.

56. Rorty, *Objectivism*, 188.

57. In Freud's construction of the self the opposition between individual(-ism) and collectivism loses much of its former urgency. "The contrast between individual and social or mass psychology, which may at first sight seem very important to us, loses very much of its urgency on careful examination." See S. Freud, "Massenpsychologie und Ich-Analyse," in Freud, *Studienausgabe*, vol. 9, *Fragen der Gesellschaft; Ursprunge der Religion* (Frankfurt am Main 1982), 65.

58. A. de Tocqueville, *De la démocratie en Amérique* (Paris 1981), 320.

59. Ibid., 318.

60. M. Kundera, *Het boek van de lach en de vergetelheid* (Houten 1990), 204. I am referring here to the Dutch translation of this novel.

61. Ibid., 208.

62. Schmitt, *Romantik*, 172, 173. Schmitt indeed discerns here the heart of the political mentality of Romanticism and we have every reason to agree with him here.

63. J. Baudrillard, "Simulacra and Simulations," in Baudrillard, *Selected Writings*, ed. M. Poster (Cambridge, Eng., 1988), 166–85. See also Chap. 1, on political representation, section 2, in the present book, where the priority of the representation to the represented is demonstrated.

64. W. Benjamin, "Das Kunstwerk im Zeitalter seiner technischen Reproduzierbarkeit," in Benjamin, *Illuminationen: Ausgewählte Schriften* (Frankfurt am Main 1969), especially 152 ff.

65. Tocqueville, *Démocratie*, 64. To place this insight in the context of Tocqueville's thought on democracy, see Chap. 6, the end of section 2.

66. In the Netherlands the implementation of the law for occupational disability (WAO) was entrusted to an institution in which the state, organizations of employers, and organizations of the employed were all represented. This institution (the Bedrijfsvereniging) soon developed into an institutional Frankenstein's monster, serving the purposes of neither the state nor the citizen and completely outside any public control. See, for this unparalleled disaster in Dutch social welfare policy, J. G. Hibbeln and W. Velema, *Het WAO debâcle* (Utrecht 1993).

67. M. Albert, *Capitalism Against Capitalism* (London 1993). Albert argues here that after the demise of Soviet communism, the new real global struggle will be the one between the economies based on the "Rhine model" (among which he includes Japan) and the Anglo-Saxon model. The superiority of the former is demonstrated, according to Albert, by the fiasco of Thatcher's social and economic policies, as well as that of Reaganomics and the disintegration of American society. Nor will it be difficult to explain the origins of the differences separating Albert's Rhine model and his Anglo-Saxon model from the perspective of the argument expounded in this chapter. It will be obvious that the Rhine model, with its affinities for reconciliation and cooperation, is the product of Romanticism, whereas Anglo-Saxon

democracy is to a much larger extent a product of the Enlightenment. In this way the postmodernist debate about the Enlightenment also has its consequences for our choice between these two forms of democracy.

68. It is illustrative that trade unions often pretend to represent the interests of the unemployed even though the interests of this group are diametrically opposed to that of the working population. This may exemplify democracy's resistance to the introduction of new principles and its tendency, instead, to recycle time and again well-known and already familiar principles. It is supported in this conservatism by the social sciences, which because of their adherence to the relevant *tertia comparationis* have made nearly impossible their own recognition of new principles or the need to establish them.

69. This characterization has to be qualified. Social and political divisions do not present themselves *sponte sua*, but only against a background of a certain more or less widely shared conception of the social and political order. In the days of the pharaohs one did not discuss social security, nor did anyone want to. From this perspective it should be observed that it has taken about a century and a half to politicize society: in the beginning of the nineteenth century politics was to the majority of the people something similar to what science or art has always been for it. That is to say, it was a business for a socially remote group of individuals without much practical relevance to most. The idea that politics matters to all of us is a fairly modern idea and seems to be gradually disappearing again. But that does not in the least mean that all social problems now have been solved—just as the political indifference of our ancestors at the beginning of the nineteenth century does not imply that theirs was a world without such problems. We should realize, instead, that there is, contrary to what we might expect, no direct link between the intrinsic gravity of social problems and the average citizen's inclination to politicize them. One may have immense political problems in a social paradise and the most harmonious of societies may be a social hell. There is a scale for the gravity of social problems and a scale for our sensitivity to them, and these two scales are quite independent of each other.

70. M. Schofield, *The Stoic Idea of the City* (Cambridge, Eng., 1991), 64. Schofield argues in the closing chapter of this book that the Stoic idea of the city and the notion of the individual as a citizen of the cosmic city laid the foundations for later Stoic natural law philosophy. This, then, provides us with the common matrix for, on the one hand, the city as a model for politics, and, on the other, natural law philosophy.

71. R. Sennett, *The Uses of Disorder* (New York 1970), 18.

72. In his better-known *The Fall of Public Man* (New York 1977), Sennett described how the public sphere, as exemplified by how people make use of the public space of the city, its streets and coffeehouses, disintegrated with the discovery of the Romantic self. In fact, the resulting opposition between public and private meant

a decisive break with Stoic conceptions of the political order. And if we observe the still essentially Stoic character of contemporary political philosophy, this may demonstrate how little political philosophy, up till now, has been successful in adequately dealing with the historical and sociological realities that came into being after the fall of the *ancien régime*. For a penetrating discussion of Sennett's oeuvre, see R. Boomkens, "Een pedagogiek van de chaos," *Feit en Fictie* 1 (1994), 63-79.

73. For *Blade Runner*, see D. Harvey, *The Condition of Postmodernity* (Oxford 1990), 308 ff.

74. F. Jameson, "Postmodernism, or the Cultural Logic of Late Capitalism," *New Left Review* 146 (1984), 53-92.

75. I am thinking of Berel Lang's notion of "styleme." See B. Lang, "Looking for the Styleme," in Lang, ed., *The Concept of Style* (Ithaca 1987), 174-83.

76. This idea is developed in A. C. Danto, *The Transfiguration of the Commonplace* (Cambridge, Mass., 1983), chap. 7.

77. J. Nelson, "Political Theory and Political Rhetoric," in Nelson, ed., *What Should Political Theory Be Now?* (Albany 1983), 229.

78. J. Vincent, *The Formation of the British Liberal Party, 1857-1868* (London 1966).

79. For a most forceful argument for studying political history as the history of politcal *style*, see I. de Haan and H. te Velde, "Vormen van politiek: Veranderingen van de openbaarheid in Nederland 1848-1900," *Bijdragen en mededelingen betreffende de geschiedenis der Nederlanden* 111 (1996), forthcoming.

80. R. Rorty, "The Priority of Democracy to Philosophy," in Rorty, *Objectivism, Relativism and Truth* (Cambridge, Eng., 1991), 190.

81. Ibid., 191.

Chapter 4

1. M. Black, "Metaphor," in Black, *Models and Metaphors* (Ithaca 1968).

2. U. Japp, *Theorie der Ironie* (Frankfurt am Main 1983), 23.

3. M. C. Brands, *Historisme als Ideologie* (Assen 1965), 35 ff., and especially M. Walser, *Selbstbewusstsein und Ironie* (Frankfurt am Main 1981), chap. 1.

4. T. Mann, *Betrachtungen eines Unpolitischen* (Berlin 1918), 587.

5. For this characterization of the Renaissance conception of how truth, freedom, and rhetoric are connected, see N. Struever, *The Language of History in the Renaissance* (Princeton 1971).

6. Mann, *Betrachtungen*, 600.

7. D. C. Muecke, *Irony and the Ironic* (London 1982), 11.

8. G. W. F. Hegel, *Vorlesungen über die Philosophie der Weltgeschichte*, vol. 1, *Die Vernunft in der Geschichte* (Hamburg 1970), 88.

9. J. G. A. Pocock, *The Machiavellian Moment in the Atlantic Tradition* (Princeton 1975), 31-49.

10. N. Machiavelli, *The Prince* (Harmondsworth 1984), 130, 131.

11. H. Fenichel Pitkin, *Fortune Is a Woman: Gender and Politics in the Thought of Niccolo Machiavelli* (Berkeley 1987), 88, 91.

12. F. Guicciardini, "History of Italy," in P. Gay and V. C. Wexler, eds., *The Historian at Work* (New York 1972), 50, 61.

13. F. R. Ankersmit, *History and Tropology* (Berkeley 1994), chap. 3.

14. See R. Rorty, *Contingency, Irony and Solidarity* (Cambridge, Eng., 1989), part II.

15. G. W. F. Hegel, *Grundlinien der Philosophie des Rechts* (Hamburg 1967), 287.

16. R. Koselleck, *Kritik und Krise* (Frankfurt am Main 1973), 8.

17. Ibid., 156.

18. Ibid., 102.

19. Ibid., 8.

20. Elsewhere I argued that the rebirth of nationalist feelings that can be observed in many countries over the last few years is a consequence of the state's loss of power and authority in the eyes of the public. Now that an uncertain and aimless state can function less satisfactorily as civil society's mirror, and as the collective expression of its needs and wishes, civil society is tempted to discover in national identity an alternative mirror for recognizing itself. An effective and responsive state is the best remedy against nationalism. See my "Commentaar op *Het nut van Nederland*," *NRC-Handelsblad*, Apr. 4, 1996.

21. As has been pointed out on other occasions in this study, it should be borne in mind that there is an inverse relationship between the state's size and its power: the strong state can only be a relatively small state.

22. J. M. Guéhenno, *La Fin de la démocratie* (Paris 1993); M. Bovens et al., *De Verplaatsing van de politiek* (Amsterdam 1995); and P. H. A. Frissen, *De Virtuele staat, politiek, bestuur, technologie: Een postmodern verhaal* (Amsterdam 1996).

23. L. von Ranke, "De Histioriae et Politices Cognatione atque Discrimine Oratio," in Ranke, *Sämmtliche Werke*, 24, *Abhandlungen und Versuche* (Leipzig 1872), 288-89.

24. In early modern Europe the term "historia" could have two meanings. In the first place the word might refer to what we still associate with the word "history." But in the second place, "historia" stood for all knowledge based on experience. The term was still understood in this way by Kant when he wrote about experimental physics: "Die Experimentalphysik ist historisch, denn sie geht auf einzelne Fälle zurück. Sobald man sie aber durch allgemeine Gesetze erklärt wird sie vernünftig. Die Historie schafft nur Gegenstände zur rationalen Erkenntnis"; cited in A. Seifert, *Cognitio historica: Die Geschichte als Namengeberin der frühneuzeitlichen Empirie* (Berlin 1976), 185-86.

25. For the premodern, Aristotelian conception of the "probable" and its use in premodern historical theory, see N. Hammerstein, *Ius und Historie: Ein Beitrag zur Geschichte im späten 17. and im 18. Jahrhundert* (Berlin 1972).

26. T. A. Spragens, *The Irony of Liberal Reason* (Chicago 1981), x.

27. "Primum mihi cura haec fuit, ut eorum quae ad ius naturae pertinent probationes referrem ad notiones quasdam tam certas, ut eas negare nemo possit, nisi sibi vim inferat. Principia enim eius iuris, si modo animum recte advertas, per se patent atque evidentia sunt, ferme ad modum eorum quae sensibus externis percipimus"; see H. Grotius, *De iure belli ac pacis* (Amsterdam 1720), xxiii. No less striking is Grotius's comparison of the certainty of natural law with that of mathematics: "Vere enim profiteor, sicut mathematici figuras a corporibus sematas considerant, ita me in iure tractando ab omni singulari facto abduxisse animum" (*De iure belli*, xxxv).

28. Spragens, *Irony*, 259.

29. M. Horkheimer and T. W. Adorno, *Dialektik der Aufklärung* (Frankfurt am Main 1973), 3.

30. Spragens, *Irony*, 255.

31. For this notion of "practical philosophy" and where it differs from "aesthetic political philosophy," see Chap. 2.

32. A. MacIntyre, "The Relationship of Philosophy to Its Past," in R. Rorty et al., eds., *Philosophy in History* (Cambridge, Eng., 1984).

33. For a more detailed and technical account of how this "scope criterion" can be justified, see my *Narrative Logic: A Semantic Analysis of the Historian's Language* (The Hague 1983), chap. 8.

34. M. Howard, "The Paradox on Which Our Future Hangs," *Times Literary Supplement*, Sept. 18–24, 1987, 117.

35. F. Nietzsche, *Over nut en nadeel van geschiedenis voor het leven* (Groningen 1983), 22, 23.

36. Japp, *Theorie*, 87.

37. This best-known form of irony was studied exhaustively under the name of "stable irony" in W. C. Booth, *A Rhethoric of Irony* (Chicago 1974).

38. Ankersmit, *Narrative Logic*, chap. 7.

39. See Chap. 5 for a comparison between metaphor and paradox—that is, the trope coming closest to irony.

40. Since in the case of figures of speech there is always a contradiction between what is literally said and what is meant, negation is an obvious strategy to penetrate into the secrets of the nature of figures of speech.

41. Cited in Booth, *Rhetoric*, 29.

42. I. Strohschneider-Kohrs, *Die romantische Ironie in Theorie und Gestaltung* (Tübingen 1960), 17

43. Ibid., 185–215.

44. Ibid., 59.

45. Ibid., 18; and Walser, *Selbstbewusstsein*, 55.

46. Strohschneider-Kohrs, *Romantische Ironie*, 37.

47. Cited in ibid., 20.

48. Cited in ibid., 22.

49. Cited in Strohschneider-Kohrs, *Romantische Ironie*, 25.

50. Walser, *Selbstbewusstsein*, 55.

51. See Chap. 3 for a discussion of Schmitt's critique of political Romanticism.

52. "Diese Ironie hat Herr Friedrich von Schlegel erfunden, und viele andere haben sie nachgeschwatzt oder schwatzen die von neuem wieder nach." See G. W. F. Hegel, *Vorlesungen über die Ästhetik* (Frankfurt am Main 1986), 95.

53. Cited in Walser, *Selbstbewusstsein*, 72.

54. Ibid., 71.

55. G. W. F. Hegel, *Vorlesungen über die Philosophie der Weltgeschichte II–IV* (Hamburg 1976), 638–47.

56. Ibid., 644.

57. See, for example, my "Freuds cultuurpessimisme," in R. A. M. Aerts and K. van Berkel, eds., *Cultuurpessimisme* (Groningen 1996).

58. S. Freud, *Civilization and Its Discontents* (New York 1961), 70, 71.

59. R. Rorty, "Philosophy as a Kind of Writing," in Rorty, *Consequences of Pragmatism* (Brighton 1982), 107.

60. S. Freud, *Studienausgabe*, vol. 1 (Frankfurt am Main 1982), 84–85.

61. I. Hassan, *The Postmodern Turn: Essays in Postmodern Theory and Culture* (Ohio 1987), 94.

62. Ibid., 39.

63. A. MacIntyre, *After Virtue: A Study in Moral Theory* (London 1981).

64. Jane Jacobs refers to this confusion of moral maps as "the Law of Systematic Moral Corruption." She observes (I believe correctly) that corruption is not a sign of moral decay but rather of ill-considered attempts to combine different moralities, more specifically the morality of commerce with that of government. See J. Jacobs, *Systems of Survival: A Dialogue on the Moral Foundations of Commerce and Politics* (London 1992).

65. B. Pascal, *Pensées et opuscules*, ed. M. Léon Brunschvicg (Paris n.d.), 244–47.

66. E. Auerbach, "Über Pascals politische Theorie," in Auerbach, *Vier Untersuchungen zur Geschichte der französischen Bildung* (Bern 1951), 65.

67. Of course we are immediately reminded in this context of Pascal's famous wager: the most prudent thing for us to do is to bet on the existence of God. For if He does not exist, little or nothing will be lost by doing so; on the other hand, if He does exist and if we had decided against His existence, we all know what most unpleasant punishment will await us on that "terrible aurore," to speak with Baudelaire, following upon our death. But I suppose that God would have sound reasons for being dissatisfied with people who decided to believe in Him exclusively on the basis of such a cynical piece of sophistry.

68. It is perhaps no coincidence that Pascal used the terms *frondes* and *fron-*

deurs — with their references to the political conflicts between 1648 and 1653 — when speaking about the Jansenists (see note 4 to the letter).

69. And at this stage in our argument we might wonder whether the different paths chosen by Descartes and Pascal respectively might be explained by a minor asymmetry between the notions of (1) truth and of (2) being in the right. "Truth" is impersonal whereas "being in the right" considers truth under the aspect of the perfection of the human being. The former has its proper locus in science, whereas the other is more suitable to the domain of morals and politics.

70. A recent one being R. Rorty, "The Priority of Democracy to Philosophy," in Rorty, *Objectivity, Relativism and Truth: Philosophical Papers*, vol. 1 (Cambridge, Eng., 1991).

71. "Mais quoi! on agit comme si on avait mission pour faire thiompher la vérité, au lieu que nous n'avons mission que pour combattre pour elle"; see Pascal, *Opuscules*, 246.

72. This is where Pascal's position is more recommendable than the one advocated by Rorty in his otherwise admirable "Priority of Democracy to Philosophy." For in Rorty's ethnocentric relativism truth tends to become victimized to toleration — it is only an argument like Pascal's that gives us the best of both worlds and will allow us to be both unflinching servants of the truth and the indefatigable apostles of toleration (in the customary sense of that word).

73. I ignore here the several different meanings that the terms "constitution" and "constitutionalism" may have and understand by the term "constitution" the formal rules that have been adopted by a political community for achieving political decisions. For a detailed enumeration of all the different though closely interrelated meanings of the term "constitution," see C. F. Friedrich, "Constitutions and Constitutionalism," in D. L. Sills, ed., *International Encyclopedia of the Social Sciences*, vol. 3 (New York 1972), 318 ff.

Chapter 5

1. Hobbes recognizes four "abuses" of speech, the second of which is metaphor; see T. Hobbes, *Leviathan* (New York 1970; Everyman's Library), 13.

2. This view of the role of metaphor in scientific discourse inspires D. McCloskey, *The Rhetoric of Economics* (Madison 1985).

3. W. E. Connolly, "Essentially Contested Concepts in Politics," in Connolly, *The Terms of Political Discourse* (Oxford 1983), 23.

4. T. Ball, *Transforming Political Discourse* (Oxford 1988).

5. Ibid., 83 ff. A similar idea is the main thesis of T. Spragens, *The Politics of Motion: The World of Thomas Hobbes* (Lexington 1973).

6. Ball, *Transforming*, 22–47.

7. J. B. White, "Rhetoric and Law: The Arts of Cultural and Communal Life," in J. S. Nelson, A. Megill, and D. N. McCloskey, eds., *The Rhetoric of the Human*

Sciences (Madison 1987), 310. See also J. B. White, *Heracles' Bow: Essays on the Rhetoric and Poetics of the Law* (Madison 1985), chap. 2.

8. White, *Rhetoric*, 316.

9. If we wish to understand Plato's political theory, according to Klosko, "the proper view is that the philosopher king is given an end at which to aim, while his political task lies in devising the proper means." See G. Klosko, *The Development of Plato's Political Philosophy* (New York 1986), 171. Louis conjectures that it was Aeschylus's *Seven Against Thebes* where Plato discovered the metaphor of the state as a ship. See P. Louis, *Les Métaphores de Platon* (Rennes 1945), 155, 156.

10. M. Walzer, *Spheres of Justice* (New York 1983), 284–87.

11. R. Bambrough, "Plato's Political Analogies," in P. Laslett, ed., *Philosophy, Politics and Society*, 105: "He [Plato] obscures the fact that, in politics as well as at sea, the theoretical knowledge and the practical ability of the navigator do not come into play until the destination has been decided upon."

12. There is a difficulty here that cannot be ignored. The difficulty presents itself most clearly when Witteveen explains Plato's metaphor as follows: "The agent functioning as the steering agent within this approach is 'the State' and the ship that is steered is 'civil society'" (my translation); see W. J. Witteveen, "Dokteren aan het schip van staat," in M. A. P. Bovens and W. J. Witteveen, *Het schip van staat* (Zwolle 1985), 25. Plato did not, of course, distinguish between State and civil society. So we have to be careful if we transpose Plato's metaphor to modern times. Bambrough explicitly embraces Plato's metaphor insofar as the metaphor suggests that State (or civil society) must be steered; see Bambrough, "Plato's Political Analogies," 105.

13. In an illuminating essay Van Gunsteren explores the implications of Plato's metaphor for our conception of the State's capacity to learn from political experience; see H. R. van Gunsteren, "Het leervermogen van de overheid," in M. A. P. Bovens and W. J. Witteveen, eds., *Het schip van staat* (Zwolle 1985).

14. J. Annas, *An Introduction to Plato's Republic* (Oxford 1981), 179.

15. Ibid., 103–4.

16. Ibid., 179.

17. George Eliot, *Middlemarch* (Harmondsworth 1965), 111.

18. D. A. Schön, "Generative Metaphor and Social Policy," in A. Ortony, ed., *Metaphor and Thought* (Cambridge, Eng., 1979), 256. See also D. A. Schön, *The Reflective Practitioner: How Professionals Think in Action* (New York 1983), 182–85.

19. Schön, "Generative Metaphor," 259.

20. Ibid., 255. See also F. R. Ankersmit, *Narrative Logic: A Semantic Analysis of the Historian's Language* (The Hague 1983), 216; and Ankersmit, "Een moderne verdediging van het historisme," *Bijdragen en mededelingen betreffende de geschiedenis der Nederlanden* 96 (1981), 464.

21. Schön, "Generative Metaphor," 262 ff.

22. Ankersmit, *Narrative Logic*, chap. 5.

23. S. H. Butcher, ed., *Aristotle's Theory of Poetry and Fine Art* (New York 1951), 77-78.

24. See, for example, K. Burke, *A Grammar of Motives* (Berkeley 1969), 503-4.

25. J. Derrida, "White Mythology in the Text of Philosophy," in Derrida, *Margins of Philosophy* (Chicago 1986), 243.

26. Ibid.

27. Ibid.

28. I. A. Richards, *The Philosophy of Rhetoric* (Oxford 1971), 96-97. For a comment on Richard's terminology, see M. Black, *Models and Metaphors* (New York 1962), 47.

29. See especially the last section of Derrida's "White Mythology," and the translator's note 2 on 209.

30. J. S. Nelson, A. Megill, D. N. McCloskey, *The Rhetoric of the Human Sciences* (Madison 1987), 1.

31. Ankersmit, *Narrative Logic*, 134-40.

32. One may think of the influential work of Hayden White and Paul Ricoeur on the role of metaphor in the humanities.

33. A. C. Danto, *The Transfiguration of the Commonplace* (Cambridge, Mass., 1983), 165-209.

34. E. H. Kossmann, "The Singularity of Absolutism," in Kossmann, *Politieke theorie en geschiedenis* (Amsterdam 1987), 134-35.

35. J. Rawls, *A Theory of Justice* (Oxford 1972), 12.

36. P. Kress, "Political Theorizing in the Late Twentieth Century: Foci, Loci and Agendas," in J. S. Nelson, ed., *What Should Political Theory Be Now?* (Albany 1983); J. G. Gunnell, "In Search of the Political Object," again in Nelson, and G. Gunnell, *Between Philosophy and Politics: The Alienation of Political Theory* (Amherst 1986), 36 ff.

37. "Durch dieses Ich, oder Er, oder Es (das Ding), welches denkt, wird nun nichts weiter, als ein transzendentales Subjekt der Gedanken vorgestellt = x, welches nur durch die Gedanken, die seine Prädikaten sind, erkannt wird, und wovon wir, abgesondert, niemals den mindesten Begriff haben können; um welches wir uns daher in einem beständigen Zirkel herumdrehen, indem wir uns seiner Vorstellung jederzeit schon bedienen müssen, um irgend etwas von ihm zu urteilen"; see I. Kant, *Kritik der reinen Vernunft* (Hamburg 1956), 374.

38. L. Wittgenstein, *Tractatus logico-philosophicus* (Frankfurt am Main 1971), section 5.633.

39. Ibid., section 5.64.

40. At first sight Plato's metaphor seems incompatible with political representation; I here call to mind the objections of Walzer and Bambrough to the metaphor mentioned in section 2. We should note, however, that the notions of distance and unity suggested by Plato's metaphor are in harmony with how political repre-

sentation has most often been conceived since the end of the eighteenth century. This conception of political representation, as defended, for example, by Burke and Sieyès, is called the mandate view of representation. Within this conception the representative is not the delegate, but the mandate of those he represents: the autonomy that is thereby accorded to the representative embodies the "distance" between the representative and the represented. Next, as Burke already emphasized, since the representative is not tied to those he represents, the representative represents the nation and not merely those who voted for him. This is where representation gives unity. See H. F. Pitkin, *The Concept of Representation* (Berkeley 1967). See also Chap. 1.

41. C. S. Maier, "Introduction," in Maier, ed., *Changing Boundaries of the Political* (Cambridge, Eng., 1987), 11.

42. J. Keane, "Introduction," in Keane, ed., *Civil Society and the State* (London 1988), 6.

43. Ibid.

44. C. Offe, "Challenging the Boundaries of Institutional Politics: Social Movements since the 1960s," in Maier, ed., *Changing Boundaries*, 91.

45. B. Constant, *De la liberté chez les modernes: Écrits politiques* (Paris 1980), 501. The distinction can already be found in a manuscript written by Constant around 1796: "Il y a au contraire une partie de l'existence humaine qui, de nécessité, reste individuelle et indépendante, et qui est de droit hors de toute compétence sociale. La souveraineté n'existe que d'une manière limitée et relative"; see Constant, *De la liberté*, 271. The distinction was anticipated by such eighteenth-century authors as Montesquieu, Hume, De Lolme, and, above all, Ferguson. When Constant was in Edinburgh in 1787, he may have become acquainted there with Ferguson's ideas on the subject; see S. Holmes, *Benjamin Constant and the Making of Modern Liberalism* (New Haven 1984), 29-31; and J. Keane, "Despotism and Democracy: The Origins and Development of the Distinction Between Civil Society and the State, 1750-1850," in Keane, ed., *Civil Society*, 35-73.

46. The subject is explored well in Holmes, *Benjamin*, chap. 4.

47. Ibid., 24.

48. H. Arendt, *De revolutie* (Utrecht 1975), 102 ff.

49. Constant's acceptance of pretext and hypocrisy is certainly not unconditional. In his major work, *De l'esprit de conquête et de l'usurpation*, Constant harshly condemns the political hypocrisy to be expected from bellicose governments: if their mentality becomes universal, "le genre humain reculerait vers ces temps de dévastation qui nous semblaient l'opprobre de l'histoire. L'hypocrisie seule en ferait la différence; et cette hypocrisie serait d'autant plus corruptrice que personne n'y croirait. Car les mensonges de l'autorité ne sont pas seulement funestes quand ils égarent et trompent les peuples: ils ne le sont pas moins quand ils ne les trompent pas"; see Constant, *De l'esprit*, 135-36.

50. Holmes, *Benjamin*, 167.

51. T. Todorov, "Speech According to Constant," in Todorov, *The Poetics of Prose* (Oxford 1977); this chapter is more convincing about the performative character of speech than much that has been written in the wake of Austin. If only for this reason, one may readily agree with Ainslie's view that "Constant a écrit dans les cent pages d'*Adolphe* un livre dont aucun critique n'épuisera les multiples significations"; see A. Ainslie, *Imagination and Language* (Cambridge, Eng., 1981), 78.

52. Holmes, *Benjamin*, 13.

53. B. Constant, *Adolphe, Cécile, Le cahier rouge* (Paris 1957), 86.

54. Constant, *Adolphe*, 37.

55. Ibid., 116.

56. If we think of Plato's metaphor, we shall recognize that with the dissolution of these boundaries the unity of civil society will also be threatened. Here one may observe a link between Plato's metaphor and the metaphor that is dominant throughout Constant's writings. It has been pointed out (e.g. by Paul Delbouille) that, on the whole, Constant's clear, Voltairian prose is inhospitable to metaphor. Nevertheless, Markus Winkler has demonstrated that the metaphor of dust (*poussière*, or *sable*) recurs again and again in Constant's writings and, moreover, that it often has a political connotation. To cite one example: "Quand chacun est son propre centre, tous sont isolés, il n'y a que de la poussière. Quand l'orage arrive, la poussière est de la fange." See M. Winkler, "Constant et la métaphore de la poussière," *Annales Benjamin Constant* 2 (1981), 10.

57. See K. G. van Wolferen, *The Enigma of Japanese Power* (London 1989), 5 ff. Some of the main themes of this excellent study, which is of as much interest to the political philosopher as to the student of Japan, can be found already in K. G. van Wolferen, "Reflections on the Japanese System," *Survey* 26 (1982), 121–50.

58. Quoted in van Wolferen, *Enigma*, 240.

59. Van Wolferen, *Enigma*, 241. See also 9–10.

60. B. M. Richardson, *The Political Culture of Japan* (Berkeley 1974), 230 ff, especially 234.

61. R. N. Bellah, *Tokugawa Religion* (Glencoe 1957), 14 ff.

62. T. Najita, *The Intellectual Foundations of Modern Japanese Politics* (Chicago 1974), 2 ff and 147–48.

63. T. Doi, *The Anatomy of Dependence* (Tokyo 1981), 31 ff.

64. Bellah, *Tokugawa Religion*, 122.

65. S. Ono, *Shinto: The Kami Way* (Tokyo 1962), 23.

66. R. Barthes, *L'empire des signes* (Geneva 1970), 58. The spirit of Saussure is all-pervasive in this remarkable book on Japan; perhaps Japan is the kind of society we may expect if the Saussurian notion of the sign becomes socialized or politicized.

67. Bellah, *Tokugawa Religion*, 87. Ono, *Shinto*, 76.

68. This is one of the leading ideas in Van Wolferen's book; see for example

chap. 8. Bellah also emphasized that in Japan religion, politics and the social order are intertwined in a way inconceivable in the West: *Tokugawa Religion*, 104, 192.

69. Van Wolferen, *Enigma*, 5.

70. Ibid., 48, 49.

71. C. Nakane, *Japanese Society* (London 1970), 69.

72. F. L. K. Hsu, *Iemoto: The Heart of Japan* (New York 1975), 212.

73. T. J. Pempel, *Policy and Politics in Japan: Creative Conservatism* (Philadelphia 1982), 3.

74. Van Wolferen, *Enigma*, 27.   75. Constant, *Liberté*, 280.

76. Van Wolferen, *Enigma*, 28.   77. Nakane, *Japanese Society*, 65.

78. Najita, *Foundations*, 117.

79. At the end of his book Sandel sums up his doubts about the deontological approach to political problems as found in Rawls in the following way: "To imagine a person incapable of constitutive attachments . . . is not to conceive an ideally free and rational agent, but to imagine a person wholly without character, without moral depth. For to have character is to know that I move in a history I neither summon nor command, which carries consequences none the less for my choices and conduct. It draws me closer to some and more distant from others; it makes some aims more appropriate, others less so"; see M. Sandel, *Liberalism and the Limits of Justice* (Cambridge, Eng., 1982), 179. It is interesting that Sandel defines these "constitutive attachments," which are systematically ignored by deontologists, in terms of dependency. Surely, Adolphe could never retire behind Rawls's "veil of ignorance."

80. See, also by T. Doi, "Omote and Ura," *Journal of Nervous and Mental Disease* 157 (1973), 258–61, where the theme of *amae* is related to the distinction between appearance and reality (*tatemae* and *honne*).

81. The verb *hohitsu* is closely related to *amae* as explained by Doi. When Doi translates *hohitsu* as "to assist," he does so in a context that is ambiguous as to whether the positive associations of "assistance" lie in giving assistance or in being assisted. And the context suggests that this ambiguity is precisely what *hohitsu* (and *amae*) is about; see Doi, *Dependence*, 58.

82. Ibid., 72.

83. Ibid., 29. The infantile origins of *amae* are discussed in G. DeVos, "Dimensions of the Self in Japanese Culture," in A. J. Marsella, G. DeVos, F. L. K. Hsu, *Culture and Self: Asian and Western Perspectives* (New York 1985), especially 147–67.

84. Doi, *Dependence*, 58.   85. Barthes, *Empire*, 45.

86. see Chap. 1.   87. Barthes, *Empire*, 110.

88. Ibid., 93.   89. Ibid.

90. Ibid., 91.   91. Ibid., 148.

Chapter 6

1. A good survey of the reception of Tocqueville from his own time up until the present is given in W. Pope, *Alexis de Tocqueville: His Social and Political Theory* (London 1986), 11–27.

2. J. Elster, *Psychologie politique (Veyne, Zinoviev, Tocqueville)* (Paris 1990), 101.

3. References to Tocqueville's own work are mostly, though not always, given in the text. The notation system adopted is as follows: *Dem. I* refers to A. de Tocqueville, *Democracy in America: The Henry Reeve Text as Revised by Francis Bowen*, vol. 1 (New York 1945; Vintage Books). *Dem. II* refers to the second volume of this work. *AR* refers to A. de Tocqueville, *L'Ancien Régime et la Révolution* (Paris 1967; Gallimard). *OR* refers to A. de Tocqueville, *The Old Régime and the French Revolution*, trans. Stuart Gilbert (New York 1955; Doubleday Anchor Books). *Rec.* refers to A. de Tocqueville, *Recollections: The French Revolution of 1848*, ed. J. Mayer and A.P. Kerr (New Brunswick 1987; Transaction Books).

4. A. de Tocqueville, *Correspondence and Conversations with Nassau Senior: From 1834 to 1859*, ed. M. C. M. Simpson (New York 1968), 140, 223.

5. Ibid., 142.

6. Ibid., 141.

7. Generalization and abstraction aspire to divine knowledge. However, the universal knowledge possessed by God is a knowledge of individuals. See *Dem. II*, 14.

8. "Il est évident que le caractère de la Réforme a dû être, je le répète, un état de liberté, une grande insurrection de l'intelligence humaine. . . . La crise du XVIme siècle n'était pas simplement réformatrice, elle était essentiellement révolutionnaire"; see F. Guizot, *Histoire de la civilisation en Europe* (Paris 1873), 338–39.

9. L. Gossman, "Michelet's Gospel of Revolution," in *Between History and Literature* (Cambridge, Mass., 1990), 215.

10. It is interesting to note that Tocqueville often uses the word "dissemination" when discussing the sociological determinants of knowledge and power; see e.g. *Dem. I*, 84, 193.

11. In democracy men "perpetually differ from themselves, for they live in a state of incessant change of place, feelings and fortunes" (*Dem. II*, 61). See also chap. 17, with the characteristic title "How the Aspect of Society in the United States Is at Once Excited and Monotonous," and *Dem. II*, 239.

12. J. Habermas, *Theorie des kommunikativen Handelns*, vol. 2 (Frankfurt am Main 1987), 489–548.

13. L. E. Shiner, *The Secret Mirror: Literary Form and History in Tocqueville's Recollections* (Ithaca and London 1988), 21.

14. Tocqueville, *Nassau Senior*, 138.

15. R. Rorty, *Contingency, Irony and Solidarity* (Cambridge, Eng., 1989), 158 ff.

16. See chap. 7, "The Paradox of Personal Independence," in R. Boesche, *The Strange Liberalism of Alexis de Tocqueville* (Ithaca and London 1987).

17. F. R. Ankersmit, *Narrative Logic: A Semantic Analysis of the Historian's Language* (The Hague 1983), 155–69.

18. F. R. Ankersmit, "Reply to Professor Zagorin," *History and Theory* 29 (1990), 175–97; and Ankersmit, "Twee vormen van narrativisme," in *De navel van de geschiedenis* (Groningen 1990), 44–78.

19. D. A. Schön, "Generative Metaphor and Social Policy," in A. Ortony, ed., *Metaphor and Thought* (Cambridge, Eng., 1979).

20. L. von Ranke, *Sämtliche Werke*, vol. 24, *Abhandlungen und Versuche* (Leipzig 1872), 288–89.

21. For a characteristic statement by Michelet about the unity the historian has to discover in the past and about the kind of metaphors that go with this search, see J. Michelet, *Tableau de la France* (Paris 1987), 136 ff. Examples of antimetaphorical historiography can be found in the writings of Ginzburg, the later work of Le Roy Ladurie, and the German historians of "Alltagsgeschichte."

22. See A. Bezanfon, "The Early Use of the Term 'Industrial Revolution,'" *Quarterly Journal of Economics* 36 (1922).

23. L. Orr, "Tocqueville et l'histoire incompréhensible: l'Ancien Régime et la Révolution," *Poétique* 49 (1982), 52. See also Orr, *Headless History: Nineteenth-Century French Historiography of the Revolution* (Ithaca and London 1990), 92.

24. Orr, *L'histoire incompréhensible*, 59.

25. Ibid., 58.   26. Shiner, *Secret Mirror*, 27.

27. Ibid.   28. See Pope, *Tocqueville*, 17–19.

29. Characteristic examples of aprioristic reasoning can be found, for example, in *Dem. II*, 50–51, 99, 312.

30. Tocqueville, *Nassau Senior*, 50.

31. Ibid., 133.

32. Ankersmit, *Narrative Logic*, 209–20.

33. See Chap. 5.

34. D. C. Muecke, *Irony and the Ironic* (London 1982), 11. See also Chap. 4.

35. H. White, *Metahistory: The Historical Imagination in Nineteenth-Century Europe* (Baltimore 1973), 191–230; similarly, Gossman speaks of Tocqueville's "ironic vision." See L. Gossman, "Michelet's Gospel of Revolution," in Gossman, *Between History and Language* (Cambridge, Mass., 1990), 207.

36. See Chap. 4.

37. Tocqueville's respect for the sublimity of historical reality, a reality that permits no aesthetic embellishment, is evident from the heated discussions he had with his friend Jean Jacques Ampère on the revolution of 1848; see *Rec.*, 67, 68.

38. Shiner, *Secret Mirror*, 21.

39. A. de Tocqueville, *Oeuvres complètes*, vol. 3, *Écrits et discours politiques* (Paris 1985), 87.

40. F. von Schiller, "Ueber das Erhabene," in Schiller, *Sämtliche Werke*, vol. 12 (Stuttgart n.d.), 191.

41. Ibid., 194.

42. Elster, *Psychologie politique*, 111.

43. Ibid., 118.

Conclusion

1. See, for example, R. Dahl, *Democracy and Its Critics* (New Haven 1989), 27; and J. G. A. Pocock, *The Machiavellian Moment: Florentine Political Thought and the Atlantic Tradition* (Princeton 1975), 129, 253. The link between democracy and the idea of the *regimen mixtum* is that both are "perspectivist" in the sense that the point of view of the magistrate always has to be supplemented by that of the citizen, and vice versa. See also my discussion of Machiavelli in Chap. 3, section 2, of the present volume.

2. C. L. de Montesquieu, *The Spirit of the Laws* (Cambridge, Eng., 1989), IV.2.

3. A. A. M. Kinneging, *Aristocracy, Antiquity and History* (The Hague 1994), 317–18.

4. We need only think of Schlegel and Müller to recognize that these high standards for what it is to be a Romantic individual were not always adopted by their theorists themselves. But so it was, of course, with honor itself.

5. This is, of course, the main thesis of Pocock, *Machiavellian Moment*.

6. See, for example, H. R. van Gunsteren and P. den Hoed, eds., *Burgerschap in praktijken*, vol. 2 (The Hague 1992) (a publication of the "Wetenschappelijke Raad voor het regeringsbeleid").

7. One is reminded here of Louis XIV's pathetic exclamation "a Dieu donc oublié tout ce que j'ai fait pour lui! [Has God then forgotten all that I did for Him!]," after having heard the news of the terrible defeat of the French at Malplaquet.

8. Ankersmit, *History and Tropology*, 42 (section 5.4.2.).

9. As was argued in R. Wollheim, "Metaphor and Painting," in F. R. Ankersmit and J. J. A. Mooij, eds., *Knowledge and Language*, vol. 3, *Metaphor and Knowledge* (Dordrecht 1993).

10. See, for example, R. Koole, "De transformatie van Nederlandse politieke partijen," *Jaarboek 1988 DNPP* (Groningen 1989), 16.

11. Van Gunsteren has recently argued that we may observe in our age the emergence of what he refers to as "the unknown society." See H. van Gunsteren, *Culturen van besturen* (Amsterdam 1994), especially chaps. 12 to 15. But we should not think of this emergence of "the unknown society" as if society now tends to withdraw behind an untransparent screen; for it is rather the death of ideology that

now prevents us from making sense of all the knowledge that we have of society. "Insight" into the nature of society has less to do with *knowledge* (of myriads of details) than with the metaphorical "point of view" enabling us to *organize* this knowledge. Thus Saffo: "It is not content, but context that will matter most a decade from now. . . . In a world of hyperabundant content, point of view will become the scarcest of resources"; see P. Saffo, "It's the Context, Stupid," *Wired*, Mar. 1994, 74, 75. See also my *History and Tropology*, 38 (thesis 4.3).

12. For a more detailed analysis of this decreased capacity of the state to learn from its mistakes, see H. van Gunsteren, "Het leervermogen van de overheid," in van Gunsteren, *Culturen van besturen* (Amsterdam 1994).

13. "Thus the typical citizen drops down to a lower level of mental performance as soon as he enters the political field. He argues and analyzes in a way which he would readily recognize as infantile within the sphere of his real interests. He becomes a primitive again. His thinking becomes associative and affective." See J. Schumpeter, *Capitalism, Socialism and Democracy* (London 1976 [1943]), 262; and P. E. Converse, "The Nature of Belief Systems in Mass Publics," in D. E. Apter, ed., *Ideology and Discontent* (New York 1964); and A. Campbell, P. E. Converse, W. E. Miller, D. E. Stokes, *The American Voter* (New York 1960).

14. K. J. Arrow, *Social Choice and Individual Values* (New York 1951); Arrow argues here that no rules that are both workable and ethically acceptable can be developed for translating the wishes of the voters into actual policy. In fact, this theorem is fatal for all conceptions of direct democracy and, from this perspective, a necessary first step to take in the transition from ideals of direct democracy to an acceptance of the aesthetic representation that I defended in Chap. 1. In a less generalized form Arrow's theorem was anticipated in M. A. Ostrogorski, *Democracy and the Organization of Political Parties* (London 1902).

15. For a more detailed argument of this thesis, see my "Politieke partijen in het tijdperk van de onbedoelde gevolgen," *DNPP* (Groningen 1995).

16. This avoids the draconic measures recommended by "bioregionalists," by the advocates of "ecocommunities" or of "ecoanarchism" such as Sale, Bookchin, Ophuls, or Dodge. Their unpractical conceptions are discussed in W. Achterberg, *Samenleving, natuur en duurzaamheid* (Assen 1994), chap. 5.

Index of Subjects

In this index an "f" after a number indicates a separate reference on the next page, and an "ff" indicates separate references on the next two pages. A continuous discussion over two or more pages is indicated by a span of page numbers, e.g., "57–59." *Passim* is used for a cluster of references in close but not consecutive sequence.

Index of Names

In this index an "f" after a number indicates a separate reference on the next page, and an "ff" indicates separate references on the next two pages. A continuous discussion over two or more pages is indicated by a span of page numbers, e.g., "57–59." *Passim* is used for a cluster of references in close but not consecutive sequence.

Library of Congress Cataloging-in-Publication Data
Ankersmit, F. R.
    Aesthetic politics : political philosophy beyond
    fact and value / F. R. Ankersmit.
        p.   cm. — (Mestizo spaces = Espaces métisses)
    Includes bibliographic references and index.
    ISBN 0-8047-2729-5 (cloth : alk. paper). —
    ISBN 0-8047-2730-9 (pbk. : alk. paper)
    1. Political science—Philosophy.   2. Aesthetics,
    Modern.   I. Series: Mestizo spaces.
    JA71.A585   1997
    320'.01'1—dc20

                                96-34474
                                    CIP

    ⊗   This book is printed on acid-free paper

Original printing 1997
Last figure below indicates year of this printing
06 05 04 03 02 01 00 99 98 97